'What does it mean to promote reconciliation in response to violent conflict? When do practices of reconciliation function to obfuscate past wrongs, silence victims, or neutralize political dissent? These are urgent questions, as institutions and policies designed to alleviate political conflict are currently being developed across the globe. Against the view that reconciliation entails social harmony and consensus, this volume offers an agonistic alternative—one that affirms *dissensus* and ongoing contestation. These essays explore, and powerfully unsettle, prevailing assumptions regarding the role of forgiveness, tolerance, healing, memorializing, and responsibility, as responses to past violence. Drawing on a dazzling array of theoretical resources, including thinkers such as Giorgio Agamben, Jean Améry, Walter Benjamin, and Walt Whitman, these essays are also grounded in, and informed by, specific cases and institutions. This collection is not only a magnificent work of political theory, but also a brilliant and timely innovation in scholarship on transitional justice.'

Bronwyn Leebaw, *Associate Professor of Political Science,*
University of California, Riverside, CA, USA

'The authors of *Theorizing Post-Conflict Reconciliation* bring the conceptual tools of agonistic democratic theory to the study of a range of hard cases of post-conflict reconciliation. The result is ground-breaking. They call into question the dominant approach of transitional justice and enable us to see these situations in a new and more complex light. The volume will be of great interest to scholars and students of both the theory and practice of reconciliation.'

James Tully, *Distinguished Professor,*
University of Victoria, Victoria, BC, Canada

Theorizing Post-Conflict Reconciliation

The founding of truth commissions, legal tribunals and public confessionals in places like South Africa, Australia, Yugoslavia and Chile have attempted to heal wounds and bring about reconciliation in societies divided by a history of violence and conflict.

This volume asks how many of the popular conclusions reached by transitional justice studies fall short, or worse, unwittingly perpetuate the very injustices they aim to suture. Though often well intentioned, these approaches generally resolve in an injunction to 'move on', to leave the painful past behind in the name of a conciliatory future. Through collective acts of apology and forgiveness, so the argument goes, reparation and restoration are imparted, and the writhing conflict of the past is substituted for by the overlapping consensus of community. And yet all too often, the authors of this study maintain, the work done in assuaging past discord serves to further debase and politically neutralize especially the victims of abuse in need of reconciliation and repair in the first place.

Drawing on a wide range of case studies, from South Africa to Northern Ireland, Bosnia, Rwanda and Australia, the authors argue for an alternative approach to post-conflict thought. In so doing, they find inspiration in the vision of politics rendered by new pluralist, new realist and especially agonistic political theory.

Featuring contributions from both up-and-coming and well-established scholars, this work is essential reading for all those with an interest in restorative justice, conflict resolution and peace studies.

Alexander Keller Hirsch is Lecturer in the Political Science Department at Northeastern University, and Research Fellow at the University of California Humanities Research Institute, USA.

Interventions

Edited by: Jenny Edkins, Aberystwyth University and Nick Vaughan-Williams, University of Warwick

'As Michel Foucault has famously stated, "Knowledge is not made for understanding; it is made for cutting." In this spirit The Edkins–Vaughan-Williams Interventions series solicits cutting edge, critical works that challenge mainstream understandings in international relations. It is the best place to contribute post-disciplinary works that think rather than merely recognize and affirm the world recycled in IR's traditional geopolitical imaginary.'

Michael J. Shapiro, *University of Hawai'i at Mãnoa, USA*

The series aims to advance understanding of the key areas in which scholars working within broad critical post-structural and post-colonial traditions have chosen to make their interventions, and to present innovative analyses of important topics.

Titles in the series engage with critical thinkers in philosophy, sociology, politics and other disciplines, and provide situated historical, empirical and textual studies in international politics.

Madness in International Relations
Psychology, security and the global
governance of mental health
Alison Howell

Spatiality, Sovereignty and Carl Schmitt
Geographies of the nomos
Edited by Stephen Legg

Politics of Urbanism
Seeing like a city
Warren Magnusson

Beyond Biopolitics
Theory, violence and horror in world politics
François Debrix and Alexander D. Barder

The Politics of Speed
Capitalism, the state and war in an
accelerating world
Simon Glezos

Politics and the Art of Commemoration
Memorials to struggle in Latin America
and Spain
Katherine Hite

Indian Foreign Policy
The politics of postcolonial identity
Priya Chacko

Politics of the Event
Time, movement, becoming
Tom Lundborg

Theorizing Post-Conflict Reconciliation
Agonism, restitution and repair
Edited by Alexander Keller Hirsch

Theorizing Post-Conflict Reconciliation

Agonism, restitution and repair

Edited by
Alexander Keller Hirsch

LONDON AND NEW YORK

First published 2012
by Routledge
2 Park Square, Milton Park, Abingdon, Oxon, OX14 4RN

Simultaneously published in the USA and Canada
by Routledge
711 Third Avenue, New York, NY 10017

Routledge is an imprint of the Taylor & Francis Group, an informa business

First issued in paperback 2013

© 2012 Editorial and selected matter: Alexander Keller Hirsch,
Contributors, their contributions

The right of Alexander Keller Hirsch to be identified as editor of this work
has been asserted by him in accordance with the Copyright, Designs and
Patent Act 1988.

All rights reserved. No part of this book may be reprinted or reproduced or
utilised in any form or by any electronic, mechanical, or other means, now
known or hereafter invented, including photocopying and recording, or in
any information storage or retrieval system, without permission in writing
from the publishers.

Trademark notice: Product or corporate names may be trademarks or
registered trademarks, and are used only for identification and explanation
without intent to infringe.

British Library Cataloguing in Publication Data
A catalogue record for this book is available from the British Library

Library of Congress Cataloging-in-Publication Data
Theorizing post-conflict reconciliation : agonism, restitution & repair /
edited by Alexander Keller Hirsch.
    p. cm. – (Interventions)
  Includes bibliographical references and index.
  1. Peace-building. 2. Restorative justice. 3. Reconciliation.
  4. Peace-building–Case studies. 5. Restorative justice–Case studies.
  6. Reconciliation–Case studies. I. Hirsch, Alexander Keller.
  JZ5538.T47 2012
  303.6′9–dc23   2011026487

ISBN: 978-0-415-78173-2 (hbk)
ISBN: 978-0-415-71365-8 (pbk)
ISBN: 978-0-203-14447-3 (ebk)

Typeset in Times New Roman
by HWA Text and Data Management, London

Contents

Contributors

Thomas Brudholm holds a PhD in Philosophy and is Associate Professor in the Department of Cross-Cultural and Regional Studies at the University of Copenhagen, Denmark. He is the author of *Resentment's Virtue: Jean Améry and the refusal to forgive* (Temple University Press, 2008), and is the editor of *The Religious in Response to Mass Atrocity: interdisciplinary perspectives* (Cambridge University Press, 2009). Brudholm has published several articles on emotional and moral responses to political violence, including 'Picturing forgiveness' (*Studies in Christian Ethics*, 24(1), 2011). Currently, Brudholm is focusing on hatred as it has been conceptualized in philosophy and as it is understood in modern discourses on hate crime and hate speech.

Sonali Chakravarti is Assistant Professor of Government at Wesleyan University, USA. She received her PhD from Yale University and is the author of 'More than cheap sentimentality: victim testimony at Nuremberg, the Eichmann trial, and truth commissions' (*Constellations*, 15(2), 2008). She is currently working on a manuscript about the significance of anger in periods after mass violence.

Erik Doxtader is Professor of Rhetoric at the University of South Carolina, USA, as well as Senior Research Fellow at the Institute for Justice and Reconciliation in South Africa. He has published widely on the theory and practice of reconciliation, including *With Faith in the Works of Words: the beginnings of reconciliation in South Africa, 1985–1995* (Michigan State UP/David Philip, 2009); *Truth and Reconciliation in South Africa—the Fundamental Documents* (Cape Town: David Philip, September 2007); *To Repair the Irreparable: reparation and reconstruction in South Africa* (Cape Town: David Philip, 2004); and *The Provocations of Amnesty: memory, justice and impunity* (Cape Town: David Philip, 2003). He is currently completing a book on the discourse of contemporary human rights and transitional justice.

Alexander Keller Hirsch is a Lecturer in the Department of Political Science at Northeastern University in Boston, as well as a Research Fellow at the University of California Humanities Research Institute. He is the author of several articles and book reviews published in such journals as *Theory and Event*; *Contemporary Political Theory*; *Law, Culture, and the Humanities*; and

Philosophy and Social Criticism. Currently, he is completing a dissertation in social and political thought at the University of California, Santa Cruz, which explores how indigenous counter-narratives trouble some of democratic theory's base assumptions.

Bonnie Honig is Sarah Rebecca Roland Professor of Political Science at Northwestern University, and Research Fellow for the American Bar Foundation in Chicago. She is the author of many books, including *Political Theory and the Displacement of Politics* (Cornell University Press, 1993); *Democracy and the Foreigner* (Princeton University Press, 2001); and *Emergency Politics: paradox, law, democracy* (Princeton University Press, 2009). Currently, she is completing a manuscript titled *Antigone, Interrupted*.

Adrian Little is Professor of the Social and Political Sciences at the University of Melbourne in Australia. He is the author of many books, including *Democratic Piety: complexity, conflict and violence* (Edinburgh University Press, 2008); *Democracy and Northern Ireland: beyond the liberal paradigm?* (Palgrave Macmillan, 2004); *The Politics of Community: theory and practice* (Edinburgh University Press, 2002); and co-editor with Moya Lloyd of *The Politics Radical Democracy* (Edinburgh University Press, 2009).

James Martel is Associate Professor and Chair of the Department of Political Science at San Francisco State University. He is the author of several books, including *Love is a Sweet Chain: desire, autonomy, and friendship in liberal political theory* (Routledge, 2001); *Subverting the Leviathan: reading Thomas Hobbes as a radical democrat* (Columbia University Press, 2007); *Divine Violence: Walter Benjamin and the eschatology of sovereignty* (Routledge, 2011); *Hope ... But Not for Us: Walter Benjamin's textual conspiracies* (Michigan University Press, forthcoming); and is co-editor, along with Jimmy Casas Klausen, of *How Not to be Governed: readings and interpretations from a critical anarchist left* (Lexington Press, forthcoming).

Paul Muldoon is Lecturer in Political Theory and Global Politics at Monash University, Australia. He has authored several articles, including most recently, 'The moral legitimacy of anger' (*European Journal of Social Theory*, 2008); 'The sovereign exceptions: colonisation and the foundation of society' (*Social and Legal Studies*, 17(1), 2008); 'Globalisation, neoliberalism and the struggle for indigenous citizenship' (*Australian Journal of Political Science*, 41(2), 2006); 'Thinking responsibility differently: reconciliation and the tragedy of colonisation' (*Journal of Intercultural Studies*, 26(3), 2005); and 'Reconciliation and political legitimacy: the old Australia and the new South Africa' (*Australian Journal of Politics and History*, 49(2), 2003).

Valérie Rosoux is Jennings Randolph Senior Fellow at the United States Institute of Peace, as well as a Senior Research Fellow at the Belgian National Fund for Scientific Research, and member of the steering committee of the Processes of International Negotiation based in The Hague at the Netherlands Institute of

International Relations. She also teaches international conflict transformation at the University of Louvain, Belgium. She is the author of 'Réconcilier: ambition et piège de la justice transitionnelle. Le cas du Rwanda', published in *Droit et société* (2009), and 'Reconciliation as a peace-building process: scope and limits', in J. Bercovitch, V. Kremenyuk and W. Zartman (eds) *Handbook of Conflict Resolution* (London: Sage Publications, 2008).

Andrew Schaap is Senior Lecturer in Politics at the University of Exeter, UK. He is the author of *Political Reconciliation* (Routledge, 2005); editor of *Law and Agonistic Politics* (Ashgate, 2009); and co-editor, along with Danielle Celermajer and Vrasidas Karalis, of *Power, Judgment and Political Evil: in conversation with Hannah Arendt* (Ashgate, 2010). He has also published widely on the subjects of reconciliation and agonism in journals such as *Constellations, European Journal of Political Theory, Contemporary Political Theory* and *Philosophy and Social Criticism.*

Michael J. Shapiro is Professor of Political Science at the University of Hawai'i at Mānoa. Among his recent publications are *Methods and Nations: cultural governance and the indigenous subject* (Routledge, 2004); *Deforming American Political Thought: ethnicity, facticity and genre* (University Press of Kentucky, 2006); *Cinematic Geopolitics* (Routledge, 2009); and *The Time of the City: politics, philosophy and genre* (Routledge, 2010). Currently, he is working on a book on method, tentatively entitled *Studies in Trans-Disciplinary Method: after the aesthetic turn.*

Ernesto Verdeja is Assistant Professor of Political Science at the Kroc Institute for International Peace Studies, and Faculty Fellow at the Nanovic Institute for European Studies, both at the University of Notre Dame, USA. He is the author of *Unchopping a Tree: reconciliation in the aftermath of political violence* (Temple University Press, 2009). Additionally, he has published numerous articles in such journals as *Constellations, Res Publica, Metaphilosophy, Contemporary Political Theory, The European Journal of Political Theory* and *Contemporary Politics.*

Acknowledgments

It is a great privilege to express my gratitude to those whose indispensable support facilitated this book's completion. To the authors I owe ultimate thanks, especially for their enthusiasm for the project as a whole and their commitment towards its publication. Particular thanks are due to Erik Doxtader and Bonnie Honig, whose incisive readings improved the introduction markedly; to Andy Schaap, whose generous and regular advice proved invaluable; and to Mike Shapiro who, luckily for us, recommended Routledge's excellent *Interventions* series in the first place. A number of enjoyable conversations with Alan Keenan proved indispensable early on as the volume was being conceived. I am also grateful to three anonymous reviewers at Routledge for their kind endorsements.

Many of the essays collected here are the upshot of two panels convened at the Western Political Science Association's 2009 annual meeting in San Francisco. Many thanks are owed to those who participated and attended those panels. Jason Frank was kind enough to serve as chair and respondent to the 'Faultlines of Contestation' panel convened at an altogether unreasonable hour of the morning. As James Martel commented at the start of the 'Scenes of Transition in Radical Democratic Perspective' panel, it truly felt as though a community of interlocutors had been assembled. Works such as this are intensely collaborative – a fact I have been vastly thankful for, given the convivial good cheer each and every one of these exceptional scholars brought to the project.

Though I can claim credit for only a modest portion of this volume, I would like also to thank those counsellors and friends at the University of California, Santa Cruz, whose influence has left an indelible impression on my work. In particular, I thank Jim Clifford and Jack Schaar, whose treasured guidance and intellectual generosity have sustained me through many projects, this one not least of all.

I would like also to thank The Routledge Publishing Group at Taylor & Francis, and especially Nick Vaughan-Williams and Jenny Edkins for their encouragement and enduring patience throughout the publication process. Nicola Parkin was an extraordinary editor, supple and responsive, possessing measured patience and fierce diligence.

Though most of the essays collected here were commissioned specifically for this project, a few are revised versions of previously published articles. I would like in closing to acknowledge those sources whose permission has been given for reprinting here. Thomas Brudholm's and Valérie Rosoux's contribution is published here with the permission of *Law and Contemporary Problems* at Duke University Press (72: 33, 2009); Bonnie Honig's essay is a revised version of an article originally published in the *TriQuarterly Review* by Northwestern University Press (2008); and Alexander Keller Hirsch's essay is a version of an article re-printed here with the permission of *Contemporary Political Theory* and Palgrave MacMillan (10: 2, 2011).

1   Introduction

The agon of reconciliation

Alexander Keller Hirsch

On the contemporary scene of geopolitical studies and international relations theory the subject of transitional justice is much invoked of late (see e.g. McAdams 1997; Minow 1999; Teitel 2000; Elster 2004; Roht-Arriaza and J. Mariecruzana 2006; De Greiff 2010; Leebaw 2011). Typically, the phrase is mobilized in reference to the recuperative period that political cultures undergo after a traumatic episode has come to pass. Reckoning with a conflict that has left a society riven, transitional justice seeks to reconstitute a shared sense of belonging – what Jean-Luc Nancy would call a 'being-in-common' – a collective social identity embodied in the mutual invocation of a communal 'we' (Nancy 2000). The founding of legal tribunals, truth commissions, official apologies, and public confessionals serve as paradigmatic exemplars. Each is established to help reconcile a society to its violent past and to shore up a new more just era 'after evil' (see Copjec 1996; Bernstein 2002; Barkan 2001; Philpott 2006; Meister 2010). As Martha Minow puts it, 'the capacity and limitations of these legal responses illuminate the hopes and commitments of individuals and societies seeking, above all, some rejoinder to the unspeakable destruction and degradation of human beings' (Minow 1999: 1).

In response to the recent spate of violent episodes and the rituals of public mourning which have cropped up to remedy them, the transitional justice literature has expanded into a now inundated field of scholarship. Since the Nuremburg trials projected techniques of redemption for victims of Holocaustic genocide at mid-century, a host of mechanisms of redress have been concocted (see Digeser 2001; Thompson 2003; Kurasawa 2007; Zolo 2009). The ethnic violence committed against Armenians, Tutsi, Bengalis, the Aché in Paraguay, Timorese, southern Sudanese, as well as countless others who have experienced mass terror and political violence in places as disparate as Northern Ireland, Chile, South Africa, Argentina, Uganda, China and Iran, exemplifies the range of scene and setting where measures of transitional justice have been taken up (see Drumbl 2007; Verdeja 2009). Interventions in the field hail from academic circles spanning the range of the humanities and social sciences – from political science, anthropology, sociology, economics and history, to literature, philosophy, theology and cultural studies.

Much of this literature has been focused on a vision of reconciliation as communitarian social harmony. Through collective acts of public apology and forgiveness, so the argument goes, reparation and restoration are imparted, and the writhing conflict of the past is substituted for by the 'overlapping consensus' of community. In 'The Moral Foundations of Truth Commissions', Amy Gutmann and Dennis Thompson defend this argument by lying down deliberative democratic principles in the service of 'mutual respect' and 'common ground'. According to Gutmann and Thompson, such principles supply a moral justification for sacrificing criminal justice in the name of the 'general social benefit' reconciliation offers. The upshot of those benefits requires that citizens 'seek common ground where it exists, and maintain mutual respect where it does not' (Gutmann and Thompson 2000: 161). In her article 'Moral Conflict and Political Consensus', Gutmann clarifies what this mutual respect would entail: 'mutual respect, the foundation upon which deliberation rests, requires citizens to strive not only for agreement on principles governing the basic structure but also for agreement on practices governing the way they deal with principled disagreements' (Gutmann 1990: 101). In other words, for Gutmann and Thompson, reconciliation means engendering relations of equanimity between historical antagonists based on reciprocal commonality, reverence and, above all, agreement.

This approach has been generally supported of late by theorists such as Bashir Bashir, Nadim Rouhana, Johnathan VanAntwerpen and Will Kymlicka who, in a recent volume – *The Politics of Reconciliation in Multicultural Societies* – defend the deliberative approach to transitional justice (Kymlicka and Bashir 2010). These thinkers equally stress the necessity of generating an overlapping consensus for a viable politics of reconciliation. As Bashir notes in his essay 'Accommodating Historically Oppressed Social Groups', 'Reconciliation should be seen as a *precondition*, not an outcome, of inclusive deliberative democracy' (Bashir 2010: 18). In other words, *pace* Gutmann and Thompson, a common agreement needs to develop between enemy contenders before any politics can take place.

In many ways, at their root, these approaches share an abiding debt to the work of political philosophers John Rawls and Jürgen Habermas. For Rawls, famously, serious conflicts must be adjudicated and resolved before political society can be cultivated. 'Faced with the fact of reasonable pluralism,' Rawls argues, 'a liberal view removes from the political agenda the most divisive issues, serious contention about which must undermine the bases of social cooperation' (Rawls 1993: xvi). Habermas, like Rawls, stresses the democratic virtue of a pre-established agreement, with the distinction that his is a 'communicatively achieved consensus' (Habermas 1996a: 21).[1] For both, agreement is idealized and rational, conducted through the public use of reason, and above all vital to the normative functioning of politics.

And yet, when applied to cases of transitional justice, several questions arise which trouble some of Rawls' and Habermas' basic assumptions. If resolve must be achieved in order for politics to begin, and deep disagreement and disrespect must be ruled out ahead of time, how ought we to cope politically with conflicts that remain fundamentally irresolvable? Does not the bracketing of difference work to suspend precisely that which must be actively confronted if reconciliation is to be achieved? How would such a model of justice which seeks to reunite a divided society by adjourning difference and discrepancy avoid promoting in practice a resolution that looks more like quietist surrender by the victim to the perpetrator than harmonizing reconciliation? How might the work done in assuaging past discord further debase and politically neutralize the victims of abuse in need of reconciliation and repair in the first place? And in what ways do the twin paradigms of victim and perpetrator fail to account for what Primo Levi described as the 'gray zone' – that space between victims and perpetrators, peopled with 'gray ambiguous persons' who may be complicit in atrocity by virtue of their unquestioning acceptance?

The essays collected here start with these questions. Their aim is not to settle, but to enrich and deepen the questions' force. More specifically, these essays are bound by the conviction that despite its exponential growth and its admirable interdisciplinary breadth, some if not most of the angles of approach, normative modes of address and popular conclusions reached by transitional justice thought fall short, or worse, unwittingly perpetuate the very injustices they aim to suture. In some cases, an injunction to 'move on', to leave the painful past behind in the name of a conciliatory future, is too quickly prescribed, resulting in the repression rather than release of the traumatic event. In still others, an insidious act of reification takes place in the call for reconciliation between hostile factions. In cases such as Rwanda or Bosnia, no originary pacific rapport characterized the relationship between those factions. In calling for *re*-conciliation or *re*-storation, the messy history of the conflict in question's gestation is obfuscated or erased from view.

Exploring the possibility for an alternative approach to post-conflict reconciliation, this volume provides an expressive contact zone between the praxis of transition, on the one hand, and the ethos of radical democratic thought, on the other. Drawing influence and insight from the exemplary work of a cluster of contemporary luminaries, such as William Connolly, Bonnie Honig, Chantal Mouffe, Ernesto Laclau, Jacques Rancière, James Tully and Sheldon Wolin, the contributors to this volume affirm the often irresolvable character of the constitutive tensions at the heart of political community. Rather than jettison serious disagreements in the name of pacifying settlement, the essays collected here affirm the *dissensus* and contestation endemic to transitional sites of reconciliation. In so doing, they find inspiration in the vision of politics rendered by new pluralist, new realist, and especially agonistic political theory.

As most readers familiar with the vicissitudes of contemporary democratic theory will be aware, the terms *agonism* and *agonistic* derive etymologically from the Greek ἀγών (agōn), signifying a brand of struggle, and in particular an athletic contest between contending agents in the midst of a religious festival. In fifth century tragic drama, the phrase was often deployed to signify the terms by which a struggle between protagonist and antagonist would be scripted in order to supply the basis of action. The concept served as an operative theme in the works of Machiavelli, Nietzsche and Weber, all of whom conjured agonism as a means of portraying politics as a mode of conflict. In tow, social and political thinkers such as Carl Schmitt, Hannah Arendt and Michel Foucault seized upon the agon, portraying political decisionism, public freedom and the microtechniques of power as occasions for agonistic engagement.

As opposed to pluralist or deliberative democrats, whose efforts are directed towards buttressing institutions and processes which would foster co-operation, reunion and appeasement, agonists assert the irreducible quality of conflict for the political. On an agonistic reading, deliberativists are charged with depoliticizing tensions and thus with neutralizing the very energies that buoy political action. Agonistic democrats also depart from the proceduralist liberalism that flows from the justice theory of Rawls and other advocates who are, as Dana Villa puts it, 'so anxious to avoid conflict that they construct a set of public institutions, and a code of public argument and justification, which leave precious little space for initiatory or expressive modes of political action' (Villa 1999: 108). Attempts to administer, bureaucratize, or otherwise domesticate the feral and fugitive quality of the political are regularly submitted to the dictates of agonistic critique (see e.g. Wolin 1989; Christodoulidis 1998; Loughlin and Walker 2007; Veitch 2007; Schaap 2009; Frank 2009).

Importantly, however, the sort of conflict agonists endorse does not resemble Georges Sorel's defense of the purging burn of revolutionary violence. Instead, it is difference, disagreement and discord, directed through channels that guard against a politics of *ressentiment*, which revitalize the political field. Agonists are interested in gauging these tensions in sites of struggle and contestation arising out of demands for cultural recognition (Markell 2003; Balfour 2008), questions of legitimation raised by declining political participation (Wolin 2008) and the constitutive exclusions upon which liberal principles of universalization are based (Connolly 2002; Honig 2003; Tully 2009; Rancière 2009; Muldoon 2010).

This volume suggests that agonism affords post-conflict thought a valuable store of insight otherwise subdued by status quo theories of transition. Though the authors below exhibit varying degrees of allegiance to this genealogy of agonistic thought, they are each alike drawn to that space where reconciliation and agonism overlap. In terms of topical variety, the essays collected here offer a panoply of vantage points from which this overlap might be viewed. A host of diverse geopolitical coordinates serve as case studies, and a range of methodological tactics are employed. In exploring what an agonistic accounting of reconciliation looks like for post-conflict societies, several important current debates are invoked and grappled with in these pages, including: the prospect for forgiveness in the aftermath of nominally unforgivable violence; the politics of loss, public mourning and memorialization; the ethics of anger and resentment; poststructuralist approaches to political subjectivity; political theologies of restitution; pluralism, multiculturalism and tolerance; the nature and meaning of political responsibility and moral repair; trauma, healing and the messianic promise of a justice 'to come'.

In Chapter 2 'Agonism and the power of victim testimony', Sonali Chakravarti asks how anger – and other such 'difficult' and 'unsocial emotions' – expressed during oral and public testimonials by those who experienced violence exposes new questions for the agonistic approach to transitional justice. In particular,

Chakravarti focuses on how such testimonials can 'allow for dissonant narratives, a rejection of narrowly rationalistic approaches, and provide a place to see patterns of political critique that would not emerge in other institutions'. Still, when victim testimony bucks against those aspects of truth commissions designed to quell enmity, it can serve as a powerful beacon for reconciliation that also pushes agonistic critique to revalue restorative justice as a measure of repairing fractured political relationships. As Chakravarti writes, 'It is not enough to say that anger is part of the remainder of politics and will continue to haunt public life …' Anger, when articulated by victims, also provides orientation for strengthening social and political ties after mass violence.

Erik Doxtader, in his contribution to the volume, 'A critique of law's violence yet (never) to come: United Nations' transitional justice policy and the (fore) closure of reconciliation' (Chapter 3), stakes out a similar point of departure. 'Today,' writes Doxtader, 'there are signs that transitional justice aims to convert – with disturbing fervor – the constitutive and agonistic quality of reconciliation into a demand (if not a command) for the adversarial, a commitment to the (prior) definition and application of a rule of law.' Doxtader's basic aim is to reflect on this turn against reconciliation's 'turning right about' and, in his own terms, 'to plot at least one of the ways in which reconciliation's place has been largely closed and then foreclosed from the premises and promises of transitional justice'. Taking the United Nations as his case study, and especially a number of its policy documents and debates that have appeared over the last decade, Doxtader traces the UN's erasure and expressed aversion to reconciliation's 'unaccountable' ambiguity. In concluding, Doxtader turns to the question of how the institution's case for standardizing the language of transitional justice recognizes the rule of law at the expense of misrecognizing the law's rule of recognition, 'that is, the fully transitional problem of how to constitute the grounds of the law's power in the wake of violence, including legal violence'. More than simple oversight, for Doxtader, the UN's presumption against reconciliation points directly to its importance – a potential for words that stand before the law and compose a critique of how the law's violence may preclude precisely the claiming of human rights that transitional justice policy presents as it ultimate warrant.

In 'Rhetorics of reconciliation' (Chapter 4), Adrian Little engages Doxtader directly. Challenging the 'rhetorical theory of reconciliation' represented in Doxtader's work on South Africa, Little contends that coming to terms with reconciliation means drawing on concepts of paradigm shift (Kuhn and Agamben), and also the insights of complexity theory (Cilliers and Zolo). In exploring this terrain, Little turns to the transitional case of Northern Ireland, and argues that 'there does not have to be a clear definition of reconciliation to underpin a conflict transformation process. Rather, reconciliation can act as a general heading under which a rhetorical space can be established that enables a more open discussion of the issues at stake in conflict transformation …' In developing this argument, Little also draws upon the Deleuzian concept of a 'disjunctured synthesis', which characterizes Northern Ireland's opposing forces, locked as they are in a reciprocal and mutual reliance upon one another.

In 'Fugitive reconciliation' (Chapter 5), Alexander Keller Hirsch follows both Doxtader, in focusing on the temporal 'to come' of reconciliation, and Little, in reading Agamben in light of an agonistic reading of transitional justice. In each case, however, Hirsch ultimately departs from the other. The chapter works both to foreground and to productively problematize theories of post-conflict reconciliation based on the perpetual deferral of accord. Through readings of Jean Améry and Sheldon Wolin the essay argues that an emphasis on messianicity as the temporal mode of political repair is ultimately less productive for what Hirsch calls an 'agonistics of reconciliation' than a more nuanced approach to what Wolin calls 'fugitive democracy'. Where the former is allied with a bedeviled politics of mutual respect, the latter affirms a more germane politics of abiding resentment. In the end, a surprising conclusion is drawn from reading agonistic reconciliation through Wolin: democracy may be a political experience reserved for scenes of transitional justice alone.

In 'Can human beings forgive?' (Chapter 6), James Martel shifts the discussion away from the 'Messianic cessation of happening' and toward another political theological motif, that of divine violence. Here, Martel engages with the philosophy of Walter Benjamin in order to consider the question of the possibility of human forgiveness in the aftermath of 'divine violence'. At first glance, writes Martel, 'Benjamin's notion of divine violence may seem to suggest that judgment and forgiveness are exclusively the province of a God that is utterly unknowable.' Martel asks, 'In the face of the awesome and irrefutable power of the divine, what can we make of the ability of human beings to make their own judgments? How are human beings able to forgive when they cannot know the bases for justice that underpin such decisions?' Provocatively, Martel suggests that, for Benjamin, we are able to forgive not despite but because of divine violence: 'Divine violence cleanses' not only the idolators themselves but also 'all of our phantasms of authority and power that take on universal, and idolatrous, pretensions. When such idolatrous forms of judgment are removed or subverted by the notion of a cleansing deity, we are returned to our own contingent and agonistic forms of justice and forgiveness.' From such a perspective, Martel writes, we can think further about what we can and cannot forgive.

In 'The unforgiving' (Chapter 7), Thomas Brudholm and Valérie Rosoux also focus on the politics of forgiveness in the context of reconciliation. From the perspective adopted in their chapter, calls for forgiveness in contemporary transitional sites such as Liberia or Rwanda, risk becoming '"distorted and cheapened by various movements that advocate it in a hasty and uncritical way"'. Seeking to 'bring more nuance to common conceptions of unforgiving victims and the resistance or refusal to forgive', Brudholm and Rosoux maintain that when forgiveness is boosted as a panacea and an absolute vitue, unforgiveness takes on the spectre of a morally impossible position. Recalling Chakravarti's chapter, Brudholm and Rosoux write: '[I]f the unforgiving survivors understood more about the background of the perpetrators, or about what ideals and values really count; if they did not confuse forgetting with forgiving; if they were more capable of managing their anger; if they thought more rationally about their own good or the good of the nation, then they would try to forgive or let go of their resentment and engage more constructively in the process of reconciliation.' And recalling Hirsch's essay, Brudholm and Rosoux elicit a reading of Jean Améry in defying stereotypical conceptions of the unforgiving victim or the refusal to forgive. Ultimately, the chapter concludes that forgiveness, when conducted in transitional contexts, remains a 'madness of the impossible'.

Michael Shapiro's essay 'Senses of justice' (Chapter 8) continues to probe the themes of law, culture, violence, retaliation, and justice by focusing on the juridico-political ramifications of Corneliu Porumboiu's *Police, Adjective*, a 2009 Romanian 'filmic text' on 'the spaces of policing', and Leonardo Sciascia's Italian detective novel *The Day of the Owl*. Drawing on readings of Agamben, Foucault, Lyotard and Deleuze in his analysis of Porumboiu and Sciascia, Shapiro lays the conceptual foundations for what he calls the 'micropolitics of justice'. This micropolitics arrays itself in a complex cartography of justice. '[J]ustice deploys itself differently in incommensurate spaces of application,' writes Shapiro, '[t]he differences in law's reception, realized as a mosaic of justice subcultures across regional spaces ...' An important distinction thus exists between formal justice, as is codified in law, and informal justice, as in belonging to political culture. Shaprio works to flesh out the tension between the two, by staging 'interferences' in Lyotard's notion of the 'differend', so often invoked in agonistic accounts of reconciliation.

In her essay, 'The other is dead: mourning, justice, and the politics of burial' (Chapter 9), Bonnie Honig draws upon a different set of texts in asking 'how should democratic societies relate to those ... killed in the process of settlement and colonization, to the victims of civil wars, conflicts or genocide?' In addressing this question, Honig reads together two improbable texts: 'a film and a play written over 2,000 years apart but which speak to each other across the temporal chasm'. The film, *Sophie's Choice*, movingly explores the tragic outcome of the divergent pulls of mourning and justice in the aftermath of genocide. *The Antigone*, stages a reflection on the politics of mourning and justice, 'two conflicting political responses to the dead'. In the end, Honig points in the direction of a different kind of 'mourning work': 'not a working through but rather a loving letting go, such as that imagined by Whitman in 'Reconciliation', where the sharedness of death itself, that ultimate other, and the power of the word, work some sort of magic and draw the living to the dead in the moment of ritual burial.'

In his chapter 'The elements of political reconciliation' (Chapter 10), Ernesto Verdeja asks what mode of reconciliation would be morally appropriate given the intensity of violence between former adversaries in Bosnia-Herzegovina. This form of reconciliation 'is achieved when previous, conflict-era identities no longer operate as the primary cleavages in politics, and thus citizens acquire new identities that cut across those earlier fault lines'. In exploring this terrain, Verdeja elaborates on two paradigms of reconciliation, generally adopted in much of the academic literature, which depart from the divisions ordinarily conceived between liberal and communitarian, restorative and realist. The approaches Verdeja works with are termed 'minimalist' and 'maximalist' respectively. The first 'identifies some basic, liminal conditions for coexistence rooted on the rule of law and the end of overt violence', while the second emphasizes 'strong social solidarity and often mutual healing and forgiveness'. In the end, Verdeja suggests neither is truly satisfactory for deeply divided societies, which ultimately require a measure of mutual recognition grounded in a conception of reconciliation as disjunctured and uneven.

In some ways, Paul Muldoon and Andrew Schaap subject this view to critique in their chapter, 'Confounded by recognition' (Chapter 11). By focusing their normative energies upon the creation of an appropriate hermeneutic of adjudication, liberal critics concerned with strengthening demands for recognition have entrenched the view of the state as a presumptively neutral arbiter and diverted attention from the underlying source of identity-based harms. On their reading, a more radical approach exposes the deeper sources of misrecognition in the identity-making practices of the state itself. Muldoon and Schaap amplify 'the more agonistic (and antagonistic) dimensions of the demand for recognition by looking at the politics surrounding two identity-based harms tangled up in the reconciliation debate in Australia: the removal of Aboriginal children from their families and the denial of Aboriginal sovereignty'. In the end, Muldoon and Schaap argue that it is only with exceptional moments – as with the Aboriginal Tent Embassy – when Aboriginal people stake a claim for prior sovereignty, that the Australian state is pressed to confront the deeper sources of misrecognition in its own desire for unity and sovereign control.

Together, these chapters form a collage, an assemblage of elements. Though they are gathered and arrayed in a purposeful order, they are also self-supporting and can be read apart from one another in any order. The essays hang together like points of light in a constellation. That said, there is a strong current that runs through them, asserting the value of challenging the way reconciliation is ordinarily conceived and executed in transitional contexts. Perennial questions of justice, power and violence are, we maintain, extended, intensified and, in some cases, upended by honing in on sites of conflict and transition in an agonistic way. In asserting as much, however, the aim is not to provide final solutions. Rather we intend to stimulate debate, encourage new orientations for social research and inspire innovative investigations into democratic theory's practical applications.

Notes

1 A similar argument is made by Stuart Hampshire, who pleads for a 'basic level of morality, a bare minimum...', see Hampshire (1989: 68, 72).

References

Balfour, L. (2008) 'Act & fact: slavery reparations as a democratic politics of reconciliation', in Bashir, B. and Kymlicka, W. *The Politics of Reconciliation in Multicultural Societies*, Oxford, UK: Oxford University Press.
Barkan, E. (2001) *The Guilt of Nations: restitution and negotiating historical injustices*, Baltimore, MD: Johns Hopkins University Press.

Bernstein, R. (2002) *Radical Evil: a philosophical exploration*, Oxford, UK: Blackwell Publishing.

Christodoulidis, E. (1998) *Law and Reflexive Politics*, Norwell, MA: Kluwer Publishers.

Christodoulidis, E. and Veitch, S. (eds) (2001) *Lethe's Law: justice, law, and ethics in reconciliation*, Portland, OR: Hart Publishing.

Connolly, W. (2002) *Identity/Difference: democratic negotiations of political paradox*, Minneapolis, MN: University of Minnesota Press.

Copjec, J. (ed.) (1996) *Radical Evil*, London: Verso Books.

De Greiff, P. (ed.) (2010) *Transitional Justice and Development: making connections*, New York: Social Science Research Council.

Digeser, P. (2001) *Political Forgiveness*, Ithaca, NY: Cornell University Press.

Drumbl, M. (2007) *Atrocity, Punishment, and International Law*, Cambridge, UK: Cambridge University Press.

Elster, J. (2004) *Closing the Books: transitional justice in historical perspective*, Cambridge, UK: University of Cambridge Press.

Gutmann, A. and Thompson, D. (1990) 'Moral conflict and political consensus', *Ethics* 101(1): 64–88.

Gutmann, A and Thompson, D. (2000) 'The moral foundations of truth commissions', in Rotberg, R. and Thompson, D. (eds.) *Truth v. Justice: the morality of truth commissions*, Princeton, NJ: Princeton University Press.

Habermas, J. (1996) 'Three normative models of democracy', in Benhabib, S. (ed.) *Democracy and Difference: contesting the boundaries of the political*, Princeton, NJ: Princeton University Press.

Hampshire, S. (1989) *Innocence and Experience*, Cambridge, MA: Harvard University Press.

Honig, B. (2003) *Democracy and the Foreigner*, Princeton, NJ: Princeton University Press.

Kurasawa, F. (2007) *The Work of Global Justice: human rights as practices*, Cambridge, UK: Cambridge University Press.

Kymlicka, W. and Bashir, B. (eds) (2008) *The Politics of Reconciliation in Multicultural Societies*, Oxford, UK: Oxford University Press.

Leebaw, B. (2011) *Judging State-Sponsored Violence, Imagining Political Change*, Cambridge, UK: Cambridge University Press.

Loughlin, M. and Walker, N. (eds) (2007) *The Paradox of Constitutionalism: constituent power and constitutional form*, Oxford, UK: Oxford University Press.

McAdams, J. (ed.) (1997) *Transitional Justice and the Rule of Law in New Democracies*, South Bend, IN: University of Notre Dame Press.

Meister, R. (2010) *After Evil: a politics of human rights*, New York: Columbia University Press.

Minow, M. (1999) *Between Vengeance and Forgiveness: facing history after genocide and mass violence*, Boston, MA: Beacon Press.

Mouffe, C. (2000b) *The Democratic Paradox*, London: Verso Books.

Muldoon, P. (2010) 'The very basis of civility: on agonism, conquest and reconciliation', in Bashir, B. and Kymlicka, W. (eds) *The Politics of Reconciliation in Multicultural Societies*, Oxford, UK: Oxford University Press.

Nancy, J-L. (2000) *Being Singular Plural*, Palo Alto, CA: Stanford University Press.

Philpott, D. (2006) *The Politics of Past Evil: religion, reconciliation and the dilemmas of transitional justice*, South Bend, IN: University of Notre Dame Press.

Rawls, J. (1993) *Political Liberalism*, New York: Columbia University Press.

Rancière, J. (2009) *Hatred of Democracy*, London: Verso.

Roht-Arriaza, N. and Mariecruzana, J. (eds) (2006) *Transitional Justice in the Twenty- First Century: beyond truth versus justice*, Cambridge, UK: Cambridge University Press.

Rotberg, R. and Thompson, D. (eds) (2000) *Truth v. Justice: the morality of truth commissions*, Princeton, NJ: Princeton University Press.

Schaap, A. (ed.) (2009) *Law and Agonistic Politics*, London: Ashgate Press.

Teitel, R. (2000) *Transitional Justice*. Oxford, UK: Oxford University Press.

Thompson, J. (2003) *Taking Responsibility for the Past: reparation and historical injustice*, New York: Polity Press.

Tully, J. (2009) *Public Philosophy in a New Key*, Cambridge, UK: Cambridge University Press.

Veitch, S. (2007) *Law and the Politics of Reconciliation*, London: Ashgate Publishing.

Verdeja, E. (2009) *Unchopping a Tree: reconciliation in the aftermath of political violence*, Philadelphia, PA: Temple University Press.

Villa, D. (1999) *Politics, Philosophy, Terror: essays on the thought of Hannah Arendt*, Princeton, NJ: Princeton University Press.

Wolin, S. (1989) *The Presence of the Past: essays on the state and the constitution*, Baltimore, MD: Johns Hopkins University Press.

Wolin, S. (2008) *Democracy Incorporated: managed democracy and the specter of totalitarianism*, Princeton, NJ: Princeton University Press.

Zolo, D. (2009) *Victor's Justice: from Nuremberg to Baghdad*, London: Verso Books.

2 Agonism and the power of victim testimony

Sonali Chakravarti

Victim testimony, the public testimony of those who experienced violence, in the context of a truth commission may be one of the best contemporary examples of an agonistic moment in political life. This chapter will examine the ways in which it embodies the characteristics of agonism while also suggesting that such testimony generates new questions for agonistic theory, especially as it pertains to transitional justice. Attention to the expression of anger in victim testimony serves as a limit case for the agonistic conception and is the focus of my argument about the potential for a relationship between agonism and the work of restorative justice.

Proponents of an agonistic conception of democracy emphasize the struggle, between forces, ideas and individuals, inherent in political life and the need to pay attention to the ways in which consensus and rationality can be limiting concepts. The writings on agonism by scholars Chantal Mouffe (2000b), Bonnie Honig (1993), and William Connolly (2002), among others, all put forth a critique of liberal democratic approaches because of the constraints, implicit and explicit, on what should be considered political. They advocate both for the creation of new political spaces and new understandings of identity, as contingent, relational, and open to upheaval and change. Connolly writes, 'Agonistic democracy breaks with the democratic idealism of communitarianism through its refusal to equate concern for human dignity with a quest for rational consensus ... Democratic agonism does not exhaust social space; it leaves room for other modalities of attachment and detachment' (Connolly 2002: x). While writing in the idiom of democratic politics, agonistic theorists put forth a new ideal of democracy, marked not by the successes of consensus or legitimacy but rather by a type of epistemic openness to a greater plurality of opinions than has been heard before. Connolly's point that 'democratic agonism does not exhaust social space' also suggests a rethinking of the ambitions of democracy in its hegemonic claims on social space. There are other ways of engaging in public that are politically relevant and not captured in even the more expansive conception of democratic agonism.

Agonistic proponents do not fear the conflict that comes from opposing perspectives in the political realm. In fact, when this type of contestation is given space to proliferate, other types of boundaries by which individuals are excluded from membership should become less salient. Chantal Mouffe writes,

Envisaged from the point of view of 'agonistic pluralism', the aim of democratic politics is to construct the 'them' in such a way that it is no longer perceived as an enemy to be destroyed, but as an 'adversary', that is, somebody whose ideas we combat but whose right to defend those ideas we do not put into question. This is the real meaning of liberal-democratic tolerance, which does not entail condoning ideas that we oppose or being indifferent to standpoints that we disagree with, but treating those who defend them as legitimate opponents.

(Mouffe 2000b: 1)

In Mouffe's understanding, advocating for the 'adversary' includes an awareness of the discursive modes through which individuals engage in political life. This necessitates acknowledging 'tolerance' often times does not extend to a large portion of the citizenry who defend viewpoints outside of conventional parameters and who are thereby not seen as 'legitimate opponents'. The tone in which their perspectives are delivered, as well as the content, make them enemies working against the ideal of liberal democratic norms. While proponents of an agonistic conception see myriad possibilities emerging from the reconsideration of these norms and an opening of alternative political spaces, the experience of victim testimony provides an unusually rich case, both because of its content and the way it acts as a challenge to the limits of agonism.

Victim testimony, as used here, refers to the oral and public testimony of victims that has been a prominent part of certain truth commissions, the most well known of which is the South African Truth and Reconciliation Commission (also known as the TRC, held between 1996–1998). Truth commissions are temporary bodies, created by the United Nations or by presidential authority, which are formed in order to investigate the events of a specific period, such as war or genocide. They have taken on a range of functions including interviewing victims of human rights violations, investigating crimes, documenting forensic evidence, and granting amnesty. Each function has a specific role to play in the period after war, but my focus is on the political significance of the public testimony of victims and, within the testimonies, on the expression of the 'difficult' emotions: emotions such as anger, resentment, and despair which occupy an uneasy place in political life. Victim testimony is often the most visible and dramatic part of a truth commission, largely because of the violence and the suffering that is being articulated, often for the first time, in the public sphere.[1] In addition to providing details about the nature of violence they experienced, the victims, in their testimonies, may include a wide range of emotional responses to the violence and its ongoing effect on their lives. In the South African Truth and Reconciliation Commission (TRC), over 2000 people testified in public within the context of hearings which took place in schools and municipal halls all over the country (Hayner 2002: 42).

Agonism and consensus

One of the foundational claims made by proponents of political agonism is the idea that consensus should not be the basis of legitimacy and it has been erroneously heralded as concomitant with democratic progress. In *The Democratic Paradox* Chantal Mouffe suggests that the belief that liberalism can be reconciled with democracy in a stable political system is the cause of delusions for many political theorists (Mouffe 2000b). For her, liberal democracy must always be a paradox that includes respect for rule of law and individual rights (liberalism) and the popular sovereignty and belief in representative government (democracy). In order to suture these two traditions, Rawls and Habermas have become reliant on schemes of rationality meant to legitimize the distribution of power or the decision-making process. Moreover, both emphasize that consensual decisions can be reached through rational argumentation. That which exists outside the guidelines of such argumentation is illegitimate and does not have a place within formal political life. Take, for example, the case of Rawls and pluralism. Mouffe acknowledges that a certain degree of pluralism of worldviews exists within Rawls' theory of the overlapping consensus, but the decision about the boundary between acceptable pluralism and excessive and unacceptable views is not based on reasonableness, as Rawls suggests, but is a political decision that cannot appeal to external justification.[2] Instead, by emphasizing that this division is a political decision, Mouffe is drawing attention to the perception of politics as an ongoing struggle between competing factions and one that must not assume that a consensus can be reached. Instead, an understanding of agonistic pluralism would be open to the variety of perspectives, especially those that would be excluded in a model that uses standards of rationality or reasonableness as filters for inclusion. The struggle and conflict between competing worldviews for power is at the crux of political life and attempting to mitigate this struggle in the name of reaching consensus through rational argument excludes consideration of language that does not contribute to a methodical accounting of causes and effects and is blind to the ways consensus-seeking distorts the full range of responses to the issue at hand.

The potential value of consensus also arises in debates over the value of victim testimony in the context of a truth commission. For example, a rationalistic account of the process after war might focus on the material details of the violence that had occurred and encourage those who testify to corroborate the stories of others to help with the gathering of evidence. This type of testimony is similar to that heard at a criminal trial, where even in the context of an adversarial process there is a consensus on the kinds of evidence deemed material and the procedures for determining its validity. At the same time, those who testify may be asked to connect their experiences to that of a larger group, or in the case of South Africa, think about how certain actions would benefit the image of the nation. All of these expectations are in line with a rational vision which highly values consensus in the context of a truth commission, both through the collection of material evidence and the creation of an overarching narrative. Such a perspective would privilege testimony based on facts over emotional expression and would want individuals to contribute to a shared collective understanding of the violence, one that was meant to encourage a sense of legitimacy and order in the current regime.[3]

In the case of South Africa, one influential perspective put forth by Archbishop Desmond Tutu was that the forgiveness of perpetrators who had committed crimes against oneself or one's family during the apartheid era was one of the most valuable sacrifices an individual could make for her country (Tutu 1999; Minow 1999: 55). Testimonies that fit within this narrative were applauded; while those which did not were sometimes curtailed or seen as dissonant with the purpose of the commission. While victim testimony in public asserts the multiplicity and incompatibility of experiences during times of mass violence, the actual breadth of perspectives about the significance and interpretation of the violence does not necessarily correlate.[4] Commissions have the ability to frame what testimonies should be valued and those that could be seen as disruptive, yet more than other political institutions, victim testimony provides a space for agonistic challenges to expectations of consensus and rationality. While truth commissions might not reach this ideal, victim testimony is crucial because it allows for the possibility of dissonant narratives, rejections of narrowly rationalistic approaches, and a place to see patterns of political critique that would not emerge in other institutions.

Agonism and the inclusion of the passions

Embedded within the debate over consensus and rational argumentation within political life is a debate about the role of emotions in politics. For Rawls and Habermas, among others, the process of building consensus cannot incorporate individual expressions of emotions as political language because such language is neither a universalizable way to persuade others, nor a basis for policy.[5] By excluding emotional language from political debate, the argument goes, individuals are less likely to be swayed by visceral and sentimental reactions to others' positions and more likely to consider concerns of equality and fairness (Rawls 2001: 32; Habermas: 1990: 65).[6]

In addition to the critique of consensus, the strong affinity between victim testimony and agonistic politics includes the centrality of emotional expression in victim testimony, a possibility which is rare in formal political institutions. The sphere of civil society and the arts certainly provide opportunities for such expression in response to the tragedies of war, but in the context of a truth commission, such testimony receives the imprimatur of the state and thus a direct connection to the work of state-sponsored transitional justice. I acknowledge that valuing such dependency on the state for legitimacy is at odds with conceptions of agonism that are committed to alternatives to formal state power. Still, my project is one that sees a potentially beneficial role for the institution of truth commissions and acknowledges that this makes the argument vulnerable to agonistic critique. The power of victim testimony, in my reading, comes not just from the openness to emotional expression within a political institution, but particularly from emotions which would fall under Adam Smith's category of the 'unsocial emotions', including anger, resentment, and despair, emotions which are seen to sever the bonds between citizens rather than strengthen them (Smith 1982). By terming them the unsocial emotions, Smith draws our attention to the tension that exists when they are expressed, but it inadvertently raises the question whether the severing or distancing of citizen relations through the unsocial emotions may, in fact, be a desirable and necessary process. In order to forge new ways of relating to fellow citizens and the state, previous norms must be destroyed and renegotiated. The expression of these emotions in victim testimony may alienate or cause discomfort in the audience, but this is not necessarily unproductive for political life after mass violence.

The unsocial emotions, referred to here as the difficult emotions, in victim testimony crystallize its significance as a manifestation of agonistic politics. The expression of anger, resentment and despair in the context of victim testimony brings to the surface struggles over history and memory, and enlarges the type of political subjectivity that is acceptable. A citizen is not only someone who can express preferences through voting or participation in political organizations, she is also someone whose experiences of physical and psychological pain are seen to be politically significant.[7] One of the most important contributions truth commissions make to the construction of the citizenry is that they challenge previous notions of who has the opportunity to express anger in a public space.

When victim testimony is open to the emotions of anger and despair and does not try to limit their expression, the possibility of consensus over the relationship between the violence of the past and the current identity of the demos is further disrupted. The expression of anger may reveal the nature and object of the speaker's ongoing distrust of institutions and fellow citizens as well as the psychological legacy of the violence which continues to shape her ability to participate in public life. The expression of despair may articulate a hopelessness regarding political responses to suffering and the temptation to withdraw from political life altogether because of the disillusionment one faces. At times, the expression of these emotions may seem irrational, especially if they are presented in a disjointed manner or if the emotions seems disproportionate to the events which caused them. They may also come across as irrational if they seem to be presenting in the political realm problems, fears, and anxieties that cannot be solved in the same place. Yet, to close the possibility of the expression of these emotions is to fall prey to both the agonistic critiques of consensus and the exclusion of passions in political life.

Anger is the emotion that emerges from testimony that is immediately at odds with expectations for political discourse. I suggest that anger threatens deliberative democratic perceptions grounded in rationality in three ways:

1   Anger disrupts the temporal narrative suggested by liberal political institutions, a narrative marked by progress and greater efficacy and objectivity. While truth commissions are about reckoning with the violence of the past, there are expectations about how certain types of reckoning aide in the restoration of political and legal order while other types prolong the chaos of violence. The expression of anger often brings aspects of the past into the present in way that does not fit with an optimistic view of the future. The expression of anger during testimony is a refusal to make oneself the worthy, selfless victim and the one most likely to garner praise from the commission. Instead, anger, often characterized as a runaway train careening off the tracks, becomes the

ongoing force of the past that has the potential to disrupt attempts at order and justice.

2   Anger is not easily universalizable into political options. It does not translate into a rational solution that can be debated for its merits and shortcomings. Consistent with the debate over the role of judgment, the subject expressing anger resists being translated into an impartial spectator who can assess the situation with attention to norms, causes, and concerns about law and fairness (Arendt 1982). The one whose testimony includes anger may not be attentive to how her reactions could not exist *en masse* without devolving into violence or anarchy.

3   The expression of anger is an imprecise way of expressing dissatisfaction about events from the past or frustration with the present. From this perspective, many causes become bundled and the presence of anger amplifies all grievances. When anger does not abate in light of mitigating evidence, this further suggests that anger is only a blunt tool for assessing the validity and significance of claims during victim testimony.

The reasons why anger is a particularly difficult emotion to incorporate into political discourse make the case of victim testimony all the more unusual. In the context of a truth commission, there are opportunities to express anger that are relevant for political life, but are often excluded from deliberation. Examples of anger strategically deployed by political leaders, or elites with political clout are not unusual and could be seen to coexist with the general discomfort with anger, but victim testimony exists outside these existing norms. In fact, the expression of anger in victim testimony can be distilled as the moment when a liberal democratic theory becomes acutely inadequate.

The emotions that are expressed in victim testimony, when administered correctly, suggest an agonistic dimension to politics that has not been fully recognized, so much so that victim testimony may fulfil Mouffe's hope for collective passions. She writes,

> Antagonism is struggle between enemies, while agonism is struggle between adversaries. We can therefore reformulate our problem by saying that envisaged from the perspective of 'agonistic pluralism' the aim of democratic politics is to transform antagonism into agonism. This requires providing channels through which collective passions will be given ways to express themselves over issues which, while allowing enough possibility for identification, will not construct the opponent as an enemy but as an adversary. An important different with the model of 'deliberative democracy' is not to render a rational consensus possible, but to mobilize those passions towards democratic designs.
>
> (Mouffe 2000b: 103)

I suggest that the expression of anger and despair in victim testimony during a truth commission can be mobilized 'towards democratic designs', which I understand to be formal institutional and political mechanisms as well as greater participation, namely through the process of testimony and response. The response to testimony exists at two moments; the first is during the testimony itself. The way a commission responds, the nature of the questions it asks and its perceived comfort with the expression of difficult emotions, shapes the nature of the testimony and whether it is able to fulfil its agonistic possibility. The commissioners have the power to curtail certain types of interpretations, or conversely, accept that such testimonies, outside of rational standards, still have political import, even if this in not immediately apparent. This does not mean accepting each testimony as constructing a blueprint for what should be included in the work of justice after violence, but a focus on the relationship between testimonies and the work of restorative justice. This type of engagement – one that accepts a range of discursive possibilities, without necessarily applauding each one, is consistent with what Connolly defines as 'critical responsiveness'. He writes, 'Critical responsiveness is critical in that it does not always accede to everything that a new constituency or movement demands. But the catch is this: The criticism is not securely guided by established codes of criteria of interpretive judgment. For some of them turn out to be part of the problem' (Connolly 2005: 127). Critical responsiveness gives a formulation to the process of loosening standards of rationality and consensus, but not abandoning the process of evaluation and exchange altogether. Moreover, Connolly's formulation mandates a self-consciousness about how expectations derived from deliberative democratic theory 'may turn out to be part of the problem'. The second moment of response comes at the end of the commission when a report is written (this is standard for truth commissions) and the report should not only focus on the evidence gathered about human rights violations, for example, but should also engage with the patterns which emerged through the expression of anger and despair. These were challenges to political expectations and should not be ignored in the desire to create a coherent, rational narrative. The report which emerges should be a recording of the struggle to make sense of the experiences of the past and the different possibilities for future political organization; it can also highlight the open-ended nature of the testimonies and the way that they resist closure.

Victim testimony brings to light the divisive issue of the place of judgment in agonistic thought. In the valorization of the passions and struggle, theories of agonism can be seen to leave the process and substance of judgment undeveloped. A discussion of agonism in the writings of Hannah Arendt is a paradigmatic example. Contra an interpretation of her work that focuses on deliberation and consensus, Dana Villa is a proponent of the agonistic spirit in Arendt's thought, drawing particularly on her understanding of the glory and virtuosity desirable in action (Villa 1992). Arendt, he notes, resists the instrumentality and teleology in both technocratic and virtue oriented politics, and takes from Nietzsche a belief in the aesthetic quality of action. In a similar way, victim testimony has been the focus of attention of literary scholars who see in it subtleties of experience and emotion not usually found in political action (Felman 2002). Yet, Villa points out that an aesthetic interpretation of action can collapse into narcissistic subjectivism;

to put it another way, the actor becomes solely concerned with the artistic quality of the action, rather than also considering its impact on collective, political life. Arendt avoids this turn, however, with her incorporation of Kant's understanding of the *sensus communis*, a generalization from particular examples which would be consistent with a common understanding. For an agonistic gesture to qualify as 'action' in the highest sense for Arendt, its value must be confirmed by the judgment of the *sensus communis*, an intellectual mechanism which provides a check on self-aggrandizement and narrow self-interest. Villa writes, 'I would like to stress, however, that Arendt's modification of her aestheticized agonism does not employ "external" measures: the appeal she makes is not to reason or dialogue but to taste. Her theory of political judgment limits an excessive agonism not by abandoning the aestheticization of action, but by completing it' (Villa 1992: 288). Villa goes on to explain that it is Arendt's ability to develop a theory of judgment based on the spectator, and the understanding we have in common with others, that insures Arendt's agonism remains relevant to political life; Arendt, he says, tames agonism with judgment. Honig resists the benefits of taming the agon, suggesting that this saps it of precisely what makes agonistic politics meaningful (Honig 1993). Instead, she points to the other divisions and boundaries Arendt employs in order to create a space for agonistic action, including the division between public and private and the role of forgiveness and promise-keeping. It is Arendt's ability to envision institutions which condition and structure action, not only her theory of judgment, which allows the agonistic spirit in her theory to flourish.

The exchange between Villa and Honig highlights the question of what forces (such as judgment) are necessary for a successful vision of agonistic politics and the case of victim testimony prompts similar concerns about whether constraints are necessary to make the emotions and content expressed more 'suitable' for political life. The question then emerges: Should there be any parameters on what type of speech is acceptable within victim testimony? Applying Villa's consideration of Arendtian judgment and the *sensus communis*, one could argue that taking into account how a spectator might react to certain types of violence found in testimony is a useful neutralizing force and should be taken into consideration in the response of the commissioners or the report. My interpretation would suggest a different approach: the institution of a truth commission is already a mitigating force acting upon the agonistic encounter and improvements in the administration of the commission can shape how they become incorporated into political life. By shape, I do not mean that truth commissions impose a coherent narrative on the testimonies where none exists, but rather synthesize the content of the testimonies such that both divergences and patterns are documented. This is consistent with my normative aspirations for victim testimony. A truth commission should not tame the agonistic spirit of victim testimony, particularly not through the censorship or ignorance of anger and despair, yet it should not think of the act of testimony only as a highly individualized, de-politicized, aesthetic performances.[8] There is a way in which institutions can strengthen agonistic politics without compromising their critical power.

Agonism and the concept of the remainder

The third way in which victim testimony manifests an important characteristic of agonistic politics is through the concept of the remainder. Honig initially developed this idea via her conceptions of virtue and *virtù* politics where she argued that within theories of virtue politics, such as those that are found in the writings of Kant, Rawls and Sandel, political stability is engendered by closing off certain possibilities, both in terms of content and emotions.[9] On the shortcomings of the virtue approach, she writes that there is 'a belief that modern disenchantment, alienation, pain, and cruelty would be diminished if only we adopted principles of right, established just institutions, whose fairness is ascertainable from a particular rational perspective' (Honig 1993: 3). In contrast, a politics based on *virtù* is open to the 'impulses, yearnings, and resentments that mark the human condition in modernity' and would allow these considerations to be voiced and contested in the public sphere (Honig 1993: 3). If political communities allow the expression of the unsocial emotions in the context of victim testimony, this is consistent with a type of *virtù* politics and should be understood as an expansion of the boundaries of what is necessary for legitimacy and a thriving political culture.

A related concept in Honig's work is that of the *remainder*, that which does not fit into an overarching narrative of virtue politics and is considered to be disruptive or irrelevant to political life. Although the remainder includes issues and sentiments that appear to be forgotten, they are not submerged completely. Instead, the remainder re-appears and upsets the political and social order in unexpected ways. Honig provides the example of how pro-choice advocates understood the politics of abortion after the *Roe v Wade* decision:

> My point is that there is a lesson to be learned from the experience of those who misread *Roe* as the end of a battle and later found themselves ill equipped and unprepared to stabilize and secure their still unstable rights when they were repoliticized and contested by their opponents. In their mistaken belief that the agon had been successfully shut down by law, pro-choice citizens ceded the agon to their opponents and found, years later, that the terms of the contest had shifted against them.
>
> (Honig 1993: 15)

In the aftermath of the *Roe* decision, pro-choice citizens underestimated the depth of feeling surrounding the morality of abortion. Moreover, they assumed the legality of abortion would greatly shape the public debate over abortion in their favor. These misunderstandings on the part of pro-choice activists gave fodder to the anti-abortion movement, increasing the degree to which the 'remainder', the ethical concerns of moderate citizens who were uncomfortable with the discourse surrounding abortion, would return and dramatically alter the political debate over its legality.

The emotions of anger and despair are part of the remainders of war and addressing their significance in the context of victim testimony is a way to incorporate them into politics. A failure to acknowledge their significance would make political communities vulnerable to the type of exaggerated return of the remainder that Honig describes above. Confronting difficult emotions after war cannot ensure that the emotions will not surface again and permeate politics for years to come, but it is the beginning of a productive conversation about how political expectations have been shaped by violence and the emotions that remain. Those who have experienced the violence of war, from the perspective of perpetrators, victims, family members and bystanders, are all changed in significant ways, especially in relation to the expectations of the state and fellow citizens. Grappling with these effects should not be seen as tangential to the work of politics in the aftermath of war, it is at the core of the process of justice. Victim testimony allows for this process and treats the complex experiences of war as appropriate for political life. Without this engagement, the emotions will not only retreat to the private sphere, they will continue to haunt everyday politics.

An example of victim testimony

The testimony of Kunyamane Arios Ranyaoa at the TRC elucidates my claims about the affinity between agonistic theory and the possibilities for victim testimony. Ranyaoa testified at the Johannesburg hearings of the TRC about his experiences as a member of the African National Congress (ANC) – Nelson Mandela's organization and the leading party in the anti-apartheid struggle – and his subsequent disillusionment with the legitimacy of its leadership. He said:

> These people acted the way I knew they'd act, because I was in Tanzania, I know how ANC officials act. If you are a rank and file person in the ANC you are nothing, we used to call rank and swine, you will forgive me for saying that, that's why I was not surprised, but this is my profound feeling, if according to the mandate given by the government, you have those powers to flex your muscles and then find out about this. I think it's a wish of the family that in a normal democracy, so to say, people under investigation concerning this, it's my deep feeling, they should relinquish their official positions, because this is not compatible with the spirit of democracy, otherwise it would be a laughing stock to talk about democracy. I think, I hate to be emotional, I always like to be rational so that things are in order, but I can't hold myself, I'm very bitter, I'm very angry.
>
> (Ranyaoa 1996)

This testimony captures the potential of testimony to upset conceptions of rational and consensus oriented politics. Although the ANC became the governing party after the first democratic elections, in his testimony Ranyaoa was not afraid to express his anger at ANC officials and question the assumptions of moral authority that were being evoked by the post-apartheid government. He did not think that the party leaders are worthy of respect and he questions the legitimacy of a truth commission which does not seem to be investigating the ANC of crimes committed against its own members.[10]

Ranyaoa is cognizant of the fact that the anger expressed in his testimony may give others reason to dismiss its accuracy. When he says 'I hate to be emotional, I always like to be rational so that things are in order', he indicates disappointment in himself for failing to meet the standard of rationality that the commissioners would prefer. He sees himself making a politically relevant statement but knows that the statement is in danger of being effaced by the tone in which it is delivered. The hierarchical dichotomy of emotional versus rational is apparent to him and he is embarrassed that his testimony falls on what he thinks is the less desirable side. He wants the audience to listen to his testimony without dismissing it, and as he is speaking, the audience hears his fear that this may not be possible and his self-doubt that he has undermined the force of this testimony.

When Ranyaoa voiced anger and bitterness toward the ANC who were widely considered to be the party of liberation, he was also going against implicit expectations of the Commissioners. Many of the Commissioners and the audience at the TRC had been members of the ANC or were sympathetic to the organization; for Ranyaoa to have been so blunt about his bitterness toward the ANC was a uncertain gesture that did not fit with the dominant narrative of forgiveness and reconciliation that the Commission had promoted. He called for an end to the hypocrisy on the part of ANC leaders who talk about the values of democracy while not admitting to the violence that existed within the organization. These claims pose a stark challenge to the legitimacy of the state.

Ranyaoa's anger signals a desire to draw attention to the illusion that all those who were part of the ANC were satisfied with the leadership and supported the ANC-led government in office. When he mentions that low-level members were called 'rank and swine', it becomes evident that he did not feel valued as a member of the organization and instead felt resentment at the fact that his contributions had been overlooked. Although he did not directly ask for recognition, it can be inferred from both the tone and content of his testimony that he desired some acknowledgement of his sacrifices for the movement and possibly a way to become involved again with political life. This suggests that a specific type of recognition may be a beneficial way for the Commission to respond to individuals such as Ranyaoa who were previously active in movements for racial justice. An acknowledgement of the particular sacrifices he made would be a step toward assessing what would need to be done to bring disillusioned citizens like Ranyaoa back into political life.

Victim testimony and the frontiers of agonism

I have focused on the ways in which victim testimony is compatible with theories of agonistic politics, but there are areas in which the relationship is more fraught. The first is the question of whether the testimonies themselves should be opened up to contestation and struggle over their content. Putting my theory about victim testimony in conversation with the literature on agonism prompts the question whether forcing those who testify to be open to questions and contrary opinions would increase its validity as an example of agonal politics. One can imagine it would: such questioning would prevent the hardening of identities and reveal the contingencies of a situation, aspects of politics which Connolly thinks are beneficial to an agonistic conception (Connolly 2002).[11] Opening up testimonies to dialogic challenges would also be a struggle, in the literal sense, over the facts of the testimony. I find that the assumptions about the value of contestation found in some of the literature on agonistic relies on the language of ever-present struggle. This assumption may inadvertently enforce a type of restrictive reciprocity on all agonistic interventions in politics. Its proponents may not want to use the term 'reciprocity' because of the way thinkers in the deliberative democratic tradition use the term to refer to the expectations of public reasons and rational argumentation. Reciprocity in the agonistic tradition does not indicate these expectations, but it is a type of adversarial dialogic engagement that is thought to be a productively destabilizing force.

In contrast to reciprocity and contestation, my hopes for victim testimony, particularly the sort which allows emotions such as anger to be voiced, raises questions about whether monologic examples of political participation should still count as moments of agonistic politics. Victim testimony highlights this issue and suggests that to further develop agonistic theory, it is not enough to leave open the meanings of 'contestation' and the struggle over hardened identities, it is time to conceptualize different iterations of agonistic democracy and how models, such as testimonies, demand an alternative way of thinking about contestation. With the case of victim testimony, contestation for its own sake, a danger to which agonistic theorizing may be vulnerable, proves to be an inadequate model. The model of testimony offers a type of engagement with a different rhythm, this would begin with the instance of testimony in which consensus and rationality are not the only modes of acceptable speech. The contingency of the identity of the speaker or the content of the testimonies is not questioned at this time, it is seen to exist alongside many other testimonials about democratic aspirations, including those stated as part of the commission itself or supported by political, civic or artistic leaders. Then comes the moment of critical responsiveness in the form of rejoinders from the immediate audience and later from those in charge of writing the report. The manifestation of agonistic struggle in victim testimony comes first with the articulation of political views which are not often heard in state-sanctioned public spaces and then with the inclusion of these testimonies in discussions about what is necessary for restorative justice.

Simona Goi's work on the abortion debate reinforces this point about the need for a theory of agonism without the implied expectation of reciprocal contestation, especially in regards to anger (Goi 2005). Following Honig's precedent, Goi references conversation about abortion as an example where rational consensus seems unattainable and where the remainders of anger are salient. Goi uses the example of the Public Conversations Project (PCP) in Boston, a non-governmental organization committed to dialogue on difficult political issues, to explore whether it is possible to foster a type of agonistic space around the topic of abortion. The

PCP sponsored the Pro-choice and Pro-Life Leaders Dialogue from 1995-2000 and while it put forth a more desirable model of discussion, Goi does not think it reaches the ideal of an agonistic space (Goi 2005).

By inviting leaders from opposing sides in the abortion debate and putting forward certain guidelines, the PCP sought to 'establish a general model for democratic interaction is that is not bound by the pressures of strategic action and tied to the rhetorical framework of hostility fostered by the mass media' (Goi 2005: 73) The guidelines included the following: individuals must not speak as representatives of organization, refrain from polarizing rhetoric, respect the confidentiality of the discussion, and assume that the purpose of the discussion was understanding, not changing the minds of those who disagreed (Goi 2005: 72). Goi describes how these assumptions were difficult for some participants and she thought that they greatly impeded their ability to speak candidly and expressively about the topic. From PCP's perspective, this was precisely the point. Certain parts of the conversation – the most polarized, inflammatory parts – are curtailed in the hope that the participants hear both their own positions and each other's in new way. The group believes that subtle shifts can happen through discussion within their guidelines and are important to later policy development. In deciding the extent to which the PCP model represents a type of agonal politics, Goi highlights two points. First, she notes that anger has no place in the PCP forum. 'Even justifiable or communal anger,' she writes, 'would not be acceptable and this results in a re-iteration of the remainders that exist in deliberative or liberal models' (Goi 2005: 75). With this finding, we again see how the expression of anger continues to foil what are perceived to be productive exchanges about political possibilities. It is not included in institutional practices even when the institution is predisposed to acknowledging its significance. Second, despite the commitment to difference in the context of the discussion, consensus still represents success. She attributes the language of consensus in part to the organizations which fund the project and set the terms for what should be seen as a successful discussion. On both these points, victim testimony is markedly different from the PCP and could thus offer a different model of agonistic politics. How anger should be incorporated and what parameters would allow for it without devolving into shouting matches has yet to be articulated. Yet Goi also identifies one of the dangers of *not* encouraging dialogic engagement – perspectives are in danger of being ignored and seen as irrelevant to decision making. Again, the particular framework for hearing and responding to anger is critical, the possibility for silencing and dismissal can happen at every stage.

The assumptions of contestation as a form of reciprocity are meant, in part, to thwart the type of marginalization Goi fears. By forcing moments of contestation, others are drawn into the exchange and forced to pay attention. By drawing attention to the monologic aspects of testimony, I do not wish to remove the significance of this and my model of victim testimony in the context of a truth commission in which there is a panel of commissioners who initiate and listen to the testimony is motivated by similar logic. However, I do not think contestation or publicity (one of Goi's suggestions) are the most compelling way to avoid marginalization. This is the issue of the relationship between agonal politics and the needs of justice.

In much of the literature about agonism the term justice seems to be tainted with the liberal interpretation of formal or procedural justice. Even though thinkers in the agonistic tradition often have strong affinities with social justice and it exists as a motivational concept, descriptions of agonistic politics should be pushed further to make connections to the work of justice. James Tully's work on recognition and freedom in an agonistic context could be a model for this type of work (Tully 2009). In the context of transitional justice, I suggest that there is a necessary relationship between the agonistic moment of victim testimony and the work of restorative justice, that is work of rebuilding trust between citizens and repairing fractured political relationships. Through the expression of anger, resentment and despair in the context of victim testimony, individuals are interpreting their experiences of past violence in light of present realities and this includes an articulation of what remain the biggest obstacles to participating in political life. For Ranyaoa, this appears to be a question of recognition for efforts on behalf of the anti-apartheid movement and an acknowledgement of the violence sanctioned by the ANC. His anger indicates the centrality of these concerns to his self-conception as a citizen and, by extension, the relationships that must be attended to in the process of restorative justice. In this way, the moment of upheaval that exists as a manifestation of agonistic politics is followed by actions that integrate the critical perspective that was expressed in the testimony with the work of justice and this necessarily demands the commitment of resources, energy and political attention.

My purpose here is not solely to mount an agonistic defence of the value of victim testimony in truth commissions, although that is a part; rather I suggest that by focusing on victim testimony as a paradigmatic case agonistic thinkers will be forced to consider new lines of inquiry. Concepts (such as reciprocity or the contingency of identity) that have been left under-defined to maintain conceptual purity or rhetorical effect come to the foreground in a study of the agonistic implications of victim testimony. I have expanded upon three main areas in which victim testimony pushes against concepts found in the agaonistic literature: the assumption about constant contestation (the heckler's veto[12]), the presence and purpose of anger, and the relationship between agonistic expression and the work of building social and political ties in a society after mass violence (the needs of restorative justice). It is not enough to say that anger is part of the remainder of politics and will continue to haunt public life; questions should emerge about different types of anger and the possibility of responding in an agonistic way. My hope is that the conversation among scholars of transitional justice, particularly of war crimes trials and truth commissions, will not focus on testimony as a way to gather facts or allow for some type of collective catharsis. Such functions are too limiting and a disservice to the salient role testimony could play in shaping the needs of justice. This would be an orientation that goes beyond the scope of a truth commissions report or verdicts of guilt. Using an agonistic lens to examine victim testimony is a way to return to one of the fundamental goals of agonistic thought – to break through the discursive constraints in liberal democratic models in a space that is still considered political.

Notes

1 For more about the value of speaking as a singular expression of the individual that goes beyond content, see Adriana Cavarero (2005).
2 'What Rawls is really indicating with such a distinction is that there cannot be pluralism as far as the principles of the political association are concerned, and that conceptions which refuse the principles of liberalism are to be excluded. I have no quarrel with him on this issue. But this is the expression of an eminently political decision, not of a moral requirement' (Mouffe 2000b: 25).
3 Richard Wilson interviewed Janice Grobelaar, an Information Manager in Johannesburg during the TRC and involved with creating the database of human rights violations. She said, 'Truth will be delivered by methodological rigor and scientific findings. The legitimacy of the TRC depends on its ability to create a truth that is acceptable, and that means a scientifically valid process that people can buy into' (Wilson 2001: 38).
4 For more on how the failure to interpret gestures, emotions, and embodied expressions hindered both the TRC Report and the scholarship that followed, see Cole 2010.
5 Hannah Arendt is relevant here for her understandings of pain and the dangers of letting private concerns masquerade as public ones (see Arendt 1958).
6 For a critique of this position, see Sharon Krause, *Civil Passions: Moral Sentiment and Democratic Deliberation* (Princeton: Princeton University Press, 2008).
7 For more on how this relates to recognition and dignity in the public sphere, see Honneth 1995.
8 Aesthetic performances can certainly be politically relevant even when they exist outside of a truth commission, but my point is to counter an overly aestheticized reading of victim testimony by scholars and commissioners who do not acknowledge the patterns of political critique embedded therein.
9 Her use of 'virtue politics' is different from the virtue ethics that is associated with Aristotle and neo-Aristotelian thinkers such as Martha Nussbaum.
10 I thank Paul Apostolidis for his suggestion that Ranyaoa's phrasing, 'I *hate* to be emotional, I always *like* to be rational' might ironically reveal the emotional component of perceptions of rationality.
11 Mark Wenman's analysis of Connolly, Tully and Mouffe explores this topic from the perspective of constitutionalism and republic politics. See Wenman 2003.
12 I thank Sonu Bedi for this formulation.

References

Arendt, H. (1958) *The Human Condition*, Chicago, IL: University of Chicago Press.
Arendt, H. (1982) *Lectures on Kant's Political Philosophy*, Chicago, IL: University of Chicago Press.
Cavarero, A. (2005) *For More Than One Voice: towards a philosophy of vocal expression*, Palo Alto, CA: Stanford University Press.
Cole, C. (2010) *Performing South Africa's Truth Commission: stages of transition*, Bloomington, IN: Indiana University Press.
Connolly, W. (2002) *Identity/Difference: democratic negotiations of political paradox*, Ithaca, NY: Cornell University Press.
Connolly, W. (2005) *Pluralism*, Durham, NC: Duke University Press.
Felman, S. (2002) *The Juridical Unconscious: trials and traumas in the twentieth century*, Cambridge, MA: Harvard University Press.
Goi, S. (2005) 'Agonism, deliberation, and the politics of abortion', *Polity* 37.
Habermas, J. (1990) *Moral Consciousness and Communicative Action*, Cambridge, MA: MIT Press.

Hayner, P. (2002) *Unspeakable Truths: facing the challenge of truth commissions*, New York, NY: Routledge.

Honig, B. (1993a) *Political Theory and the Displacement of Politics*, Ithaca, NY: Cornell University Press.

Honig, B. (1993b) 'The politics of agonism: a critical response to "Beyond good and evil: Arendt, Nietzsche, and the aestheticization of political action", by Dana R. Villa', *Political Theory* 21.

Honneth, A. (1995) *The Struggle for Recognition: the moral grammar of social conflicts*, Cambridge, UK: Polity Press.

Krause, S. (2008) *Civil Passions: moral sentiment and democratic deliberation*, Princeton, NJ: Princeton University Press.

Minow, M. (1999) *Between Vengeance and Forgiveness: facing history after genocide and mass violence*, Boston, MA: Beacon Press.

Mouffe, C. (2000b) *The Democratic Paradox*, London: Verso.

Rawls, J. (2001) *Justice as Fairness: a restatement*, Boston, MA: Harvard University Press.

Smith, A. (1982) *The Theory of Moral Sentiments*, Indianapolis, IN: Liberty Fund.

Tully, J. (2009) *Public Philosophy in a New Key*, Cambridge, UK: Cambridge University Press.

Tutu, D. (1999) *No Future without Forgiveness*, New York: Doubleday.

Villa, D. (1992) 'Beyond good and evil: Arendt, Nietzsche and the aestheticization of political action', *Political Theory* 20.

Wenman, M. (2003) 'Agonistic pluralism and three archetypal forms of politics', *Contemporary Political Theory* 2.

Wilson, R. (2001) *The Politics of Truth and Reconciliation in South Africa: legitimizing the post-apartheid State*, Cambridge, UK: Cambridge University Press.

3 A critique of law's violence yet (never) to come

United Nations' transitional justice policy and the (fore)closure of reconciliation

Erik Doxtader

> There is apparently no moment in which a decision can be called presently and fully just; either it has not yet been made according to a rule, and nothing allows us to call it just, or it has already followed a rule – whether received, confirmed, conserved or reinvented – which in its turn is not absolutely guaranteed by anything; and moreover, if it were guaranteed, the decision would be reduced to calculation and we couldn't call it just.
>
> Jacques Derrida

In transition: For the law, the promise of reconciliation remains and must remain yet to come; asked of its own limit, the question of good faith with which reconciliation begins, the law replies with a timeless warrant for a system of precedent which disavows that the founding of its (founding) rule of recognition is an occasion to undertake a critique of violence in which the norm of its exception is not negated but (re)turned to the present as a potential for constitutive power. Before the law, reconciliation arrives to what remains, a history that cannot stand and which lacks standing, a silent and thus barbaric precedent that nevertheless holds the potential for beginning again, an exceptional transformation that does not forgive its own risk of bad infinity, the wait that sacrifices accountability in the name of becoming in relation.

For transition: In early 1995, the South African Parliament's Joint Committee on Justice opened public hearings dedicated to debating the rationale, form, and power of what would become the Truth and Reconciliation Commission (TRC). Controversial from the start and rooted in an old and complex discourse of reconciliation, the TRC was staunchly defended at the hearing by then Minister of Justice Dullah Omar. In his testimony, responding in part to Amnesty International's objection that the TRC's vested power would contravene global norms, violate international human rights law, and condone a dangerous impunity, Omar argued that amnesty, if viewed in conjunction with the TRC's "victim-centered" approach, afforded South Africa a chance to "deal with our past on a morally acceptable basis and make it possible to establish the rule of law. But much more important than that, Mr. Chairperson, to establish the rule of law on the basis of the recognition of human rights and the building of human rights culture in our country." Going further, Omar then put the matter more plainly: "we are building a future for South Africans" and as "there is a conflict between what the international community is saying and what is in the interests of the people of South Africa then I think that we will have to live with that kind of conflict" (Omar 1995: 55).

We will have to live with that kind of conflict. What kind of conflict is this kind of conflict? Taking exception to one law in the name of remaking another, Omar's defense of reconciliation opposes the familiar commonplaces of law with the promise of a conflict with which we must live, a form of contention that crafts the ground for productive (dis)agreement from within historical reasons for violence and opens a space in which to begin dialogue over the meaning of human rights in the wake of a system that was fundamentally anti-human.[1]

We will have to live with that kind of conflict. Can we live with(in) it? For many, Omar's position was not simply inhospitable but a degradation of the form of life that it claimed to honor. Although unsuccessful in their petition to the South African Constitutional Court, victims of apartheid-era violence challenged the announced aims of the TRC legislation by laying bare the sacrifice that attends setting reconciliation before the rule of law and arguing that the state's abridgment of the constitutional right to seek redress from perpetrators transformed the choice to reconcile into nothing less than coercion.

We will have to live with that kind of conflict. If we cannot live with this conflict, how can it be resolved? Must we league ourselves with Jody Kollapen, the former chair of South Africa's Human Rights Commission, and his contention that "[w]e focused too much on reconciliation in the first years of democracy." Pushed too far, according to Kollapen, reconciliation serves only to cover the "everyday problems" of transformation. Left unchecked, its idle talk of miracles and rainbows degrades the real work of justice.

Relatively little is understood about whether it is possible to live with the conflict between reconciliation's constitutive potential and the defining norms of the international human rights project. With respect to the South African case, the question has never really received a full hearing. When it is considered, the problem is usually distorted by the myopic assumption that reconciliation in South Africa began with the TRC, a body that while quite important neither displayed a philosophical flair in its thinking about reconciliation nor fully resisted the legitimacy and identity politics that cut against inquiry into the concept's complex roots.[2] Thus for all the praise and blame thrown its way, one of the Commission's legacies is an evident reluctance to grapple with a key piece of the puzzle, a history that Nelson Mandela articulated precisely in a 1999 speech to Parliament:

> [W]e need to remind ourselves that the quest for reconciliation was the fundamental objective of the people's struggle, to set up a government based on the will of the people, and to build a South Africa which, indeed, belongs to all. The quest for reconciliation was the spur that gave life to our difficult negotiations process and the agreements that emerged from it.
>
> (Mandela 1999)

These words about words may yet matter. Without rendering South Africa into a model or even a leading light, they speak directly to the conflict that inheres within reconciliation and to which it may well be given.[3] Here, what Mandela recollects is that the work of reconciliation is a rhetorical struggle with the question of transition, the question of discovering a language that holds the potential to compose and move with(in) transition's "between," a space and moment in which things are not as they have been and not yet to (be)come.[4]

While it admits to no singular reply, the question *qua* question of reconciliation's place in a time of transition that may be "no time at all" is one that seems to be less and less on our minds. The ensuing silence suggests that lines have been drawn, some of them implicit and presumptive; it is an indication of an evident and growing tendency to cast reconciliation as a bit player if not a soothing but expendable jester in the larger and serious drama of promoting transitional justice. This may be an infelicitous development, one that correlates to a certain reluctance amongst the architects and heroes of transitional justice – as a global discourse and international practice – to spare a thought for how the idea of the "transitional" may condition and alter the arc of the "justice" promised in transitional justice. If the now well-tooled machine of transitional justice takes reconciliation to be a conflict with which it can live without, it may do so at the risk of transition itself, a now-time in which the desire to stabilize history's contingency in the name of the future rests heavily on the making (of) words that begin the work of opening the hard heart to the terms of ethical-political life.

Today, there are signs that transitional justice aims to convert – with disturbing fervor – the constitutive and agonistic quality of reconciliation into a demand (if not a command) for the adversarial, a commitment to the (prior) definition and application of a rule of law. In this essay, my basic aim is to reflect on this turn against reconciliation's "turning right about" and to plot at least one of the ways in which reconciliation's place has been largely closed and then foreclosed from the premises and promise of transitional justice. While it is possible to discern something of this dynamic in both academic and non-governmental literature on transitional justice, my interest here is with the United Nations, a relative latecomer to the transitional justice game and a motley body that has nevertheless come to reflect and direct something of the mainstream consensus regarding the proper aims and methods of transitional justice.[5] Looking across and within a number of policy documents and debates that have appeared over the last decade, I begin by tracing the UN's announced interest in transitional justice and the precise way in which it has sought to incorporate the "option" of reconciliation into a "necessary" rule of law.[6] In light of what I take to be the UN's erasure and expressed aversion to reconciliation's "unaccountable" ambiguity, I then turn to the question of how the institution's case for standardizing the language of transitional justice recognizes the rule of law at the expense of misrecognizing the law's rule of recognition – that is, the fully transitional problem of how to constitute the grounds of the law's power in the wake of violence, including legal violence. More than simple oversight, I suggest, the UN's presumption against reconciliation points directly to its importance – a potential for words that stand before the law and compose a critique of how the law's violence may preclude precisely the claim(ing) of human rights that transitional justice policy presents as its ultimate warrant.

In making this wager, I seek neither to lay the evident shortfalls of transitional justice at the UN's step nor to simply reverse field and reclaim reconciliation's "prior" standing. While not widely known, Richard McKeon's thoughtful work on human rights warns against both paths, particularly as they involve conceptual approaches that may actually perpetuate conflict to the degree that they fail to grasp how political, social, and ethical forms of violence, "have the peculiarity, shared by other practical inquiries, that [the] discussion may itself become part of the data of the problem" (McKeon 1947: 79).[7] It will not do to battle transitional justice's *logomáchia* (against reconciliation) any more than it will do to tritely propose reconciling transitional justice to itself. The problem at hand is thus fundamentally rhetorical, something that almost no one wants to hear but which may be important in both understanding reconciliation's *ethos* and the way in which it seeks to discern the potential for disagreement from within the midst of violence. While some see this work only as evidence of a forked albeit silver tongue, it may be far better understood as the movement of theory, a movement that provokes the question of how transitional justice and reconciliation might come to reflect on the transitional power of the word as something more and less than instrument or miracle.

Transitioning to the rule of law's justice

The problems that compose the constellation of transitional justice have long occupied the United Nations, even as the concept of transitional justice itself is a relatively new addition to its policy debates.[8] In 2005, then Secretary General Kofi Annan invoked the Millennium Declaration as evidence of the UN's growing awareness of the difficulties involved in attempting to "build human rights and rule of law provisions into peace agreements and ensure that they are implemented" (Annan 2005: 35). Echoing both the unresolved debate within the Philosopher's Committee that laid a groundwork for the 1948 Universal Declaration of Human Rights and Hannah Arendt's wonder in the wake of the Eichmann trial as to whether national or international tribunals could ever meaningfully adjudicate the "sins of the fathers," Annan's announcement was conditioned on the idea that the UN had a longstanding obligation and urgent need to "address the injustices of the past and to secure sustainable justice for the future" even as the organization lacked a specific institutional facility to "assist countries in their transition from war to peace" (Annan 2004: 7).

Beyond the economy of international tribunals, the gap between one of the UN's apparent premises and its practice has been the source of significant debate in the organization's constituent offices and bodies. Here, beginning with a sketch of the UN's initial attempts to define transitional justice, I offer a somewhat extended but by no means complete reading of this debate, a reading that focuses on how the UN has problematized the meaning of justice in "transitional situations" and the ways in which this grammar has been used to justify policy that delineates methods by which divided societies can best move from past to future. Undertaken variously by the Security Council, the General Assembly, the Human Rights Council, the United Nations Development Programme (UNDP), and the Office of the High Commissioner for Human Rights, this work has proceeded through three discernable and interlocking phases. Viewed over time and as a whole, UN policy makes a case for a standardized language of transitional justice that progressively winnows reconciliation from the pursuit of justice grounded in the creation and application of the rule of law.

In a 2004 report entitled "The Rule of Law and Transitional Justice in Conflict and Post-Conflict Societies," Annan drew from a set of Security Council discussions in order to argue that the "notion of 'transitional justice'" is best defined as "the full range of processes and mechanisms associated with a society's attempts to come to terms with a legacy of large-scale abuses, in order to ensure accountability, serve justice and achieve reconciliation" (Annan 2004: 4). Two years later, the UNDP offered the more elaborate and also slightly circular position that, "transitional justice covers the ways in which societies in transition from authoritarian rule to democracy, or from armed conflict to peace, address legacies of gross and systematic humans rights and other violations such as large scale corruption." Maintaining that such work rests on the "four essential pillars" of "truth-seeking mechanisms, criminal trials, reparations programmes, and institutional and legal reforms," the UNDP's interpretation is largely congruent with the Human Rights Council's more formal 2007 claim that transitional justice rests on the rights of individuals to truth, justice, reparation, and identity (United Nations Development Programme 2006: 1; Human Rights Council 2006: 4).

Together, these familiar definitions demonstrate that transitional justice is pitched to a number of goals, all of which have been deemed central to the "international community's efforts to enhance human rights, protect persons from fear and want, address property disputes, encourage economic development, promote accountable governance, and peacefully resolve conflict" (Annan 2004: 4). Moving beyond the prosecution of perpetrators to "helping war-torn societies re-establish the rule of law and come to terms with large-scale abuses," the "normative foundation" of contemporary transitional justice policy is claimed by UN leadership to rest on the set of "universally applicable standards" comprised by its own charter and the larger terms of international human rights and humanitarian law (Annan 2004: 3, 5). With extra-national legitimacy and composed of forensic and non-judicial mechanisms for the "peaceful settlement of disputes and the fair administration of justice," transitional justice, according to Annan's 2004 report, focuses on "a context marked by devastated institutions, exhausted resources, diminished security, and a traumatized and divided population" and endeavors to respond to "a lack of political will for reform, a lack of institutional independence within the justice sector, a lack of domestic technical capability, a lack of material and financial resources, a lack of public confidence in Government, a lack of official respect for human rights, and more, generally, a lack of peace and security" (Annan 2004: 3).

Thus, the UN's announced vision of transitional justice begins in the silence of the aftermath, a sort of silence in which Blanchot hears a cry, a voiceless and patient cry that exceeds sense and suspends meaning (Blanchot 1995: 51). Somehow, *stasis* must become *kairos,* a time that remains, a moment which holds the potential to "address" violence and a power to "come to terms" that does not refuse the question of its own violence (see Agamben 2005). A bit more concretely, the hope of UN transitional justice policy turns on the question of how to begin the making of a beginning (again). Over the last decade, the organization has proffered three answers. Grounded in the root metaphors of accountability, balance, and juridical power, these replies shed light on the complexity of the UN's current definition of transitional justice and betray more than a little about the respective place and role of reconciliation and rule of law in the institution's attempt to promote the "mutually reinforcing imperatives" of justice, peace, and democracy.

1. Impugning impunity. The longstanding referent if not precedent for UN transitional justice norms and policy is a 1997 report, entitled "The Question of Impunity of Perpetrators of Human Rights Violations (civil and political)" (United Nations Commission of Human Rights 1997). Submitted to the then standing Commission of Human Rights, the report begins with an explanation of its motives, an argument as to how amnesty for political prisoners held by dictatorial regimes was converted in the 1970s and 80s from a "symbol of freedom" that could catalyze political-democratic reform to a form of "self-amnesty" that provided rulers with an "insurance on impunity" which, according to a 1988 decision by the Inter-American Court for Human Rights, trampled the rights of those who had suffered gross violations of human rights (see Velasquez-Rodriguez v. Honduras: 1988). Bringing the matter forward into the post-Cold War era, the report also makes the now fashionable claim that the apparent value of indemnity and amnesty in promoting dialogue and peace negotiations between belligerents had been abused by those seeking "to strike a balance between the former oppressor's desire for everything to be forgotten and the victim's quest for justice" (United Nations Commission of Human Rights 1997: 2).

Developed over the course of nearly ten years and written largely under the supervision of Louis Joinet, then the UN's Special Rapporteur on amnesty, the 1997 report responds to these defining problems with some forty-two principles "in reference to victim's legal rights." Many of these protections are now commonplaces of transitional justice theory and practice. Under the banner of the individual and collective "right to know" and its corollary "duty to remember," the report contends that victims of human rights violations must be able to discover the truth behind their suffering and that the State has a steadfast obligation to guard against "the perversions of history that go under the name revisionism or negationism" (United Nations Commission of Human Rights 1997: 3). In turn, the right to justice is deemed to prohibit amnesty to perpetrators of violations, at least in so far as it might compromise the ability of victims to assert their right to receive a "fair and effective remedy, ensuring that their oppressors stand trial and that they obtain reparations" (United Nations Commission of Human Rights

1997: 4). Along with prosecution, such effective remedies included restitution, compensation, and rehabilitation, all of which were held as a means for the restoration and "formal public recognition" of victims' dignity (United Nations Commission of Human Rights 1997: 4).

At its close, the 1997 report presents its principled actions to combat impunity in the form of a UN General Assembly resolution, the pre-amble of which contends that there is "always a risk" that States will disregard human rights and undertake those barbarous acts which have outraged the conscience of mankind. Deemed repugnant to the letter and spirit of the UN Charter, this timeless danger is taken as a warrant for the adoption and the provision of rights spelled out in the report, without which "there can be no effective remedy against the pernicious effects of impunity" and no recognition of victims' interests. Moreover, the report contends explicitly that the fight against impunity follows directly from the view that "there can be no just and lasting reconciliation unless the need for justice is effectively satisfied" (United Nations Commission of Human Rights 1997: 9). If not circular and self-sealing, this claim proposes that reconciliation – as closure that requires knowledge of its object – necessarily follows from the development and promotion of the rights to truth (knowledge), justice, and reparation. On this interpretation, the report thus seems quite correct when it maintains that its announced principles are "intended not to thwart reconciliation," at least as the latter is understood as a state of peace. The difficulty appears with the follow-up argument. Declaring that before a "new leaf can be turned, the old leaf must be read," the report warns of "distortions in certain reconciliation policies" and then cites a 1993 UN report's claim that those released from the shackles of barbarism frequently "find themselves caught in the mechanism of national reconciliation, which moderates their initial commitment against impunity" (United Nations Commission of Human Rights 1997: 7, 9). Now cast as an open-ended process instead of a future condition, reconciliation is the very risk of the atrocity that human rights doctrine seeks to eradicate. There is no middle ground. The law must come first. In this defining proto-view of a transitional justice that is not yet named as such, reconciliation is a safe hope but a practice best deterred.

2. Creating an undecidable balance. The authors of the report on combating impunity can be forgiven for not predicting the tremendous upsurge of interest in reconciliation that took place in the late 1990s. The intrigue can be explained in a variety of ways, although it is surely linked closely to the unexpected form of the South African transition and the way in which the country and its flamboyantly led TRC recuperated reconciliation in the wake of its troublesome application in Latin and South America.[9] In any case, reconciliation's turn of the century currency across and then outside the African continent is reflected in UN policy as it shifts from a largely if not strictly legal vision of transitional justice to a view premised on the need to balance effective legal remedies and the promotion of reconciliation. The creation of this balancing test approach takes place over a period of several years and grows out of a series of debates in which a variety of UN bodies struggle with the question of how to define reconciliation and set it into meaningful constellation with standing norms regarding the priority of law's rule.

The beginning of this debate appears clearly in a September 2003 Security Council meeting dedicated to the theme "Justice and the Rule of Law: The United Nations Role." Framed by several heartening and failed transitions, along with unhappiness over the pace of trials in Rwanda and the former Yugoslavia and frustration in getting Pinochet, Taylor and others into the dock, the gathering, according to the opening speaker, Jean Marie Guéhenno, aimed to confirm the "emerging unanimity" about the "critical role of the rule of law in building a sustainable peace in post-conflict settings" and recognize that, for the UN and its departments, "The restoration of the rule of law is a *sine qua non* for the sustainable resolution of conflict and the rebuilding of secure, orderly and humane societies" (J.M. Guehenno, United Nations Security Council 2003: 3). What follows this declaration, a moment of agenda-setting that appears to impose several basic limits on the so-called debate, is an exchange that closes with precisely the questions which one might expect to see at the start: "To what law are we referring" and what does "rule of law" mean in respect to the international community's interest in the promotion of peace and justice.

If only in reverse, this question provokes several significant lines of argument. Initially, the idea of the rule of law is used to encapsulate and justify the 1997 *Principles on Combating Impunity* at the same time that it is granted a constitutive role in the work of "stabilizing societies emerging from conflict," "building democratic institutions," and "ensuring the success of "peace-keeping" (United Nations Security Council 2003: 11, 16, 3). To these ends, the rule of law is tasked to perform a number of functions. It serves as the measure of accountability and the grounds for convening national and international tribunals dedicated to the achievement of "post-conflict justice." In the name of dispute resolution and "harmonious coexistence," along with legislative transparency, it underwrites the creation of "all components of the criminal justice chain," including a stable judiciary and the police (Mr. Spatafora, United Nations Security Council 2003: 3–4). Beyond these structures, according to one representative, the rule of law is the basis for developing, consolidating and ensuring the consistency of criminal law and its procedures, a process of invention that aims to build community on the grounds of "mutually agreed upon principles" (Mr. Spatafora, United Nations Security Council 2003 3–4). As the representative from Japan put it, the promise of "universal justice" (Mr. Haraguchi, United Nations Security Council 2003: 9) through rule of law rests heavily on the normative law-making functions of the UN system.

The line is a fine one. While many representatives underscore that law cannot be imposed onto nations and that "local traditions" must be recognized, the larger claim that runs across the debate is that the UN's defining concern for the rule of law is necessary precisely to the degree that, "Where *no* justice or rule of law exist, frustration and bitterness will accumulate, and a society that is supposed to be united for development will instead become fragmented and divided, and descend into a vicious circle of conflict and poverty" (Mr. Haraguchi, United Nations Security Council 2003: 9). This argument is crucial. In the midst of transition, nations are held to confront if not manifest a void, a so-called vacuum in which it is "necessary to rebuild all aspects of the legal system" while, at the same time, ensuring the respect and legitimacy of that system *through* the delivery of justice to "victims of crimes or atrocities" (Mr. MacKay, United Nations Security Council 2003: 10).

It is here that, at the apparent limit of law, reconciliation enters and becomes relevant to the Security Council's deliberations. Defended by some representatives as a means of creating the trust needed to reconstruct and support judicial remedies to violence and held out by others as a complement to legal forms of nation-building, reconciliation is presented as evidence that "the relentless pursuit of justice may sometimes be an obstacle to peace" and a practical way to balance the political, social, and humanitarian-legal demands of transition (Mr. Rasi, United Nations Security Council 2003: 18). Over the course of the debate, this argument to balance reconciliation with rule of law proves decisive. Rooted in the position offered by the South Korean representative, that "somewhere between amnesty and uncompromising justice, each society must strike its own delicate balance," reconciliation is deemed a supplement to law, an ambiguous excess that accounts for law's limit but does so in a manner that does not undermine its prior – impunity-combating – power (Mr. Kim Sam-Hoon, United Nations Security Council 2003: 31). Thus, the defining dilemma, according to New Zealand's spokesperson, is "finding the appropriate balance between justice on the one hand and reconciliation on the other, because it will obviously not be possible to put an end to the culture of impunity for the gravest international crimes if amnesties are granted for them" (MacKay, United Nations Security Council 2003: 11).

Aligned with the threat of impunity and its attending injustice, reconciliation enters the (still unnamed as 'transitional justice') equation as (thin) compensation for the lacking but still prior precedent of law and the rule of its justice. Several months later, in January 2004, the Security Council undertook to check its math in a session dedicated to "Post-Conflict National Reconciliation: The United Nations Role." An explicit counterpart to its rule of law debate, the central problem was evident in the discussion's opening remarks. After the reading of a letter sent by Desmond Tutu, an epidictic appraisal of the South African transition as moment in which a nation walked "the path of forgiveness and reconciliation" and became a beacon of hope for others "hagridden with conflict and strife," the Assistant Secretary General of Political Affairs, Tuliameni Kalomoh, reversed field and claimed that reconciliation "may require the settling of the past, an accounting of prior wrongs and an acceptance of responsibility for abuses" and then, going further, concluded that "an essential part of reconciliation is to isolate those who are most responsible and have committed the most egregious violations in order to bring them to justice" (Mr. Kalomoh, United Nations Security Council 2004: 4, 5).

Two visions of transition – one offers no account of justice, the other is concerned with little else.[10] Neither affords a substantive interpretation of reconciliation nor offers an assessment of whether it contributes to the definition, recognition, or protection of human rights. Over the course of two days and some thirty speeches, members of the Security Council replied to this silence with a variety of claims about the nature of reconciliation and its appropriate place in the work of transitional justice. Responsible for convening the debate, the Chileans offered one of the more nuanced definitions when they argued that: "Reconciliation is not a utopian objective; it is the collective response of a society emerging from a crisis whose fabric has been torn asunder. Reconciliation puts an end to the cycle of violence, laying the foundation for a new coexistence" (Mrs.Valenzuela, United Nations Security Council 2004: 2). Both a reply to *stasis* and given to inventing grounds for interaction, reconciliation is figured here as a relational good, a contingent capacity to restore the desire and constitute the capacity for dialogue. In situations characterized by distrust, trauma, and the echoing roar of the gun, reconciliation aims less to restore the social fabric than open a moment in which to weave the fabric of sociality. According to the representative from Sierra Leone, this work is "the single most important aspect of post-conflict peace management" and best defined as the process of creating a "deep sense of belonging" and cultivating the "desire to participate" in those forms of engagement that recognize the need for compromise in the face of discord (Mr. Rowe, United Nations Security Council 2004: 7). More than non-lethal co-existence and less than outright consensus, according to the Peruvian representative, reconciliation "signifies the process of building a new social contract based on democratic institutions aimed, above all, at eradicating social exclusion, which is the breeding ground of civil conflicts of national self-destruction" (Mr. De Rivero, United Nations Security Council 2004: 16).

With several others, these interpretations support the idea that "national reconciliation is both a process and a goal" (Mr. De Rivero, United Nations Security Council 2004: 16). But how, asks one representative, does the process of reconciliation make a new social contract in a situation "in which a society's harmonious relations have been ruptured ..." (Mr. De Rivero, United Nations Security Council 2004: 16)? Over the course of the debate, this constitutive work is cast largely in terms of reconciliation's capacity to elicit and disseminate truth – the experience of victims, the motives of perpetrators, and the remnants of history (and bodies) buried by authoritarian regimes. With a therapeutic value that is discussed only in passing and cast by one speaker as a form of restorative justice, the most common defense of reconciliation as truth-telling is that it constitutes one way to recognize the rights of victims, particularly as it composes a referent for reparation and provides information that can be used to facilitate the indictment and prosecution of perpetrators.[11] For the moment, the importance of this claim is the strict distinction that it attempts to draw: attached to and promoted by extra-judicial bodies (truth and/or reconciliation commissions), reconciliation's production of truth makes a contribution to the provision of that justice of which it is not a part.

Working from a relatively nuanced account of the contingency that attends political transition, there are some participants in the Security Council debate who argue – against the grain – that reconciliation is either prior to the work of law or, more moderately, that it compensates for the fact that "the rule of law is an essential element in establishing democracy, but it is not enough in itself" (Sir Parry, United Nations Security Council 2004: 22). Without a "single model" and concerned to constitute both the shared meaning of time and a time of shared meaning, reconciliation may, according to one representative, "lay a path from a past where justice was denied to a present where it is not yet fully attainable, and to a future where it will be an integral part of the social order" (Mr. Baja, United Nations Security Council 2004: 25). If the past cannot serve as precedent and the future is not given, reconciliation is an event that "takes time" to compose the present, a moment in which the meaning of the collective good and the form of ethical life is an open question. For most, however, the view that "It is for each society to decide whether it wishes to achieve reconciliation through the criminal justice system or by recourse to other mechanisms" is an occasion for worry, a concern that led several representative to recall the balancing test that appeared in the Council's debate on the rule of law (Kofi Annan, quoted in United Nations Security Council 2004: 26). Speaking to the matter directly, France's representative argued that "national reconciliation often requires a balance between the imperatives of justice and the defence of universal values, on the one hand, and taking into account the circumstances inherent in a situation or a particular culture, on the other ... However, that which is inviolate must be respected" (Mr. Dulcos, United Nations Security Council 2004: 22). Recalling the ambiguity with which the Council's debate began, this position is echoed and used to argue that the lack of a "single model for reconciliation" must not obscure that "consistency must be seen as one of the cornerstones of reconciliation in post-conflict situations" (Ms. McAskie, United Nations Security Council 2004: 10). What this appears to mean is that reconciliation's varied and various modes must be "tempered with a clear commitment to ending impunity for serious violations of international humanitarian and human rights law" (Ms. McAskie, United Nations Security Council 2004: 11). Even if the rule of law is not a sufficient condition for *any particular* – a phrase that overwrites the meaning of particularity – transitional situation, and even if reconciliation may contribute to the provision of justice, its pursuit with "misplaced vigour" demonstrates in no uncertain terms that a "balance is essential" in order to ensure reconciliation does not condone or result in amnesty that serves to "prevent truth and justice from emerging" (Mr. Nambiar, United Nations Security Council 2004: 19). Now back to the idea that reconciliation is an outcome, a state that follows from the implementation of the three pillars of truth, justice and reparation, transitional justice rests on the unanswered question of what *holds* the balance that separates and links the promise of reconciliation and the power of rule of law.

3. Making the Good (Standard) Word (of Law). Not long after the close of the Security Council's debates, the idea of "transitional justice" as such appears and begins to play a prominent role in UN discourse. By mid-1994, just around the time that South Africans were turning their attention to the question of how to make good on the 1993 interim constitution's amnesty mandate, the concept is mobilized to address the hanging question of how post-conflict societies *should* conceive the connection between rule of law and reconciliation-based approaches to transition and resolve the way in which this relation is *best* embodied in policy. Over the course of several years, this normative approach leads UN actors to standardize the meaning and consolidate the justification of transitional justice, a process in which the idea of balancing reconciliation and rule of law is supplanted by a position that figures reconciliation as a subsidiary form and function of law.

The move to contain reconciliation's role in juridical conceptions of transitional justice began with a return to the 1997 principles on combating impunity. Going backwards to go forward, the Commission on Human Rights tasked Dianne Orentlicher, an academic well known for her defense of post-conflict prosecutions, to revisit and revise the principles in the name of developing a "comprehensive strategy" dedicated to ensuring that "states meet their obligations to protect human rights through effective measures of truth, justice, reparations and other guarantees of non-recurrence" (Commission on Human Rights 2004: 2).[12] Presented to the Commission in February 2004, Orentlicher's position makes for somewhat odd although not especially surprising reading. Holding that there is "no 'one-size-fits-all'" response to serious violations of human rights and noting that the success of efforts to combat impunity rests heavily on the involvement of victims and NGO-supported dialogue that can give voice to "citizens' understanding of justice," a point that is made through some consideration of the work undertaken by South Africa's TRC, the report's larger claim is that the original principles "have already had a profound effect" and that "disappointing results" in particular transitional situations are due to local failures to implement a "mutually reinforcing repertoire of strategies" (Commission on Human Rights 2004: 4). Quite subtly, this claim recalls the risk of reconciliation's distraction, the danger of backsliding noted in the 1997 principles and which, when brought forward, holds the suggestion that the question of transitional justice requires a far more categorical than balanced reply.

Just such an approach appears with the release of the Secretary General's August 2004 report, *The Rule of Law and Transitional Justice in Conflict and Post-Conflict Societies*. With explicit reference to the Security Council's earlier discussions, the report begins by advocating for and then articulating a "standard language" of transitional justice for the United Nations. Wary of the "multiplicity of definitions and understandings" of such concepts as "justice, the rule of law, and transitional justice," the Secretary General contends that "a common understanding of key concepts is essential" in order to "define our goals and determine our methods" for the "promotion of justice" and the "consolidation of peace" (Annan 2004: 3–4). With reconciliation notably absent from the terms to be defined, the report's work is striking for the way in which it derives the meaning of transitional justice – "the full range of process of mechanisms associated with a society's attempt to come to terms with a legacy of large-scale past abuses, in order to ensure accountability, serve justice, and achieve reconciliation" – from those goods that are held to compose the "rule of law" which sits "at the very heart" of the UN's mission (Annan 2004: 4).

Defined *inter alia* as a "principle of governance" that renders individuals, institutions, and the State itself "accountable to laws that are publicly promulgated, equally enforced, and independently adjudicated," the rule of law is deemed necessary to ensure the legitimacy of transitional justice in the face of national variation and local indecision (Annan 2004: 5). In this regard, the importance of not being seen to "prescribe a particular formula for transitional justice" and the need to give "due regard" to "indigenous and informal traditions for administering justice" is made explicitly conditional on their "conformity with international standards" (Annan 2004: 12). This standard, however, presupposes that such traditions are coherent and meaningful, an assumption that the report calls subtly into question when it details the prior need to fill the "rule of law vacuum" which leaves traditional or national remedies subject to political distortion, a lack of public knowledge, institutional legitimacy crises, minimal resources, and the presence of general lawlessness (Annan 2004: 5).

From the UN's vantage, to look into a divided society is to see that the terms with which it can "come to terms" must come from the outside. Put differently, the Secretary General's standard(ization) of language underwrites a logic of transitional justice in which the (prior) necessity of defining and unilaterally applying the (universal) rule of law is justified through an appeal to the value of "local choice" at the same time that this choice is characterized as a risk to the larger aims of policy; the underlying and unspoken assumption of the UN's position is thus that the contingency of transition either confounds the capacity to choose or subverts the principles on which decisions must rest. The danger in either case is a (re)turn to violence.

With the vocabulary fixed and the rules set, the potential of reconciliation begins to fade. Offering an extremely narrow and selective reading of the Security Council's earlier debates, the Secretary General's position devotes no attention to the various meanings of reconciliation, situates its "use" solely within the context of truth commissions – defined as such – and relies almost wholly on the position advanced in the 1997 principles – reconciliation is a synonym for the state of peace that follows *from* political reconstruction and a process of truth-telling that can yield information which serves the ends of prosecutions that fulfill victims' right to justice and, to a lesser degree, reparation. If the matter has to be expressed as a balance, this means not that competing goods must be weighed, but that a single standard – rule of law – should serve as the arbiter of what transitional initiatives are appropriate and valuable. This is especially true in the matter of amnesty, a deviation from the rule and deviance fed by overbroad hopes of reconciliation.

By the end of 2004, the UN's now standardized discourse of transitional justice increasingly relies on the rule of law to subsume and then progressively obscure the language and practice of reconciliation. In early 2005, the Human Rights Commission's resolution on "Democracy and the Rule of Law" affords no role to reconciliation in the "fragile process" of democratization and appeals to a series of General Assembly resolutions to claim that the promotion of human rights in transitional settings hinges primarily if not exclusively on an "effective rule of law" (Office of the High Commissioner of Human Rights 2005: 2–3). This discounting of reconciliation is evident as well in the Secretary's General's 2005 report, "In Larger Freedom," a document that declares an end to the debate over the language of transitional justice policy and then suggests that discussion on the matter represents nothing less than a deadly threat to the extent that fails to close the gap between "rhetoric and reality" (Annan 2005: 135).[13] While banal, this precise distinction has played a legitimizing role in the recent push to incorporate an explicit "right to truth" into the fabric of transitional justice policy.

Worthy of an inquiry unto itself, this proposed protection has roots in the 1997 report on combating impunity, specifically its claim that "Every people has the inalienable right to know the truth about past events and about the circumstances and reasons which led, through systematic, gross violations of human rights, to the perpetration of heinous crimes" (United Nations Commission of Human Rights 1997: 10).[14] In the late 90s and the first few years of the new century, this position found the most traction with those that were justifiably disappointed by the work of Latin and South American truth commissions, particularly as they failed to shed light on the fate of those abducted and disappeared over the course of conflicts. In fact, Article 24 of the recently ratified 2006 *Convention for the Protection of All Persons From Enforced Disappearances* holds explicitly that victims have "the right to know the truth regarding the circumstances of enforced disappearances." With an extremely broad definition of the crimes that fall within its purview, the Convention has bolstered efforts to ground larger transitional justice policy on a right to truth that, according to a 2007 General Assembly resolution, "presupposes the disclosure of the whole and complete truth about the events that occurred, the specific circumstances attending them and the individuals involved, including the circumstances in which the violations were committed and the reasons for their commission" (Report of the Office of the High Commissioner for Human Rights 2007: 16).

Deemed inalienable and non-derogable, the "right to truth" has helped codify the limited view of the "transition" that conditions transitional justice, one defined by a proceduralist case for the priority and presence of truth and reparation within "any peace and reconciliation scheme" (Report of the Office of the High Commissioner for Human Rights 2007: 13).[15] In this respect, the exemplar of the UN's reduction of reconciliation to an administrative supplement of rule of law may well be the High Commissioner's 2006 report, "Rule-of-Law Tools for Post-Conflict States." Attributed to Priscilla Hayner, a commentator known for her largely descriptive work on truth commissions, the report takes the form of a handbook for would-be transitional societies and is addressed exclusively to those elements of transitional justice that qualify as a "rule-of-law tool" and thus serve the ends of strengthening prosecutions and combating "all aspects of impunity" (Report of the Office of the High Commissioner for Human Rights 2006: 1). In this context, reconciliation is offered only the smallest of roles in the work of transition. Characterized tritely as "a very long and slow process," it is portrayed as a way of unduly raising public expectations and then divorced from the question of how to design an effective truth commission. It is difficult not to view this separation as artificial, particularly when one considers the nominal and legislated aims of the South African TRC – treated in the handbook as a curiosity – and similar bodies that have followed in its wake. So too, the report discounts claims made in the Security Council's debate as to how many truth commissions seek to instigate a process of national and local reconciliation, ones that aim less to feed momentum for prosecutions than to open space for citizens to reflect on the contingent meaning of justice and undertake meta-political agreements that reconstitute the law's power and legitimacy. Even more remarkable is the claim that the difficulties involved in assessing reconciliation-oriented initiatives evidence the necessity of criminal prosecutions, despite the fact that reconciliation may well be addressed to the underlying question of what justice means – and for whom – in transition and beyond. Thus, as with the Secretary General's 2004 position, the tool in the toolbox turns out to be a ratchet, a largely uncalibrated instrument designed to tighten (but not question) the language of transitional justice and seal its juridical framework from reconciliation's leakage, an outpouring of expression that may well contain the potential for precisely the dialogue that the UN claims to value and which it concedes is a basic if not necessary element of (re)constituting the form of historically divided nations.

Recognizing the transitional rules

What's left to say? Over the course of a decade, the UN's discourse of transitional justice moves from a concern to combat impunity that speaks of reconciliation as an abstract outcome of accountability's aftermath to the creation of a vague balance that concedes the constitutive power of reconciliation's speech while legislating against its force, and then, finally, to a positive vocabulary that sets reconciliation's speaking wholly into the service of law's prior rule. As declared, the UN's rendering of transitional justice leaves little room for reconciliation. And, for some, this appears a relief; the UN's position sets reconciliation's shifty words in their proper place and puts its shifting meaning under good and stable management.

There may be good reasons to doubt this apparent comfort. As the UN's common language of transitional justice calls for the (re)creation of human relations and yet appears to sanction the process of their invention, one cannot help but wonder whether and to what degree the potential of reconciliation has been misplaced. To see why, I want to turn from the specific terms of policy and reflect on the dynamics of the conceptual constellation that contains the UN's vision of transitional justice. Here, I am particularly interested in how the UN's defense of rule of law conditions its interpretation of the transitional element of transitional justice and whether this view sets the UN to justify the foundations of law in a manner that leaves it blind to the problem of legal violence, a form of conflict and source of deep division that may undermine the UN's case against reconciliation's constitutive potential to open and enable the transitional work of composing the law without the banister of its precedent.

Transitional justice begins in the midst of transition. While this seems obvious enough, there is something curious if not almost passive-aggressive about the UN's account of what it means to enter into a "state of transition." In some sense, the phrase itself holds the problem, at least insofar as a moment of change is named in a manner that works to conserve the integrity of its form. However, if we are willing to set aside both the idioms of political science *qua* science and the idyllic aspirations of revolutionary "politics," it may be important to recall the eventfulness of transition, the ways in which transition opens space for invention, a creativity that is neither evidence of unbounded freedom nor a simple teleological arc. At least in the wake and midst of deep division, the hope for the new appears and takes shape in a time and space that provides no (self) certain place to stand. An intransitive time, the transitional is a moment and mode of (im)potentiality; in it, what *is* is equally what *is not*.[16] Both conceptual and historical, this undecidability troubles (but does not negate) the grounds of both acting and judging: precedent is suspect; language lacks for a stable referent; the meaning, direction and value of history is open to fundamental question. In short, confronted with that which is not here (now) or there (then) or yet (to come), the experience of transition involves struggling with(in) an uncomfortable and ambiguous middle: What is (not) between us? How do we move between the times? What makes and accounts for the difference between violence and ethical life?

If the UN's policy project is animated by, although perhaps not addressed to, these questions, its subsequent replies serve to bracket, discount, and then manage the contingency that "defines" the transitional moment. Initially, its approach rests on a distinction between transitional justice and nation-building. Consistently, the former is deemed to begin *after* states have been (re)constituted, *after* the work of constitution-making has been started if not largely completed. While this cut endows the state in transition – as an *object* of transitional justice – with a certain stability, the distinction is complicated if not confounded by the UN's claims about the *subject* – the terms, scope, and value – of transitional justice policy. For instance, the 2004 Secretary General's report contends that the issue of transitional justice includes the drafting of new constitutions, establishing tribunals, strengthening judicial institutions, and (re)developing civil society (Annan 2004: 5–6). If so, things are not so clear-cut after all. Blurring the difference between transitional justice and the transitional work that is frequently set under the headings of democracy-building, democratization, and democratic consolidation, the UN's policy claims implicitly and explicitly to encompass significant constitutive work: defining a new social compact, negotiating the conditions of institutional legitimacy, establishing shared ground rules for reading and interpreting history in the name of accounting for and defusing sources of conflict, and creating public forums given to the negotiation of collective interest and disagreement about how to relate competing individual and collective needs.[17]

The UN's case for transitional justice may well be coy. Its vision of transitional justice involves an oscillation that is never explained, a movement in which policy presupposes what transition is tasked to create and also calls for the creation of that which can be supposed in order to ground the transition from past to future. Put differently, the UN plays rather fast and rather loose with two crucial but quite different questions: What has to happen for transition? What happens in transition? Nowhere is the blurring of these problems more apparent than in the UN's argumentation about the necessity and right of truth (telling). Here, in the wake of violence and the gross violation of human rights, the transitional moment is held out as a "scene of address," a time and space in which there is both an opportunity and (dire) need to speak: testimony must be heard; accounts of violence must be articulated; dialogue must begin and take root; citizens must find their voices and reinvest themselves in civic discourse; acknowledgement must be given and felt.[18] At the same time, the UN's description of transition figures it as a moment and bearer of *stasis*, a time of "language trouble" that calls into question the space, meaning, and power of address (see Cassin 2001).

Fragile and uncertain, the experience of transition comes with no assurances about the capacities of speaking and listening that underpin the right to (tell and hear) truth. Victims lack for voice at the same time that perpetrators ration their own; as history's meaning and historical rules for interpretation are deemed suspect to the degree that they are linked with the violence of the past, shared space and common vocabularies are scarce; understanding is thwarted by a lack of trust, an unwillingness to address or engage with those guilty of evil; norms and hopes of legal and socio-political recognition founder and fail when they are deemed compulsory or when victims are subjected (sacrificed) to the assumption that their experience "begs for response"; the perceived connection between argumentation and violence undermines the desire for substantive engagement and stifles collective debate.[19]

While we could extend this list of symptoms, all of which point to a simultaneous rhetorical limit and opportunity, an (im)potential, the underlying point is that the transitional is an event and an experience that throws open the question of how human beings might begin to (re)invent the meaning of relationality and (re) negotiate the terms of their relations. Yet, the irony of the UN's declaration that the (declared) right to truth is a necessary element of transitional justice is that it does not concede the possibility that the truth of language may abide in and through its taking place as transitional; the non-derogable demand for truth to be told stands wholly outside the scene of transition's (non)address. And it does so in order to fiat the expression, hearing, and rhetorical production of a truth (telling) that presupposes the prior and successful work of meta-transitive discourse which questions how individuals can relate through speech and the ways in which truth (telling) best serves, if at all, the ends of politics, justice, and civic life.[20] Given for truth, the UN's word remains an unexplained and unhinged gift.

This inheritance beckons the law. In the name of fostering understanding that yields account and accountability, the latter an adversarial event that may find its limit in the midst of transitional uncertainty about what *is* and thus what can be meaningfully opposed to what, the right to truth (and its telling) points to the UN's second significant view of transition, an argument as to how its contingency must be deterred in the name of combating impunity. The claim is two-fold: amnesty is a threat to transition and transition constitutes the threat of amnesty. On the one hand, the UN is adamant that there be no exception, no impunity for those guilty of atrocity. To provide amnesty is to allow history to haunt, corrupt, and ultimately thwart the move from old to new; transition is thus best conceived as an objective space or grid given to the prosecution of those who would fate its collapse. Fusing the principled and the pragmatic, the UN's case is that the intrinsic value of "doing justice" is equally a way of assuring that transitions are not derailed by the recuperation of perpetrators, denialism, and resentment; the refusal of amnesty, in all forms, paves the road from past to future by ensuring the production of "a historical record that leaves no room for misinterpretation" (United Nations Security Council 2004: 7). On the other hand, the UN's acknowledgment of the sheer uncertainty of transition signals the unacknowledged possibility of a temporal and conceptual breach that exceeds the grasp of law, in part because of the way in which it renders the meaning of precedent suspect and thus calls for the (re)making of legal norms and directed reflection on how to best define law's (historical) relationship to justice.

While it has larger implications, the point for now is that the UN's view of transition serves to deny its discretionary if not constitutive quality, particularly with respect to how it may open a moment of choice in which to question the reasonable, realistic, and ethical means of "dealing with the past." And, it is nearly impossible to deny that there will be a deal. For indeed, amnesty happens, if for no other reason than the reality of plea-bargaining. But, the instances where this inevitability is addressed, the arguments that unsettle the unilateral direction of transition by pointing to the *de facto* necessity of unaccountability, are virtually erased from the UN's larger policy position. This erasure is difficult to miss when one traces how the UN scrubs itself clean of the South Africa transition and the latter's attempt to wed a "victim-centred" approach to historical violence with a public amnesty in which perpetrators were invited to exchange testimony about the nature, motivation, and proportionality of their crimes for a permanent indemnity from prosecution.[21] Even the South African representatives that participated in the 2003 and 2004 Security Council debates soft-peddled the dynamics of this process and its underlying wager that there are forms of amnesty which count not as amnesia but as processes that take the question of defining and preserving memory out of the law's hands in order to motivate public-civic meta-discourse that holds the potential for acknowledgement which proceeds in the grammar and voice of the first person.[22] At the UN, however, the argument runs in precisely the opposite question. Set against the "impunity gap" that opens with(in) and attends transition, the UN neither admits nor condones any amnesty. Where it "must" occur, a hedge that appears without comment, the right to truth and its telling is mustered and defended as a way to fill the gap. It is *homo narrans* that will save the day. Even if the day is one that calls the capacity to narrate into fundamental question, there is little doubt that the law will stitch the pieces and provide the true story(line).

Both for and against a transition that may or may not be transitional, the UN offers the rule of law – lots of it. With multiple forms, objects, premises, and powers, it is the rule of law that sits at the centre of the UN's vision of transitional justice. It may be ambiguous, this rule of law, but its claimed integrity and value is not subject to doubt and rarely open to question, at least after the 2004 Security Council debate. This self-certainty performs an important function and creates a notable dilemma. Providing the means by which the UN can overwrite and then subsume the contingency of transition, law's alleged priority brackets the history of law itself. This dynamic is curious and potentially troublesome as it suggests that the UN's assumption of law rests on a misrecognition of the rule of recognition that it endeavors to create and defend.

To develop this idea, it is first important to reflect very briefly on the fact that the nature and status of rule of law in humanitarian and human rights law is an open question. Frequently characterized as "soft law," declarations from bodies such as the General Assembly and the Human Rights Council/Commission are frequently read by national and some international courts as non-binding except insofar as they have provoked or constituted widespread "agreement, consensus, and custom."[23] In turn, the view that UN decisions are best understood through the lens of (potentially) customary law has fueled debate over how to interpret the institution's normative definition and defence of rule of law. Working between minimalist and maximalist positions, Gerhard Casper maintains that international rule of law can refer variously to the consistent application of law, the protection of more or less universal civil, political and human rights, formal assurances of the capacity to participate in government, and substantive rules ensuring the opportunity to undertake (economic) exchange (Casper 2004: 1–4).

This wide-ranging account squares with a number of traditional interpretations, wherein the rule of law is concerned variously with the democratic creation of law, the codification of norms that bind government to pre-existing law, the preservation of personal autonomy against governmental intrusion, and the maintenance of a separation of governmental power.[24] Looking broadly, one relevant and admittedly substantive interpretation has it that "democracy is an inherent element of the rule of law" and that "the rule of law does not mean merely a formal legality which assumes regularity and consistency in the achievement and enforcement of democratic order, but justice based upon the recognition and full acceptance of the supreme value of the human personality and guaranteed by institutions providing a framework for its fullest expression" (Tamanaha 2004: 111). In the context of the UN, this interpretation resonates with Kofi Annan's 2004 definition, a position that accompanied his first significant statements on transitional justice as such. In Annan's terms, the rule of law:

> [R]efers to a principle of governance in which all persons, institutions, and entities, public and private, including the State itself, are accountable to laws that are publicly promulgated, equally enforced, and independently adjudicated, and which are consistent with international human rights norms and standards. It requires, as well, measures to ensure adherence to the principles of supremacy of law, equality before the law, accountability to the law, fairness in the application of the law, separation of powers, participation in decision-making, legal certainty, avoidance of arbitrariness and procedural and legal transparency.
>
> (Annan 2004: 4)

In their sympathetic critique of UN transitional justice policy, Solomon and Tolbert read this position to say the rule of law must, at bottom, "address the crimes committed during the conflict, create sound infrastructure, and build functioning institutions." Advocated repeatedly in UN discourse, such efforts, according to Solomon and Tolbert, demonstrate the merit of avoiding a "false dichotomy" between "traditional rule of law development work and efforts to build rule of law in post-conflict societies"(Solomon and Tolbert 2006: 30–31). If so, the UN's view recalls Casper and Jeremy Waldron's respective claims that the rule of law is a "cluster of values" and defined by "human rights norms" such that it provides both a sense of legal certainty and a set of "organizing rules of political and public life" (Casper 2004: 3).

With something of a nod to Hayek, the UN defends rule of law partly on the grounds that it situates life on the grounds of stable expectation. In the UN's position, this stability has a double referent and function. On one side, the rule of law is a normative benchmark that fills the "vacuum" of transition by determining when prosecutions are necessary and guiding the adjudication of charges set against individuals who committed those gross violations of human rights that prefaced transition and which risk its success. On the other side, the rule of law is a development initiative dedicated to rebuilding a nation's judiciary, establishing norms of due process, and ensuring that citizens have the ability to both access an effective remedy for their grievances and contribute to the creation of the legal system.

In UN accounts, the double function (and site) of rule of law expresses the tension between its contention that successful transitions are prefaced by adherence to a prior (universal) rule of law and its claim that local customs and interpretations of rule of law have priority in defining the nature and arc of a transition. Viewed over time, transitional justice policy shifts between these positions. The movement is tactical; the UN warrants the claim that its (customary) rule of law contains, expresses, and enforces the meta-political choices and norms that underwrite nation-building by appealing either to a near natural rights view of human rights or by attributing a (local-cultural) consensus about the demands of transition in a way that pre-empts the ability of transitional states and societies to compose the grounds and the terms of such a consensus. The apparent gain of this position is that the UN assumes a capacity to manage the complexity of transition by claiming that the unaccountable act of constitution is either given – its already and magically happened, as a once off event – or an act that is subsumed entirely by (and produced through) a prior (historically given) measure of law. Put in slightly different terms, the UN defends rule of law as both the basis and defining outcome of transition. In between, the re-cognized but unrecognized (unacknowledged) work of constitution is taken for granted or defined as the pursuit of a timeless justice, a set of stable moral obligations that govern the contingent and indeed unaccountable creation of political-ethical life.

The UN's transitional justice policy would reduce politics to the impunity that it seeks to ban. More than an argument about the value of rule of law in defining democratization and promoting human rights, it attempts to build and defend a "*rule of recognition*," a set of unifying and normative statements that codify what the rule of law *is* in the context of transition(al) (justice) and why these necessary components should be accepted as appropriate (valid), useful, and binding.[25] Yet, as the UN composes the terms and assumptions of transitional justice, as the rule of recognition enables a larger system, it does so only by bracketing two basic problems, both of which suggest that the attributed force of the rule evades the question of its own formation by supplanting the good faith of its constitution with a law deemed beyond justification.

The first problem concerns the history of the rule itself. At no point, at least in no policy document on transitional justice that I have found, does the UN – or any of its representatives – offer a reflection on the sponsoring role of law in atrocity or the questions of integrity and legitimacy that follow from the commission of what Hannah Arendt called "legal crimes" (Arendt 2006: 277).[26] On Arendt's well-known reading, such offences are not so much formal or jurisdictional issues as a rending of the socio-political-judicial fabric itself; they are crimes that bequeath a (paralytic) silence about what law can do and how it may or may not serve the justice to which it professes obedience. Even in the most hopeful case, the situation in which the UN's transitional justice policy embodies a spirit of productive support to nations working through transition, the position is simply mute on the question of why the so-called vacuum of transition may, in fact, be the radical absence of the rule of law that follows from the violence that has been carried out in and through its name. In the wake of apartheid, for instance, what does rule of law mean? Why would law not proceed under the weight of a crippling legitimacy crisis – which it did – and how is it possible to rebuild a shared belief in the meaning of law, if the act of declaring its rule (of recognition) simply replicates the form of violence that has defined the past and enforced deep division? In short, the transitions that rule of law endeavors to manage suggest in many cases that recovering the potential of law requires law to make a constitutive exception to the priority of its own rule; the deformation of the rule must give way to question of its own formation (Arendt 2006: 255).

This then is the second blind spot: the rule of recognition that appears within the UN's case for transitional justice supplants the "arguable character of law" with a demand for re-cognition that sanctions questions as a form of impunity.[27] In other words, the UN's rule of law is predicated on an act of auto-poiesis that defends the need for citizens to participate in the authorship of law and retracts such an opportunity by presupposing that consensus on the form and content of law already exists. By way of a tactical balance or a flexible positivism, the UN's position either overwrites the local constitution of law or deems it a risk to the degree that is not accountable for the (sovereign) power that it creates. Both gestures yield an unproductive hypocrisy, at least to the degree that the UN's own (customary) rule of law refuses to recognize the conditions under which the potential of custom is composed.

The stabilized/standardized meaning that is alleged to abide in and follow from the rule of recognition which underwrites transitional justice points to why UN policy comes to cast the relation-making promise of reconciliation as the threat of illegality. Intuitively, reconciliation appears to have little place in the UN's discourse of transitional justice, save perhaps as a tool at the bottom of the box or as a foil that serves to validate the primacy of rule of law. Ironically, the UN's objection that reconciliation's words yield no "real" deeds is an altogether apt way of characterizing how it then figures reconciliation into policy; a subject for discussion and not to be excluded from the recipe, the UN's talk about reconciliation shows little interest or understanding of how its words may matter. Thus, the UN proposes, reconciliation is important precisely to the degree that transitional societies accept that it means what the UN says it means. The idea that its meaning may be held within the relationships that it creates and (re)forms is supplanted by the consistently espoused view that reconciliation is an outcome, a state of "just" peace that follows – and can only follow – from the larger and prior work of transitional justice. Indeed, the claimed difference between so-called genuine and false reconciliation is held to rest on whether particular reconciliation initiatives develop from and produce practical instantiations of the rule of law.

As the fuzzy aura of reconciliation's (false) promise is thought to interrupt and undermine the work of transition, the UN places a high premium on its institutionalization. Almost exclusively, reconciliation is discussed and set within the context of quasi-juridical truth commissions that are legitimate insofar as they are legally created and accountable. Only within this setting can reconciliation be seen to have a processual quality, a capacity to promote truth-telling and recover a history that defies "mis-interpretation." Yet, this power remains unexplained at the same time that the UN offers no account of how such bodies are sites if not lightening rods for political-public controversy over how citizens and institutions can best articulate experience, interpret history, and assess its relevance. The hermeneutic equivalent of the problem of how to create law's rule of recognition, this matter is not open to debate. Underneath this ban, the UN's position presupposes the capacity and desire to speak in prototypical ways – an interest in language that is "given" through the right to truth that truth commissions are tasked to protect and which serves to illustrate why any opposition that does appear counts as a risk of revisionism. Thus, by collapsing the undecidability of transition into a determinate time and space and installing a "common language" into a situation that may well be "defined" by a need to discover the conditions and terms of meaningful expression, the UN trades the relational for the teleological. With disturbing parallels to how the Dutch Reformed Church used the promise of reconciliation – in the next life – to rationalize apartheid, this move figures reconciliation as that which is yet (but never) to come and relieves claims about its value from the burden of demonstrating when it is appropriate, how it works, or the ways in which it amasses power. Strictly a procedure, there is virtually no sense in which reconciliation might do constitutive work.

The UN's conceptual and practical reduction of reconciliation is particularly stark when one compares the terms of standing policy with the variety of claims about reconciliation's power that were made during the Security Council's 2004 debate. In distinction to the Peruvian claim that reconciliation "signifies the process of building a new social contract based on democratic institutions aimed, above all, at eradicating social exclusion, which is the breeding ground of civil conflicts of national self-destruction," the policy-making that follows pays little mind to the possibility that reconciliation signifies the (im)potential of signification, the pre- and meta-political capacity to discover the grounds for that dialogue which allows for the expression of interest and the formation of shared norms that underwrite collective (inter)action (United Nations Security Council 2004: 16). At best, transitional justice offers a balance, a scale that presents reconciliation and rule of law as equally significant elements of transition, but which is itself held – at the fulcrum – by the rule of law. If it is not simply rigged, this tether is warranted by the unconditional need to combat impunity and the presumption, reaching back to the 1997 principles, that reconciliation holds the temptation and the mechanism for amnesty. Thoroughly manichean, UN discourse shows no willingness and affords little space to consider illiberal yet public forms of amnesty, a legislated release from the law's precedent in exchange for disclosure that has proven useful in demonstrating the transitional limits of law and creating incentives, along with a provisional vocabulary, for civic debate in which citizens face the question of memory – for themselves – and take up the question of how to define and relate the force of law and the obligations of justice.[28] In referring to such instances, including South Africa's transition, the UN complicates its announced respect for local custom and decision-making about the form and content of transitional justice by hailing an "authentic experience" that is claimed to demonstrate the universality of (at least an interest in) justice and, simultaneously, used as evidence that "indigenous tradition" is an expression of violent pathology that needs to be quieted.[29] All (not) told, this silence is telling.

An unjust reconciling of transition's rules

If the wind is blowing the other way, if reconciliation is increasingly viewed as suspect and left with only a tangential role to play in transitional justice's expansive agenda, then perhaps the UN's position is a leading light and a soft landing, a way to wean the devotees from a flavour of the month that has gone sour behind their backs. Such a possibility deserves a full and fair hearing, although perhaps not a trial – reconciliation may not deserve a place at the transitional justice table. All the songs from (and to) its choir will not change that, particularly if they simply serve to mimic the discourse to which they are opposed; the rule of law's claimed priority and subsequent discounting of reconciliation will not be altered by appealing to the latter's law, even if it is higher. The better option, if we are interested to pursue the matter, may involve letting our guard down just a bit and deferring the extended case for what reconciliation *might* do in order to ask after the cost of the UN's position and whether its lack of interest in the potential of reconciliation's relational if not transitional words sits in an interesting tension with any of its own announced goals.

It does. To see why, it is useful to recall, just briefly, Jeremy Bentham's well known characterization of the natural rights doctrines that helped build the modern human rights regime. As it's usually quoted, Bentham proclaimed these rights to be "nonsense on stilts." What he actually said, in reference to the "perpetual abuse of words" and "terrorist language" of the 1791 French Declaration of Rights was "Natural rights is simple nonsense: natural and imprescriptible rights, rhetorical nonsense, nonsense upon stilts" (Bentham 2002: 330). Today, at least on one register, it seems that the tables have turned. In seeking to contain reconciliation with(in) the rule of law, the UN's discourse of transitional justice may well count as nonsense without stilts. Indeed, there is no rhetoric about it, at least in the sense that reconciliation's difficult words are held to have little value outside of their ability to provide material to support prosecutions. With this presumption, policy fails to ask after the question of language in transition; it denies that historical violence may render its underwriting discourse suspect and it rules out the possibility that the meaning of transition rests heavily on the invention of words that shed light on law's (founding) violence. In the UN's expressed terms, the imperative to produce truth (which cannot be heard) in the name of law marks the prohibition of rhetorical work that aims to (re)constitute the grounds on which those who have been deemed exceptional, those who have been left to wait "outside" the purview of human rights, can gather the potential for "making-claims," a capacity for shared although not necessarily consensual expression that would seek to fashion transition rather than let it unfold as a matter of fate.

There are a number of ways of unpacking and explaining this dynamic. One path is through the question of whether the UN's discourse on transitional justice founders on what Hannah Arendt, writing just as the law was being mobilized in the name of legislating apartheid, identified as the paradoxical origins of human rights. Developed in *The Origins of Totalitarianism*, the gist of Arendt's position is well known. In her terms:

> The paradox involved in the loss of human rights is that such loss coincides with the instant when a person becomes a human being in general – without a profession, without a citizenship, without an opinion, without a deed by which to identify and specify himself – and different in general, representing nothing but his own absolutely unique individuality which, deprived of expression within and action upon a common world, loses all significance.
>
> (Arendt 1948: 383)

On this view, the need for human rights appears at that moment when human beings, reduced to the terms of bare life, have no recognizable basis to claim them. Whether within the sovereign law of states or the globalist legal framework of "one world," the meaning of what it means to be a human being endowed with rights is located, according to Arendt, in an abstract sense of being, a subject imbued with precisely the inalienable protections to which they have been denied. Lacking community and thus the grounds of politics, the human being in general suffers from the "innocence of the persecuted," a fate of invisibility and an inability to find standing within and before the law. In this way, Arendt writes:

> The fundamental deprivation of human rights is manifested first and above all in the deprivation of a place in the world which makes opinions significant and actions effective. Something much more fundamental than freedom and justice, which are rights of citizens, is at stake when belonging to the community into which one is born is no longer a matter of course and not belonging no longer a matter of choice, or when one is placed in a situation

where, unless he commits a crime, his treatment by others does not depend on what he does or does not do. This extremity, and nothing else, is the situation of people deprived of human rights. They are deprived, not of the right to freedom, but of the right to action; not of the right to think whatever they please, but of the right to opinion.

(Arendt 1948: 376)

More fundamental than justice? In this aftermath, neither the actuality of atrocity nor the exigence of a crime against humanity "fit" into that justice which presupposes the standing of subjects, a "given" capacity for appearance and expression that is severely disrupted if not negated by violence and which leaves the subject to plead with a language that law can neither hear nor understand. In this moment, as the human hangs in the balance, or confronts the potential of transition, Arendt finds that only friendship, sympathy, or the "great and incalculable grace of love" will suffice (Arendt 1948: 382). More precisely, the deprivation of human rights holds the call to forge relations without reason, a potential that figures the constitutive power of (inter)action before the law.

The beginning of human rights, the beginning to which transitional justice professes its allegiance, appears at the limit of the words to which it calls. As with Adorno's contention that philosophy leagues with barbarism as it forsakes rhetoric, the (re)turn from general to particular being, from *zoe* to *bios*, unfolds in the relational potential of language (Arendt 1948: 382). Quite literally, this is the thought for which the UN's reading of transitional justice has no place. Focused on the mechanics of transition rather than the undecidability of the transitional, it seeks and defends a method to bridge past and future such that the bridge itself is of little importance, a temporary throughway understood only as a contingency to be "consolidated."

And yet, Arendt gives pause to this approach. In her estimation, the question is how the transitional present may open and hold open a gap between the past and the future, a moment in which we are called to speech, a speaking that is a doing, and more important, a speaking that holds a power of beginning, the linguistic birth in which humans appear before others, express their interests and experiences, and fashion the potential for collective action (Arendt 1958: 198–199).[30] *Zoe* (be)comes toward *bios* with the word, the speech that affords an encounter in which self and other are (re)presented in mutual vulnerability. The grounds of an acting and judging that moves meta-transitively, perhaps even transitionally, between the work of constitution and an understanding (perhaps, a forgiveness) of its inevitable cost, the potential of language stands in contrast, and indeed challenges, the "perfect functionality" of reason that seeks "the elimination of the new" and supplants it with the "tranquillity of the cemetery" (Birmingham 2006: 27)

Today, one reason to listen closely to the UN's evolving account of transitional justice is to hear just this sort of "peace," a silence that resounds with the question of what to do if "those who desperately appeal to human rights are often those who are in no position to be recognized as claimants before a tribunal that has already decided against them"?[31] This decision is not the denial of rights, but a failure on the part of the law to account for the violence that follows from its inability to recognize the subject that abides in the very zone of indistinction on which the law depends for the power of its rule. No easy task, the opening of this gap, in Derrida's terms, is a trial of undecidability, a standing before law with constitutive words that take exception to its jurisdiction and challenge its rule of recognition; it is a struggle of "recognizing" that refuses a sovereign voice in the name of exceeding the expression of sovereignty's legal grant of recognition (Derrida 1989: 963).[32]

If the standardized language of transitional justice would deter this struggle, it does so by forbidding its place, the "taking place of language" that takes (its) place before the law and asks after the making (of) relations that embody the work of transition.[33] Pegged to a level of clarity that interprets ambiguity as a threat to the integrity of transition, transitional justice may well rest on a rule that misrecognizes (its) language, a self-sealing norm that precludes it from explaining transition itself and which emerges through a commitment to the law of the excluded middle at the cost of discovering words that turn between what *is* and what *is not, a* "turning right about" that has defined the conceptual work of reconciliation since antiquity.[34] At the heart of Aristotle's account of the end of the rule of thirty tyrants and Hegel's "reply" to the causality of fate, reconciliation *asks* after the limit of the law in order to find those words that exceed the grasp of its violence and enable its constitutive critique. For a beginning that invites a becoming (of the human) in relation, reconciliation's question inaugurates the beginning of a difficult politics, an engagement for and through language that provokes the question of transition, the question of beginning anew by moving in relation without (self) certainty.

A word that calls for(th) the question of words. Too often undermined by the unwieldy and brittle promise of multiculturalism and distorted by cut and dried appeals to forgiveness that rarely resonate, reconciliation's rhetorical character may yet help to unravel something of the contemporary "New York consensus" over the nature of transitional justice and the trouble that attends its thin account of transition. What are the elements of this character, this *ethos* that beckons and defies words? Most simply, reconciliation operates as a rhetorical potential, an idea that while arguably redundant means that reconciliation begins with(in) a call to language at the apparent limit of expression.[35] Beyond what may or may not happen in the pre-structured confines of truth commissions, reconciliation begins in the midst of history's betrayal, at a moment when combatants confront an inability to realize their own historical goals in the face of opponents that are held not only in contempt but thought irrational, untrustworthy, and in the ancient meaning of the term, barbaric.[36]

Such *stasis* is a common condition. While this may mean that it is a feature of many types of conflict, the more important point here is that this *stasis* is a plague on everyone's house; it is a limit experienced by all combatants, an opposition that they hold in common.[37] Unable to move forward or backward, opponents are beckoned if not thrown into a present, a moment that resembles Benjamin's understanding of a now-time which troubles history's linear movement. The beginning of reconciliation, this *kairos* is less an "opportune time" than a time in which instrumental opportunity is demonstrably self-defeating – for all parties. Left then with the choice of endless, total conflict or a path of becoming as they are not, the time at hand is a remnant that calls for(th) words.[38] Yet, it is precisely here where the conceptual train so frequently runs off the tracks and where advocates of reconciliation so often render it a naïve ideal. This calling toward language, a calling that marks the potential of a beginning (anew), is not a moment of mutual understanding or intersubjective consensus, an agreement that could only signal a simple return, a turning back to the given language beneath the conflict which thus risks its repetition.[39] Instead, within this threat of return, reconciliation discerns an occasion and indeed a calling to undertake a sort of "talk-about-talk," a proto-discourse given first and foremost to constituting the terms, grammar, and norms for disagreement about the meaning and value of individual and common interest.

Reconciliation's beginning is the turn from (self)negating violence to a language of potentially productive opposition.[40] As a "turning right about," if we read "right" expansively, this turn is treasonous. It proceeds in a middle voice that brushes against the grain of combatants' expressed historical commitments and repudiates their (sovereign) power to define the future. Moreover, the derivation of a common vocabulary of disagreement from *within* a common opposition deactivates or suspends the oaths and promises that compose and express individual and collective identity. This break is no doubt a sacrifice, one with no attending guarantees. Even in Paul's account, the Word of reconciliation offered not grace but the contingent gift of words for no good reason, a release from the violence of law in the name of becoming otherwise in relation. Yet, it is precisely this transgression, a coming to speak as one is not, that demonstrates the good faith whereby reconciliation gathers the potential to move from the tentative encounter of talking-about-talk to the deliberative question of whether and how to (re)constitute not only the rule of law but its underlying rule of recognition, the relational good(s) that circumscribe its power and to which it is dedicated. Although frequently written off as the "negotiated settlement" or "peace accord" that simply precedes transitional justice, this dynamic – as a performance of reconciliation – not only makes such a distinction naive but indicates how the work of "coming to terms" with the past risks the assumption and imposition of a victor's justice to the extent that it relegates reconciliation to the *outcome* of a rule of law which may be viable and meaningful only as it has emerged through a *process* of reconciliation that is both constitutive of ethical life and a form of political constitution-making (see Orentlicher 2007: 12).[41]

A language of potential and a potentiality of language, reconciliation's power is law-breaking, both for its refusal of the given word and its gift of words that enact transition, a turning-between that exposes the contingency of law in the name of its (re)constitution.[42] And, it is so criticized. From within transitional justice policy that holds out the rule of law as the superior, if not the only, means of protecting human rights and promoting the formation of human rights cultures, reconciliation's potential appears as an unjust exception to a universal rule.

More specifically, reconciliation's work is perceived to support the closed door production of "elite pacts" and condone, at the very least, the idea of amnesty. Thus defying accountability, it leaves victims outside the fold or folded into the promise of a better life that hinges on their willingness to sacrifice (once again) their principles and interests. Taken individually and together, these criticisms are live questions, particularly as they suggest that reconciliation does not necessarily cut open the paradox identified by Arendt. That said, if the power of Arendt's position lies in its ability to identify the exception – the state of exception – on which human rights rest, then the (im)potential of reconciliation may be important precisely for the way in which it inaugurates and supports a critique of law's violence.

Such a critique may well move along the lines of Benjamin's attempt to grapple with the conditions under which humans can begin to "reconcile their interests peacefully without involving the legal system" (Benjamin 1996: 245). While this not the space to undertake a full reading, Benjamin's position is suggestive at several levels. Lamenting the fact that governing institutions forget the contingency of their founding and intent to concede nothing to pacifism's inability to grapple with cases, Benjamin endeavors to show how the violence that attends the making and conservation of law opens into the question of whether there is an "unalloyed means of agreement" that would not so much overcome law's violence as expose its operativity. While Derrida and others have focused heavily on Benjamin's subsequent distinction between mythic and divine violence, a distinction that does bear on the possibilities of reconciliation's messianic power, it is the brief middle passage of the critique that proves most provocative (see Derrida 1989).[43] Here, the potential for agreement that takes exception to law's violence, what Benjamin would later refer to as the normality of law's sovereign state of exception, abides in a "technique of civil agreement" that refuses the form of the legal contract and "holds no sanction for lying" (Benjamin 1996: 245). This refusal is important, according to Benjamin, as it provides a way of demonstrating that, "there is, in the end, apart from all virtues, one effective motive that often enough puts into the most reluctant hands pure instead of violent means: it is the fear of *mutual* disadvantages that threaten to arise from violent confrontation, whatever the outcome might be" (Benjamin 1996: 245). Again, the shared perception of *stasis* beckons that word which stands before the law and questions its fate.[44]

If this provocation toward the discovery (not the accomplishment) of "understanding" is more than a resemblance to the turn that marks reconciliation's beginning, Benjamin's ensuing concern to extricate man from the fate of bare life (*zoe*) suggests that the faith of reconciliation's productive opposition holds the potential for words that compose the relationality of life (*bios*) in a manner that discloses what law may covet most: the (in)distinction between the inside and outside of law.[45] Put more simply, reconciliation offers not only a way of locating the legal violence that concerned both Benjamin and Hannah Arendt, but opens a space to reflect on how such violence can be interpreted and addressed (and perhaps redressed). Circling the hinge of the law's exception, the locus from which it offers standing (the announced standards regarding the conditions for making a meaningful claim to the law), reconciliation troubles the precedent with which law justifies its decision to grant or deny the expression on which the provision of human rights rests. Such inquiry marks not the negation of law but the beginning of an effort to refigure its power through the disclosure and constitution of its rule of recognition. In this light, if it must somehow contain an amnesty, reconciliation's potential is the question of what might (yet) come with a refusal to submit to the rule that indemnifies law's steadfast reluctance to ask after its own discourse and the costs of its creation.

Conclusion

As transition: It is the (im)potential of reconciliation that holds the question of transition, a question regarding the movement in words that struggle for a beginning which abides in the taking place of language that exceeds law's rule. Facing this question, if we are to hear it and thus gather something of the possibility for critique in the wake of the aftermath to which transitional justice is addressed, it will not suffice to reply with the commonplace that reconciliation and transitional justice are best bundled into a "unity *as* difference," a bond defined by an agreement to disagree and the idea that having the most options at the ready is necessarily the best option; so too, its close cousin, the "can't we all just get along?" (with others and other concepts) school of thought offered up by so many who favour reconciliation, may be no less (ob)noxious than the legalistic bureaucrat's methodical and methodological call to follow rules that refuse an account of their constitution. These *topoi* are tired. They figure a problem at the expense of a question, a question of an *agon* that now appears doubled: reconciliation and transitional justice are each conflicted at the same time that they stand at odds with one another. If so, we might then do well to bear in mind that the *agon* in antiquity was frequently the uncertain hope to arrive at a destination, a space of spectacle, contest, and speech to which one travelled and that defined the figure of theory, the *theoros* called to take leave of the city and proceed toward that which upon return required translation.

In the arena of human rights that is quite quick to chastise reflection as undue and dangerous delay, the struggle for transitional justice and reconciliation – and the struggle between them – may be to resist this presumption against theory, one that has ironically produced paralysis and an indefensible gap between practitioners-activists and scholars-critics.[46] Today, it may well be that *both* reconciliation and transitional justice have foreclosed something of the (conceptual) movement that energizes their potential and speaks to the question of their (non)relation. As idea and practice, reconciliation has become inert within its own vernacular, a lexicon of forgiveness, story-telling, and commission-speak that promises insight while declining the complexity of expression's creation and interpretation; and even more troublesome, it has all but failed to explain or justify its constitutive risk, the turn against self-interest and identity that opens space to make and remake the form and content of human relationships. Pointing to this undue gift, the promises, premises and policies of transitional justice have been inoculated with a piety that would take transition by right, an appropriation (with a rather poor track record) that disavows the need to think the relation between peace and justice and which severely discounts the complexity of the interplay between law and ethical life. Taken together, these limits are questions as such, questions that may open (into) transition, a movement and struggle with the deeds of words that may (yet) enable the "turning right about" which marks the (im)potential of a (civic) friendship about which we have yet to think.

Notes

1 For an important supplement to Omar's argument, see Kader Asmal, Louise Asmal, and Ronald Roberts (1996).
2 Given its task, I take the former as something less than a criticism. At a larger level, however, I do not believe that the meaning and significance of reconciliation in South Africa is comprehensible without an understanding of reconciliation's long and contested role in South African politics and culture, not least its defining role in the struggle against apartheid and the constitutional negotiations that culminated in the production of the 1993 interim constitution. For an account of this rhetorical history, along with a close examination of the TRC's creation, including the definition of its rather identitarian premise, see Erik Doxtader (2009). In practical terms, the conflation of reconciliation with the work undertaken by the TRC has produced a simplistic understanding of the transition from apartheid, one that has supported criticism of the Commission that confuses its work with its legislative mandate. For instances of the latter, see Soyinka (1999) and Mamdani (1996: 22–25).
3 As will become apparent, conventional wisdom counsels that one should not begin with reconciliation in the South African case. To do so, according to the growing international consensus, is to mistake an exceptional instance for the norm; if it ever did, the argument goes, South Africa's turn from apartheid to non-racial constitutional democracy can no longer serve as a model for critical inquiry into the (appropriate) form and tensions of transitional justice. Yet, beyond the fact that the country's history of reconciliation has been quite misunderstood, there are hints that this exceptionalism, a yoke that is frequently hung around South Africa's neck, offers an apt starting point precisely because it illustrates the ambiguous object of transitional justice and points to the often unspoken choices (prejudices) that underwrite its study. Put differently, my concern for the South African case that opens this essay and which reappears over its course may offer a way to reflect on Ruti Teitel's claim that transitional justice is "present at a threshold of choice" and that it follows from and is "related to exceptional political conditions" (Teitel 2003: 86–87).
4 This rhetorical view of reconciliation is one that I have developed elsewhere at some length. See Erik Doxtader (2003).
5 This is not the place to undertake a survey of the trends within the literature on transitional justice or rehearse its central premises. Yet, in both academic literature and materials issued by civil society organizations, there are some clear signs that efforts to define and promote transitional justice are distancing themselves from the idea and practice of reconciliation; the dynamic does not seem to run in the opposite direction, although there are certainly strands of thought regarding reconciliation that rather piously segregate themselves from larger policy debates. With respect to the former, Paige Arthur, a Deputy Director of Research at the International Center for Transitional Justice, has recently offered a "conceptual history" of transitional justice that goes to rather extraordinary lengths to avoid discussions of reconciliation, an omission that is particularly evident in Paige's near complete failure to wrestle with the concepts that were in play at a 1994 conference in South Africa, an event that

helped frame the (problematic) case for the TRC's creation. See Paige Arthur (2009). While outside what I can consider here, there is work that has begun to ask after the economy of transitional justice discourse, particularly in the non-governmental sector and with an eye toward relative concerns for reconciliation and other conceptions of transitional justice. See, for instance, VanAntwerpen (2009). The recent study by Fletcher, Weinstein, and Rowen undertakes an expansive survey, although not one that includes significant discussion of how reconciliation does or does not factor into the experience of contingency that complicates transitional justice initiatives. See Laurel Fletcher and Harvey Weinstein with Jamie Rowen (2009). Weinstein is the co-editor of the *International Journal of Transitional Justice*, a relatively new periodical and one which offers some insight into the relative priority of reconciliation within the field.

6 In this essay, I am primarily interested in UN policy discourse as a discourse that both problematizes the meaning and elements of transitional justice and yields normative claims about its development, promotion and application. Oddly enough, this discourse has not featured significantly in academic treatments of transitional justice, an omission or aversion that is plainly evident in Leigh Payne's voluminous bibliography on the subject (available online at http:users.polisci.wisc.edu/tjdb/bib. htm). One problem that attends a reading of UN policy discourse is its uncertain status; both the left and the right have found reasons to doubt the institution's veracity and power, a suspicion not unrelated to the question of whether its international law is in fact law, a matter that I discuss below. Finally, as I am primarily interested in the announced interplay between different modes of transitional justice within UN discourse, my focus here is not on reading the discourse surrounding the formation of the International Criminal Court and its role in the development of transitional justice.

7 Also see, Richard McKeon (1944) and McKeon (1968).

8 With respect to the field of transitional justice as a whole, there are debates over its precise origins and boundaries. With the caveats noted above, see Arthur (2009). Among others, works that shed important light on the field's development and the diversity of approaches to transitional justice include, Ruti Teitel (2000); Elster (2004); Hess and Post (1999).

9 The momentum was fed by calls within Africa to model the South African case, not least in Burundi and Sierra Leone. In the former, Nelson Mandela took an active role in leading negotiations that closely resembled the South African constitutional talks. In the latter, a number of individuals from South Africa's TRC helped design Sierra Leone's truth commission, a body that has been criticized for not taking stock of the particular dynamics of the conflict it sought to understand. At a larger level, the South African case provoked a substantial and still growing body of more or less critical literature. See, for instance, Robert Rotberg and Dennis Thompson (2000); Veitch (2007); and Borer (2006). For different reasons, see Boraine (2001). Having served as the South African TRC's Vice-Chairperson, Boraine was the leading force behind the creation of the International Centre for Transitional Justice, a New York-based organization that has exerted significant influence on a variety of transitional justice initiatives. For an insightful and very useful reflection on the lessons of the South African case and their larger relevance, see Villa-Vicencio (2009).

10 Here, the objection could be made that Tutu's position entails an advocacy of restorative justice, an idea that emerged in the South Africa case, at least, over the course of the TRC's tenure and which has yet to capture the international communities imagination outside of a relatively small circle.

11 It is curious here to compare the idea that reconciliation may count as or contribute to meaningful reparation with later claims which set reparation as a precondition to reconciliation. This latter idea is evident in the 1997 principles and a number of later UN documents. See, for instance, Commission on Human Rights (2003).

12 Also see Diane Orentlicher (1991); Diane Orentlicher (2007).

13 Also see Office of the High Commissioner for Human Rights (2005); and Commission on Human Rights (2005).
14 For an opening analysis of the right, see Yasmin Naqvi (2006).
15 Also see: Office of the High Commissioner for Human Rights (2005); Commission on Human Rights (2006); and Human Rights Council (2006).
16 A fuller formulation of this rendering of potential (*dunamis*) can be found in Giorgio Agamben (2000). The objection could be made that this view of transition unduly ignores the variety of socio-political transitions, a set of forms that political science has labored to schematize, although without always considering the ways in which those participating and caught up in these events are confronted with the experience of "making anew," a beginning which does not have to count as revolutionary in order to call into question the grounds of individual and collective action, particularly in the wake of historical division that renders hermeneutics a contested enterprise. At this level, as I discuss shortly, typologies of transition frequently supplant their rhetorical operativity with methodological accounts that risk presupposing the product(ion) of transition.
17 These issues play fundamental roles in contemporary democratization literature, a field that has not been put into significant play with transitional justice even as their overlap is substantial. See, for instance, Diamond (1999).
18 Here, I borrow from and rely somewhat on Judith Butler's account of the scene of address. See Butler (2005). See also Cavarero (2004).
19 For two of the best treatments of the issue, see Ross (2003) and Sanders (2007).
20 On this point, Arendt's reflections on the awkward production of truth are particularly instructive, not least as she anticipates something of the dilemma that attends the work of transition. See Arendt (1993).
21 For accounts of the process that go beyond the usual descriptive fair, see Villa-Vicencio and Verwoerd (2000); and Krog (1998).
22 This apparent and discomforting reversal echoes the first formal defence of amnesty, the institutionally sanctioned presence of oblivion that appeared with the overthrow of the Thirty Tyrants in 403 BC. Not so much has changed since these difficult days in Athens, at least if we are able to disavow the conflation of amnesty and amnesia in order to think how an edict against forms of recollection that invoke law's rule of retribution may give way to a memory that reconstitutes the grounds of speaking, the potential of *logos* to (re)establish the exchange, the constitutive relation, that turns enmity towards (civic) friendship. In the form of an oath that meta-transitively figures the citizen-subject in a way that subverts the violence of its own self-certainty, this (then secular) gift of the reconciling word invents the potential for asking after the transitional relationship between politics and justice. The terms and underlying logic of the Athenian amnesty are best detailed by Nicole Loraux. Jon Elster's recent account of the amnesty in his work on the history of transitional justice is largely derivative of Loraux's crucial account of amnesty's memorial operativity. Too, Elster rather underplays the way in which reconciliation – as more than a state of affairs – figures the amnesty as a constitutive form of public memory. See Loraux (1998); and Elster (2004). One of the tasks that remains to be undertaken is a close consideration of how Hannah Arendt's account of forgiveness bears on Loraux's demonstration that amnesty may serve, in some cases, to compose the commons, the domain of political appearance that Arendt seeks to recover. With respect to the South African amnesty, in particular, see Charles Villa-Vicencio and Erik Doxtader (2003).
23 For accounts of international human rights law as a form of customary law, see Lori Fisler Damrosch, et al, (2001); and Casper (2004).
24 In part, I draw here from Tamanaha's useful overview of historical and competing schools of thought about the nature, scope and force of rule of law. See Tamanaha (2004).

25 For detailed discussions on the law's rule of recognition, see Joseph Raz (1980); Raz (1983); Casper (2004: 3–5). For another important account of the tension that defines the position of rule of law in society see Jürgen Habermas (1986).

26 The problem is particularly acute in those transitions that endeavor to preserve legal continuity, a turn that does not mitigate the transitional question of (re)making the legitimacy of the legal system. For instance, see Doxtader (2009: 250–254).

27 On the arguable character of law, see MacCormick (2005).

28 As I suggest below, amnesty thus construed enables an important exception to law's state of exception.

29 For a crucial reflection on this problem, see Povinelli (2002: 54–56).

30 For an excellent discussion of Arendt's concern for speech and its action in the context of human rights, see Birmingham (2006: 26–27).

31 Worth reflection, the whole thought is: "What of those political places where no debate about right is possible because no claim to right has been recognized as valid? To argue that it is up to individuals to claim rights through a debate is to miss the political urgency: those who desperately appeal to human rights are often those who are in no position to be recognized as claimants before a tribunal that has already decided against them" (Birmingham 2006: 27).

32 In this latter formulation of the problem, I follow Düttmann's difficult but powerful critique of the struggle for recognition as it is developed in the literature on multiculturalism and the way in which the latter renders recognition into a procedure at the cost of understanding the struggle itself, an abiding "recognizing" that does not afford the ground for given or stable identity. See Düttmann (2000).

33 Agamben has thought carefully about this idea, the taking place of language, and I rely somewhat on his position in appealing to the notion here. See Agamben (1991).

34 This is a complicated matter, one that turns partly on the connection in antiquity between the concepts of recognition, reconciliation, and discovery. The connection is most apparent in Aristotle's poetics. Here, the finding (out) of discovery (*huerisis/heurêma*) reveals and transforms that which seems to be into what it is not. The defining quality of recognition (*anagnorsis*), this turn is explained by Aristotle as an event that changes ignorance to knowledge and reverses (*peripeteia*) affiliations of love and hate. Literally and figuratively, recognition entails "turning right about," an upset and transition that involves not only the acquisition of knowledge but an understanding that cuts and composes ethical and moral relationships, including the self's relation to itself. Understood as "a change from enmity to/for friendship," this turn is also a basic characteristic of reconciliation (*diallagê*, *kattallagê*, and *sunallagê*). The matter is complicated further in Hegel, as he leaves the vocabulary of reconciliation in his early theological writings for the grammar of recognition in the *Phenomenology*. I have considered the implications of this shift elsewhere; see Doxtader (2007).

35 The point is small but important given Aristotle's definition of rhetoric as a potential (*dunamis*). For a leading discussion of the matter, see Farrell (1993).

36 That is, the other, from outside the city, who lacks the capacity for meaningful let alone trustworthy speech.

37 In Hegel, one name for this condition is bad infinity. The mutual recognition of *stasis*, or in Derrida's terms a shared moment of undecidability that precludes the trial that gives way to a decision, may be one way of marking the ground of reconciliation, at least if one works from the view that reconciliation is not something which can be imposed by a third party. While this "voluntarism" is troubled by the status of language, to the degree that it stands as a third, the interpretation is useful as it concedes something to the question of what kinds of conflict are (not) open to reconciliation, a limit that many general defenses of reconciliation have failed to consider to the effect of feeding the juridical case for transitional justice. By the same token, however, the latter has become fond of the ruse that warrants a rule of law based approach solely on the grounds that not all conflicts may admit to reconciliation.

38   On this point, see Agamben's crucial account of *kairos* and its relation to the giving (up) of vocation (Agamben 2005).

39   In what may be one of the subtlest retorts to the call for reconciliation, Constand Viljoen, a former General in the South African Defence Force, once urged, "Let us not spend a single day in masochistic retroversion." While it may misunderstand reconciliation's middle voice, at least as Hayden White would have it, the point, in part, is that reconciliation may be a category mistake to the extent that there is no "originary" condition to which parties might (re)turn. Andrew Schaap has formulated a thoughtful and indeed elegant reply to this objection, one that echoes with my argument here as to how reconciliation may open with a more or less extended period of meta-discourse given to opening the question of how to forge the commons and in what terms. See Schaap (2008).

40   In other work, I have developed a much fuller account of reconciliation's beginning as the invention of a language that offers the potential for productive opposition. See Doxtader (2003). I would then agree with Schaap's recent claim that reconciliation may lay the basis for an "overlapping dissensus" that enables an "agonistic politics that is potentially constitutive of a political community." See Schaap (2008: 251). Approaching the matter in the context of reconciliation's risk of assimilation, Schaap then suggests that it was only possible to speak of reconciliation in South Africa *after* the brokering of the 1993 constitution. As suggested above, I have difficulty following this position, at least if it amounts to a historical claim. At a philosophical and rhetorical level, as Schaap suggests with his turn to Rancière, the issue, if conceived as a line drawn by law, points to the importance of questioning if not resisting notions of transitional justice that fail to consider reconciliation's *claimed* meaning and *expressed* power (as a performance of reconciliation) within the context of constitution-making, a context that reconciliation may well open. Independent of Schaap's argument, the matter also points to the entrenched presumption in human rights discourse that there is little need to think beyond the terms of the French and American revolutions.

41   Moving beyond (or rather, within) reconciliation's movement, there is an important resonance between the weak messianic quality of reconciliation and the project of constitution, where the latter, in Kenneth Burke's terms, is a "calculus of motives" that holds and holds open the moment of its creation, a beginning whose cost must itself be reconciled. See Burke (1969). In this regard, Habermas' account of the extended time of constitution-making is instructive. See Habermas (2000). The interplay between reconciliation and the messianic rests heavily on Agamben's recovery of the concept from its popular eschatological connotation (Agamben 2005).

42   The former is addressed in Boraine (2000).

43   In the context of my argument here, there is an element of Derrida's reading of Benjamin that must be and most certainly cannot be "reckoned with," that is, the terms of Derrida's post-script, in which he asks whether Benjamin's defence of divine violence can be tolerated in the wake of the Holocaust. That such a reading may be unfair, that it exceeds the bounds of 'productive' critique, a line that Benjamin himself calls into question, I take to be central to Derrida's very point, particularly in light of his claims regarding the important and even indefatigable relation between deconstruction and justice, a relation that itself must face the trial of its undecidability, not perhaps unlike that conciliatory gesture which cannot exceed the costs of its words that would claim to appear before the truth of law's rule. For a very relevant and closely argued reflection on Benjamin's position, see McNulty (2007).

44   For a perplexing and instructive consideration of this point, see Benjamin (1996).

45   Here, I rely partly on Agamben's reading of Benjamin's well known reflections on history. See Agamben (2005); and Agamben (1998).

46   While it stops a bit short of considering the operativity of human rights discourse, David Kennedy's attention to the importance of the discourse as such makes a crucial case. See Kennedy (2005).

References

Agamben, G. (1991) *Language and Death: the place of negativity,* trans. K. Pinkus, Minneapolis, MN: University of Minnesota Press.

Agamben, G. (1998) *Homo Sacer: sovereign power and bare life,* trans. D. Heller-Roazen, Palo Alto, CA: Stanford University Press.

Agamben, G. (2000) *Potentialities: collected essays in philosophy,* trans. D. Heller-Roazen, Palo Alto, CA: Stanford University Press.

Agamben, G. (2005) *The Time that Remains: a commentary on the letter to the romans,* trans. P. Dailey, Palo Alto, CA: Stanford University Press.

Annan, K. (2005) 'In larger freedom: towards development, security and human rightsfor all', Report of the Secretary General, 21 March, available online at http://daccessods.un.org/access.nsf/Get?Open&DS=A/59/2005&Lang=EA/59/2005.

Annan, K. (2004) 'The rule of law and transitional justice in conflict and post-conflict societies', United Nations Security Council, Report of the Secretary General, 23 August.

Arendt, H. (1948) *The Origins of Totalitarianism*, New York: Schocken Books.

Arendt, H. (1958) *The Human Condition*, Chicago, IL: University of Chicago Press.

Arendt, H. (1993) 'Truth and Politics', in *Between past and Future: eight exercises in political thought*, New York: Penguin Books.

Arendt, H. (2006) *Eichmann in Jerusalem: a report on the banality of evil*, New York: Penguin Books.

Arthur, P. (2009) 'How transitions reshaped human rights: a conceptual history of transitional justice', *Human Rights Quarterly* 31, pp. 3221–3267.

Asmal, K.L. and Roberts, R. (1996) *Reconciliation Through Truth*, Cape Town, ZA: David Philip Publishing.

Benjamin, W. (1996a) 'The Critique of Violence', in Bullock, M. (ed.) *Walter Benjamin: selected writings volume 1, 1913–1926*, Cambridge, MA: Harvard University Press.

Benjamin, W. (1996b) 'Fate and Character', in Bullock, M. (ed.) *Walter Benjamin: selected writings, volume 1, 1913–1926*, Cambridge, MA: Harvard University Press.

Bentham, J. (2002) 'Nonsense upon stilts or pandora's box opened', in Schofield, P., Pease-Watkins, C. and Blamires, C. (eds) *The Collected Works of Jeremy Bentham: rights, representation and reform*, Oxford, UK: Clarendon Press.

Birmingham, P. (2006) *Hannah Arendt and Human Rights: the predicament of common responsibility*, Bloomington, IN: Indiana University Press.

Blanchot, M. (1995) *The Writing of the Disaster*, trans. A. Smock, Lincoln, NB: University of Nebraska Press.

Boraine, A. (2001) *A Country Unmasked: inside South Africa's Truth and Reconciliation Commission*, Oxford, UK: Oxford University Press.

Boraine, A. (2000) 'A Language of Potential', in James, W. and van der Vijver, L. (eds) *Reflections on Truth and Reconciliation in South Africa*, Cape Town, ZA: David Philips Books.

Borer, T. (2006) *Telling the Truths: truth telling and peace building in post-conflict societies*, South Bend, IN: University of Notre Dame.

Burke, K. (1969) *A Grammar of Motives*, Berkeley, CA: University of California Press.

Butler, J. (2005) *Giving an Account of Oneself*, New York: Fordham University Press.

Casper, G. (2004) 'Rule of law? whose law?', *Center on Democracy, Development and the Rule of Law*, working paper #10, Stanford Institute for International Studies, available online at http://pesd.stanford.edu/publications/rule_of_law_whose_law/.

62   *Erik Doxtader*

OK

Cassin, B. (2001) 'Politics of memory: on treatments of hate', *The Public-Javnost: Journal of the European Institute for Communication and Culture* 8, pp. 9–22.

Cavarero, A. (2004) *For More Than One Voice: toward a philosophy of vocal expression,* trans. P. Kottman, Palo Alto, CA: Stanford University Press.

Commission on Human Rights (2003) 'Civil and political rights – the right to a remedy and reparation for victims of violations of international human rights and humanitarian law', 10 November.

Commission on Human Rights (2004) 'Promotion and protection of human rights – Impunity', 27 February.

Commission on Human Rights (2005) 'Administration of justice, rule of law and democracy – report of the sessional working group on the administration of justice', 10 August.

Commission on Human Rights (2006) 'Promotion and Protection of Human Rights – Study on the Right to Truth', 8 February.

Damrosch, L.F., Henkin, L., and Murphy, S.D. (eds) (2001) *International Law: cases and materials, fourth edition,* St. Paul, MI: West Group Publishers.

Derrida, J. (1989) 'Force of law: the mystical foundation of authority', *Cardozo Law Review* 11.

Diamond, L. (1999) *Developing Democracy: toward consolidation,* Baltimore, MD: Johns Hopkins University Press.

Doxtader, E. (2003) 'Reconciliation: a rhetorical concept/ion', *Quarterly Journal of Speech* 89, pp. 267–92.

Doxtader, E. (2007) 'The faith and struggle of beginning (with) words: on the turn between reconciliation and recognition', *Philosophy and Rhetoric* 40(1), 119–146.

Doxtader, E.(2009) *With Faith in the Works of Words: the beginnings of reconciliation in South Africa, 1985–1995,* Cape Town, ZA: David Philip/Michigan State University Press.

Doxtader, E. and Villa-Vicencio, C. (eds) (2003) *The Provocations of Amnesty: memory, justice and impunity,* Cape Town, ZA: David Philip Publishers.

Düttmann, A. (2000) *Between Cultures: tensions in the struggle for recognition,* London: Verso.

Elster, J. (2004) *Closing the Books: transitional justice in historical perspective,* Cambridge, UK: Cambridge University Press.

Farrell, T. (1993) *Norms of Rhetorical Culture,* New Haven, CT: Yale University Press.

Fletcher, L. and Weinstein, H. with Rowen, J. (2009) 'Context, timing and the dynamics of transitional justice: a historical perspective', *Human Rights Quarterly* 31, pp. 163–200.

Habermas, J. (1986) 'Law and morality', *Tanner Lectures on Human Values,* 1 and 2, available online at http://www.tannerlectures.utah.edu/lectures/documents/habermas88.pdf.

Habermas, J. (2000) 'Constitutional democracy – a paradoxical combination of contradictory principles', paper presented at the Northwestern School of Law, 23 October, available online at http://www.mediafire.com/?gdnkzwmzwiw.

Hess, C. and Post, R. (eds) (1999) *Human Rights in Political Transitions: Gettysburg to Bosnia,* New York: Zone Books.

Human Rights Council (2006) 'Resolution 9/11 – Right to Truth.'

Human Rights Council (2007) 'Implementation of General Assembly Resolution 60/251 of 15 March 2006: "Human Rights Council – right to truth: report of the Office of the High Commissioner for Human Rights"', Fifth Session, 7 June.

Kalomoh, T. (2004) 'Post-conflict national reconciliation: role of the United Nations', UN Security Council, 4903rd Meeting, 26 January.

Kennedy, D. (2005) *The Dark Sides of Virtue: reassessing international humanitarianism*, Princeton, NJ: Princeton University Press.

Krog, A. (1998) *Country of My Skull: guilt, sorrow, and the limits of forgiveness in the new South Africa*, New York: Random House.

Loraux, N. (1998) 'Of amnesty and its opposite', in *Mothers in Mourning*, trans. C. Pache, Ithaca, NY: Cornell University Press.

MacCormick, N. (2005) *Rhetoric and the Rule of Law: a theory of legal reasoning*, Oxford, UK: Oxford University Press.

MacKay, D. (2003) 4,835th Meeting of the UN Security Council, 30 Sept, 2003, available online at https://www.civcap.info/fileadmin/user_upload/UN/S_PV_4835.pdf.

Mandela, N. (1999) 'Opening address by President Nelson Mandela in the special debate on the Report of the Truth and Reconciliation Commission', 25 February, available online at http://www.info.gov.za/speeches/1999/99225_trc-ma99_10201.htm.

McKeon, R. (1944) 'Discussion and resolution in political conflicts', *Ethics* 55(4), pp. 236–237.

McKeon, R. (1947) 'Economic, political and moral communities in the world society', *Ethics* 57(2).

McKeon, R. (1968) 'Philosophy and history in the development of human rights', in Kiefer, H. and Munitz, M. (eds) *Ethics and Social Justice*, Albany, NY: SUNY Press.

McNulty, T. (2007) 'The commandment against the law: writing and divine justice in Walter Benjamin's critique of violence', *Diacritics* 37(2), pp. 34–60.

Naqvi, Y. (2006) 'The right to truth in international law: fact or fiction', *International Review of the Red Cross* 88(862), pp. 245–273.

Office of the High Commissioner for Human Rights (2005) 'Basic principles and guidelines on the right to a remedy and reparation for victims of gross violations of international human rights law and serious violations of international humanitarian law – human rights resolution 2005/35', April.

Office of the High Commissioner for Human Rights (2005) 'Democracy and the rule of law – human rights resolution 2005/32', April.

Office of the High Commissioner for Human Rights (2005) 'Right to truth – human rights resolution 2005/66', 20 April.

Office of the High Commissioner for Human Rights (2006) 'Rule of Law Tools for Post-Conflict States', available online at www.ohchr.org/Documents/Publications/RuleoflawVettingen.pdf.

Office of the High Commissioner for Human Rights (2007) 'Implementation of General Assembly resolution 60/251, entitled "Human Rights Council"--right to truth', available online at www2.ohchr.org/english/bodies/hrcouncil/docs/a.res.60.251_en.pdf.

Omar, D. (1995) 'Testimony delivered to parliament's joint committee on justice with regards to the promotion of national unity and reconciliation bill', 31 January, Archives of Parliament, Cape Town, South Africa.

Orentlicher, D. (1991) 'Settling accounts: the duty to prosecute human rights violations of previous regime', *Yale Law Journal* 100.

Orentlicher, D. (2007) 'Settling accounts revisited: reconciling global norms with local agency', *International Journal of Transitional Justice* 1, pp. 10–22.

Povinelli, E. (2002) *The Cunning of Recognition: indigenous alterities and the making of Australian multiculturalism*, Durham, NC: Duke University Press.

Raz, J. (1980) *The Concept of a Legal System*, Oxford, UK: Oxford University Press.

Raz, J. (1983) *The Authority of Law*, Oxford, UK: Oxford University Press.

Report of the Office of the High Commissioner for Human Rights (2007) 'Implementation of general assembly resolution 60/251 of 15 March 2006 entitled "Human Rights Council – right to truth"', 7 June.

Ross, F. (2003) *Bearing Witness*, Cape Town, ZA: Pluto Press.

Rotberg R. and Thompson, D. (eds) (2000) *Truth v. Justice: the morality of truth commissions*, Princeton, NJ: Princeton University Press.

Sanders, M. (2007) *Ambiguities of Witnessing: law and literature in the time of a truth commission*, Palo Alto, CA: Stanford University Press.

Schaap, A. (2004) 'The rule of law and transitional justice in conflict and post-conflict societies', available online at www.un.org/Docs/sc/sgrep04.html.

Schaap, A. (2008) 'Reconciliation as ideology and politics', *Constellations* 15(2).

Solomon, A. and Tolbert, D. (2006) 'United Nations reform and supporting the rule of law in post-conflict societies', *Harvard Human Rights Journal* 19.

Soyinka, W. (1999) *The Burden of Memory, the Muse of Forgiveness*, Oxford: Oxford University Press.

Tamanaha, B. (2004) *On the Rule of Law: history, politics, theory*, Cambridge, UK: Cambridge University Press.

Teitel, R. (2000) *Transitional Justice*, Oxford, UK: Oxford University Press.

Teitel, R. (2003) 'Transitional justice genealogy', *Harvard Human Rights Journal* 16.

United Nations Commission on Human Rights, 'The administration of justice and the human rights of detainees--question of the impunity of perpetrators of human rights violations,' revised final report prepared by Mr. Joinet pursuant to sub-commisssion decision 1996/119', 2 October 1997, available online at http://www.unhchr.ch/huridocda/huridoca.nsf/(Symbol)/E.CN.4.sub.2.1997.20.Rev.1.En.

United Nations Development Programme, 'UNDP and transitional justice: an overview', January 2006.

United Nations Security Council (2003) 'Justice and the rule of law: the United Nations role' available online at www.undp.org/.../rule%20of%20law%20and%20transitional%20justice.pdf.

United Nations Security Council. (2004) 'Post-conflict national reconciliation: 30, September, the United Nations role of',available online at www.un.int/.../Statement%20on%20post-conflict%20reconciliation.doc.

VanAntwerpen, J. (2009) 'Moral globalization and discursive struggle: reconciliation, transitional justice and cosmopolitan discourse', in Hammack, D. and Heydemann, S. (eds) *Globalization, Philanthropy, and Civil Society: projecting institutional logic abroad*, Bloomington, IN: Indiana University Press.

Veitch, S. (ed.) (2007) *Law and the Politics of Reconciliation*, Hampshire, UK: Ashgate. United Nations Development Programme (2006) 'UNDP and transitional justice: an overview', 1 January.

Velasquez-Rodriguez v. Honduras (1988) Inter-American Court of Human Rights, no. 4.

Villa-Vicencio, C. (2009) *Walk with us and Listen: reconciliation in Africa*, Washington, DC: Georgetown University Press.

Villa-Vicencio C. and Verwoerd, W. (eds) (2000) *Looking Back, Reaching Forward: reflections on the Truth and Reconciliation Commission of South Africa*, Cape Town, ZA: UCT Press, 2000.

4   Rhetorics of reconciliation

Shifting conflict paradigms in Northern Ireland

Adrian Little

The concept of reconciliation has endured a chequered development in the last twenty years. Not surprisingly, given its prominence in conflict transformation processes in South Africa in the 1990s, the primary usage of the concept of reconciliation was as a normative good (Hamber and van der Merwe 1998; Lederach 1997). Buoyed by the ostensible success of the South African example, pressure groups, NGOs and peace activists in a variety of political settings commandeered the idea of reconciliation to bolster their arguments (Bar-Siman-Tov 2004). However, as events unfolded in South Africa, and as the difficulties in establishing shared understandings of reconciliation emerged in combination with the problematic translation of theoretical aspirations into meaningful political institutions, a more critical perspective on reconciliation has become a central part of social and political debates on conflict transformation in recent years. These critical accounts are often still receptive to the idea that reconciliation may be a worthwhile vision to aspire to but are less forthright in the pursuit of a normative vision of reconciliation *per se*.

Before going on to address these perspectives in more detail, it is worth briefly outlining the key concerns of this chapter. It begins by evaluating three different perspectives that fall under the broad rubric of critical theories of reconciliation. Two of these approaches, agonistic and narrative accounts of reconciliation, have been addressed in more detail elsewhere (Little 2011, 2012a). The focus here however is on the rhetorical theory of reconciliation which is most commonly associated with the work of Erik Doxtader on the experience of reconciliation in South Africa. In short, this approach contends that there does not have to be a clear definition of reconciliation to underpin a conflict transformation process. Rather, reconciliation can act as a general heading under which a rhetorical space can be established that enables a more open discussion of the issues at stake in conflict transformation – wrongdoing, violence, reparation, mourning, justice for victims and so forth – than had hitherto been the case. For Doxtader, reconciliation played precisely such a transformative role in South African politics in the mid-late 1990s despite the contested nature of the concept and disagreements about how it should be institutionalised.

This chapter analyses this argument in the much different contextual environment of Northern Ireland. Moving on from a foundational argument that

Northern Ireland reflects a 'disjunctured synthesis' whereby the opposing forces are locked into and rely upon their opposition to one another (Little 2012a), I use the example of Northern Ireland to question the extent to which a rhetorical device or a range of rhetorical practices can engender significant shifts in social and political paradigms. This requires a discussion of the concept of paradigm shift such as in the work of Thomas Kuhn (1996) and more recent developments of these theoretical models in the work of Giorgio Agamben for example (Agamben 2009). These arguments, when coupled with some of the insights of complexity theory (Cilliers 1998; Zolo 1992), provide a more nuanced understanding of conflict paradigms and their resilience than is evident in the dominant normative understandings of reconciliation and, I argue, a more developed account of the possibilities and difficulties of conflict transformation than is at work in even the critical theories of reconciliation that have become more popular in recent years. This not to say that there is not a significant role for reconciliation in conflict transformation processes but that the precise nature of that role is highly dependent on the contextual circumstances of a particular conflict situation and, thus, that the idea of a particular rhetorical device as a transformative catalyst, while not impossible, faces numerous obstacles in established social and political institutions and practices.

Critical approaches to reconciliation

For analytical purposes it is useful to separate critical approaches to reconciliation into three main groups: agonistic theories, theories of reconciliation as rhetoric, and narrative understandings of reconciliation. Each of these approaches has different understandings of the nature of reconciliation and varying implications for politics and policy. First, for agonistic theorists it is important that we develop a more sophisticated account of conflict and its inherent role in political organization (Mouffe 2000). Agonistic accounts of reconciliation are based on the need to foreground divisive issues and the disputes they engender but also to seek a more inclusive polity that is not constrained by the narrowing pursuit of consensus (Schaap 2008). Second, rhetorical approaches to reconciliation also recognise the inevitability of conflict but emphasise the potential of rhetorical devices to provide a conceptual backdrop against which groups can engage across difference (Doxtader 2003). Like agonism, these rhetorical approaches can be viewed as an attempt to domesticate political conflict but they attempt to use rhetorical mechanisms rather than political structures as the primary means of facilitating engagement across conflictual political difference. Thirdly, narrative perspectives also embrace the inevitability of conflict but are less oriented towards forging political common ground than is the case with agonistic and rhetorical approaches (Moon 2006). Narrative accounts do not prioritise reconciliatory perspectives over conflictual arguments in quite the same way that the agonistic and rhetorical approaches tend to do. The key point here is that rather than trying to either domesticate or override disputatious standpoints, narrative approaches to reconciliation are based upon the centrality and inevitability of conflict to politics. By this understanding, conflict is part of the ontological condition of political life and, however much we try to overcome it, it can never be eradicated. Therefore, the politics of reconciliation needs to take account of not only those perspectives that are overtly conciliatory but also – and more significantly – those which are non-reconciled and continue to articulate a disruptive, disagreeable political message (Little 2007). Let me now turn to the agonistic and rhetorical perspectives in a little more detail.

The agonistic approach is one that recognizes the inevitability of political conflict and so provides a critical alternative to more normative approaches which preference the potential for peace and harmony over disagreement (Schaap 2008: 249). In this vein, Paul Muldoon contends that provided 'the objective is restoring legitimacy (rather than that of restoring order), the possibility of grounding the state upon dialogically constructed forms of consensus rather than ideologically veiled modes of coercion remains open' (Muldoon 2003: 187). Arguably though, the pursuit of a more agonistic polity underplays the complex nature of conflict and the difficulty of establishing a shared 'political community' grounded in dialogue as the basis of legitimacy (Little 2002). Agonistic accounts pre-suppose the possibility of a dialogic process of reinvention to renegotiate the terms of 'political association' as part of a 'new liberal political formation' (Muldoon 2003: 196) rather than identifying the contentious nature of these objectives in many conflictual societies.

The problem with agonistic accounts is the difficulty of establishing a founding order of reconciliation which can act as an agreed basis on which to conduct a more inclusive but conflictual form of political engagement. For example, Schaap attempts a 'noncontroversial' definition of reconciliation as 'a public reckoning with a history of political violence and oppression and their legacy in order to enable people divided by that past to coexist within one political community and to recognize the legitimacy of its law' (Schaap 2008: 250). However, this seems a rather controversial definition insofar as, in societies as diverse as Northern Ireland and Australia where reconciliation has been articulated, we can see quite substantial degrees of opposition to such public reckoning of violence, the notion of a divided rather than singular political community, and suspicion of – if not outright opposition to – the system of law inflicted as part of a particular jurisdiction. Thus, it is dangerous to over- determine reconciliation in the construction of an agonistic *modus vivendi* because there is a danger of replicating the limitations of normative liberal approaches albeit with a wider constituency and greater scope for disagreement.

An alternative formulation in the critical reconciliation literature emanating from South Africa is the rhetorical approach which focuses on the creation of a space for dialogue even where the process and the events it seeks to make sense of are highly contested. By this account 'reconciliation is a mode of rhetorical history-making' (Doxtader 2001: 225) which both generates further drives for reconciliation as well as constituting a mindset in which these contested events of the past could be addressed directly. This suggests that prior agreement on reconciliation was not vital and that, on the contrary, 'reconciliation rhetorically constituted a referent for interaction, a bridge between incommensurable views of South Africa's past and future' (Doxtader 2001: 244). This account emphasizes the utility of reconciliation as a 'dialogic event' rather than an institutional political process which would reach particular outcomes. Reconciliation was almost an umbrella term which allowed for contestation within the South African context. However, this does not mean that reconciliation would have the same cachet in transforming other conflicts – in South Africa it had a functional utility insofar as it was capable of acting as a rhetorical space to permit engagement. However, as we shall see, in other societies like Northern Ireland, it is likely to close down spaces for engagement or generate significant political conflict.

The rhetorical approach is a subtle move beyond agonistic accounts which rely more heavily on pre-conceived ways of performing politics or ultimately the need for legitimization of a particular political community. Instead, rhetorical arguments provide an 'oppositional view of reconciliation [that] unsettles its dialectical aspirations towards the transcendent' (Doxtader 2003: 268). The implication of this argument is that reconciliation in South Africa should be viewed as a framing device which established the paradigm within which the competing sides could work through their differences. However, there is still a lacuna in the rhetorical approach concerning the opportunities for the articulation of non-reconciliatory arguments. There is a risk then that the rhetorical approach privileges conciliation over other more critical and disputatious accounts of the events of the past. Moreover, as will become clear in the discussion of the contested nature of reconciliation in Northern Ireland, an alternative rhetorical device would have to be articulated to perform a similar function in societies where the concept of reconciliation was more controversial. The question remains then of which concept we use to frame these kinds of engagements, where it comes from and who decides that it is fit for purpose.

The key question to be addressed in the remainder of the chapter is the extent to which the use of the concept of reconciliation to open up a rhetorical space for conflict transformation in South Africa can be applied to other contested political environments. In applied terms, the chapter takes the example of Northern Ireland as a counterpoint to the South African experience in order to clarify some of the issues that emerge in different, complex political contexts. This helps to clarify some of the key theoretical concerns that the chapter identifies – namely, the nature of social and political paradigms and the ways in which rhetorical devices can change and shift those paradigms in the face of ingrained systemic practices and the institutions which help to sustain them. The first step in this analysis is to identify precisely what we understand by paradigms and the ways in which they might be said to be in processes of transition.

Paradigm shifts in complex societies

The concept of paradigm shift has become prominent in the social sciences through the work of Thomas Kuhn as a means of explaining the ways in which the framing of social phenomena can change over the course of time as the epistemological foundations of what we know develops (Kuhn 1996; Nickles 2003). Since the original thesis was expounded by Kuhn, the notion of paradigm shift has become a focus of debate for a number of theorists including (obliquely) Michel Foucault, Alain Touraine (2007), and, most recently, Giorgio Agamben (2009). For the purposes of understanding the potential of rhetoric, the key question is the extent to which it can influence the shifting of interpretive paradigms (Finlayson and Martin 2008). This question relates to the discursive possibilities of the linguistic reframing of social phenomena and whether such a process is only marginally capable of affecting significant paradigmatic change in the face of the ingrained structural practices of existing institutional paradigms. More specifically, given the highly adaptive nature of complex social and political systems, to what extent can shifts in the use of political language exact sufficiently significant substantive change on the institutional frameworks that give practical meaning to the linguistic constructions of politics such that a paradigmatic shift could be said to have taken place? If a shift in paradigms involves the emergence of a 'new and more rigid definition of the field' (Kuhn 1996: 19), what is the role of rhetoric in their establishment?

Complex paradigms

These accounts of paradigms and the manner in which they reproduce and change also need to be placed in the context of social and political complexity. There is insufficient space here to rehearse the arguments around complexity theory (Cilliers 1998) and its application in both conceptual debates and to specific conflict scenarios (but see Little 2008, 2009a and 2009c for the former and 2009b for the latter in relation to Northern Ireland), but it is worth summarising some of the key aspects of complexity in the social sciences to help us to understand what is at stake in talking about paradigm shifts in complex, conflict-ridden societies. Three dimensions of social complexity are worth devoting particular attention to: path dependence, emergent properties and adaptive systems. By briefly commenting on each in turn, the affect that complexity can have on the possibilities for continuity and change (and, thus, paradigm shifts) will become apparent.

Path dependence is a well-established term in the social sciences. It alludes to the way in which social and political practices and ideas emerge from a value-laden, historical trajectory. As such, when we debate political ideas in any given context and their implications for political action, we always do so within a pre-established set of parameters which frame debates and limit the possibilities of how we might define 'rational' or 'practicable' actions or 'attainable' outcomes. Path dependence helps us to understand the shifting ways in which ideas and practices develop and the genealogy of the tools we have at our disposal for addressing social and political conflicts. The problem of path dependence is that it can enshrine and reify particular accounts or practices which constrain the possibilities of conflict transformation. Indeed, in most conflict scenarios at their most intractable, it is the ingraining of particular ideas and their institutionalisation in the political architecture that serves to preclude obvious political progress. At the same time however, political conflicts and the modes of their transformation (e.g. peace processes) do not proceed in isolation. Every conflict is constantly being transformed although that transformation can both further reify and amplify conflict or lead to some mode of better management of the issues at stake. In the example of somewhere like Northern Ireland then, the peace process of the 1990s involved both a rearticulation of pre-established theories of conflict resolution while, simultaneously, the institutions that were created through the 1998 Belfast Agreement arguably strengthened some of the ethno-national identifications which gave rise to the conflict in the first place (Little 2004, 2009b, see also Ruane and Todd 2007).

The second dimension of complexity that requires particular exposition is the concept of emergent properties. This idea alludes to the generative aspect of complex systems. That is, complex systems do not only emerge from particular historical trajectories but they also contribute to the reproduction of those systems in innovative and unforeseen ways. Complex systems are traditionally viewed as neither static nor linear. Instead, they are in a constant process of redevelopment that, given the complicated interaction of a multiplicity of variables, often generate unpredictable, non-linear outcomes. That is, complex systems are dynamic and the manner in which they deal with path dependent, historical trajectories does not merely reproduce or replicate those trajectories but instead reforms them in fresh, innovative ways. Complex systems are then a chaotic mix of orderly and disorderly phenomena – a blend of path dependence (and a degree of predictability) combined with newly emerging features that recast that path dependence in unforeseen ways. Again, to use Northern Ireland as an example, the Belfast Agreement was at one and the same time a reflection of established theories of political change as well as a new formulation of those established theories which both reflected the changed social realities of the 1990s and recast the political situation for a new era. Coupled together, path dependence and emergent properties highlight the elements of continuity and discontinuity that complexity invokes.

The third and final aspect that pertains to this argument is the notion of complex societies as adaptive systems. For our purposes, this refers specifically to the ways in which the institutions and structures of a complex political system are able to adapt to the changing nature of their constituent parts. Thus, just as the elements within a system react to the emerging challenges to their path dependent trajectory, so too must the system embody a dynamic of change. Complex systems cannot survive if they are so tightly wedded to one particular aspect of their social and political formulation that a shift in that aspect draws the system into crisis. Instead, complexity requires adaption precisely because of the inherently disorderly nature of complex systems and the unpredictable, internally complex nature of their elements in interaction with one another. This is particularly significant if we return to our theme of paradigms and the ways in which they might be said to shift. Insofar as complex systems are always in a stage of renewal and redevelopment to accommodate their inherent disorderliness, then so too must the prevailing paradigms within those systems be adaptive. That is, paradigms in complex societies must be capable of being differentially identified to accommodate the changing nature of the phenomena they refer to and of which they are comprised. In other words, if it were the case that paradigms disintegrated when one of their constitutive elements changed then we would be in a process of permanent change and collapse. Instead, what we can see is that paradigms are adaptive – or, more precisely, can be read as adaptive – in such a way that they have longevity despite the changing phenomena through which they are understood to exist.

Rethinking paradigms

In the recent work of Giorgio Agamben, however, the structural conditions in which social paradigms emerge are made clear using from a line of interpretation derived from Foucault and Kuhn. Using the latter's formation of the paradigm in particular, Agamben advances the view that a:

> paradigm is simply an example, a single case that by its repeatability acquires the capacity to model tacitly the behavior and research practices of scientists. The empire of the rule, understood as the canon of scientificity, is thus replaced by that of the paradigm; the universal logic of the law is replaced by the specific and singular logic of the example. And when an old paradigm is replaced by a new paradigm that is no longer compatible with the previous one, what Kuhn calls a scientific revolution occurs.
>
> (Agamben 2009: 11–12)

This relates to Foucauldian theories insofar it is not so much the precise rules of scientific conduct that influence Kuhn but the ways in which the paradigmatic structures of scientific conduct affected their interpretation of those rules. Similarly, Foucault 'questioned the traditional primacy of juridical models of the theory of power in order to bring to the fore multiple disciplines and political techniques through which the state integrates the care of the life of individuals within its confines' (Agamben 2009: 12). Here Agamben highlights the parallels between Foucault's notion of disciplinary power and Kuhn's interpretation of the epistemological foundations of what he saw as 'normal science'. This helps to explain why the propensity for error in the construction of scientific knowledge is not an impediment to the formation of particular paradigms and the perpetration of errors need not lead to fundamental shifts in political or scientific paradigmatic structures (Little 2012b).

From Agamben's perspective then, the emergence of paradigms is an analogue process whereby key social and political events form the basis of the construction of paradigms and surrounding contemporaneous developments come to be interpreted within the same paradigmatic structure. As such the paradigm is not settled, pre-given and superimposed on social and political events. Instead, it emerges as a way of interpreting and making sense of phenomena. The paradigm is populated by events which both regenerate and develop the paradigm into new formations. Or, as Agamben puts it in his analysis of Victor Goldschmidt's work on Plato, the:

> paradigm is never already given, but is generated and produced ... by 'placing alongside,' 'conjoining together,' and above all by 'showing' and 'exposing' ... The paradigmatic relation does not merely occur between sensible objects or between these objects and a general rule; it occurs instead between a singularity (which thus becomes a paradigm) and its exposition (its intelligibility).
>
> (Agamben 2009: 23)

Clearly, language is central to the ways in which paradigmatic structures develop, are maintained and are reproduced but, without archetypal events to make sense of linguistic framing, then we risk losing sight of the practical and institutional dimensions of creating and shifting paradigms. Rhetorical constructions are pivotal to the maintenance of certain institutional structures and their adaptive capacity but this is somewhat different from the notion of rhetoric as instigating paradigmatic change. If, following Agamben, we accept that all phenomena are an instantiation of a paradigm and that the paradigm can only be reproduced through these instantiations, then there is no origin to the paradigm – it is not a singular event that creates the paradigm archetypically but rather the paradigm is embodied (differently) in different phenomena and events. Thus the paradigm 'is a form of knowledge that is neither inductive nor deductive but analogical. It moves from singularity to singularity' (Agamben 2009: 31).

In terms of rhetoric then, paradigms develop and reproduce through the use of language in ways that both reinforce existing structures and – due to elements of semiotic and semantic dissonance – potentially disrupt established elements of the paradigm. In complex systems paradigms reproduce at least partially through their adaptive capacity such that paradigm shifts can be difficult to initiate and even harder to reproduce sufficiently to achieve the kind of longevity we usually attach to notions of the paradigm. What emerges for theories of rhetoric is the very clear role that it can play in the maintenance and reproduction of paradigmatic structures insofar as the repetition of particular language and rhetorical devices can serve to reinforce 'signature' concepts like democracy. These concepts cannot be sustained without rhetorical reinforcement given both the dissonance between their theoretical elements and foundations and actual practices and institutions on the one hand and also the dissonance between the multiplicity of interpretations of the signified and its relation to the signifier on the other (Agamben 2009: Chapter 2). Rhetoric, then, is vital to the reproduction of paradigmatic concepts and their institutions – what is less clear is the extent to which rhetoric can, of itself, help to enact paradigmatic change in the way that rhetorics of reconciliation may be claimed to have provided a key part of the profound shift in South African politics in the 1990s.

Discourses of reconciliation in Northern Ireland

Unsurprisingly, given the temporal proximity of the South African transition, the early stages of the Northern Ireland peace process in the 1990s gave rise to some discussion of reconciliation as an important factor in the nascent process of conflict transformation. Moreover, key analysts of social and political transition came together to highlight potential lessons that Northern Ireland could learn from reconciliation processes in South Africa (Hamber and Kelly 2004). In more recent years, however, reconciliation has been far less evident in Northern Irish political discourse and it has become clear that, in the context of Northern Ireland, it is a highly contentious concept that is likely to generate as much dissent as it is to inspire peaceful transition. Indeed, for many unionists in Northern Ireland, the discourses of reconciliation that emerged in the early stages of the peace process amounted to little more than a rather poorly concealed republican Trojan Horse (Little 2012a). Whether or not this is true, it should be noted that the major republican party, Sinn Féin, has also been sceptical of reconciliation regarding it as a rather vague, middle class concept designed to facilitate a 'shaking hands and moving on' approach that failed to deal adequately with the past. Indeed, such is the significance of historical narratives to different interpretations of the Northern Ireland conflict, that this sense that reconciliation might lead to the past being brushed under the carpet was one of the few issues around which opposing political actors were able to agree on as problematic (Little 2000). It is worth noting that only one political party, the nationalist Social and Democratic Labour Party (SDLP), has been consistently supportive of the idea of reconciliation as a process utilising the rather orthodox understanding of the concept that has emerged from some of the mainstream writing on South Africa and elsewhere.

It is clear, even from the most cursory analysis, that reconciliation has not played the same kind of role in conflict transformation in Northern Ireland as it has done in other transitional processes elsewhere in the world. The evidence suggests that there may well be rhetorical tools that might facilitate political change in different scenarios but that it is more difficult to identify a *particular* concept such as reconciliation that can play a transformative role across varying complex contexts. In Northern Ireland for example, the conceptual tool that was used most frequently at the time of the signing of the Belfast Agreement was 'parity of esteem' (Thompson 2002) rather than reconciliation. While this too generated considerable political disagreement and conflict, it serves to underline the ways in which different conflicts might require specific rhetorical devices to activate the kind of political change that is deemed appropriate. In Northern Ireland, during the 1990s peace process, the concept of reconciliation was so laden with specific – and, for some people, pejorative – undertones that it was hard to operationalise it in such a way that might lead to less rather than more political conflict. While, of course, from a post-structuralist perspective, all of the political language we use is laden with certain assumptions and pre-suppositions, this problem is at its most acute when we are trying to deal with the tensions and conflicts of deeply divided societies. Indeed, the pre-suppositions that particular terminologies invoke, may be precisely those ideas and practices which animate and reproduce the conflict.

In Northern Ireland there is a particular touchstone around the notion of victimhood and how discourses of reconciliation pertain to interpretations and narratives of the conflict. As long as the narratives that explain the conflict vary so radically, then any strategy for grappling with the conflict must invoke a particular story of what took place in the past and why. This reflects Foucault's contention that the way in which we make sense of peace always involves a rewriting of the story of war (Little 2009c). Thus, to argue for reconciliation without reaching some kind of agreement on the source of conflict – even if that is as little as agreeing to disagree – is inherently problematic. In Northern Ireland, especially where at times the conflict has been construed as a zero-sum game, then the pre-condition of a degree of prior understanding and consensus on which to base reconciliatory processes is a difficult obstacle to overcome.

Specifically, in the Northern Irish context, there is a substantive disagreement about who the 'real' victims of the conflict were in a way that was not such a factor in the South African transition (even though, obviously, disagreements existed there too). In particular, many unionists in Northern Ireland are deeply opposed to the idea that there might be some kind of moral equivalence between the different people who died or were injured during 'the Troubles'. The risk of this moral equivalence for unionists is that it upsets their narrative of what actually took place during the Northern Irish conflict – that is, of a just and fair society that was undermined by the actions of terrorists who sought to bring about radical social change through violent tactics to achieve their vision of a united Ireland. By this account, certain groups – mainly republican paramilitaries – were to blame for 'the Troubles' and their victims are the authentic and legitimate claimants of the status of victimhood. By this account, the security forces were merely trying to maintain peace and order while the loyalist paramilitaries, although not regarded as blameless, were reactionaries against the republican campaign without which they would not have needed to exist. From many unionist perspectives then, any argument that required all victims of the Troubles (including members of paramilitary organisations alongside innocent civilians and members of the security forces) to be regarded as holding the same status is deeply problematic, if not completely unjustifiable. This is why, in the context of Northern Ireland, the notion of reconciliation was nowhere near as effective in acting as a rhetorical device for transmitting change as was the case in South Africa. The very terms in which Northern Ireland was constructed and the narratives employed to make sense of that reality were at odds with a reconciliatory agenda which regarded all those who suffered during 'the Troubles' as having the same status.

What this reading of the status of reconciliation in Northern Ireland points to is the difficulty of applying the concept as a transitional device in all scenarios. Different societies have moved towards peace without reconciliation and others have been much more explicit in articulating a reconciliatory agenda as a way of facilitating peace. In other words, in some conflict transformation processes it has proved productive to try to address the past head on, to be clear about wrongdoing, to seek truth and, in some instances, to attribute blame. In other situations, however, it is precisely the process of such raking through the coals of the past that might give rise to further conflict and act against some kind of transitional process. The point of the argument here is not to suggest that there is an appropriate normative model that can be applied to different conflict settings and their modes of transition but to recognise, instead, the deeply contextual nature of understanding conflict in different complex societies. If this is the case then rhetorical approaches to political conflicts need to recognise the fluidity in the ways in which rhetoric can affect political conflicts and the various political practices and institutions which have emerged from their historical trajectory. From this perspective, the problem in Northern Ireland is that the narrative accounts of the past, although by no means reducible to a 'two traditions' paradigm (Little 2004), are set up in contradiction to one another. That is, many of the narratives of the past in Northern Ireland only make sense if there is an alternative narrative proclaiming the alternative position. Elsewhere I have referred to this as a Deleuzean 'disjunctured synthesis' (Little 2012a) whereby alternative and incommensurable accounts of the past actually rely upon one another as a buttress to provide meaning to one another. In this situation, conflict transformation is not so much about finding 'truth' as a matter of seeking accommodation between conflicting accounts in such a way as to make a conflict more liveable rather than something that is to be transcended through political processes such as reconciliation. This notion of 'disjunctured synthesis', however, focuses on the continuation of conflict in transitional settings rather than conflict being something that can be resolved. Undoubtedly, reconciliation can have a role in either of these approaches but it is a much more difficult concept to operationalise where the sources of the conflict remain a matter of considerable disagreement and dispute.

Conclusion: rhetoric, paradigms and contingency

In the argument thus far, we have noted the role that rhetoric potentially plays in conflict transformation processes and, in particular, the role of the rhetoric of reconciliation in the transitional process in South Africa. At the same time, however, and from a more theoretical standpoint, it is equally clear that there are substantive structural obstacles to fundamental shifts in social and political paradigms such that the potential of rhetoric as a transitional tool may be limited. In particular, in terms of reconciliation, there is a substantial risk that rhetorical devices act as filters that enable some perspectives to be aired and to attain public credence while others languish on the margins having been policed out of the space of acceptable discourse (Rancière 1999). Questions remain, then, as to how conflict transformation processes driven by particular rhetorical foundations such as reconciliation are capable of including and engaging with non-reconciled perspectives. This is particularly important in complex societies emerging from a trajectory of conflict because the foundations of conflict are not something that can be packaged as 'history' – instead the conflicts are regenerated afresh in the ways in which we seek to transform them. In this instance, non-reconciled perspectives are likely to play a significant role in the political discourse of a conflict-ridden society. Perhaps it is fair to say that the conditions in South Africa in the early 1990s were more conducive to the creation of a process where non-reconciled perspectives had little political cachet. This is not to say that all those involved in the Truth and Reconciliation Commission (TRC) were completely reconciled but that those people may have seen instrumental value in participating in reconciliatory processes in a way that was less evident in Northern Ireland (or Australia for that matter). What this suggests is that the capacity of rhetoric to influence change is highly dependent on the structural context in which it is promoted – it is never likely to have the power to bring about paradigmatic shifts in its own right and is, to some extent, dependent on political contingency.

Clearly then, rhetoric can potentially play a major part in paradigmatic shifts but it is highly dependent on structural conditions. An obvious example of this would be the way in which religion played such a pivotal role in the development of the South African model of reconciliation (Doxtader 2009). Here, religion was able to play the role of the honest broker in a way that is fairly unimaginable in Northern Ireland, for example. Thus, in one context such as South Africa, reconciliation, based on religious discourse, might be a means of opening up transformative discourse, while in another like Northern Ireland, it might be a way in which traditional divisions and conflicts are brought back to the fore of political discussion. Herein lies the rhetorical potential of reconciliation as a tool for understanding historical issues but it is less clear that it is so capable of providing a rhetorical device for dealing with the conflict in the present. If, following a Foucauldian analysis (Little 2009c), we understand that even the way in which we address the past rewrites narratives about conflict for the present, then the capacity of any rhetorical device (and reconciliation in particular) to fundamentally shift the terms in which political debate is conducted should be treated with considerable caution. To be clear, it is obvious that the rhetoric of reconciliation was a powerful contributor to conflict transformation in the South African context (although the degree to which the conflict has been transformed is a matter of some contention). However, the role of rhetoric is closely tied to and hard to separate from the shift in social and political paradigms that took place through the interaction of a range of domestic and international pressures.

In conclusion, the structural conditions in situations such as Northern Ireland are much less conducive to the seductions of rhetorical devices such as reconciliation. This is not to say that particular rhetorical devices do not have a role to play in conflict transformation but that, even in Northern Ireland thirteen years after the Belfast Agreement, relative peace seems much more important to many people than the chance to reconcile and face up to the conflicts of the past and their resonance in the present. Put simply, the structural context of Northern Ireland was less conducive to reconciliation as a key contribution to conflict transformation than might have been the case in situations like South Africa which had different structural constraints. So, the key point is that the power of rhetoric in any specific social and political context is dependent on the structural environment and this is particularly the case where we are dealing with issues of deeply divided societies and forms of conflict transformation. Moreover, those structural contexts are not static but, in complex societies, are highly dependent on the shifting terrain of politics and the contingent emergence of new structural constraints that emanate from changing political events (Schedler 2007). From this perspective, the elevation of any particular rhetorical device such as reconciliation as something with applicability across different conflict scenarios is fraught with danger. Rhetoric is a powerful political tool in any political environment but its impact is always constrained by the structural context and its progress is continually at the behest of social and political contingencies.

References

Agamben, G. (2009) *The Signature of All Things*, New York: Zone Books.

Bar-Siman-Tov, Y. (2004) 'Introduction: Why reconciliation?', in *From Conflict Resolution to Reconciliation*, Oxford: Oxford University Press.

Cilliers, P. (1998) *Complexity and Postmodernism: understanding complex systems*, London: Routledge.

Doxtader, E. (2001) 'Making rhetorical history in a time of transition: the occasion, constitution, and representation of South African reconciliation', *Rhetoric and Public Affairs* 4(2), pp. 223–260.

Doxtader, E. (2003) 'Reconciliation – a rhetorical concept/ion', *Quarterly Journal of Speech*, 89(4), pp. 267–292.

Doxtader, E. (2009) *With Faith in the Works of Words: the beginnings of reconciliation in South Africa, 1985–1995*, East Lansing, MI: Michigan State University Press.

Finlayson, A. and Martin, J. (2008) '"It Ain't What You Say ...": British political studies and the analysis of speech and rhetoric', *British Politics*, 3, pp. 445–464.

Hamber, B. and Kelly, G. (2004) 'A working definition of reconciliation', working paper, Belfast: Democratic Dialogue.

Hamber, B. and van der Merwe, H. (1998) 'What is this thing called reconciliation?', *Reconciliation in Review* 1(1).

Kuhn, T. (1996) *The Structure of Scientific Revolutions*, Chicago: University of Chicago Press, 3rd edition.

Lederach, J-P. (1997) *Building Peace: sustainable reconciliation in divided societies*, Washington, DC: United States Institute of Peace Press.

Little, A. (2002) *The Politics of Community: theory and practice*, Edinburgh: Edinburgh University Press.

Little, A. (2004) *Democracy and Northern Ireland: beyond the liberal paradigm?*, London: Palgrave.

Little, A. (2007) 'Between disagreement and consent: unravelling the democratic paradox', *Australian Journal of Political Science* 42(1), pp. 143–159.

Little, A. (2008) *Democratic Piety: complexity, conflict and violence*, Edinburgh: Edinburgh University Press.

Little, A. (2009a) 'The complex agon', in A. Schaap (ed.) *Law and Agonistic Politics*, Aldershot: Ashgate.

Little, A. (2009b) 'Sunningdale for slow learners? towards a complexity paradigm', in Taylor, R. (ed.) *Consociational Theory*, London: Routledge.

Little, A. (2009c) 'The Northern Ireland paradox', in A. Little and M. Lloyd (eds) *The Politics of Radical Democracy*, Edinburgh: Edinburgh University Press.

Little, A. (2011) 'Debating peace and conflict in Northern Ireland: towards a narrative approach', in Hayward, K. and O'Donnell, C. (eds) *Political Discourse and Conflict Resolution: debating peace in Northern Ireland*, London: Routledge.

Little, A. (2011a, forthcoming) 'Disjunctured narratives: rethinking reconciliation and conflict transformation', *International Political Science Review*.

Little, A. (2012b, forthcoming) 'Political action, error and failure: the epistemological limits of complexity', *Political Studies*.

Moon, C. (2006) 'Narrating political reconciliation: truth and reconciliation in South Africa', *Social and Legal Studies* 15(2), pp. 257–275.

Mouffe, C. (2000) *The Democratic Paradox*, London: Verso.

Muldoon, P. (2003) 'Reconciliation and political legitimacy: the old Australia and the new South Africa', *Australian Journal of Politics and History* 49(2), pp. 182–196.

Nickles, T. (ed.) (2003) *Thomas Kuhn*, Cambridge, UK: Cambridge University Press.

Rancière, J. (1999) *Disagreement: politics and philosophy*, Minneapolis, MN: University of Minnesota Press.

Ruane, J. and Todd, J. (2007) 'Path dependence in settlement processes: explaining settlement in Northern Ireland', *Political Studies* 55(6), pp. 442–458.

Schaap, A. (2008) 'Reconciliation as ideology and politics', *Constellations* 15(2), pp. 249–264.

Schedler, A. (2007) 'Mapping contingency', in Shapiro, I. and Bedi, S. (eds) *Political Contingency: studying the unexpected, the accidental, and the unforeseen*, New York: New York University Press.

Thompson, S. (2002) 'Parity of esteem and the politics of recognition', *Contemporary Political Theory* 1(2), pp. 203–220.

Touraine, A, (2007) *A New Paradigm for Understanding Today's World*, Cambridge, UK: Polity Press.

Zolo, D. (1992) *Democracy and Complexity: a realist approach*, Cambridge, UK: Polity Press.

5 Fugitive reconciliation

Alexander Keller Hirsch

Ours is a time distinguished by catastrophic violence. Such an aphorism has so oft been repeated that it has become quite nearly platitudinous. The horrible inventory of the twentieth century's brutal excesses – from Chile to Bosnia; Armenia to Darfur; Cambodia to Rwanda – is recounted so regularly that the catalogue's pang no longer seems to strike the same chord it once did. It is almost as though we have become resigned to the fact of violence, accustomed to expect its terror. When, at the century's close, Eric Hobsbawm typified ours as an 'age of extremes' (1996), or Jonathan Glover announced this as 'the epoch of genocide' (2001), no one seemed to blink.

If the question of the prevalence of violence in the contemporary world has long been settled, that of how to reckon with it, how to cope with the loss rendered in its aftermath, remains insufficiently resolved. An entire sub-field of social and political thought has been fashioned to concoct reconciliatory measures for post-conflict societies left riven in the wake of some traumatic episode.

Despite their good intentions, in practice, many commentators have observed, these measures all too often fail to achieve the standard of reconciliation set for themselves (see Krog 2000; Christodoulidis 2000; Barkan 2001; Thompson 2003; Schaap 2005; Verdeja 2009). In some cases, the effort to assuage the pain of the past results in the sublimation of, rather than confrontation with, the events in need of redress. In still others, transition is equated with the exigency to 'move on', to reunite a divided society through the soothing of tensions engendered between historical antagonists. Such measures work to promote a collective social amnesia in the wake of some terrible episode, embodied in the notorious slogan 'forgive and forget'. In this case, reconciliation tends to look like an assimilative resolution. Here, transition is figured less as a mode of true justice and more as one of quietist surrender by the victim to the perpetrator (see Mamdani 2002).

Part of what this chapter seeks to make plain is that these misgivings of transitional justice regimes stem from an underlying lapse in the theoretical understanding that compels them. There is inherent to transitional thought an impetus to resolve what all too often remains irresolvable, to repair what turns out to be irreparable. The drive to smooth over deep and writhing differences between adversaries, despite their deservedly stubborn discord derives, on this account, from a certain tradition of modern and contemporary social and political thought commonly referred to as political liberalism.

There are at least two components of that tradition worth mentioning in this regard. The first is the 'overlapping consensus' liberal political projects take as their *a priori* condition of possibility. When it comes to scenes of transitional justice, it has persuasively been argued, this tendency to disparage disagreement in the name of social consistency and political accord too often amounts to an amnesiac reaction to the traumatic past, which bars the very course of reconciliation (see Veitch 1999).

The second component of concern regards political liberalism's insistence on addressing conflict through the medium of constitutional law (see Loughlin 2007). The law, in its administration of justice, tends to elide the complexity and contingency of a given crime, reducing its particularity to a universal standard of guilty behaviour in order to prescribe acceptable punitive measures. The trouble here is that reconciliation in transitional contexts, where the atrocity in question out paces our capacity to calculate and thus rationally address it, requires an accommodation of the nuance of contingency and particularity. Reconciliation depends upon the understanding that things could have been otherwise. Were the atrocity viewed as the outcome of some inevitable cause, no need for reconciliation would be required, as no guilty agent would be ultimately responsible. One apt commentator put it thus: 'Where law is reductionistic, reconciliation is reflexive; where the law is over-determined by closure, reconciliation requires openness' (Christodoulidis 2000: 12).

Responding to these perceived lapses in transitional thought, some scholars have recently turned to agonistic theories of radical democracy – and especially to the provocative work of William Connolly, Bonnie Honig, Chantal Mouffe and James Tully – in order to foreground an alternative theory of political reconciliation. This makes sense for several reasons. In the agonist's world we are enjoined to the very mode of hostile opposition that liberal transitional justice is so often at pains to mollify. If the latter can be characterized by the effort to disavow animosity in the name of harmonizing settlement, the former is enlivened by the will to *dissensus*. On this view, friction, divisiveness, and rupture are all considered characteristically endemic to political life. Thus agonism affords post-conflict thought a valuable point of departure otherwise subdued by normative theories of transition; namely, the source and thrust of the disharmony generated out of the conflict itself. Additionally, rather than presume at the start that the trauma of the past must be mediated vis-à-vis the medium of constitutional order, agonistic models tend to emphasize instead the transformative power vested in aesthetic, affective, and cultural modalities. In place of the social contract an ethos of the political is envisaged. Here, the juridical inclination to restrain and set limits upon political orders is replaced with an openness to the contingency of possibility (see Keenan 2003).

This essay serves both to accentuate the agonistic approach to post-conflict reconciliation, as well as to submit it to the dictates of critique. The aim will not be to refute theories of agonistic reconciliation so much as to challenge and productively complicate them. This challenge is framed in two interrelated parts. The first concerns what agonists commonly refer to as 'agonistic respect', 'critical responsiveness' or, alternatively, 'agonistic mutuality'. As Monique Deveaux correctly notes, 'Instead of encouraging citizens to bracket their moral and cultural disagreements, agonistic democrats suggest that we cultivate oppositional *yet respectful* civic and political relations and practices' (Deveaux 2000: 61). Though they are quick to suggest that an agonistic mode of mutual respect implies a far more dynamic conception of social interdependence than does the liberal doctrine of tolerance, I remain incredulous insofar as some proponents of agonistic reconciliation tacitly endorse a *necessarily* non-violent tactic of recovery in the name of such interdependence. The question I pose asks: If agonism takes liberal forms of democracy to be reprehensible insofar as they jettison serious disagreement in the name of resolution, how does it avoid reiterating such a logic in demanding that conflicts be sorted out vis-à-vis an *a priori* civic relation of respectful mutual submissiveness? Does not the insistence on framing a respectful non-violence between antagonists in divided societies betray agonism's otherwise practical suspicion of such attempts to determine in advance what is to count as legitimate political action?

My second challenge concerns a categorical correlate to agonistic respect, a site many agonists have turned to in their focus for a renewed vision of reconciliation and restitution, namely that of ethical and political responsibility (see Muldoon 2005). Though I agree that critical theories of responsibility can viably be woven into the common fabric of an agonistic critique of transitional justice, I remain dubious insofar as those theories take mutual respect to be responsibility's main condition of possibility. In arguing against such a notion, I take as my case in point Giorgio Agamben's reconceptualization of ethical responsibility in his *Remnants of Auschwitz: the witness and the archive* (1999). Though often compelling, eloquent, and most certainly provocative, I take Agamben's concept of '(non) responsibility' – which is to say, an 'unassumable yet unavoidable' ethical imperative – ultimately to endorse the view I find infeasible for a theory of agonistic reconciliation. In the end, Agamben inadvertently undermines the agency of victims of atrocity in vesting too much confidence in a form of post-conflict agonistic respect he terms 'intimacy'. The reason for this problem stems, as shall be seen, from Agamben's misplaced confidence in the political upshot of messianic time.

In exploring the possibility for an agonistic mode of reconciliation contrary to Agamben's theory of (non)responsibility, I turn to democratic theorist Sheldon Wolin, and especially his vision of 'fugitive democracy'. Through a close reading of Wolin, an impression of reconciliation can be fleshed out, rich and thick with political possibility. Key to this impression is Wolin's understanding of political time, altogether at odds with the messianic conception underpinning Agamben's conception of infinite apology. Though Wolin, unlike Agamben, rarely links his work to the project of reconciliation, I argue that the effort to do so yields fascinating and important theoretical results which push this line of thinking beyond the precipice of what even Agamben could imagine. Following Wolin's compelling logic through to the end, a radical, albeit tentative, conclusion can be drawn: democracy may be a political experience reserved for transitional contexts alone.

In many respects, what follows can be read as an effort to unpack what is laid above. Before turning to an exegesis of the intervention I see Wolin staging in the agonistic reconciliation literature, it is imperative to first trace, however schematically, that literature's contours. The coming section seeks to do just that. In outlining the vicissitudes of this recent field, I clarify Agamben's notion of (non)responsibility. As shall be seen, Agamben misappropriates philosopher Jean Améry's ethics of resentment in a bid to articulate an otherwise compelling model of post-juridical justice. In thinking *contra* a reductive caricature of Améry, Agamben misses an opportunity to avow the important political role resentment plays in sustaining conflict. The penultimate section turns to Wolin. Read as a theorist of reconciliation, Wolin's accounting foreshadows a fecund notion. In a sense, Wolin can be seen to inherit and democratize the line of thinking Améry initiated with his *At the Mind's Limits: contemplations by a survivor on Auschwitz and its realities* (1980). Finally, I conclude by touching on the notion that democracy may itself be a momentary experience of the political reserved exclusively for scenes of reconciliation.

Agonism and the politics of repair

Though it is important to stress that there is no single uniform doctrine by which all agonists abide, there is indeed an appreciable overlap amongst them (Schaap 2009). Of foremost significance here is the irreducible contestation agonists take to be vital to democratic politics. Unlike deliberative democrats – such as Jürgen Habermas, Seyla Benhabib and Amy Gutmann – who emphasize the political consequence of public discourse in civil society and underscore rational and consensual agreement as the objective of politics, agonists remain wary of the prospects for rational collective decision making altogether. Rather than strive toward consensual union, agonists insist that politics is about resisting the urge to defuse the hostility of opposition. Indeed, as William Connolly has put it, agonism means safeguarding the space in which antagonistic social forces fail to subdue one another: '[I]t affirms the indispensability of identity to life, disturbs the dogmatization of identity, and folds care for the protean diversity of human life into the strife and interdependence of identity/difference' (Connolly 1995: x). On this score, the effort to elide conflict is seen as complicit in a certain project of de-politicization, insofar as the political amounts to what Chantal Mouffe, in a vein similar to Connolly, describes as 'a vibrant clash of democratic positions and passions'. For Mouffe, '[i]nstead of trying to erase the traces of power and exclusion, democratic politics requires us to bring them to the fore, to make them visible so that they can enter the terrain of contestation' (Mouffe 2000b: 34–35). Thus, in line with what Jacques Rancière has recently argued, agonists privilege a logic of disparity rather than common identity, in which the politically relevant 'common of the community' consists primarily in its divisions, which constitute a structure of difference that 'escapes the arithmetic of exchange and reparation' (Rancière 1999: 12).[1]

It isn't particularly difficult to see why theorists critical of the normative thrust of transitional justice studies would be attracted to such an agonistic critique. The understanding, so often viscerally espoused in the field, of reconciliation as the restoration of a relationship shared between alienated co-members of a single moral community would be viewed sceptically by an agonist, who would question both the prospects for future rehabilitation as well as the verifiability of that broken community's originary social coherence. Mark Warren captures this perspective nicely in writing that agonism 'keeps alive the idea that politics involves struggles to find ways of expressing injustices, over and against the pressure, built into social life, to routinize conflict resolution' (Warren 2003). To conceive of reconciliation as a project of harmonics is to neglect what Andrew Schaap refers to as 'the risk of politics'. For Schaap, this risk refers to the possibility that the struggle for reconciliation may just as likely divide as forge mutuality between estranged factions (Schaap 2005). The risk consists in the prospect that the furrows that divide constituencies after some evil has come to pass may prove irrevocable and binding. In the end, an agonistic account of democracy remains important for transitional justice studies, Schaap maintains, insofar as it affirms this risk, however paradoxically, as the precondition for reconciliation itself.

Several theorists have sustained this position of late. Lawrie Balfour, for one, appropriates agonistic thinking in staging an important intervention in the debates surrounding reparations for slavery in the United States. In a recent essay Balfour argues that agonism 'emerges from an appreciation of differences that cannot simply be managed, forgotten, or transcended and a commitment to equality that resists the kinds of seamless narratives of national belonging that have been so effective at silencing African American claims' (Balfour 2008: 96). In a similar take, Alan Keenan has turned to the transitional context of Sri Lanka in order to argue that due to the scale of atrocity committed on both sides of the conflict (Sinhalese and Tamil), 'both to each other as well as to the fabric of society within which the conflict is embedded generally', no justice, understood as post-conflict resolution and consensus, 'can ever truly be achieved' (Keenan, forthcoming). As Keenan puts it, 'Pressing for "reconciliation" now or any time soon could only produce "victors" reconciliation' – a forced "we" or new "Sri Lankan" identity that continues the same attempt at violent erasure of competing, different, multiple group identities.' In his essay 'Aftermaths of evolution: forgiveness as agonistic reconciliation', post-colonial scholar David Scott tacitly endorses Keenan's point in asking how the understanding of certain kinds of conflict as intractable, 'and certain forms of justice as thereby necessarily constrained and limited', alters the way we understand political pasts (Scott, forthcoming). Scott's essay is exemplary in its exploration of agonistic critique of transitional justice in that it explores how forgiveness rituals can serve either to enable or betray the memory of collapsed revolutionary pasts. Ultimately, the essay works especially to emphasize how a most genuine form of 'agonistic relationality' – which, for Scott, represents a modality of 'justice as conflict', in the sense Judith Shklar or Stuart Hampshire might sanction – might be posed between former adversaries.

Underpinning each of these accountings of reconciliation is another feature of agonistic thought, commonly referred to as 'agonistic respect'. For Schaap, the fundamental task the problem reconciliation faces is not merely how to resist the proclivity for conflict suppression, but also how to transform a relation of total abhorrence between antagonists into one of 'civic enmity'. As Schaap puts it, agonism 'aims to mediate conflict in such a way that the other is not perceived as an "enemy to be destroyed" but as an "adversary", i.e. one with whom we disagree vehemently but whose right to contest the terms of our political association we respect' (Schaap 2006: 268). Rather than endorse the reactionary application of force or violence against one's opponent, agonistic reconciliation seeks to address past conflict in reverent terms, albeit ones conducive to the dissonance of disagreement.[2] Ernesto Verdeja also affirms this view in his book *Unchopping a Tree: reconciliation in the aftermath of political violence*, arguing that, 'Reconciliation is ultimately a condition of mutual respect between former adversaries that necessitates the reciprocal recognition of moral worth and dignity' (Verdeja 2009: 180).

The impetus for these attitudes stems in part from Connolly's insistence, made perhaps most expressly in *Identity/Difference*, that agonism inheres in a 'critical responsiveness' and a measure of abiding respect. Though folded into 'the inevitable element of conflict', identity, Connolly argues, depends upon a difference anterior to itself in order to provide for its very ontology. For Connolly, one's identity ultimately relies upon the difference against which it appears to be arrayed in conflict; and this reliance bespeaks something of an underlying mutual respect forged between nominal opponents.[3] As he explains, agonistic respect, as an 'ethos of critical responsiveness', departs from the liberal doctrine of tolerance, which misrecognizes 'the relation of connection and strife between alternative identities' (Connolly 1995: xvii). Agonistic respect, for Connolly, 'cuts deeper than tolerance' in its active avowal of the interdependence of identity and difference.

The trouble I see arising out of this line of thinking concerns its uncanny resemblance to, despite its stated departure from, the liberal doctrine of forbearance and mutual surrender agonists are otherwise right to mistrust. The Rawlsian dread of 'serious contention' is openly disparaged in agonist circles, even as a reluctance to espouse a politics of difference that goes 'all the way down' delimits agonistic critique. In exploring my reservation concerning the appropriation of an ethos of respect for a theory of agonistic reconciliation more fully, I turn now to an appraisal of one particularly fashionable luminary of contemporary critical thought, Giorgio Agamben. Often cited in the agonist literature, perhaps especially for the seminal role he has played in cultivating the renaissance in Schmittian scholarship of late, Agamben has become a major interlocutor, if not a source of inspiration, for radical democratic thought generally (see Norris 2005; Arditi 2007; Little 2009).

Messianic healing and (non)responsibility

Though he no where explicitly links his work to the agonistic reconciliation literature, Agamben does invoke and work within the parameters of its central tropes – violence, witness, guilt, conflict, shame, testimony, forgiveness, revenge, healing, and punishment, for instance – and is therefore well worth mining for relevance. As I argue below, something like Connolly's brand of critical responsiveness is transmuted into a general theory of ethical responsibility for post-conflict society in Agamben's work, and especially in his acclaimed text, *Remnants of Auschwitz*. Especially in terms of his thinking on the subjects of resentment and shame, elements which help comprise his theory of intimacy, Agamben can be seen to foreground the principles of agonistic respect in his reading of responsibility. In this sense, Agamben can be seen as emblematic in the unwitting espousal of a politics of tolerance that is otherwise sceptical of the prospects for moral agreement in the post-conflict milieu. Before turning to that implication, it is important first to briefly work out what Agamben explicitly endeavours to achieve with that text generally.

Following from a host of critical thinkers – from Adorno to Lyotard – who have sought to come to terms with the unfathomable violence of the Third Reich's 'Final Solution', Agamben structures his account as a reading of the coterminous relation between testimony and survival. In terms as concise as they are eloquent, Agamben articulates the fundamental problem in stipulating the conditions of reconciliation for the surviving witnesses:

> On the one hand, what happened in the camps appears to the survivors as the only true thing and, as such, absolutely unforgettable; on the other hand, this truth is to the same degree unimaginable, that is, irreducible to the real elements that constitute it. Facts so real that, by comparison, nothing is truer; a reality that necessarily exceeds its factual elements – such is the aporia of Auschwitz.
>
> (Agamben 1999: 12)

Unforgettable and yet unimaginable, as powerful as it is unrepresentable, Auschwitz necessitates a measure of responsibility that exceeds the juridical imagination. 'One of the most common mistakes,' argues Agamben in an agonistic tone, of those who write of reconciliation in the aftermath of the camps, 'is the tacit confusion of ethical categories and juridical categories ... Almost all the categories that we use in moral judgments are in some way contaminated by law: guilt, responsibility, innocence, judgment, pardon' (Agamben 1999: 18). This is because, for the law, the ultimate aim is directed not toward justice, but rather *res judicata* – which is to say, judgment as such. This much, Agamben writes, can be learned from Kafka, Levi and Arendt.

The alternative conception of responsibility Agamben invokes thus abandons the juridical model in favour of a properly ethical one. In particular, the form this ethics takes is one where the distinction between human and non-human is suspended (see Ziarek 2008). The figure that embodies this indistinction, Agamben tells us, is the *Muselmann*, the one who cannot speak, the true witness of the camps. This figure represents an extreme form of survival who, in the words of Catherine Mills, 'no longer sustains the sensate characteristics of the living but who were not yet dead' (Mills 2009: 83). *Muselmann* thus names the 'living corpses' – what Levi refers to as 'the drowned' – the 'anonymous masses' of the camps who, though lost of the vital capacity to live, remain as of yet undead. Transformed into the *Muselmann* in the camps through the channels of bio-political interpellation, the Jew assumes this status at the threshold between human and inhuman. For Agamben, the suggestion that the *Muselmann* is the true witness of the camps reveals that 'the value of testimony lies essentially in what it lacks; at its centre it contains something that cannot be borne witness to and that discharges the survivors of authority' (Agamben 1999: 52). The fundamental task of the witness, then, resolves in bearing witness, however paradoxically, to the impossibility of witnessing itself.

The motivating force behind Agamben's account of witnessing is his notion of '(non) responsibility'. Not to be confused with some nihilistic amorality, (non) responsibility signifies 'a confrontation with responsibility infinitely greater than we could ever assume' (Agamben 1999: 21). On this score, the only appropriate measure of responsibility taken for a catastrophe of such formidable proportion as the Holocaust would be an 'unassumable' one. Despite its unassumability, (non) responsibility remains an imperative toward which its subjects must remain true. As Agamben puts it, the confrontation with a responsibility greater than that we could ever assume also necessitates that we 'remain faithful to it, that is, *assert* its unassumability' (Agamben 1999: 21). Thus, Agamben's can be read as a vision of (non)responsibility as an infinite project, without end – unachievable and yet interminable, in the messianic sense – as unattainable as it is unavoidable.[4]

In *The Time That Remains*, a treatise devoted entirely to the exploration of the messianic conception, Agamben clarifies the connection he forges between time and redemption in *Remnants*: 'That messianic "healing" happens in *kairos* (occasion) is evident, but this *kairos* is nothing more than seized *chronos* (time). The pearl embedded in the ring of chance is only a small portion of *chronos*, a time remaining' (Agamben 2005: 69). In other words, for Agamben, the punctual instant of healing takes place in and through time, but this time is a time 'always about to come, a time not yet present … the time of the end rather than the end of time' (Agamben 2005: 62–64). Insofar as Agamben's (non)responsibility can be read as a theory of reconciliation, the healing resolution of justice would remain a perpetually pending expectation, realized ironically in the act of staving itself off. Though the moment of forgiveness, the very *telos* of reconciliation, is restlessly deferred by (non)responsibility's irredeemability, the obligation to strive however fruitlessly toward it is affirmed nonetheless (see Kaufman 2008).

In qualifying his position, Agamben argues contrary to philosopher and Holocaust survivor Jean Améry who, in holding fast to an ethics of resentment, 'simply refuses to accept that what happened, happened'. In his *At the Mind's Limits*, Améry writes that after Auschwitz, 'a forgiving and forgetting is induced by a social pressure that is immoral'(Agamben 1999: 101). By contrast, 'the moral person demands annulment of time – in the particular case under question, by nailing the criminal to his deed' (Améry 1980: 72). Agamben reads Améry's appeal to the 'annulment of time' as a tacit plea for Auschwitz's eternal return. And yet, as Agamben writes, 'One cannot want Auschwitz to return for eternity, since in truth *it has never ceased to take place*; it is always already repeating itself' (Agamben 1999: 121). This interminable recurrence is due of course to the unassumability of responsibility for Auschwitz's brutality, and especially to the impossibility of bearing witness to it. As Agamben puts it, in a crucial passage,

> It is no longer a question of conquering the spirit of revenge in order to assume the past, willing its return for eternity; nor is it a matter of holding fast to the unacceptable through resentment. What lies before us now is a being beyond acceptance and refusal, beyond the eternal past and the eternal present—an event that returns eternally but that, precisely for this reason, is absolutely, eternally unassumable.
>
> (Agamben 1999: 102–103)

Though a remarkable formulation, a certain tautology characterizes Agamben's stance here. On the one hand Auschwitz is constructed as perpetually immanent due to its unassumable disposition, and yet on the other hand, as Agamben makes clear in his last sentence laid above, that event's unassumability is owed precisely to its ceaseless presence. Thus, the unassumability of responsibility for Auschwitz is both what sets in motion the event's 'eternal return' and also what results of it. Auschwitz is both generated out of and yet generative of its own ethical unassumability.

This tension can be clarified in turning to the experience of 'shame', what Agamben terms this unassumability's most fitting affective correlative. 'To be ashamed,' writes Agamben, 'means to be consigned something that cannot be assumed' (Agamben 1999: 105). Shame is defined by Agamben, quite explicitly, as an ontological equivalence between subjects who appear on the surface of things to antagonize one another, and yet ultimately rely upon a reciprocal bond of mutual coalescence. Agamben exemplifies this definition of the shame that encompasses the subject of (non)responsibility in a peculiar, albeit fascinating, discussion of 'the domain of sadomasochism'. Importantly, there exists a certain dialectical relation, not unlike that between master and slave in Hegel's oeuvre, between the figure of the masochist – which to say, he who is 'infinitely receptive' – and the sadist – who, by contrast, is 'infinitely impassive'. For Agamben, however,

> The master-slave dialectic here is the result not of a battle for life and death, but rather of an infinite 'discipline,' a meticulous and interminable process of instruction and apprenticeship in which the two subjects end by exchanging their roles. Just as the masochistic subject cannot assume his pleasure except in the master, so the sadistic cannot recognize himself as such ... if not by transmitting pleasure to the slave through infinite instruction and punishment.
>
> (Agamben 1999: 108)

The masochist relies for his very sense of being upon the sadist, whose own identity is fixed in place only through his relation to the masochist. Thus, the chiasmus of their affiliation belies their apparent discord, and this 'indistinction of discipline and enjoyment in which the two subjects coincide is *precisely shame*'. The flush of shame experienced in the dialectical resolution and relational surrender between masochist and sadist gives way to a form of agonistic respect Agamben calls 'intimacy'. Defined as 'of being consigned to a passivity, to a making oneself passive in which the two terms are both distinct and inseparable', intimacy – what Agamben, in a Kantian mood, sometimes refers to as 'auto-affection' – characterizes what Connolly otherwise refers to as an appreciation for the existential interdependence that lies beneath the semblance of difference and dispute.

Here is where the tautology of time's relationship with (non)responsibility can most poignantly be glimpsed. The problem is that where Agamben's messianism dictates deferred sublation between antagonists, his theory of the intimate alliance of shame suggests an always already reconciled opposition. The restlessness of a time 'to come' is violated by the passivity of intimacy. The ceaselessness of the messianic is contradicted by the seamlessness of intimate indistinction. The very *telos* messianism would otherwise adjourn is altogether confirmed in the harmony of coterminous identity. The circular logic Agamben formulates, namely that Auschwitz's necessary eternal presence is both the source and effect of its unassumability, is a symptom of this deeper tension in his work. Even as he insists on its ineliminable perpetuity, Agamben ensures Auschwitz's erasure in suggesting the prospect for reconciliation depends upon 'the intimacy that betrays our non-coincidence'. In this movement the postponement of reconciliation's moment of positive-affirmative closure is betrayed as surely as is identity's non-coincidence.[5]

Just as Connolly sees deference for the structure of identity underlying difference as the animating principle of his politics of becoming, so too does Agamben see a dialectical resolution between masochist and sadist underpinning his ethics of (non)responsibility. Herein, however, lies the rub for Agamben, insofar as his theory of intimacy can, as I have suggested, be likened to mutual respect. There is first of all the trouble Stanley Fish addresses in his poignant critique of mutual respect, namely that such respect often serves as a device of exclusion for regimes that seek to manage and minimize conflict (Fish 1999). Rather than promote a broadminded sensitivity toward difference, such respect in practice too often serves to politically neutralize those who would otherwise legitimately cleave to their hostility. To this critique, I would add that the restriction agonists like Connolly place on what sort of action counts as agonistic – that it be constituted through non-violent, respectful terms, for instance – contradicts the otherwise powerful notion that a post-foundational politics of becoming ought not prescribe strictures of political legitimacy. To restrict the bounds of action is to engage in the very 'totalitarian' thinking theorists like Connolly despair of. Likewise, in arguing that the sadomasochistic experience of shame necessarily precedes, even as it results from, the opening of a space of testimony – a space of reconciliation – Agamben unwittingly opposes his own messianic commitment to illimitable openness, contingency, and amenability.

Fugitive democracy, conditioned by bitter experience

In his now well-known essay, 'Fugitive Democracy', Wolin formulates a theory that is, in some ways, akin to Agamben's own. In his great effort to replace the institutionalized form of the political with a temporalized one, for instance, Wolin elaborates a conception of democratic action that resonates on some level with Agamben's messianism. And yet, as shall be seen below, Wolin intimates a theory of memory that resonates with Améry's ethics of anger, thus replacing the ethos of respect underpinning Agamben's (non)responsibility with a conception of temporal disjuncture I shall call 'fugitive reconciliation'.

Before turning to his theory of democracy in earnest, it is useful to explore first the effect Wolin's reading can have on theories of reconciliation, if only to stress up front his departure from Agamben. In a brief but characteristically penetrating meditation, 'Injustice and Collective Memory', Wolin muses about the reconciliation movements launched to rectify the internment of Americans of Japanese descent during World War II. Referring to the so-called Japanese relocation camps where scores of American citizens were detained, Wolin writes:

> For nearly three decades the vast majority of Americans repressed the memory of the camps … Yet over the past decade various official measures for indemnifying the detainees for some portion of their losses and for extending a national apology have been passed or are pending … What dictated this about face? Was it less a question of injustice remembered than of a radical change in the American perceptions of Japan rather than of the Nisei, an official recognition on the part of American policy makers, both governmental and corporate, of the extraordinary power now possessed by Japan and hence of its vital importance to global political and economic strategies? Is it a part of the gradual downgrading of World War II … and is the depreciation of World War II connected with the apparent fact that ever since the cold war began in earnest, American policy makers have been as concerned to repress the fact that the Soviet Union was once an ally as to forget that among America's present allies are three former enemies?
>
> (Wolin 1990: 35–36)

To ask why public memory works in this way, Wolin tells us, is to ask how 'forgetfulness is established as a condition of a certain form of society'. Forgetfulness refers here not to expediency, or oversight, or even blocked recollection. Instead, Wolin proposes that 'we consider it in a context where the self must renounce some part of itself or of its own experience if it wants to be accepted into political society. In the act of reconstituting the self into a civic self, forgetting becomes a rite of passage and as such a condition of membership' (Wolin 1990: 36). Forgetfulness, then, amounts to the thinly veiled impulse toward suppressing differences. The social contract liberal political theorists have conventionally taken to represent the means of constituting a pacific political society out of the traumatic past of man's violent state of nature represents for

Wolin the very principle of forgetfulness. For Wolin, 'the covenant was a device to incorporate social amnesia into the foundation of society. If men could forget, mutual absolution was possible, allowing society to start afresh without inherited resentments' (Wolin 1990: 38).

The stubborn bond between forgetfulness and obliviousness to difference, is vividly illustrated in Wolin's lucid terms. Mutual respect – which is to say, the collective assumption of a certain 'mutual absolution' necessary for the conception of civic belonging liberal political societies take to be foundational – can take place only through the rite of forgetting. If inherited resentments abide, and the social wound of a public past is left open and festering, no mutual respect can consequently be forged. As Wolin puts it in reference to the early modern liberal tradition,

> Hobbesian and Lockean men have passions, interests, even experiences, but they seem not to have, or only barely to have had, the searing experiences of those for whom social categories have symbolized social wounds. The trade off is equality for remembrance, or rather a certain kind of equality – not equality as an ideal that is necessarily at war with power (because power presupposes inequality) but equality as a fiction that serves to legitimate power.
>
> (Wolin 1990: 40)

For Wolin, memory stands as 'the guardian of difference' (Wolin 1990: 40). Thus, the repression of difference through an act of collective forgetting offers us, on Wolin's view, a measure of political equality that amounts to little more than hegemonic subordination.

Taking seriously Wolin's critique, one can stand Agamben's position on its head. Insofar as intimacy can be read as a mode of mutual absolution – which is, after all, in Agamben's own terms 'where the "I" stands suspended in disjunction' – the relational surrender it entails can be read as a plea for forgetfulness. Though he calls for its eternal presence, Aushwitz would thus fade into obscurity, insofar as Agamben's understanding of shame, and the intimacy it elicits, remains the place where testimony and reconciliation take place.

In a different essay, 'Fugitive Democracy', composed roughly in the same period, Wolin introduces an alternative to such a politics of forgetting. Wolin opens his essay with a nuanced take on constitutional democracy's most writhing internal contradiction. Constitutional democracy, Wolin argues, is in fact *not* democratic. A constitution, by necessity, normalizes political behaviour by laying down strict principles for how democratic action should be governed:

> Thus a constitution in settling limits to politics sets limits as well to democracy, constituting it in ways compatible with and legitimating of the dominant power groups and interests in society. Constitutions are not only about what is legal and what illegal political activity, but they regulate the amount of politics let in.
>
> (Wolin 1996: 41)

Constitutionalism 'domesticates' the power of ordinary citizens through structures of authority that set the terms for proper avenues of political participation. 'The citizen is shrunk to the voter: periodically courted, warned, and confused but otherwise kept at a distance from actual decision-making and allowed to emerge only ephemerally in a cameo appearance according to a script composed by the opinion takers/makers' (Wolin 1996: 26). Institutionalization marks the attenuation of democracy: '[L]eaders begin to appear; hierarchies develop; experts of one kind or another cluster around the centres of decision; order, procedure, and precedent displace a more spontaneous politics: in retrospect the latter appears as disorganized, inefficient' (Wolin 1996: 19).

Opposed to its constitutionalization then, Wolin proposes a vision of democracy fundamentally resistant to domestication – it is rendered unenclosed, unrestrained. Impulsive and unprompted, democracy is destined to be volatile and precarious.[6] Wolin cites the lines enshrined in Dion Cassius's famous phrasing: 'If any democracy has ever flourished, it has been at its peak for only a brief period, so long as the people were neither numerous enough nor strong enough to cause insolence because of their good fortune, or jealousy because of their ambition' (Wolin 1996: 41) Democracy is the net result of the extraordinary release of human energies which, from time to time, bursts through the present, only to recoil inevitably back into the ether from which it came.[7] One might say that, for Wolin, democracy is fated to be a moment rather than a form.[8] In a crucial passage, Wolin summarizes:

> Democracy needs to be reconceived as something other than a form of government: as a mode of being which is conditioned by bitter experience, doomed to succeed only temporarily, but is a recurrent possibility as long as the memory of the political survives. The experience of which democracy is the witness is the realization that the political mode of existence is such that it can be, periodically lost. Democracy is a political moment, perhaps the political moment, when the political is remembered and recreated. Democracy is a rebellious moment that may assume revolutionary, destructive proportions, or may not.
>
> (Wolin 1996: 22)

Democracy remains evanescent and fleeting, episodic and fugitive, given to disappear, to evaporate at the very moment of its materialization.[9] Importantly, the rebellious spirit it embodies suggests no given *a priori* form. Unlike Agamben's notion of the intimate, respectful, bond animating the thrust of messianic healing where ostensible antagonists 'end by exchanging roles', for Wolin the democratic moment may take on 'revolutionary, destructive proportions, *or may not*'. Schaap's risk of politics is thus affirmed far more radically in Wolin's formulation in that he refuses to engage in a politics of prescription and resists the inclination to set the terms of political action in advance. Indeed, just the opposite, for Wolin, the political act amounts to the 'wholesale *transgression* of inherited forms'.

Additionally, rather than imply that the memory of disharmony needs be eschewed in order to launch the auto-affection necessary for testimonial reconciliation, Wolin goes the contrary direction, avowing the political value of collective remembrance. For Wolin, the impetus for the political is not shame, but rather memory. So long as those 'conditioned by bitter experience' remember the conditions of possibility for political experience its renewal remains utterly attainable. Memory, for Wolin, refers to 'the formation, interpretations, and retention of a public past'. Even if reconciliation, expressed as a modality of the political, 'lapses in the course of time', its resurgence is potentially realizable, insofar as it can be defined as a moment of remembrance.

I would like to suggest that Wolin's fugitive politics can be divorced from Agamben's ethics of (non)responsibility, precisely in terms of its resistance to messianic temporality. Instead of a theory where reconciliation is nominally forever delayed, Wolin sketches a notion of time where the moment of the political – or, on the reading I'm giving here, the moment of reconciliation – would represent an epiphanic flash. Reconciliation, an experimental temporal struggle, would ebb and flow. In place of Agamben's theory of pure potentiality, Wolin intimates one of perpetual possibility. Rather than something that is about to come, reconciliation would be conceived as something *which actually takes place*, albeit fleetingly, bursting onto the scene only to vanish at the moment it is sublimated into an institutionalized form. For Wolin, the recurrence of the disruptive, spontaneous moment of reconciliation would persist everlastingly so long as its memorialization remains unbroken.

When Wolin's theory is put into conversation with the position of Améry's Agamben rejects, resentment appears a forceful vector of political memory. Resentment here, for Améry, is not to be understood as *ressentiment*, that affective experience strongly coloured by Nietzsche's picture of the loathsome and pathological 'man of *ressentiment*'. This is a man consumed in his own self-poisoning, deceitful and vindictive hypersensitivity; a man spoiled by his own spiteful and envious obsessions.[10] Such is the true object of critique in Agamben's conception of messianic healing. By resentment, however, Améry means to distance an unabashed ethics of anger from the debilitating and malevolent paralysis of *ressentiment*.

To do this he appeals to the 'time-sense' each relates to (see Brudholm 2008). On the one hand, *ressentiment* 'nails the victim to the past, blocks exit to the future, and twists or dis-orders the time-sense of the person trapped in it' (quoted in Brudholm 2008: 105).[11] The victim's inability 'to look but forward' is due in no small part to his entrenched *ressentiment*. Thus, *ressentiment* ensnares the victim in the temporality of the trauma which befell him, where 'the past is produced by, or even takes the place of the present' (Améry 1980: 68).[12] For Améry, the '*ressentiment*-ful' victim is trapped, twisted, because of a desire for 'two impossible things: regression into the past and nullification of what happened' (Améry 1980: 68).[13] Ironically, despite his critique of Améry, this is a conception of time that is characteristic of Agamben's, insofar as messianic healing takes Auschwitz to be always already happening and therefore entrapping. Resentment, on the other hand, works to retrieve the victim from his past, to call him into the present condition of his suffering – as does Wolin's democratic memory, conditioned by bitter experience – where he can actively engage his perpetrator.[14] This does not however mean that Améry calls, as I've suggested Agamben ultimately does, for a silencing of the past:

> It is impossible for me to accept a parallelism that would have my path run beside that of the fellow who flogged me with a horse whip. I don't want to become the accomplice of my torturers; rather, I demand that the latter negate themselves and in the negation coordinate with me. The piles of corpses that lie between them and me cannot be removed in the process of internalization, so it seems to me, but on the contrary, through actualization, or, more strongly stated, by *actively settling* the unresolved conflict in the field of historical practice.
>
> (Améry 1980: 69)[15]

Like Agamben, here settlement refers to something unfulfilled, but not in the sense of its messianic unassumability. Rather, for Améry, settlement is deferred because it refers to an irresolvable conflict. Where Agamben sanitizes the conflictual aspect of reconciliation in an appeal to intimacy, Améry asserts the heated and agonized memory of horror, 'the inexpiable thing', lived in resentment. In place of the victim's desubjectification, resentment resubjectifies the otherwise dehumanized *Muselmann*, and thus supplies for a renewed form of emotional testimony. Indeed, resentment stands as testimony itself to 'our allegiance to the moral order itself ... an order represented by clear understandings of what constitutes unacceptable treatment of one human being by another'.[16]

Améry repeatedly denies being motivated by a desire for revenge. He doesn't, as he asserts, live in the 'bloody illusion' that revenge could compensate for his suffering or resolve the twisting of his sense-time. Rather, for Améry, resentment connects susceptibility to the reactive emotions with the stance of holding people responsible. And this is where the most precise difference between the two can be seen: Améry replaces Agamben's respect with resentment as the ground upon which responsibility and responsiveness is founded for a politics of reconciliation. So long as the victim clutches to his existential antipathy the memory of what was lost to violence cannot fade. Here, resentment amounts to the affective equivalent to democratic collective remembrance for post-conflict societies. And this is what, if we follow Wolin to the end, reconciliation would mean in the agonistic mode: a wild and disorderly temporal rupture where the resentments of the victims of atrocity accumulate and split open the present, and the startling invocation of a bygone past continues to haunt the present as a fugitive moment.

This is a conception of reconciliation agonists should be attracted to. Insofar as agonism asserts the political value of contestation and heteronomy, the virtues of remembrance, resentment, and non-identity ought replace those of intimacy, respect and similitude as the hallmarks of a theory of responsibility. The 'time-sense' that corresponds to this agonistics of reconciliation would be fugitive rather than messianic, conceived as one where resolution appears in the chronoscape of time so long as animosity, emblazoned in public memory, is guarded against rapprochement.

Another way of putting this would be to say that Wolin and Améry offer us a means of viewing reconciliation that goes beyond the now well worn debates in literary and psychoanalytic theory over whether collective mourning ought be construed as a mode of decathexis (see Baer 2000; Durrant 2004; Eng and Kazanjian 2003; Santner 2006). The question these debates often orbit around asks how the subject of loss can best reconstitute itself and so figure a future untrammelled by infinite repetition. On the one hand are those who favour unswerving and limitless grief along with the concomitant construal of 'communities of loss' and social networks of solidarity forged of a shared bereavement (see Butler 2004). On the other hand are those who argue for the disinvestment of melancholic energies from the lost object and a future project untethered to the painful past (see Brown 1999). Wolin and Améry argue on the side of both and/or neither. The cathartic moment of reconciliation is achieved, thus a 'moving on' is made possible, and yet that moment is prone to return as the 'differentia of time', that instant in which the sequential relation of past to present explodes.[17]

Perhaps, it might be argued, under 'normal' social circumstances, which is to say conditions of relative historical tranquillity where no spectre of violence or trauma troubles the instantiation of present collective order, the intimacy suggested in mutual absolution and agonistic respect ought to be taken as altogether germane. This argument would suppose that it is the exceptionality of certain forms of violence and the distinctiveness of the consequent post-conflict context that makes the preservation of resentment in memory a necessary correlate to reconciliation. In societies devoid of distress and a history of suffering mutual respect would be a more feasible, if not desirable, *a priori* condition for politics.

I would like to close by alluding, however rudimentarily, to a different point of view. In his 2004 work *The Dark Side of Democracy: explaining ethnic cleansing*, Michael Mann makes the rather stark claim that the relative success all stable modern liberal democracies enjoy is due in no small part to their having been historically rooted in practices and processes of genocide. Mass violence, Mann claims, is endemic to modernity, insofar as the founding of the liberal state has traditionally depended upon colonial appropriation, imperial reterritorialization, civil war, ethnic cleansing, and the like. If Mann is correct, one can argue contrary to the position that suggests reconciliation is a political experience reserved for states of exception alone.[18] On his view, modernity itself can viably be defined as the promulgation of transitional contexts, insofar as founding and violence are coterminous.[19] Following Mann, I would suggest, we late-moderns can be seen as mired in the framework of the post-conflict milieu, insofar as inconsolable loss, transhistorical suffering, and posttraumatic ruin characterize the political landscape generally.

Notes

1 See also Michael Shapiro's essay 'Time, Disjuncture, and Democratic Citizenship', Chapter 12 in Connolly and Botwinick (eds) (2001).
2 One might suggest that agonistic reconciliation, when phrased in terms of respect, is arrayed against Fanonian postcolonial theories which stress the constructive role violence and revenge can play in post-conflict scenarios. On the Fanonian connection here, see Homi Bhabha (1984).
3 Though filtered through a poststructuralist lens, in a sense, this is German Sociologist Georg Simmel's point, that conflict is a 'form of sociation', that, however ironically, 'conflict itself resolves the tension between contrasts' (Simmel 1964: 14).
4 Not unlike Derrida's theory of justice, Agamben's (non)responsibility for atrocity retains the structure of an unfullfillable promise, one whose resolution remains everlastingly 'to come' (Derrida 2004). It ought to be noted here that though I see important consistencies between Agamben and Derrida, Agamben himself is careful to distinguish his from Derrida's approach. On Agamben's critique, see the work of Adam Thurschwell, and in particular 'Cutting the Branches for Akiba: Agamben's Critique of Derrida' in ed. Norris (2005).
5 Though it is hasn't been articulated in these terms, my critique here does resonate with those recently formulated by Dominic LaCapra (2003), J.M. Bernstein (2004), and Geoffrey Hartman (2002). They each emphasize, in their own respective terms, the frames of reference lost in the parochial focus on the figure of the *Muselmann* – what I am here characterizing as the epitomization of sadomasochistic intimacy. Bernstein in particular writes of his distate for Agamben's inability to 'veer off from the space of impossible sight to the wider terrain: from victims to the executioners, to the nature of the camps, to the ethical dispositions of those set upon reducing the human to the inhuman'.
6 Wolin's critique of constitutional power, as well as his articulation of the constituent act altogether at odds with constitutionalism, can be read as akin to Negri's in *Insurgencies*. See Jason Frank (2010) and Andreas Kalyvas (2005).
7 It would be interesting to compare Wolin's notion of a democracy which bursts forth periodically to Rene Girard's notion that a scapegoat is necessary to sacrifice from time to time in order to avoid the terrible violence which festers due to mimetic contagion. On democracy and sacrifice see Anne Norton, 'Evening Land' (2001), in *Democracy and Vision: Sheldon Wolin and the vicissitudes of the political* (Princeton, NJ: Princeton University Press); also, John Fortuna, 'Democratic Sacrifice', unpublished paper presented at the annual meeting of the Western Political Science Association, San Diego, March 2008.
8 See Nicholas Xenos' excellent essay in ed. Connolly (2001), 'Momentary Democracy'.
9 On Polybius' remarks, see Scott-Kilvert, I. (1980) *The Rise of the Roman Empire*, New York: Penguin Classics.
10 As Jeffrie Murphy puts it, '*Ressentiment* is, by definition, an irrational and base passion. It means, roughly, "malicious envy". It thus makes no sense to speak of rational or justified or honorable ressentiment' (Murphy 2004)
11 In full the quote reads: 'It did not escape me that *ressentiment* is not only an unnatural but also a logically inconsistent condition [*Zustand*]. It nails every one of us unto the cross of the ruined past. Absurdly, it demands that the irreversible be turned around, that the event be undone. *Ressentiment* blocks the exit to the genuine human dimension, the future. I know that the time-sense of the person trapped in *ressentiment* is twisted around, dis-ordered, if you wish, for it desires two impossible things: regression into the past and nullification of what happened. In any event, for this reason the man of *ressentiment* cannot join in the unisonous peace chorus all around him, which cheerfully proposes: not backward let us look forward, to a better, common future' (Améry 1980: 134).

12 See Jenny Edkins (2003: 59). The psychological concept of *hypermnesia* also seems to approximate the nature of the twisted time-sense of the person trapped in *ressentiment*. Hypermnesia, according to William Niederland, is the all too clear and strongly emotionally inflected memory of traumatic experiences of persecution and the related shattering of the self. In a description of a female Holocaust survivor suffering from hypermnesia, Niederland notes that, although she is oriented in time and space, her state of health is controlled by undigested memories of past horrors. She still sees how her bloodstained brother was led away; she hears the screaming of infants and clings to her beaten mother, and in a certain sense she is still staying with the dead and dying of the concentration camp. She is, as Niederland observes, 'well aware that all these events happened a long time ago, and yet she cannot get away from the memories and agonizing fantasies. In other words, she still lives in the concentration camp ...' (Niederland 1981: 101).

13 *Ressentiment*'s modification into what Améry terms, the 'modality' of the past also brings to mind Jean-Paul Sartre's notion that the emotions are 'magical transformations' of the world. Sartre sees the emotions as attempts to 'live through the relations between things and their potentialities where not governed by deterministic processes but by magic'. According to Sartre, in the emotional experience the subject 'magically' tries to escape an unbearable reality. Being unable to escape a danger by normal means, the person may 'faint to fear' – that is, annihilate the dangerous world 'magically'. See Sartre (1993).

14 This is potentially linkable to Jean-Paul Sartre, and especially what he terms 'bad faith'.

15 My emphasis. This passage is especially interesting to correlate to Fanon's psychoanalytic understanding of racially charged colonization, see Frantz Fanon (2008) *Black Skin, White Masks*, New York: Grove Press.

16 See Wood (1999).

17 The 'differentia of time' is Walter Benjamin's felicitous phrase (2002: 456).

18 On the deconstruction of the state of exception thesis, see also Jason Frank (2010).

19 This is a view eloquently theorized by Walter Benjamin (2002) and later refined by Derrida (2004).

References

Agamben, G. (1999) *Remnants of Auschwitz: the witness and the archive*, New York: Zone Books.

Agamben, G. (2005) *The Time That Remains: a commentary on the letter of the Romans*, Palo Alto, CA: Stanford University Press.

Améry, J. (1980) *At the Mind's Limits: contemplations by a survivor on Auschwitz andits realities*, Bloomington, IN: University of Indiana Press.

Arditi, B. (2007) *Politics on the Edges of Liberalism: difference, populism, revolution, agitation*, Edinburgh: Edinburgh University Press.

Baer, U. (2000) *Remnants of Song: trauma and the experience of modernity in Charles Baudelaire and Paul Celan,* Palo Alto, CA: Stanford University Press.

Balfour, L. (2008) 'Act & Fact: slavery reparations as a democratic politics of reconciliation', in Kymlicka, W. and Bashir, B. (eds) (2008) *The Politics of Reconciliation in Multicultural Societies*, Oxford, UK: Oxford University Press.

Barkan, E. (2001) *The Guilt of Nations: restitution and negotiating historical injustices*, Baltimore, MD: Johns Hopkins University Press.

Bernard-Donals, M., and Glejzer, R. (eds) (2003) *Witnessing the Disaster: essays on representation and the Holocaust*, Madison, WI: University of Wisconsin Press.

Benjamin, W. (2002) *The Arcades Project*, Cambridge, MA: Harvard University Press.

Bernstein, J.M. (2004) 'Bare life, bearing witness: Auschwitz and the pornography of horror', *Parallel* 10(1), pp. 2–16.

Bhabha, H. (1984) 'Of mimicry and man: the ambivalence of colonial discourse', *October* 28, pp. 125–133.

Botwinick, A. and Connolly, W. (eds) (2001) *Democracy and Vision: Sheldon Wolin and the vicissitudes of the political*, Princeton, NJ: Princeton University Press.

Brown, W. (1999) 'Resisting left melancholia', *Boundary 2* 26(3), pp. 19–27.

Brudholm, T. (2008) *Resentment's Virtues: Jean Améry and the refusal to forgive*, Philadelphia, PA: Temple University Press.

Butler, J. (2004) *Precarious Life: the power of mourning and violence*, London: Verso Press.

Christodoulidis, E. and Veitch, S. (eds) (2001) *Lethe's Law: justice, law, and ethics in reconciliation*, London: Hart Books.

Christodoulidis, E. and Veitch, S. (2000) 'Truth and reconciliation as risks', *Social and Legal Studies*. 9(2), pp. 179–204.

Copjec, J. (ed.) (1993) *Radical Evil*, London: Verso Books.

Connolly, W. (1995) *Ethos of Pluralization*. Minneapolis, MI: University of Minnesota Press.

Connolly, W. (2002) *Identity/Difference: democratic negotiations of political paradox*. Minneapolis, MI: University of Minnesota Press.

Derrida, J. (2004) *Rogues: two essays on reason*, Palo Alto, CA: Stanford University Press.

Deveaux, M. (2000) *Cultural Pluralism and Dilemmas of Justice*, Ithaca, NY: Cornell University Press.

Durrant, S. (2004) *Postcolonial Narrative and the Work of Mourning: J.M. Coetzee, Wilson Harris, and Toni Morrison*, Albany, NY: SUNY Press.

Edkins, J. (2003) *Trauma and the Memory of Politics*, Cambridge, UK: Cambridge University Press.

Elster, J. (2004) *Closing the Books: transitional justice in historical perspective*, Cambridge, UK: Cambridge University Press.

Eng, D. and Kazanjian, D. (eds) (2003) *Loss*, Berkeley, CA: University of California Press.

Fish, S. (1999) 'Mutual respect as a device of exclusion', in Macedo, S. (ed.) *Deliberative Politics: essays on democracy and disagreement*, Oxford, UK: Oxford University Press.

Frank, J. (2010) *Constituent Moments: enacting the people in postrevolutionary America*. Durham, NC: Duke University Press.

Glover, J. (2001) *Humanity: a moral history of the twentieth century*, New Haven, CT: Yale University Press.

Gutmann, A. and Thompson, D. (1998) *Democracy and Disagreement*, Cambridge, MA: Harvard University Press.

Hartman, G. (2002) 'Testimony and authenticity', *The Yale Review* 90(4), pp. 1–15.

Hobsbwam, E. (1996) *Age of Extremes: a history of the world, 1914–1994*, New York: Vintage Press.

Honig, B. (1993) *Political Theory and the Displacement of Politics*, Ithaca, NY: Cornell University Press.

Kalyvas, A. (2005) 'Popular sovereignty, democracy, and the constituent power', *Constellations* 12(2): 223-244.

Kaufman, E. (2008) 'The Saturday of messianic time (Agamben and Badiou on the apostle Paul)', *South Atlantic Quarterly* 107(1), pp. 37–54.

Keenan, A. (2003) *Democracy in Question: democratic openness in a time of political closure*, Palo Alto, CA: Stanford University Press.

Keenan, A. (Forthcoming) 'Agonism and reconciliation in post-war Sri Lanka', working paper, cited with permission of author.

Krog, A. (2000) *Country of My Skull: guilt, sorrow, and the limits of forgiveness in the new South Africa*, New York: Three Rivers Press.

LaCapra, D. (2003) *History in Transit: experience, identity, critical theory*, Ithaca, NY: Cornell University Press.

Lara, M. (ed.) (2001) *Rethinking Evil: contemporary perspectives*, Berkeley, CA: University of California.

Little, A. (ed.) (2009) *The Politics of Radical Democracy*, Edinburgh, UK: University of Edinburgh Press.

Loughlin, M. and Walker, N. (2007) *The Paradox of Constitutionalism: constituent power and constitutional form*, Oxford, UK: Oxford University Press.

Mamdani, M. (2002) *When Victims Become Killers: colonialism, nativism, and the genocide in Rwanda*, Princeton, NJ: Princeton University Press.

Mann, M. (2004) *The Dark Side of Democracy: explaining ethnic cleansing*, Cambridge, UK: Cambridge University Press.

Meister, R. (2010) *After Evil: a politics of human rights*, New York: Columbia University Press.

Mills, C. (2009) *The Philosophy of Agamben*, Montreal: McGill University Press.

Minow, M. (1999) *Between Vengeance and Forgiveness: facing history after genocide and mass violence*, Boston, MA: Beacon Press.

Mouffe, C. (2000b) *The Democratic Paradox*, London: Verso Books.

Mouffe, C. (2006) *The Return of the Political*, London: Verso Books.

Muldoon, P. (2005) 'Thinking responsibility differently: reconciliation and the tragedy of colonisation', *Journal of Intercultural Studies* 26(3), pp. 237–254.

Murphy, J. (2004) *Getting Even: forgiveness and its limits*, Oxford, UK: Oxford University Press.

Negri, A. (1999) *Insurgencies: constituent power and the modern state*, Minneapolis, MN: University of Minnesota Press.

Niederland, W. (1981) 'The survivor syndrome: further observations and dimensions', *Journal of the American Psychoanalytic Association* 29(2), pp. 413–425.

Norris, A. (2005) *Politics, Metaphysics, and Death: essays on Giorgio Agamben's* Homo Sacer, Durham, NC: Duke University Press.

Rancière, J. (1999) *Disagreement: politics and philosophy*. Minneapolis, MN: University of Minnesota Press.

Rawls, J. (1999) *Collected Papers*, Cambridge, MA: Harvard University Press.

Roht-Arriaza, N. and J. Mariecruzana, (eds) (2006) *Transitional Justice in the Twenty- First Century: beyond truth versus justice*, Cambridge, UK: Cambridge University Press.

Santner, E. (2006) *On Creaturely Life: Rilke, Benjamin, Sebald*, Chicago, IL: University of Chicago Press.

Sartre, J-P. (1993) *The Emotions: outline of a theory*, New York: Citadell Press.

Schaap, A. (2005) *Political Reconciliation*, London: Routledge.

Schaap, A. (2006) 'Agonism in divided societies', *Philosophy and Social Criticism*. 32(2), pp. 255–277.

Schaap, A. (2009) *Law and Agonistic Politics*, London: Ashgate Press.

Scott, D. (Forthcoming) 'Aftermaths of revolution: forgiveness as agonstic reconciliation', working paper, cited with author's permission.

Scott-Kilvert, I. (1980) *The Rise of the Roman Empire*. New York: Penguin Classics.

Simmel G. (1964) *Conflict and the Web of Group-Affiliation*, New York: Free Press.

Teitel, R. (2000) *Transitional Justice*, Oxford, UK: Oxford University Press.

Thompson, J. (2003) *Taking Responsibility for the Past: reparation and historical injustice*, New York: Polity Press.

Veitch, S. (1999) '*Pro patria mori*: law, reconciliation and the nation', in Manderson, D. (ed.) *Courting Death: the law of mortality*, London: Pluto Press.

Verdeja, E. (2009) *Unchopping a Tree: reconciliation in the aftermath of political violence*, Philadelphia, PA: Temple University Press.

Warren, M. (2003) 'What can and cannot be said: deliberating sensitive issues', paper presented to the Conference on Deliberative Democracy and Sensitive Issues, Amsterdam, 25–26 March.

Wood, N. (1999) *Vector's of Memory: legacies of trauma in postwar Europe*, Cambridge, MA: Berg Books.

Wolin, S. (1990) *The Presence of the Past: essays on the state and constitution*, Princeton, NJ: Princeton University Press.

Wolin, S. (1996) 'Fugitive democracy', Benhabib, S. (ed.) *Democracy and Difference: contesting the boundaries of the political*, Princeton, NJ: Princeton University Press.

Ziarek, E. (2003) 'Evil and testimony: ethics "after" postmodernism', *Hypatia* 18(2): 197–204.

6 Can human beings forgive?

Ethics and agonism in the face of divine violence

James Martel

This chapter will engage with the philosophy of Walter Benjamin in order to consider the question of the possibility of human forgiveness in the face of divine violence. At first glance, Benjamin's notion of divine violence may seem to suggest that judgment and forgiveness are exclusively the province of a God that is utterly unknowable. For Benjamin, when human beings make judgments, they inherently risk idolatry and mythology, a hubristic replacement of the true (divine) font of justice with some imagined (and false) alternative. In the face of the awesome and irrefutable power of the divine, what do we make of the ability of human beings to make their own judgments? How are human beings able to forgive when they cannot know the bases for justice that underpin such decisions? In this chapter, I will argue that for Benjamin we are able to forgive not despite but because of violence. Divine violence cleanses, not only those who are punished, but also all of our phantasms of authority and power that take on universal, and idolatrous, pretensions. When such idolatrous forms of judgment are removed or subverted by the notion of a cleansing deity, we are returned to our own contingent and agonistic forms of justice and forgiveness. From such a perspective we can think further about what we can and cannot forgive.

In addition to considering Benjamin's own work, I will also a consider Arendt and Derrida's respective considerations of forgiveness. I will argue that these thinkers have something to gain from Benjamin's understanding (even as Benjamin's work is aided by their work as well) insofar as it allows them to avoid some of the traps and dilemmas that trouble their own considerations.

Korah's punishment

In his "Critique of violence" (1978a), Walter Benjamin illustrates the power of divine violence when he tells the story of Korah, an idolatrous man who rebelled against the rule of Moses as God's lieutenant on earth. Korah's punishment was to be swallowed up by the earth, along with his followers, leaving no trace behind. For Benjamin, this instance of divine punishment "strikes privileged Levites, strikes them without warning, without threat, and does not stop short of annihilation. But in annihilation it also expiates" (Benjamin 1978a: 297). In this immediate moment of divine justice, both punishment and atonement are simultaneous acts. This is an absolute verdict and broaches no compromise or negotiation.

Benjamin compares the divine violence promulgated against Korah with the mythical violence seen in the punishment of Niobe. Niobe's children were killed by poison arrows shot by Apollo and Artemis after she bragged that, while their mother only had two children, she had fourteen. Benjamin focuses on the fact that Niobe's punishment involved bloodshed while Korah's did not. He writes:

> Mythical violence is bloody power over mere life for its own sake, divine violence pure power over all life for the sake of the living. The first demands sacrifice, the second accepts it.
>
> (Benjamin 1978a: 297)

In contrasting these two forms of violence, mythical and divine, Benjamin is making a distinction between a kind of violence (or power) based on human-centered phantasms and a form of violence that cannot be known or judged by human beings but which in turn serves as the basis for judgment over us. Mythical violence is the violence and authority of the phantasmagoria. It is a form of idolatry wherein we ascribe truths and realities to mythical deities which serve as a ghostly echo of our own, outwardly projected delusions (our own attempts, as it were to 'speak for God'). Mythical violence must be rendered in blood because we need a marker to make such a delusional power 'real' and legible to us. It is a 'bloody power over mere life for its own sake' because it has no cause but itself, no truth that it has not itself produced. Human existence is reduced to 'mere life' [in German: 'das bloße Leben'] because human beings, while the author of such mythologies, are reduced to shadowy figures in its wake.

Divine violence on the other hand, which, Benjamin tells us (at the end of the Critique) "may be called sovereign violence" is executed "for the sake of the living" (Benjamin 1978a: 300).[1] It needs no sign, no bloody manifestation, for it is not mediated by representation at all but is a direct manifestation of divine will and authority. And yet, despite its immediacy, we read divine violence through our own distorting, and mythological, lens. Benjamin tells us that "myth bastardize[s divine violence] with law" (Benjamin 1978a: 300). Here we see that in some sense, mythological violence is not unconnected to divine violence; it is a pale and distorted mirror of divine will. It is our own, failed attempt to produce a law and an authority that is true.

For all our misreading of divine violence, for Benjamin there remain opportunities to avoid idolatry. He speaks in the "Theses on the philosophy of history" of a "Messianic cessation of happening," a break in the otherwise seamless fabric of the myths that constitute our reality (Benjamin 1968: 263). In such moments – as may already be perceived in the story of Korah – the authority of idolatry, its ability to stand in for and determine our reality, is shattered and/or removed. Here, we might (but also might not) learn to read the world differently. The possibility of such a cessation is, for Benjamin, all that we require from the divine in order to avoid being totalized by mythology.

Human and divine judgment(s)

Even if divine violence potentially allows us a cessation from idolatry, what does such an intervention actually mean for our own ability to make judgments or to forgive? By its very nature, divine violence seems so opaque, so illegible, that it appears impossible to think that human beings could also dare to make their own judgments, to either punish or forgive crimes or evil deeds that have been fomented against them. Insofar as the chief instance that Benjamin offers of divine violence involves the case of Korah, a man who challenged the rule of God, it seems that the overall effect of Benjamin's narrative is, if anything, to stifle our right to think, judge and forgive on our own terms. Does not his notion of "mythology" doom any and all of our attempts at judgment from the outset? Must we not be, like Korah, infinitely suspect in all that we do, say and think? If what we produce is inherently idolatrous, mythological and wrong, where then, if anywhere, can one find in Benjamin's work any inkling that human beings have the right and ability (or power) to forgive? On what basis would such forgiveness be made?

In fact, even in the story of Korah, we can see that forgiveness is not occluded but actually modeled by God's awesome power. Recall that "in annihilation [divine violence] also expiates." Korah is swallowed up but his sin is also forgiven. This is not the case in the mythological violence enacted against Niobe; she is turned into a weeping rock, forever mourning her children. Her punishment is thus endless. Perhaps, we might say, the fact that divine punishment expiates also permits or models our own acts of expiation and forgiveness.

This point can perhaps be seen even more explicitly in one of the very few texts where Benjamin actually directly references forgiveness, the 1921 fragment entitled "The meaning of time in the moral universe." There, Benjamin speaks of "the tempestuous storm of forgiveness which precedes the onrush of the Last Judgment" (Benjamin 1996: 286). This divine storm, like God's punishment of Korah "is not only the voice in which the evildoer's cry of terror is drowned; it is also the hand that obliterates the traces of his misdeeds, even if it must lay waste to the world in the process" (Benjamin 1978a: 312). Here again, we see that an act of divine violence (even extreme violence) is also an act of forgiveness, of obliterating the crime along with the criminal.

Quite paradoxically, it seems that in fact for Benjamin, the source of our own ability to judge and forgive is *also,* in a sense, divine. In his *Theologico-Political Fragment*, Benjamin tells us that in many ways the small and human perspective which seeks happiness, and the infinite divine perspective which produces justice are complete opposites and have no point of intersection. And yet, he concedes that:

> If one arrow points to the goal toward which the profane dynamic acts, and another marks the direction of Messianic intensity, then certainly the quest of free humanity for happiness runs counter to the Messianic direction; but just as a force can, through acting, increase another that is acting in the opposite

direction, so the order of the profane assists, through being profane, the coming of the Messianic kingdom. The profane, therefore, although not itself a category of this Kingdom, is a decisive category of its quietest approach.

(Benjamin 1978b: 312)

Here we see, as is often the case with Benjamin, that there is a kind of relationship, however unexpected it may seem, between divine and human forms of judgment. Although they are unrelated, unconnected and even oppositional, divine and human actions (and thereby judgments and forgiveness) are mutually implicated.

Although unfathomable, the "quietest" approach of the Messianic Kingdom for Benjamin sustains and promotes human life in all of its locality and specificity (a concept that is reinforced by Benjamin telling us that divine violence is executed "for the living"). In this sense, a contemplation of divine violence might just return us to ourselves, to our own perspectives (once they are cleansed of idolatry). Keeping the unknowability of the divine foremost in our minds, our own judgments, our own ability to forgive, become legible as such. We can engage in such acts, not as a myth we project onto God, but as a set of guesses, prayers and gestures.

Redemption and forgiveness

As already noted, Benjamin does not discuss forgiveness much per se. In "The meaning of time in a moral universe," true forgiveness is depicted as an act that comes only through an inhuman time span (and, as we have seen, from a superhuman divine judge). Benjamin writes:

[T]ime not only extinguishes the traces of all misdeeds but also – by virtue of its, duration beyond all remembering or forgetting – helps, in ways that are wholly mysterious to complete the process of forgiveness, though never of reconciliation.

(Benjamin 1996: 287)

It may be that for forgiveness to be "complete," we must turn to such a superhuman perspective (a perspective that Benjamin takes great pains to point out is utterly denied to us). Yet perhaps an "incomplete" form of forgiveness – a human and political form – can be derived from the convergence between his most basic theology and his understanding of politics more generally. For Benjamin, as we have already seen, the "sin" that we must be forgiven for is idolatry. The "phantasmagoria" he describes is a miasmic force of misrepresentation and idolatry which produces the faux reality that we occupy and subscribe to whatever our politics or intentions may be. Although Benjamin usually ascribes the phantasmagoria to commodity fetishism, it seems that human idolatry stems back all the way to Adam's original sin of seeking knowledge against God's command. For Benjamin, knowledge itself is idolatrous, a form of misreading which represents an original (and Satanic) rebellion against God's authority. Thus, in the *Origin of German Tragic Drama,* he writes:

> The Bible introduces evil in the concept of knowledge. The serpent's promise
> to the first men was to make them "knowing both good and evil." But it is
> said of God after the creation: "And God saw everything that he had made,
> and, behold, it was very good." Knowledge of evil therefore has no object.
> There is no evil in the world. It arises in man himself, with the desire for
> knowledge, or rather for judgment.
>
> (Benjamin 1998: 233)[2]

When Benjamin writes "there is no evil in the world," he means evil as an
independent force, something that lies autonomous from human error. In fact,
everything and everyone that God has made is "very good" and it is only our
misperception that produces evil at all. Evil is thus a product of our subjective
misreading; it stems from our quest for knowledge. Benjamin goes on to say that
"[t]his knowledge [is] the triumph of subjectivity and the onset of an arbitrary rule
over things ..." (Benjamin 1998: 233).[3]

Yet, for Benjamin, the solution to the problem of knowledge is not to abandon
our subjectivity in favor of some external "truth" (to do so would be to engage in a
greater idolatry still). Instead, we must go deeper, in a sense, into our subjectivity,
into realizing our radical isolation from God. Insofar as God will always appear
to us via our own mythology and phantasms, we must turn away from God, as it
were, to preserve God as an aporia. We do this, in part, through allegory, through
a trope that renders the signs and images that constitute our reality legible to us
as such. In this way the objects that form our reality cease to serve as idols and
become instead reflections of the broken and ruined nature of the postlapsarian
world we occupy. In the *Origin*, Benjamin speaks of an:

> about-turn, in which the immersion of allegory has to clear away the final
> phantasmagoria of the objective and, left entirely to its own devices, re-
> discovers itself, not playfully in the earthly world of things, but seriously
> under the eyes of heaven.
>
> (Benjamin 1998: 232)

If the very idea of objectivity is a part of the phantasmagoria, we need a new
relationship with reality itself, with the objects that form the "objective" world.
Rather than see ourselves as fallible, yet potential beacons for truth (with objects
and symbols making such transmissions possible), we must accept our fallenness,
our utter subjectivity. It is this acceptance that, however paradoxically, realigns us
with the divine redemption that is always ours (even though we don't know it). It
is in this way that the two "arrows" of human subjectivity and divine truth, though
pointing in different directions, become realigned. We are thereby returned to our
status as being "under the eyes of heaven" (or, perhaps more accurately, such a
status becomes legible to us, once again, without telling us anything else about
divine will or judgment).

In this way, redemption – and by extension, forgiveness – comes mainly from
our own acts of resisting idolatry (albeit with the help of moments of divine

intervention, as we have seen). When and if we can stop "knowing" the universe, we can return to our original state of redemption, a state that never left us (if anything, we left it). In this way, and only in this way, can we be said to be "forgiven" (at least incompletely). And in this way we in turn can perhaps learn to forgive (both ourselves and one another).[4]

Here, we can see more clearly how for Benjamin moments of messianic interruption coincide exactly with human acts of resistance; if the messiah were to "save" us once and for all, we would be returned utterly to our delusion (because, as we have already seen, acts of divine violence are "bastardized" by mythology). And if we had no messianic moments of interruption, our idolatry would be similarly irremediable (because there would be no way to get outside of our faux subjectivity, our "arbitrary rule over things").

To put this discussion more firmly in the lexicon of forgiveness, we cannot wait to be "forgiven" by God. God's forgiveness lies outside of human time and human hope. In some sense, our problem lies not with God but with ourselves; our guilt is perpetuated by our own hubris, by knowledge itself. Thus we must in effect, forgive one another. Forgiveness must be a political rather than a theological function (or perhaps more accurately the theological function must eclipse itself so that the political function becomes possible). Forgiveness must be something that we do together in the face of an unknowable God who nonetheless models to us (and permits us) the possibility of forgiveness. Forgiveness must be, like redemption, a state of surrender, a capitulation toward our subjectivity and away from our (false) power over the signs and objects of the world (including one another).

Derrida's forgiveness

Such an understanding of forgiveness is quite different from Derrida's notion and it is worth spending some time looking at Derrida's concept of forgiveness to highlight the dissimilarities. Although Derrida is in many ways deeply indebted to Benjamin, I will argue that his turn towards a "religion without religion" and "messianism without a messiah" entails a theology that cannot quite help us to forgive (see Caputo 1997: 99). By contrast, I'd say that Benjamin offers us a messianism *with* a messiah, albeit one that does almost nothing for us. Whereas Benjamin's God enters into the world and remains a force (however weak and unknowable), Derrida's understanding of the deity or messiah is something that "trembles" in the world – it is always immanent but never quite present, always to come and never quite here. The differences, I think, are telling for their respective notions of forgiveness.

In his essay "On Forgiveness," Derrida notes that forgiveness in our own time is too often confused with reconciliation, with the kinds of negotiated and political outcomes that follow great political crimes (i.e. "crimes against humanity") such as the holocaust and apartheid. For Derrida, the purpose of major and public trials (like Nuremburg in Germany) or processes (like the Truth and Reconciliation Commission in South Africa) is to produce a return to normalcy, where people who have done terrible things can live with their victims in a way that allows the country to continue to function. Yet, Derrida warns us that:

> Forgiveness is not, it *should not be*, normal, normative, normalizing. It *should* remain exceptional and extraordinary, in the face of the impossible: as if it interrupted the ordinary course of historical temporality.
>
> (Derrida 2001: 32)

In his understanding of forgiveness, Derrida parts company both with Hannah Arendt (about which more will be said shortly) and Vladimir Jankélévitch, insofar as both of those thinkers argue that we can only forgive what we can understand and what we can punish. "Inexpiable" crimes like the holocaust (Jankélévitch argues) cannot be forgiven at all (see Jankélévitch 2005; Derrida 2001; Copjec 1999).[5] For Derrida, these thinkers are ceding forgiveness to the "sovereign" impulse (a harsh commentary in Arendt's case, as we'll see further, insofar as she dedicates a great deal of her own thought to combating sovereignty). The sovereign decides who can and cannot be forgiven. It decides on the meaning of a crime and it alone has the right to absolve (or not absolve) us from that crime.

For Derrida on the other hand, forgiveness must be excluded from the realm of sovereignty and politics entirely. He "insist[s] ... on the necessity of maintaining the reference to an economical and unconditional forgiveness: beyond the exchange and even the horizon of a redemption or reconciliation" (Derrida 2001: 38). He calls forgiveness "heterogeneous to the order of politics or of the juridical as they are ordinarily understood" (Derrida 2001: 39). For Derrida:

> [a] pure and unconditional forgiveness, in order to have its own meaning, must have no 'meaning', no finality, even no intelligibility. It is a madness of the impossible. It would be necessary to follow, without letting up, the consequence of this paradox, or this aporia.
>
> (Derrida 2001: 45)[6]

Derrida tells us that he is "torn" between the pragmatic requirement of reconciliation on the one hand and a vision of pure forgiveness on the other. He insists that this "torn-ness" is in fact necessary in order to temper the sovereign tendency towards mandating and negotiating forgiveness (and hence ensuring that there is no actual forgiveness at all). He argues that insisting upon an a-political and a-juridical form of forgiveness (despite its impossibility and its "madness") "alone can inspire here, now, in the urgency, without waiting, response and responsibilities" (Derrida 2001: 51).[7]

Derrida concludes his essay by arguing:

> What I dream of, what I try to think as the "purity" of a forgiveness worthy of its name, would be a forgiveness without power: *unconditional but without sovereignty*. The most difficult task, at once necessary and apparently impossible, would be to dissociate *unconditionally* and *sovereignty*. Will

that be done one day? It is not around the corner, as is said. But since the hypothesis of this unpresentable task announces itself, be it as a dream for thought, this madness is perhaps not so mad …

(Derrida 2001: 59–60)

The inside and the outside

Derrida and Benjamin do not seem to be in agreement here. As we have seen, for Benjamin – at least by analogy to his understanding of redemption – forgiveness must be political, a thing we do ourselves, with one another, while for Derrida it must not. As mentioned earlier, I think that the difference here stems from their different understandings of theology and also what constitutes an "inside" and an "outside" from and to the human perspective. For Derrida, we need the "outside" perspective that forgiveness offers. It is "impossible" and a "madness" which is "perhaps not so mad …" Yet, from a Benjaminian perspective, even the idea of a pure forgiveness, a dream that is private and a secret (Derrida says "I must respect its secret") risks becoming another form of idolatry (Derrida 2001: 55). We know that God's forgiveness of us is ultimately "complete" but to presume any access to or insight about that forgiveness is to commit the gravest form of idolatry. In the Benjaminian scheme, the solution to the subjectivity of forgiveness (which risks a "sovereign" solution – i.e. more mythology) is not to turn to a "mad" vision of a redemptory and pure form of forgiveness – a way to haunt and subvert the sovereign wish – but rather to turn deeper into that subjectivity, as we have already seen. Just as for Benjamin allegorical knowledge – a product of the fall and a sign of our distance from truth – is part of the way back towards redemption, so too must our subjective acts of forgiveness become the means by which to make forgiveness something other than mythological. Whereas Derrida's messiah stands just beyond our reach (or not even just beyond, since the redemption it might offer is not "around the corner"), Benjamin's messiah is always with us (the famous "*weak* Messianic power" that he attributes to every generation) (Benjamin 1968: 254). As we have seen, his messiah does nothing except interfere with our tendency to fetishize it. By voiding itself as a cite of idolatry (as it voided Korah), the messianic function serves to return us to the necessity of our own judgments, that is to say, it (potentially) leads us to politics.

Benjamin's understanding of God is both more and less alien than Derrida's. It is more alien because for him, the divide between human beings and God is even more utter than it is for Derrida. Because of the threat of idolatry, we must in essence not even think about what God wants from us, least we succumb to more mythology. God can't tell us anything at all (and is not in this way even "immanent" the way the divine is for Derrida). In contemplating the absolute blank of God, we are thus returned to our own devices. We must dare to judge, and to forgive as a response to God's willingness to remove idolatry (and idolators) from the world.

But Benjamin's God is also closer than Derrida's insofar as his God actively serves to void the site of the divine from all forms of idolatry. In that sense,

Benjamin's God or messiah is also *here* and *now*. With this crucial aid, we can see that forgiveness – and redemption – *are* possible and, indeed, required of us; we are not fated to always be mired in idolatry.

Derrida, in other words, fears the site of the political because it is *too human*. It is subjective, negotiated and marked by sovereignty. But for Benjamin, such a state is not our only option as human beings. Under the conditions of fetishism, we tend towards mythology, towards a terrestrial sovereignty that is the opposite of a "divine sovereignty" that cleanses and expiates. But with the possibility that we don't have to engage in idolatry another form of politics emerges, a more democratic and agonic form that is not overridden by the phantasms of sovereignty. *This* human response, I would argue, must be political and it is neither private nor impossible. It can only done by and between human beings who know that they have neither a sovereign nor a divine source of rescue, but only one another.[8]

Arendt and forgiveness

And, in this formulation, we begin to see the convergence between Arendt and Benjamin when it comes to the question of forgiveness (this, despite their many and important differences). Indeed, I will argue that when we read Arendt and Benjamin in conjunction, we get a clearer sense of the possibility of what might be called a "politics of forgiveness" than we would taking either thinker in isolation.

As I see it, Arendt's understanding of forgiveness may help to render the politics of Benjamin's conceptions (or the conceptions I have inferred to Benjamin) more clear. Similarly, Benjamin's turn to theology helps Arendt to better avoid Derrida's charge about the sovereign nature of her understanding of forgiveness (a charge with some basis, as I will explain further), as well as helping her overcome her general sense of pessimism and helplessness about the state of politics and the possibility of forgiveness.

In many interesting ways, Arendt's understanding of forgiveness echoes Benjamin minus his intensely theological orientation. For Arendt "what saves man ... comes from the outside" (Arendt 1958: 236). However she hastens to add that it comes " not to be sure outside of man" (Arendt 1958: 236). For Arendt, the capacity to forgive comes only from and by other human beings, but it remains a "miracle" to us nonetheless.[9]

Arendt sees forgiveness as an explicitly political activity insofar as we cannot forgive ourselves but only other people.[10] In her own understanding, forgiveness is crucial to the possibility of human politics because without it we would not be able to dare to act at all. Given the irreversibility of our actions, and given that we can never know with full accuracy what the consequences of our actions will be, we require forgiveness to be able to risk both action and speech. Otherwise we would "be confined to one single deed from which we could never recover" (Arendt 1958: 237).

In this sense, we see the similarities between her views and Benjamin's. Here again is an agonic and human centered form of judgment and forgiveness. Here too, the divine and theological functions of forgiveness are superseded by human gestures. Finally here too, forgiveness involves risk; it is part of how we face the void of uncertainty and doubt that comes in the absence of divine and sovereign assurances.

The dangers of ideology

And yet, for all her convergence with Benjamin, Arendt is troubled by the fact that her version of human centered politics is always threatened, virtually impossible. Arendt explicitly links forgiveness to promising, a faculty that in her view is both essential for the practice of politics and also always under threat. In *The Human Condition,* she famously writes that:

> The possible redemption from the predicament of irreversibility – of being unable to undo what one has done though one did not, and could not, have known what he was doing – is the faculty of forgiving. The remedy for unpredictability, for the chaotic uncertainty of the future, is contained in the faculty to make and keep promises. The two faculties being together insofar as one of them, forgiving, serves to undo the deeds of the past ... and the other, binding oneself through promises, serves to set up in the ocean of uncertainty, which the future is by definition, islands of security without which not even continuity, let alone durability of any kind, would be possible in the relationship between men.
>
> (Arendt 1958: 237)

Here we see her clearest and best articulation of how forgiveness crucially fits into a politics that is based on human plurality, on collective and mutual acts. This is a politics, as already mentioned, that directly addresses the void left by divine sanction. And yet, despite this seeming optimism, Arendt sees that in fact communities based on promising and forgiveness – agonic, local and explicitly political though they may be – ultimately founder in the face of ideological doctrines that supplant the political experience altogether.

On Revolution is perhaps the book that most clearly lays out this dilemma. There, she lauds the virtues of local political practices in revolutionary America, France and Russia, but in each case (more quickly in the latter cases but even in the American case) these "council" based systems of politics were overtaken by "parties," ideologically based, top down organizations. Arendt tells us:

> In the conflict between the two systems, the parties and the councils, came to the fore in all twentieth-century revolutions. The issue at stake was representation versus action and participation. The councils were organs of action ... [the parties] knew well enough that no party, no matter how revolutionary it was, would be able to survive the transformation of the government into a true Soviet Republic.
>
> (Arendt 1987: 273)

Here, two models of politics compete for ascendency – one diffuse and anarchic; the other ideologically driven and statist. In each case, she notes, the parties took over and destroyed the revolutions from within.

For Arendt, parties are agents of sovereignty. Arendt sees sovereignty and ideology as stemming from the prevalence of the will in modern times. The will, which sees the world only in terms of its own private perspective and advantage, denies human plurality and seeks to impose its own internal phantasms outwardly through ideology. Sovereignty is the expression of the will in its most hegemonic and pervasive form. Putting the matter plainly, Arendt tells us that "if men wish to be free, it is precisely sovereignty they must renounce" (Arendt 1968: 165).

Given this conviction, it may seem peculiar that Derrida accuses Arendt of having recourse to sovereignty in her own rendition of forgiveness. To some extent, Derrida may be conflating her position with that of Jankélévitch. He may be confusing her own brand of politics, her own collective basis for forgiveness, with the kind of sovereign politics that are practiced by states. And yet, in some sense, he is right; Arendt *does* turn to sovereignty to some extent and does compromise with it.[11]

For example she writes in *The Human Condition* that:

> Sovereignty, which is always spurious if claimed by an isolated single entity, be it the individual entity of the person or the collective entity of a nation, assumes, in the case of many men mutually bound by promises, a certain limited reality.
> (Arendt 1958: 245)[12]

Perhaps "a certain limited reality" is the best that Arendt can hope for, but even such a relatively hopeful argument pales in the face of her own acknowledgement that in fact there is no compromise with sovereignty and parties (as her analysis in *On Revolution* shows).[13] With the loss of the power of the councils, the power of forgiveness, promising and judgment disappears as well; even politics itself becomes impossible under such conditions.

It may be that Arendt seeks to compromise with sovereignty, despite all the dangers it poses because she is convinced that parties always win out and because she sees that will and sovereignty are the inevitable condition of modernity. In other words, given her position in time, she seems to have no choice but to find a way to live with sovereignty and make the best of it. But the price of this compromise, it seems, is despair, a sense that her own vision of politics can never come to pass in a modern setting.

It is at this juncture that it seems to me that aligning Arendt more closely with Benjamin may help to protect the kinds of politics she seeks from the forces of ideology. I would argue that what is missing from Arendt's analysis is Benjamin's concern with fetishism. Insofar as she regards the prevalence of the will as being endemic to modernity, Arendt seems trapped, as we have seen, in her (and our) own time. She is nostalgic for a period of time (ancient Greece and Rome) when politics was (at least she claims) engaged with differently, more in keeping with her own goals.

Yet, in Benjamin's analysis, our current predicament comes not from an inviolable and unalterable force like "the will" (which we can do nothing about) but rather from the effects of commodity fetishism, from the phantasms that are produced by the phantasmagoria. This kind of ideology can and must be fought. A greater awareness of the dangers of fetishism – even for the left – marks Benjamin's life work and hence is of service to Arendt's own goals. It gives her an option for fighting with rather than resigning herself to (and compromising with) the very forces that threaten what she most cherishes about political life.

Conclusion: a politics of forgiveness?

Taking Arendt and Benjamin together, we get a fuller vision of what a politics of forgiveness might look like. Since Benjamin does not discuss forgiveness itself all that much (especially not at the level of the human being), we have to make analogies, as we have seen, to his ideas of redemption, to his theology and rhetorical analysis in order to think about what forgiveness might look like as a political practice. Arendt on the other hand gives us a much fuller vision of a politics of forgiveness but she hampers her vision with her own pessimism, by her own sense that in modern times, politics can be nothing other than the practice of false ideologies imposed on humankind by the non agonic, non local and apolitical forces that can be collectively called sovereignty. Both of these thinkers share, as we have seen, an orientation towards human centered politics, but Benjamin's theology, however paradoxical it may seem, actually makes such a human centered politics more possible.

Derrida too has something to add to this conversation in his own insistence that politics – and hence forgiveness – have nothing of the sovereign in it. But he misplaces, I argue, his view of forgiveness onto the screen of am impossible, unavailable sense of justice that haunts the actions that we do actually perform (producing his "torn-ness" which I see to some extent as disabling his politics). Fundamentally, I see Derrida as attempting a similar project to Benjamin (often based on Benjamin's own writings). Yet, I think a greater attention to the power of fetishism would – in Derrida's case as in Arendt's – better enable him to embrace a human centered form of politics (the politics I see him as actually pursuing) with less ambivalence, less of a sense that something was being occluded or left out (the "outside" perspective).

With Benjamin himself, we get both a sense of how forgiveness must be political (but not sovereign, a difference that Derrida does not quite recognize in his essay on forgiveness) and also how a sense of God's judgment (or "justice," however we want to speak about true and unknowable sources of decision making) is perpetually unavailable. Benjamin's sense of justice – and hence the source of the possibility of our forgiveness – is not just out of reach, always arriving but never quite here. It is actually not "here" at all as far as we are concerned. At the same time, Benjamin also shows us a sense of God or messianism that intrudes forcefully into our world (but only to cleanse the world of its own idolization, as we saw with Korah). With such a messianism and with such an emphasis on human centered politics – a politics cleansed of dangerous idolatry in a way that Arendt does not envision – we can return to an agonic form of forgiveness. We can also turn to an agonic form of politics in which our actions do not perfectly determine us even as they are not foreordained by phantasms of truth and justice. With such a possibility the fact that we must forgive does not come into conflict with our own anxieties about judgment (i.e. we do not need to be "torn").

To be clear, such a politics will not automatically be just or good. Agonic politics are not in and of themselves perfect or complete (quite the contrary); we will continue to make mistakes, to forgive for ill-conceived reasons. But without the overwhelming effect of idolatry, it becomes possible to engage in a politics where the outcome and the value judgments to measure such outcomes are not preordained, predetermined in ways that bypass politics itself. In such a circumstance, even our forgiveness can become, as it were, subject to forgiveness, a product of a human centered politics that knows that the messiah is already here and is, for all intents and purposes, only ourselves.

Notes

1 Actually, in the original German, it is not literally sovereign violence, but the power of rule. What in English is rendered as "may be called sovereign violence" says in German "mag die waltende heißen" [literally may be called ruling, in the sense of caretaking"]. The German term for sovereignty is not explicitly used.
2 Although Benjamin goes on to distinguish the knowledge of good and evil from the knowledge of facts, thus preserving the possibility of a non idolatrous human knowledge after all.
3 He is speaking here specifically of allegorical knowledge.
4 For Benjamin, each of us, idolator and non idolator alike, is seeking good, seeking to reproduce the lost unity of paradise. Even the greatest idolator may be successful in his or her attempts to produce truth, yet such success would be completely opaque to them (as it would be for the non-idolator as well).
5 For his text see Vladimir Jankélévitch (2005). In a related text, Derrida cites Arendt in *The Human Condition* to make his case that for Arendt, forgiveness "is always a correlate of the possibility of punishment." He quotes her saying there that "men are unable to forgive what they cannot punish and…they are unable to punish what has turned out to be unforgivable." Jacques Derrida "To Forgive" in John D. Caputo, Mark Dooley, and Michael J. Scanlon, eds. (2001: 30). See also "On Forgiveness: A Roundtable Discussion with Jacques Derrida" in that same volume. For a set of treatises on the "inexpiable" see Joan Copjec, (ed.) (1999).
6 He also tells us that "Forgiveness is thus mad. It must plunge, but lucidly into the night of the unintelligible" (Derrida 2001: 49).
7 Derrida reproduces this kind of torn-ness for example in "To Forgive" when he writes: "Thus forgiveness, if it is possible, if there is such a thing, is not possible, it does not exist as possible, it only exists by exempting itself from the law of the possible, by impossibilizing itself, so to speak, an din the infinite endurance of the im-possible as impossible …" (Derrida 2001: 48).
8 In some sense Derrida is after the same thing that Benjamin: a form of politics that does not merely replicate what we already have. But given Benjamin's focus on fetishism and its dangers, it becomes possible with Benjamin to have a politics that is not merely "to come" but is already here.
9 In considering the primacy of politics over theology she writes:

It is decisive in our context that Jesus maintains against the "scribes and Pharisees" first that it is not true that only God has the power to forgive and second that this power does not derive from God – as though God, not men, would forgive through the medium of human beings but on the contrary must be mobilized by men towards each other before they can hope to be forgiven by God also. Jesus' formulation is even more radical. Man in the gospel is not supposed to forgive because God forgives and he must do 'likewise' but 'if ye from your hearts forgive' God shall do "likewise." (Arendt 1958: 239)

Thus forgiveness is for Arendt a human miracle, something of our own devising (without necessary precluding or negating the possibility of God's forgiveness, as we see here).

10 Arendt contrasts forgiveness with vengeance which "remains bound to the process, permitting the chain reaction contained in every action to take its unhindered course" (Arendt 1958: 240). She goes on to write that: "forgiving in other words, is the only reaction which does not merely re-act but acts anew and unexpectedly, unconditioned by the act which provoked it and therefore freeing from this consequences both the one who forgives and the one who is forgiven" (Arendt 1958: 241).

11 I make this argument in Martel (2008).

12 She goes on to write: "The sovereignty of a body of people bound and kept together, not by an identical will which magically inspires them all, but by an agreed purpose for which alone the promises are valid and binding, shows itself quite clearly in its unquestioned superiority over those who are completely free, unbound by any promises and unkept by any purpose. This superiority derives from the capacity to dispose of the future as though it were present, that is, the enormous and truly miraculous enlargement of the very dimension in which power can be effective" (Arendt 1958: 245).

13 Another way that Arendt compromises with sovereignty can be seen in *On Revolution* when she peculiarly sides with Madison to some extent against the anti-federalists, despite the fact that by her own analysis the anti-federalists represent the "councils" and Madison represents a "party." For a good explication of this tendency, see, Lisa Disch "How Could Arendt Glorify the American Revolution and Revile the French? Placing *On Revolution* in the Historiography of the French and American Revolution," p. 2. This is a paper she presented at the University of Pennsylvania in January 2008 (among other places). Cited with permission from the author.

References

Arendt, H. (1958) *The Human Condition*, Chicago, IL: University of Chicago Press.

Arendt, H. (1968) *Between Past and Future: eight exercises in political thought*, New York: Penguin Books.

Arendt, H. (1987) *On Revolution*, New York: Penguin Books.

Benjamin W. (1968) 'Theses on the philosophy of history', in *Illuminations: essays and reflections*, New York: Schocken.

Benjamin W. (1978a) 'Critique of violence', in *Reflections: essays, aphorisms, autobiographical writings*, New York: Schocken.

Benjamin W. (1978b) 'Politico-theological fragment" in *Reflections: essays, aphorisms, autobiographical writings*. New York: Schoken.

Benjamin W. (1996) 'The meaning of time in the moral universe', in Bullock, M. and Caputo, J. (1997) *The Prayers and Tears of Jacques Derrida: religion without religion*, Bloomington, IN: Indiana University Press.

Caputo, J.D., Dooley, Mark, and Scanlon, Michael J. (eds.) (2001) *Questioning God*, Bloomington: Indiana University Press.

Copjec, J. (ed.) (1999) *Radical Evil*, New York: Verso Books.

Derrida, J. (2001) *On Cosmopolitanism and Forgiveness*, New York: Routledge.

Jankélévitch, V. (2005) *Forgiveness*, Chicago, IL: University of Chicago Press.

Jennings, M. (eds) *Walter Benjamin: selected writings, volume 1, 1913–1926*, Cambridge, MA: Belknap Books.

Jennings, M. (1998) *The Origin of German Tragic Drama*, New York: Verso.

Martel, J. (2008) '*Amo Volo Ut Sis*: love, Williand and Arendt's reluctant embrace of sovereignty', *Philosophy and Social Criticism* 34(3).

7 The unforgiving

Reflections on the resistance to forgiveness after atrocity

Thomas Brudholm and Valérie Rosoux

Enraged by calls upon the Nazi victims to forgive, Vladimir Jankélévitch once asserted that forgiveness 'died' in the Nazi extermination camps (Jankélévitch 1996: 552). If the murderers wished for forgiveness they should go and ask the children who were burned alive. If the survivor had a moral task to consider, it was the unending preservation of a resentful and unreconciled memory of those who were murdered (Jankélévitch 1996: 565–572). At about the same time, in the 1960s, Hannah Arendt took notice of widespread German sentiments about the possibility of immediate reconciliation. According to Arendt, the sentiments revealed the degree to which the systematic mendacity – the escalating self-deception – of the Third Reich had been internalized by the people (Arendt 1978: 52).

Today, the belief in the possibility and value of forgiveness and reconciliation is in considerable vogue (Griswold 2008; Walker 2006). Jankélévitch and Arendt responded to popular sentiments, but within the last two decades, the advocacy of forgiveness has also become the business of nongovernmental organizations (NGOs), health-care workers, and conflict mediators.[1] Forgiveness is encouraged by religious leaders chairing truth and reconciliation commissions, as well as by political leaders publicly pleading with victims to forgive.[2] Yet, more than that, the interest in the topic has gained an explosive momentum among scholars around the world. Forgiving is examined as a personal virtue, as a rational and therapeutic response, and as a necessary condition for social and political reconciliation through the overcoming of emotions like resentment and vindictiveness (see e.g., Enright and North 1998; Murphy 2003; Schaap 2005). An increasing number of critical studies are being published; but the mainstay of the literature on the practice and value of forgiveness as a means to reconciliation has been marked by laudatory approaches that take for granted that forgiveness is morally, politically, and therapeutically superior to resentment and other 'negative' attitudes (see Philpott 2007).

The need for more critical reflection arises, not the least, from attention to current public appraisals of forgiveness in so-called post-conflict societies. In places like Rwanda, Sierra Leone, Liberia, and South Africa, religious leaders publicly praise or recommend unconditional forgiveness, or urge people to marvel at the wish of a victim that she may be forgiven by the man who injured her grievously and killed others (see Tutu 1999: 147). State officials help ex-perpetrators post prefabricated letters that mimic what could perhaps have been a genuinely contrite sign of remorse and repentance (Mujawayo and Belhaddad 2006). According to its advocates, forgiveness is the best or the only path to personal as well as social healing and reconciliation. To opt for forgiveness is, or so it seems, to side not only with virtue but also with prudence. Not to forgive is ultimately a sign of a regrettable lack of rationality or moral virtue. Perhaps this is one reason why victims can be encouraged or expected to forgive even when the plea for forgiveness seems both cheap and calculated. In Liberia, an exceptionally brutal, former Liberian rebel leader accompanied his confessions of a horrible and vast catalogue of crimes not just with a plea for forgiveness, but also with a counsel of forgiveness as 'the right way to go' and the key to national healing (see Paye-Leyleh 2008). The apparent ease and self-confidence with which even mass murderers can request, counsel, or expect forgiveness is bewildering to the observer, but it can be unfathomable to the survivor. As Francine, a survivor of the carnage in Rwanda, responds to the very idea of being approached by an ex-genocidaire asking for forgiveness, '[I]f he has worked at killing for a whole month, even on Sundays, whatever can he hope to be forgiven for?' (Hatzfeld 2004: 196). This expression of a sense of limits is precisely what is absent when forgiveness gets 'boosted' as an unqualified virtue or sociopolitical good.

From the perspective adopted in this article, the trends and cases mentioned above substantiate the observation that we live in a time in which the virtue of forgiveness risks becoming 'distorted and cheapened by various movements that advocate it in a hasty and uncritical way' (Murphy 2008: ix). There is a strong need for a sustained and extensive ethical reflection on the advocacy and practice of forgiveness, not the least in the context of transitional justice and reconciliation. This essay is intended to address just one small part of this more comprehensive undertaking. More precisely, we would like to bring more nuance to common conceptions of unforgiving victims and the resistance or refusal to give.

Advocates of forgiveness naturally tend to privilege 'forgivers' as examples of the kind of moral character, humane generosity, civic virtue, or sheer prudence that is needed if the goal of reconciliation is to come closer. Those who say they will not forgive might be mentioned, admonished, or received with expressions of understanding or even respect, but their motivations and reflections are seldom seriously investigated. Indeed, when forgiveness is boosted as a panacea and an absolute virtue, unforgiveness takes on the spectre of a morally impossible position: if the unforgiving survivors understood more about the background of the perpetrators, or about what ideals and values really count; if they did not confuse forgetting with forgiving; if they were more capable of managing their anger; if they thought more rationally about their own good or the good of the nation, then they would try to forgive or let go of their resentment and engage more constructively in the process of reconciliation. Relentless, backward-looking resentment must be the sign of some kind of moral failure or irrationality on behalf of its holder.[3]

In order to complement and challenge given conceptions of unforgiving victims, this article considers several actual examples of resistance with particular concentration on the reflections of two genocide survivors, namely Jean Améry and Esther Mujawayo. This focus on the voices of two individual survivors is deliberate and tied to the very nature of the problem being addressed here. By drawing on the reflections of unforgiving victims themselves, we wish to challenge the way in which they are represented by third-party advocates of forgiveness. And by attending to the voices of particular individuals, we hope to defy stereotypical or purely theoretical conceptions of 'the' unforgiving victim or 'the' refusal to forgive.[4]

The morality of resistance

Jean Améry was born in Austria as Hans Maier in 1912. His father was an assimilated Jew and his mother a Catholic. With the rise of the Nazi regime, Maier's Jewish ancestry became potentially fatal, and in December 1938 he fled to Belgium and joined the resistance. He was soon caught, tortured by the Gestapo, and sent to a number of concentration and extermination camps, including Auschwitz. Upon liberation from Bergen-Belsen, Maier returned to Brussels, and in 1955 he began publishing under the French anagram Jean Améry. Améry used his own life and experiences as the object of literary experimentation or philosophical elucidation. Among his later writings, one finds works on suicide, and the proximity between his life and his work was, sadly, also evident in them: in 1978, Améry took his own life in a hotel room in Salzburg.

Améry's collected works span nine thick volumes, but his most influential work probably remains *Jenseits von Schuld und Sühne (Beyond Guilt and Atonement)*, which was published in 1965.[5] The book consists of a series of essays in which Améry tries to articulate philosophically the experiences and post-war situation – the *conditio inhumana* – of the surviving Nazi victim. In spite of declarations that his intent was only to describe, the essays also testify to a wish that they would be a cause of change. That is, the essays were not only the attempt of a surviving victim to examine his own ruined life, but also a revolt against the way German society dealt with its past. During the first couple of decades following 1945, a desire among Germans to 'turn the page' or 'forgive and forget' was foremost. For Améry this was morally impossible, and with *Beyond Guilt and Atonement* he explicitly addressed his German contemporaries who, as he put it, 'in their overwhelming majority do not, or no longer feel affected by the darkest and at the same time most characteristic deeds of the Third Reich' (Améry 1980: xiv). More specifically, Améry struggled against a post-war *Zeitgeist* that he perceived as impregnated with 'hollow, thoughtless, utterly false conciliatoriness' (Améry 1980: xiv). In this situation, he not only refused to forgive: Améry explicitly denounced forgiving 'induced by social pressure' as immoral, and he discordantly scorned those who were – all too early and easily in his opinion – 'trembling with the pathos of forgiveness and reconciliation' (Améry 1980: 65, 72). As a rejoinder to common notions of the vengefulness of the unforgiving victim, Améry stated his conviction that a 'loudly proclaimed readiness for reconciliation by Nazi victims can only be either insanity and indifference to life or the masochistic conversion of a suppressed *genuine* demand for revenge' (Améry 1980: 71).

What accounts for this resistance to, and even disdain of, the advocacy and endorsement of forgiveness in the aftermath of the Holocaust? Evidently Améry's denigrations are directed towards certain pathetic, thoughtless, hollow, immoral ways of promoting or embracing forgiveness and reconciliation. Indeed, it is possible to read Améry as an illustration of what might be at stake when the talk of forgiveness becomes indistinguishable from escapist forgetting or unconditional acceptance. That is to say, the virtue of forgiving can easily be co-opted as a banner under which victims are actually urged to *condone* what happened – to move on, look ahead, bury the past and forget what, after all, happened so long ago. Thus, Améry's indignation could in principle be tied to a strong commitment to 'genuine' forgiveness and to a belief that contemporary discourses compromised and perverted the real thing. Yet, even though Améry can be read as a strong challenge to advocates of forgiveness to reflect on the line between sentimental and sound forms of forgiveness-advocacy, it seems most certain that his contempt of and indignation for the advocacy of forgiveness was *not* due to a personal allegiance to forgiveness. Yet, and this is most interesting, the values and commitments that Améry was concerned about (and that he believed to be compromised by the cheap and thoughtless advocacy of forgiveness), are not necessarily incompatible with the values and commitments that inform at least some well-reflected approaches to forgiveness (see Griswold 2008).

To understand what lies behind Améry's attitude, we need to take a closer look at his essays in *Beyond Guilt and Atonement*, the chapter on 'Ressentiments' in particular. It is impossible to do justice here to the complexity of Améry's reflections on these issues, but four reasons why his resistance to forgiveness was so vehement can be pinpointed: human dignity, recognition, accountability, and coexistence. These are the main conceptual points of the moral explanation offered by Améry to illuminate for his contemporaries just why he neither could nor would let go of his ressentiments or endorse their calls for forgiveness.

1. Human dignity

Beyond Guilt and Atonement is, in part, an attempt to 'rehabilitate' not just resentment, but the 'man of resentment' (Améry 1980: 64) – the common assumption that humanity and moral virtue are automatically behind displays of a willingness to forgive, reconcile, and 'move on,' whereas prolonged display of ressentiment and irreconcilability are the reflex of a morally flawed or deficient character. Trying to counter this picture, Améry articulates his own normative view on the proper allegiances of what he calls 'the moral person,' and the most central virtue invoked is the 'moral power to resist' (Améry 1980: 72). The sort of forgiving objected to by Améry was precisely promoted by pleas to accept that what happened, happened; that it was already long past, and that one would do well to look to the future rather than dwell on the irreversible past. According to Améry, to give in to such pleas would be unworthy of human beings qua moral beings (Améry 1980: 72). To give in to the social pressure and the implied attitudes of individuality, morality, and time would constitute a demeaning moral lapse. It is as if Améry asks: What kind of person would be able and willing to accept the call to forgive, forget, or reconcile in the given context (that is, under the circumstances of massive impunity and escapist forgetfulness)? As Améry viewed the situation, it would require a person willing to submerge his individuality into the needs and consensus of social opinion – a demeaning relinquishing of the moral experiences and demands of the individual (Améry 1980: 71). The ease with which the deindividualized person forgives might be celebrated from the perspective of a hasty societal interest in political stability and nation-building. Améry insists in spite of its tense relationship with concerns about the social collective.

What Améry calls the 'insensitive and indifferent person' is further characterized by his relationship to time and the healing it may bring about (Améry 1980: 71). Améry stipulates as unworthy the attitude that the future per se should be considered more important than the past, and that what is past should, simply qua past, be considered unimportant. According to Améry, this is an intolerable form of human subjugation – a moral defeat to the social and biological, or allegedly 'natural,' consciousness of time with its bias for the future. Equally incompatible with his notion of human dignity is the notion that one may allow the sheer passing of time to heal the wounds of the past. From within the 'natural' perspective on time, forgetting and the kind of healing that time brings about may be suggested as a way in which to 'get over' historical wrongs. The future-oriented person who allows 'what happened to remain what it was [and] lets time heal his wounds' might be considered healthy from a therapeutic perspective (Améry 1980: 71). But Améry retorts on moral grounds: 'Man has the right and the privilege to declare himself in disagreement with every natural occurrence, including the biological healing that time brings about. What happened, happened. This sentence is as true as it is hostile to morals and intellects' (Améry 1980: 72).

2. Recognition

Another reason Améry wanted to have nothing to do with what he called the 'pathos of forgiveness and reconciliation' (Améry 1980: 65) had to do with his belief that it would do nothing to address the chasm between survivors like himself, on the one hand, and 'the world which forgives and forgets' on the other (Améry 1980: 75). What was needed was an honest, if disturbing, confrontation with the Nazi past and its unrecognized implications for the present. To 'forgive' or to be 'conciliatory' in the face of continued denial and evasion would simply allow what happened to remain what it was. Améry was concerned that the rhetoric and pathos of forgiveness and conciliation would simply ratify or accelerate the general lack of recognition of what he called the 'moral truth' of the Nazi past (Améry 1980: 70). What truth? The recognition, put all too briefly, that what had happened, or what was done, was utterly unacceptable and unjustifiable. Part of the reason Améry did not want to let go of his resentment was his belief that it (and with it, an impossible but essential demand that what had happened had not happened) harbored a truly moral understanding of what happened as absolutely unacceptable, as something with which there can be no reconciliation. Convinced that the urgent task was to uncover and to face the moral truth of what had happened, Améry insisted on the moral value of his resentments: '[M]y resentments are there,' as he put it, 'in order that the crime become a moral reality for the criminal, in order that he be swept into the truth of his atrocity' (Améry 180: 70).

3. Accountability

The third point follows closely from the issue of recognition. According to philosopher Richard Wallace, resentment is distinguished by a connection with normative expectations. It is 'caused by the belief that an expectation to which one holds a person has been breached' (Wallace 1994: 12). What Améry expected, and what he held his contemporaries accountable to, was a moral response to the Nazi past, that is, an assumption of personal guilt or collective historical responsibility, or both. He brandished his ressentiments against denial, evasion, and cheap reconciliation. As expressed in and with his essays, his ressentiments maintained the stance of holding Germany responsible for its twelve years under Hitler: 'In the midst of the world's silence our ressentiment holds its finger raised' (Améry 1980: 78). Thus, what he craved was not bloody revenge, but reassurance from the relevant moral communities that they could be trusted (again).[6]

4. Coexistence

Beyond Guilt and Atonement was published in the hope that it could 'concern all those who wish to live together as fellow human beings' (Améry 1980: xiv). The preservation of resentment and the opposition to the rhetoric of forgiveness and reconciliation were related to a desire to be released from a deep sense of abandonment and loneliness. Améry held the world – and his German contemporaries in particular – to the demand of his ressentiments for an impossible undoing of the past. Evidently, he did not require satisfaction of this absurd demand, but he wanted his contemporaries to join his – the victim's – moral view of what had happened. Thus, although Améry refused any reconciliation with the past, his whole endeavor was aimed toward a reconciliation between people. In other words, in his mind, the condition of social reconciliation was a refusal of historical reconciliation. Améry struggled against an increasing sense of loneliness and abandonment – caused, in the first instance, by the persecution, torture, and evils of the Nazi past, but maintained and solidified by the subsequent history of denial and evasion of dignity, recognition, accountability, and true care for the other, that is, of coexistence.

5. Loneliness

'Ressentiments' ends on a bitter note, with Améry's articulation of deep-seated mistrust about whether his call for accountability will be heeded (Améry 1980: 81). As he puts it, 'the world which forgives and forgets' has sentenced him to loneliness (Améry 1980: 75). He feels condemnable as Shylock, 'but already cheated of the pound of flesh too' (Améry 1980: 75). Améry's ordeal, left with the mistrust and abandonment intensified by unanswered calls for reassurance and responsibility, is first fully expressed in the essay following 'Ressentiment,' the last essay of *Beyond Guilt and Atonement*. In stark contrast to his 'moral daydream' of a restoration of human solidarity and responsibility, this essay now presents us with the point of view of a person who has almost resigned himself to a sense of inescapable abandonment and mistrust:

> Every day anew I lose my trust in the world. ... My neighbor greets me in a friendly fashion, Bonjour, Monsieur; I doff my hat, Bonjour, Madame. But Madame and Monsieur are separated by interstellar distances; for yesterday a Madame looked away when they led off a Monsieur, and through the barred windows of the departing car a Monsieur viewed a Madame as if she were a stone angel from a bright and stern heaven, which is forever closed to the Jew. ... Without trust in the world I face my surroundings as a Jew who is alien and alone, and all that I can manage is to get along within my foreignness ... I was unable to force yesterday's murderers and tomorrow's potential aggressors to recognize the moral truth of their crimes, because the world in its totality did not help me to do it. Thus I am alone, as I was when they tortured me. Those around me do not appear to me as anti-humans, as did my former torturers; they are my co-humans, not affected by me and the danger prowling at my side.
>
> (Améry 1980: 94–96)

The temptation to forgive: Esther Mujawayo

From April to July 1994, more than 800,000 people (the majority of them Tutsis)[7] were killed in a horrifying genocide in Rwanda. Afterwards, the prosecution of all the enocidaires was simply impossible. In 2003, about 80,000 people accused of human-rights crimes were packed into jails, often in insalubrious conditions, still waiting to come before the court. To face the concrete impossibility of any exemplar justice, various measures were taken: the liberation of 10,000 prisoners for health or age reasons, the increasing number of collective proceedings, and the launching of a new version of a traditional conciliation procedure, the *gacaca*.[8] Up to a certain point, the Rwandan response to the genocide seemed to illustrate the experience once articulated by Hannah Arendt, namely that there are certain crimes '[that one] can neither punish nor forgive' (Arendt 1998: 241). But the Rwandan authorities have not remained in Arendt's aporetic, stringently dubious, situation. Indeed, they explicitly called for forgiveness, presenting it as the key to the reconstruction of the national community. For example, since 2002 President Paul Kagame has explicitly encouraged forgiveness on a national level.[9] In April 2006, at the twelfth commemoration of the Rwandan genocide, Kagame emphasized again the notion of forgiveness in underlining the importance to 'confront the truth, to tolerate and to forgive for the sake of our future, to give the Rwandans their dignity' (Kagame 2006).

However, in spite of official policy and public pressure from NGOs and churches, the encouragement of forgiveness is rarely embraced among survivors. This section provides a closer look at some of the voices of resistance, Esther Mujawayo's in particular (Mujawayo and Belhaddad 2006: 17). Born in Rwanda in 1958, she is a sociologist and a psychotherapist. In 1994, she lost hundreds of relatives – including her mother, father and husband – during the genocide. She now lives in Düsseldorf, Germany, and works in the field of trauma therapy with refugees. She wrote about her experience in two books entitled *Survivantes* (2004) and *La fleur de Stéphanie* (2006). What one finds in these writings is not the often-praised voice of the forgiving and conciliatory victim. To the contrary, even though Mujawayo endorses a gradual rapprochement between Rwandans in the long run, she clearly expresses her refusal to forgive, and talks of the inclination to forgive as a temptation.48 More than that, she talks about the interest in post-atrocity forgiveness as an 'obsession' – not on behalf of the survivors, but on behalf of the authorities, NGOs, and other agents of reconciliation (Mujawayo and Belhaddad 2006: 127).

What accounts for such 'negative' attitudes to the advocacy of forgiveness? Of course, a comprehensive exploration is impossible here, but focusing on three different and partly successive reactions depicted by most of the Rwandan survivors will to some extent illuminate what lies behind this kind of resistance. The first is summarized by a single word: silence. The second is a strong refusal to forgive. The third, more global, one is a distancing from any 'politics of reconciliation.' Each of these reactions indicates the limits of a forgiveness presented as a miraculous formula for reconciliation.

1. Silence

Although questions of forgiveness loom large in current discourse on reconciliation, the issues faced most urgently by genocide survivors do not always or necessarily involve either forgiveness or anger or its overcoming. Instead, the response to past atrocity can engage deep sadness, fear, loss of trust and hope, and other emotions that might lead to silence rather than to calls for justice and accountability. In her first book, Esther Mujawayo depicts the initial reaction of most of the survivors after the genocide: 'No one ... explicitly asked us to be quiet, [but] we have immediately felt that we had to [be]' (Mujawayo and Belhaddad 2004: 20).

The sheer difficulty of finding proper words, as well as listeners, is not the only reason for this first reaction. Many survivors decided to be silent because they felt guilty, ashamed, or afraid. The paradoxical guilt experienced by many of the other survivors around Esther Mujawayo resulted from the fact that they – and not the others – survived, that they could not save their loved ones, or that they could not find their loved ones' bones. As for the shame, this feeling is often linked with the violence – especially sexual violence – that they underwent. Even though eighty percent of the women who survived were raped, the reality of this specific violence is still a taboo (Mujawayo and Belhaddad 2006: 196). According to representatives of the Association of Genocide Widows (AVEGA), '[T]he rape, you bear it silently, in such a shame that no one could even imagine. But you, you always feel like a stink inside your body and a grime that itches your skin' (Mujawayo and Belhaddad 2004: 201). This shame and constant humiliation – reinforced by the stigmatization of any one Tutsi, systematically identified with a cockroach during the genocide (Bagilishya 2004) – are so deep that the roles seem reversed: 'The survivor is ashamed to meet the killer of his close relatives; he [the survivor] is the one who is afraid, who feels humiliated to see the perpetrator walking like that. He feels so guilty' (Mukayiranga 2004: 783).

This sense of the survivor's guilt and shame can be associated with another cruel inversion of the roles during the genocide – when the victims themselves asked for forgiveness from their perpetrators. Several witnesses explained that, in front of the *Interahamwe*, victims were indeed asking for forgiveness in order not to be tortured for too long (Hatzfeld 2004: 198). The fear expressed by the survivors can be explained by various elements: angst about not being believed, anxiety in front of recently liberated perpetrators, and a general feeling that they would be bothering everybody. With the 'un-listenable' mingling with the unspeakable, both tendencies imply a loss of confidence in the world and the loss of any sense of personal safety. Facing these extreme difficulties, the Rwandan victims have to make an immense effort to testify in front of a sometimes-hostile gathering, to express publicly tragic facts (above all, sexual violence), to denounce neighbors, or even members of their own family. As Mujawayo noticed, in these circumstances forgiveness is not the primary concern of the survivor (Mujawayo and Belhaddad 2004: 127). Arguably, this kind of 'distancing' from the entire issue of forgiveness is not an example of resistance to forgiveness in the sense of active and focused opposition, like that of Améry. But the situation is prone to feed into a kind of loathing and disdain that is as significant as the more explicit forms of opposition. Consider for example this remark by Innocent Rwililiza, as quoted in one of Jean Hatzfeld's books on post-genocide Rwanda:

Actually, who is speaking about forgiveness? Tutsis, Hutus, liberated prisoners, their families? None of them, it is the humanitarian organisations. They import forgiveness in Rwanda, and they wrap it in dollars to convince us. There is a Forgiveness Plan as there is an Aids Plan, with meetings of popularization, posters, little local presidents, very polite Whites in cross-country and turbo vehicles. … We, we speak about forgiveness to be well considered and because subsidies can be lucrative. But in our intimate talks, the word 'forgiveness' is strange, I mean constraining.

(Hatzfeld 2007: 25)

2. Clear Refusal to Forgive

Beyond this first reaction, Mujawayo insists on her resistance to any kind of forgiveness toward perpetrators. She says,

[T]he more I think about that, the more I ignore what forgiving means, except this mini-settlement that I make with myself to hold out for a pretended moral appeasement, to 'win' against hatred … Today, as the years go, I accept better, I finally accept that, no, I will not forgive.

(Mujawayo and Belhaddad 2004: 126)

This position relies on two main reasons: on the one hand, the lack of energy to adopt an empathetic view of perpetrators, and, on the other, a deep discontent with what might be called a 'cheap' repentance. Speaking about the killers, Mujawayo explains that empathy must follow a return of her energy:

I don't want to understand them, at least, not yet. I want to proceed step by step: within ten years maybe. I don't want to understand … I say to myself that some people are paid for that, for understanding the killers – politicians, humanitarian staff, right-thinking people … all those whose work is to get into contact with criminals. Myself, I don't need that. I don't want to understand them and I don't want to excuse them. They did it … and I want them to pay for that and not to sleep soundly.

(Mujawayo and Belhaddad 2004: 87)

This refusal to understand the 'other' to some extent results from the immense fatigue felt by survivors who have so many other priorities in the current Rwandan context. Before thinking about the potential scope of empathy, Mujawayo wants 'some bread for those who survived' (Mujawayo and Belhaddad 2004: 189). However, apart from the inappropriate character of any 'duty to understand' (Mujawayo and Belhaddad 2004: 87), she does not deny the humanity of each Rwandan, including perpetrators: 'Yes, there is a human touch in each of us, and therefore in each of them, and who knows what we could have done in their place' (Mujawayo and Belhaddad 2004: 120).

Mujawayo's attitude seems to be characterized by a constant effort to take into consideration the ambivalence and complexity of the situation. Underlining the loneliness that goes with the experience of victims, she does not expect any kind of revenge in order to appease this feeling. Nonetheless, she maintains that victims have the right not to be above resentment. Being a psychotherapist, she does not feel any guilt when she faces her own resentment. Taking lucid account of the limits of her powers, she knows and she accepts that, for most survivors, full empathy would be unattainable and even counterproductive. Like Améry, she seems to consider resentment as a deeply human attitude.[10]

The second reason for survivors' resistance to forgiveness is that forgiveness does not make sense when perpetrators do not express any remorse. According to Mujawayo, '[M]ost of the killers do not ask forgiveness, they say sorry … Or they ask it with the certainty that this request … inherently merits a positive answer' (Hatzfeld 2007: 87). To her, the notion of forgiveness is not the same for the killer and the survivor. For the perpetrator, it represents a potential reduction of sentence, whereas for the victim it appears either as something beyond reach or as a sacrifice.

Against this background, Mujawayo wonders, 'To forgive whom in fact? The one who writes you his letter of repentance?' This question denounces the quasi-administrative letters written by perpetrators in order to be liberated as soon as possible. To Mujawayo, these documents at best mimic a true acknowledgment of responsibility and a genuine address to the survivors. In La Fleur de Stéphanie, she gives an example of the hundreds of similar letters sent to survivors:

> Musange, province of Gitarama
>
> Object : [T]o ask forgiveness [of] Nyirakanyana Madalina's family
>
> I, N.V., son of K., I am writing to Nyirakanyana Madalina's family, asking them forgiveness because I was one member of the group that took her from M.P.'s house (a neighbour). ... This group was directed by M.F. ... [a list of 11 members follows]. These are those with whom we took her together to the river Nyabarongo but I, at that moment, I stopped on the riverside. Then, I ask you, the members of Nyirakanyana's family, forgiveness; to the State, I also ask to forgive me, to God too I ask forgiveness, and I hope that you will forgive me as well. Peace of God with you.
>
> [Following is a signature, a name, and fingerprints.] A last sentence specifies: 'This letter is notified to the gacaca coordinator of M[.] Muhanga.'
>
> (Hatzfeld 2007: 127–129)

To Mujawayo, this kind of statement, always identical (same phrases, same structure) is almost indecent because it does not express any regret or any personal responsibility: everyone is hiding his own behavior behind 'the group as such' (Mujawayo and Belhaddad 2004: 127). Many survivors confirm that not a single prisoner came and expressed remorse for what he did. In some cases, prisoners decided to confess their crimes, but they did it in a mechanical way, and even required the victims' forgiveness – most often taken for granted. There are pressures in favor of forgiveness all around (from official authorities, churches, and NGOs); survivors discredit mainly what they consider as only a pretense of forgiveness.

The absence of authenticity is apparent in many gestures leading theoretically to forgiveness: 'Humanitarian organizations ... spend millions of dollars in order to make us forgiv[e] and bind each other by friendship. But survivors do not want to bargain their word against little compensations' (Hatzfeld 2007: 101). This account likewise illustrated the hollowness of the victim's forgiveness in response to the hollowness of the perpetrator's request for the same:

> Two people came at home to ask me for forgiveness. They did not come willingly, but in order to avoid the prison. It is difficult to explain to a father how one has cut his daughter or for the father to ask these people how they have cut her. Then, we did not say anything but polite phrases ... To listen to them or not to listen to them was the same[.] I listened to them in order [for] them to go away quicker[,] letting me alone with my grief. When they left,

the persons added that they had been kind with me since they missed me in
the marshes. Me, I pretended to thank them.

(Hatzfeld 2007: 104)

This strategy, used largely by criminals to avoid too many years in prison, creates
an overwhelming sense of injustice in the victims. In some cases, as the former
prisoner Elie Mizinge explains, perpetrators even regret not having 'finished their
job. They blame themselves for negligence, more than for spitefulness. ... Waiting
to start again' (Hatzfeld 2004: 198). However, the external pressure is perceived
as so intense that some survivors tend to internalize a certain obligation to forgive.
As another victim said to her former perpetrator, 'The government forgave you
and I cannot refuse it to you' (Gakenke and Umutara 2005). Similarly, several
other survivors explain that they agreed to forgive because the 'power' – the State
or the Church – asked them to do so (Hatzfeld 2007: 19).

3. A Global Distancing from any 'Politics of Reconciliation'

In Rwanda, as well as in other places, like South Africa, forgiveness has been
publicly encouraged as the only, or at least as the most important, condition for
reconciliation. Unsurprisingly, the resistance of many victims to public pleas
for forgiveness can seep into a more general animosity against the process of
reconciliation. Many survivors denounce the so-called 'politics' or 'ideology' of
reconciliation:

Reconciliation. This word became unbearable to me and to most of the
survivors who[m] I know. To me, it is even perfectly indecent after genocide
... 'To reconcile,' as it is written in the dictionary, consists in making
people at odds agree again ... Do I have to consider that what happened in
Rwanda between April and July 1994 is the product of a dispute, a quarrel,
a disagreement[,] and therefore that it would not be understandable not
to reconcile? Do the people who use this word all the time realize that its
meaning is fundamentally simplistic?

(Mukarwego in Braeckman 2004)

Moreover, the public advocacy of forgiveness and reconciliation is permeated
with promises of healing, peace, and harmony. At this juncture, forgiveness and
reconciliation can take on the quality of a temptation, a lure of redemption. The
words of Mujawayo on this point are univocal:

I really hope that I will not give in to ... the 'national reconciliation' camp ... To
have a grudge against somebody requires an important mental resistance: you
are thinking about it all the time and this feeling consumes you so much that,
just to appease it a little bit, you sometimes find yourself having the temptation
to forgive. If, furthermore, governmental politics presents forgiveness as
a national priority ..., I do fear the easiness of such project: all of us would

be beautiful, we would finally have become nice, everything would be well cleaned and then, that would start again! But what would start again in fact?
(Mujawayo and Belhaddad 2004: 17)

Beyond this general resistance to any official 'politics of reconciliation,' Mujawayo is ready to conceive a gradual *rapprochement*, on a people-to-people level, among Rwandans. If she refuses to forgive, literally, she does not totally reject the concept of reconciliation 'because there is no other possible choice' (Mujawayo and Belhaddad 2004: 130).

All those I met in Rwanda, until the survivors working on the field ... never think about forgiveness ... However, all of them work in favour of a reconciliation. Because to reconcile does not mean to forgive. To take up with neighbours again, starting with the ability to greet each other, is important for all the reasons that I have already emphasized: our culture cannot be conceived without these traditions, these rituals.
(Mujawayo and Belhaddad 2004: 130–131)

The record of Esther Mujawayo manifests the unavoidable tension between the need to look forward and the absolute necessity of respecting the intimate experience and personal pace of each survivor. In this regard, the challenge is paramount. As Mujawayo emphasizes, '[T]his is not the end of the genocide that really stops a genocide, because inwardly genocide never stops' (Mujawayo and Belhaddad 2004: 197). The same experience is echoed in the words of another: 'The survivor remains inconsolable. He resigns himself but he remains in revolt and powerless. He does not know what to do, the social environment does not understand him, and he does not understand himself either' (Mukayiranga 2004: 777).

Concluding reflections

Persons who refuse to forgive are often and easily seen as somehow exemplifying various moral failures (of judgment understanding, et cetera) or psychological (and thus more-or-less understandable) shortcomings. Yet, although the refusal to forgive can be testimony of self-righteous rigor, vengeance, or a reduction of wrongdoers to what they have done, it is essential that the discussion of forgiveness and its alternatives take more seriously the possibilities and sources of various kinds of more or less legitimate resistance. The cases of Jean Améry and Esther Mujawayo deviate from the common 'imaginaries' of the agents of unforgiveness. Neither of them is consumed by hatred or out for bloody revenge: they suffer and a tempered measure of rage suffuse the writings of Améry in particular, but their reasoning and aims are not deluded, self-preoccupied, or morally demeaning. Moreover, though Améry and Mujawayo might be exceptions in some regards, we surmise that there are many other cases of similar sobriety and complexity. Consider, for example, the case of Primo Levi (who repeatedly stated that he did not forgive), Vladimir Jankélévitch, or a host of other examples from Rwanda and South Africa.

One of the important 'lessons' emerging from these and similar cases is the inadequacy of an overly individualized focus on the survivor and her personal or community issues. Whether one thinks of Améry or Mujawayo, it is impossible to account for their attitudes without attention to their perceptions of their social contexts and, in particular, the attitudes of their communities. After mass atrocity, the preservation of resentment or resistance to forgiveness might be largely dependant on perceptions of the attitudes prevalent among entire social groups, authorities, and so on. In Mujawayo's case, the relevant others are not only the majority of criminals and their families – who rarely expressed any kind of remorse – but also the Tutsis who arrived in Rwanda after 1994 and who are therefore not still-wounded survivors. Even though they of course do not deny the genocide, they are preoccupied mainly with the need to concentrate on building the future. To some extent, they seem to be bored by the victims' expectations or claims (Mujawayo and Belhaddad 2004: 20). Another significant point has to do with the nature of victims' resistance to forgiveness. Whereas advocates of forgiveness tend to represent or imagine opposition in the form of the total refusal to forgive, the examples from Rwanda testify to more-reasoned and condition-dependent forms of resistance. One will not forgive because of the absence of repentance (or because of the cheap and hollow way in which a perpetrator is encouraged to 'forgive'), because of the urgency of other issues, and so forth.

Vladimir Jankélévitch once observed that forgiveness can be recommended in such ways as to make people disgusted with it (Jankélévitch 1996: 55). This is an important point, because it indicates the reason why victims and survivors in many different places respond negatively to social or official encouragements of forgiveness after mass atrocities. Yet what if forgiveness is recommended in proper and respectable ways, in a way that avoids placing pressure on victims to forgive, that stops short of pathologizing or diminishing unforgiveness, and that is receptive to legitimate alternatives? Even then, it is highly questionable whether reconciliation is well served by being closely tied to an advocacy of forgiveness. Forgiveness overburdens reconciliation insofar as the latter is thought to build on a general endorsement of the former. Unless drastically redefined to suit political processes, forgiveness should perhaps be respected as an anomaly – a sometimes highly admirable and laudable gesture, but something that should, as Jacques Derrida put it, 'never amount to a therapy of reconciliation' (Derrida 2001: 41), something that 'must remain a madness of the impossible' (Derrida 2001: 39).[11]

Notes

1   Even though the role of NGOs, health-care workers, and mediators has not significantly changed, the emphasis put on forgiveness seems to be quite recent.
2   As the chairman of the Truth and Reconciliation Commission in Sierra Leone, Bishop J.C. Humper, put in his foreword to the report of the commission, 'Learning to forgive those who have wronged us is the first step we can take towards healing our traumatised nation' (Humper 2004: 2, 3).

3 For an extensive examination of this aspect of the advocacy of forgiveness, see
   Brudholm (2008: 21–62). For an examination of ways in which advocating forgiveness
   risks jeopardizing the needs and autonomy of the victims, see generally Brudholm
   (2009).
4 As we are featuring the written work of two victims who are extraordinarily lucid in
   explaining their resistance, it should be mentioned that we do not pretend to represent
   'the victims' as a general category, but rather to illustrate the possibility of an often-
   neglected normative stance.
5 The English translation is *At the Mind's Limits: contemplations by a survivor on
   Auschwitz and its realities* (1980).
6 For the conceptualization of resentment as tied to reassurance, see Walker (2006).
7 Estimates for the total number killed in the genocide vary from 500,000 to more than
   1 million. According to the official census report of the Rwandan authorities (quoted
   by Paul Kagame in April 2006), 937,000 Tutsi and Hutu opponents were killed.
   According to Alison Des Forges (1999), around 500,000 were killed.
8 The *gacaca* court system started in 2002. In total there are 12,103 igacaca icourts
   established nationwide, presided over by 169,442 *inyangamugayo* (persons of
   integrity) – the local judges elected among the populace. The purpose of these courts is
   to gather survivors, witnesses, and suspects of genocide in order to establish the truth
   and to stop the culture of impunity by singling out those who actively participated in
   the killings. On the scope and limits of the *gacaca* courts, see Ingelaere (2008).
9 'The committed sins have to be repressed and punished, but also forgiven. I invite
   the perpetrators to show courage and to confess, to repent, and to ask forgiveness'
   (Kagame 2006). And later: 'It is important that culprits confess their crimes and ask
   forgivenss to victims. On the one hand, the confession appeases their conscience, but
   above all these avowals comfort the survivors who can then learn, even though it is
   painful, how their close relatives were killed and where their bodies were abandoned'
   (Braeckman 2004: 103).
10 For an elaboration on this point, see Veltesen (2006).
11 The viability and propriety of forgiveness (variously understood) in the political realm
   has been debated intensely in recent years. See Digeser (2001); Griswold (2008); and
   Philpott (ed.) (2006).

References

Améry, J. (1980) *At the Mind's Limits: contemplations by a survivor on Auschwitz and its realities,* trans. S. and S. Rosenfeld, Bloomington, IN: Indiana University Press.
Arendt, H. (1978) *Eichmann in Jerusalem: a report on the banality of evil*, New York: New Grove Press.
Arendt, H. (1998) *The Human Condition*, Chicago, IL: University of Chicago Press.
Bagilishya, L. (2004) 'Discours de la négation, dénis et politiques', in Coquio, C. (ed.) *L'histoire trouée: négation et témoignage*, Paris: L'Atlante.
Braeckman, C. (2004) 'Les fantômes d'Immaculée hauntent toujours les collines', in *Le Soir*, 7 April 2004.
Brudholm, T. (2008) *Resentment's Virtue: Jean Améry and the refusal to forgive*, Philadelphia, PA: Temple University Press.
Brudholm, T. (2009) *The Religious in Response to Mass Atrocity: interdisciplinary perspectives*, Cambridge, UK: Cambridge University Press.
Des Forges, A. *Leave None to Tell the Story: genocide in Rwanda*, Washington, DC: Human Rights Watch.
Enright, R., and Joanna North (1998) *Exploring Forgiveness*, Madison, WI: Universityof Wisconsin Press.

Gakenke and Umutara (2005) 'Penal reform international: rapport de synthèse demonitoring et de recher csur la Gacaca', available online at http://www.penalreform.org/resources/rep-ga7-2005-pilot-phase-fr.pdf.

Griswold, C. (2008) *Forgiveness: a philosophical exploration*, Cambridge, UK: Cambridge University Press.

Hatzfeld, J. (2004) *Machete Season: the killers in Rwanda speak*, New York: Picador.

Hatzfeld, J. (2007) *La stratégie des antilopes*, Paris: Soleil.

Humper, J.C. (2004) 'Foreword', *Sierra Leone Truth and Reconciliation Commission: witness to truth*, available online at http://www.usip.org/publications/truth-commission-sierra-leone.

Ingelaere, B. (2008) 'The Gacaca courts in Rwanda', in Huyse, L. and Salter, M. (eds) *Traditional Justice and Reconciliation after Violent Conflict: learning from Africa experiences*, Washington, DC: IDEA Books.

Jankélévitch, V. (1996) *Forgiveness*, Chicago, IL: University of Chicago Press.

Kagame, P. (2006) 'Address at the twelfth commemoration of the Rwandan genocide', April 7, available online at http://www.gov.rw/government/president/speeches/2006/07_04_06_genocide.html.

Lemarchand, R. (2001) 'Rwanda et Burundi: génocides croisés', in Charny, I. (ed.) *Le livre noire de l'humanité: encyclopédi mondiale des genocides*, Paris: Privat.

Mujawayo, E. and Belhaddad, S. (2004) *Survivantes: Rwanda, historie d'un genocide*, Paris: Editions de l'Aube.

Mujawayo, E. and Belhaddad, S. (2006) *La Fleur de Stéphanie: entre reconciliation et déni*, Paris: Flammarion.

Mukayiranga, S. (2004) 'Sentiments de rescapés', in Coquio, C. (ed.) *L'histoire trouée: négation et témoignage*, Paris: L'Atlante.

Murphy, J. (2003) *Getting Even: forgiveness and its limits,* Oxford, UK: Oxford University Press.

Murphy, J. (2008) 'Foreword' to Brudholm, T. *Resentment's Virtue*, Philadelphia, PA: Temple University Press.

Paye-Layleh, J. (2008) 'I ate children's hearts, ex-rebel says', BBC NEWS, Jan. 22.

Philpott, D. (ed.) (2006) *The Politics of Past Evil: religion, reconciliation and the dilemmas of transitional justice*, Notre Dame: University of Notre Dame.

Philpott, D. (2007) 'Religion, reconciliation, and transitional justice: the state of the field', Social Science Research Council Working Paper, available online at http://programs.ssrc.org/religion/reconciliation.pdf.

Schaap, A. (2005) *Political Reconciliation,* London: Routledge.

Ternon, Y. (2001) *L'Innocence des victims: au siècle des genocides*, Paris: Desclee de Brouwer.

Tutu, D. (1999) *No Future without Forgiveness*, New York: Image.

Veltesen, A.J. (2006) 'A case for resentment: Jean Améry versus Primo Levi', *Human Rights* 44(5).

Walker, M. (2006) *Moral Repair: reconstructing moral relations after wrongdoing*, Cambridge, UK: Cambridge University Press.

Wallace, R. (1994) *Responsibility and the Moral Sentiments*, Cambridge, MA: Harvard University Press.

8 Senses of justice

Bodies, language and space

Michael J. Shapiro

> What might be called the intersentient plastic life of our sensory sociality goes unacknowledged, unplumbed, and unarticulated in its potential.
>
> (Cristolphe Wall-Romana)

> Justice does not exist only in words, but first of all it exists in words.
>
> (Carlos Fuentes)

Introduction: a cinematic text

In Corneliu Porumboiu's film *Police, Adjective*, the detective, Cristi (Dragos Bucur), exhibits a tension between his official policing obligations and his conscience. He has been assigned to the surveillance of high school hashish smokers in his Romanian city, Brasov, and is ultimately ordered to set up a sting so they can be arrested and prosecuted. Much of the film focuses on Cristi's physicality. The camera follows his movement about the city on foot, as he trails the suspects; it zooms in on his standing around for hours, trying to keep warm (by stuffing his hands in his pockets and drawing his sweater over his chin and mouth) as he watches them gather and smoke; and it frames tableux of his proletarian eating practices (as he breaks up bread into his stew), his drinking until he's a bit tipsy (as he sits and ponders his dilemma in a bar), his attempts to connect with his wife (as he lounges and watches television while she listens to loud music on her computer next to him, and sits with her eating and conversing at the dining table), and his foot tennis game (played in a foursome) in which he releases tension. In the film narration, Cristi is a quintessential aesthetic subject, for *Aisthitikos*, the ancient Greek word from which aesthetics is derived, refers to the pre-linguistic, embodied, or feeling-based aspect of perception; "Aesthetics is born as a discourse of the body"(Eagleton 1990: 13).

This sense of aesthetics is effectively enacted in Cristi's personal approach to justice, which is based on his corporeal apprehension of crime and punishment. In two office scenes, one a conversation with a prosecutor and one with his superior, the captain of his precinct, he attempts to resist the demand that he entrap and arrest the teenagers. Significantly, Porumboui avoids point of view shots; "the camera adopts studies, mid-shot neutrality with few if any flourishes" to effect a third person, story-telling aesthetic (Corless 2010: 40). The viewer stands as a detached witness to Cristi's movements and conversations. While speaking with the prosecutor early in the film narrative (shot a mid distance from the side), Cristi reveals what has affected his reluctance to make the drug entrapment and arrest. He reports that while on his honeymoon in the Czech Republic, he saw people smoking hashish with impunity. It therefore strikes him as unfair to impose a law that will undoubtedly change once Romania catches up with other more progressive European states. At the end of the film narrative, in an interview with his captain, he attempts to resist the demand that he set up the sting, saying that it would bother his conscience to bust "crazy kids" and subject them to a seven-year prison term for "smoking a joint." He adds that it would that it would make him feel bad.

However in the conversation with the captain, Cristi is at a marked linguistic disadvantage, which the viewers can appreciate because they have been prepared by an earlier scene. As he sits watching television while his wife is listening to a song loudly broadcast from her desktop computer, Cristi remarks that "the song doesn't make any sense." When his wife asks why he thinks that, he repeats a couple of lines: "what would the field be without the flower; what would the sea be without the sun" and says "what else would it be? It would still be the field and the sea." His wife, who turns out to be a linguistic pedant and an advocate of the official Romanian grammar, points out that the lines are a figure of speech known as an *anaphora*. Cristi, who lacks an appreciation of figurative language, asks why the song doesn't just say what it means directly. Subsequently, they converse about the report he is compiling about the hashish smokers. She says that she read it when he left it on the coat rack and that it contains a grammatical mistake; a particular construction has been changed by the Romanian Academy. Cristi responds passively, saying simply that he'll change it, although he thinks that official language policy is "crazy."

At the film's climax, Cristi again finds himself in a language confrontation. When summoned by his captain, who asks why he is not proceeding with the sting, he insists that he won't carry it out because if he did, his conscience would bother him. Cristi's refusal is reminiscent of Herman Melville's Bartleby in his "Bartleby, The Scrivener," who responds with increasing frequency to his employer's request for fulfilling tasks or explaining his recalcitrance, with the phrases "I would prefer not to" and "I prefer not to" (Melville). As Gilles Deleuze points out, because the "prefer" construction is not an outright refusal, it does not effect Bartleby's transition from one employed, fulfilling his obligations as a law-copyist, to one shirking them (Deleuze 1997). Even when prompted by his employer: "Every copyist is bound to help examine his copy. Is that not so? Will you not speak," the response remains, "I prefer not to." Eventually, Bartleby's repetition of the phrase permeates the discourse of the office as a whole. The Lawyer and the other clerks find the word creeping into their statements unbidden. And ultimately, after Bartleby has deflected all attempts to get him to examine his

Figure 8.1 Cristi and his wife, from *Police, Adjective*

and other copies, he gives up copying as well; the "formula annihilates 'copying'" (Deleuze 1997: 71) and "erodes the attorney's reasonable organization of work and life" (Rancière 2004a: 146). For purposes of comparison, Cristi and Bartleby both resist the sense-making that predicates the hierarchy of tasks within their respective vocations. However, Bartleby succeeds where Cristi fails. In Bartleby's case, he has an employer who lacks the phrases to contest his formula. The formula "stymies the speech acts that a boss uses to command" (Deleuze 1997: 73). Unable to engage in effective discursive contestation, the lawyer "concocts a theory explaining how Bartleby's formula ravages language as a whole" (*ibid.*) and leads to a logic that permits Bartleby to stop copying altogether. Bartleby has effectively "invented a new logic, *a logic of preference*, which is enough to undermine the presuppositions of language as a whole" (*ibid.*). In contrast, Cristi lacks an effective formula. As a result, he is helpless in the face of the ones thrown at him by the police captain. While Bartleby has a formula that "severs language from all reference" (*ibid.*: 74). Cristi's reference is confined to himself (his conscience and feelings). While Bartleby's formula casts him outside of all prescribed positioning, Cristi's attempt to step outside fails; he is repositioned by the captain's words within the extant policing roles.

After stating, "You're not making sense," the captain challenges Cristi by asking a colleague to write Cristi's reasons for his recalcitrance on a chalk board and then asking his secretary to bring in a Romanian dictionary. The board's transcript reads, "Conscience is something within me that stops me from doing something bad that I'd afterwards regret" – to which the captain responds, "So you have a feeling, an intuition." In response to Cristi's statements – the kids are just "crazy" rather than being serious criminals and thus that it would not be moral to impose such a penalty (moreover, arresting them would make him feel bad) – the captain reads definitions of Cristi's oppositional concepts from the dictionary (conscience, morality, justice), all of which, when uttered without benefit of the alternative discursive contexts within which they might be understood, suggest that his position is based on idiosyncratic resistance to his official policing obligations. And ultimately, lacking linguistic facility, Cristi cannot find words adequate to his sensibilities. What he needs are words that "exceed the function of rigid designation" in order to be able to translate what he senses into an intelligible discourse on crime and justice that opposes effectively "those who claim to speak correctly" (Panagia 2000: 115).

Generalized beyond the particular confrontation in the film, the police captain's insistence on correct speech is anathema to a consideration of the politics of crime, punishment, and justice. Toni Morrison lyrically captures the depoliticizing aspects of the anachronistically rigid language of policing through the perspective of *her* conceptual persona (a blind woman) in her Nobel Prize acceptance speech:

> [I]t is unyielding language content to admire its own paralysis ... Ruthless in its policing duties, it has no desire or purpose other than maintaining the free range of its own narcotic narcissism, its own exclusivity and dominance ... Unreceptive to interrogation, it cannot form or tolerate new ideas, shape other thoughts, tell another story, fill baffling silences. Official language smitheryed to sanction ignorance and preserve privilege is a suit of armor polished to shocking glitter, a husk from which the knight departed long ago.
> (Morrison 1993)

Of course Porumboiu's film as a whole is able to provide what his character, Cristi, cannot – a conceptual exploration of the relationships among sense, space, discourse and justice. Among other things, architecture is one of the film's major characters. In addition to showing how "language creates and defines reality," Porumboiu shows the way the spaces of the police station – with its "seemingly endless doors and corridors" (*ibid.*: 42) that control access of subordinates – constitutes much of the experience of policing. Heeding the film's provocations on the spaces of policing, I turn to an elaboration of the space–justice relationship.

The spaces of the justice

The challenge that the linguistically limited Cristi mounts unsuccessfully is not only about language. He attempts as well to enlarge the spatio-temporality of justice. In his conversation with the prosecutor, he connects his small city, Brasov, to the rest of Europe and imagines a future in which Romanian drug penalties are abrogated as his country catches up with the tolerant climate in other European states. Once Cristi reveals to the prosecutor that his reluctance to pursue young hashish smokers was reinforced while he was in Prague on his honeymoon, there ensues an exchange of seemingly idle talk that implicitly involves contestation about the spatial boundaries of the city's drug policing. After Cristi reports that some of Prague's buildings have gold roofs, that he saw a "theater with an entire ceiling of gold," and that Prague is known as the Golden City, the prosecutor brings the conversation's focus back to Brasov: "Did you know that the Black Church in Brasov once had a golden roof?" "Yes," says Cristi, "It burnt down." Undeterred, the prosecutor suggests that the government should renovate that roof, restoring its gold: "Then we could call Brasov The City of Gold; sounds great, yes?" When Cristi counters that "Prague is a much larger city," the prosecutor says, "Well then, we could call it the Little Prague ... We'd have Bucharest as 'Little Paris' and Brasov as 'Little Prague'... Sounds great, doesn't it?"

Although verbally, Cristic accedes, saying *Da* (yes), his body in this scene, as in other conversations in the film, is recalcitrant. While the prosecutor is leaning back in his chair and exhibiting a posture of self-satisfaction, Cristi's is troubled and resistant; it is hunched over and tense. Here, as throughout the film, Cristi is the kind of aesthetic subject that is not simply an instrument of the film narrative. Rather, he is the kind of subject who, unlike those bodies in classic cinema whose "density" is abandoned as they function as "simply vehicles for a story [as they move about in] the service of narrative articulations," is one found in some contemporary films that "dis-organize the body – by means of revealing its fragmented nature, [and] by extracting from it the 'yoke of unity' and consciousness, by giving it back the complexity of its own determinations" (Amiel 1998: 7). Although unable discursively to oppose the policing structure, Cristi's body retains its "density" and "complexity," and in this scene's conversation is able to evoke what Paolo Virno calls a "spontaneous epistemology" embedded in such seemingly idle talk. "Idle talk," Virno points out, reveals aspects of political opposition because it is often a form of "social communication" that breaks away from "every bond or presupposition" (Virno 2004: 89). In this case, the spontaneous epistemology is an embodied knowledge, coming from within and reinforced by an experience of alternative legal spaces. It is enacted through Cristi's corporeally displayed resistance to capitulating to Brasov's parochial policing mentality. By the end of the film, Cristi's resistance is broken, leaving him as a suborned body as the outcome appears as an event of "linguistic domination"(Ruthrof 1992: 331). However, although the politics of language is a primary frame within which the film cries out for analysis (and I do so below), much of the politics of the film can also be captured in the analysis of the relationship between justice and space toward which the encounters in the film gesture.

An effective conceptual rendering of such a spatial analysis is available by analogy in Michel Foucault's treatment of the spaces of disease. At the outset of his investigation of the history of the medical gaze, Foucault discerns three levels of spatialization. At the primary level, disease exists in medical language – in a classificatory system, expressed as "an area of homologies" (Foucault

1973: 15). At a second level, it is located in "the space of the body," and finally, once medicine becomes a governmental task, it is located in a third space, an administrative structure where it is subject to an intensification of surveillance by a proliferating series of official agencies, including "a policing supplement" (*ibid.*: 19). To apply those levels of spatialization to the location of justice in Porumboiu's *Police, Adjective*, we can surmise that justice is located first of all in the languages of the law (specifically in the local codification of the law's narrow, dictionary-assisted languages of transgression and policing obligations), second in Cristi's body, and third in the law's administrative agencies – prosecutors, police officer hierarchies, and policing functionaries (forensic specialists, filing clerks, among others). Moreover, just as in the history of medicine where a proliferation of agencies developed when medicine became "task for the nation," so in the case of the history of punishment, the state's monopolization of disputes has meant that proscribed forms of drug use also evoke a policing supplement, which includes an "intensification of surveillance" that requires complex intra and inter-agency cooperation (quotations from *ibid.*). However, while Foucault's spatial analysis of medicine provides an apt analogy for understanding the specific case that the film addresses, we need a more historically situated perspective to grasp more generally what the film implies with its image and narrative provocations. In what follows I give the primary conceptual contributions of the film some historical depth.

Bodies, discourse, spaces: achieving historical distance

In order to gain a politically perspicuous view of the way Porumboiu's film mobilizes the tensions between Cristi's sense of justice and its location within the extra-corporeal spaces he cannot control or effectively address, we need to defamiliarize contemporary justice-space relationships. As Foucault has noted, when referring to his "method," to be able to grasp "the history of successive forms" and appreciate how peculiar the contemporary form is, he had "to stand detached from it, bracket its familiarity, in order to analyze the theoretical and practical context with which it has been associated" – hence his analysis of the way sexuality was problematized in ancient Greece (Foucault 1985: 3). In a similar methodological gesture, the classical historian, Paul Veyne, says that he is interested in analyzing Roman history because of the way it allows him to see the present: "Rome ... takes us out of ourselves and forces us to make explicit the differences separating us from it" (Veyne 1982: 176).

Where can we go historically to bracket the familiarity of the problematic in Porumboiu's fictional (yet very realistic) Brasov, recognizing that the contemporary spatial strategy for responding to crimes is dominated by agencies whose ultimate horizon involves mechanisms of confinement (hence the seven-year term facing the young hashish smokers). While there are many historical venues and periods that would serve as an effective defamiliarizing contrasts, the system of law and justice in medieval Iceland is perhaps the best historical moment we can use to "take us out of ourselves" because it had no institutions of confinement and no centralized state to administer punishment. As the writers of Icelandic Sagas teach us, medieval Iceland had a singular way of identifying political affiliation and allocating legal protection. A person's affiliational identity was not that of the modern citizen subject. It was primarily biopolitical rather than territorial inasmuch as it was tied to family and clan heredity. Nevertheless, one's legal identity could migrate into a spatial mode because the movement from inside the law to outside of it (being outlawed) could be juridically determined at a yearly meeting of the clans at the Icelandic *Althing*. For example, if a person was charged with murder and thereby ordered pay compensation to a victim's family or clan, failure to come up with the payment would outlaw the perpetrator. Once outlawed, a person could be killed with impunity. In Giorgio Agamben's terms, the perpetrator would become "bare life," one without legal or political standing, and thus without the protections of community qualification; he (always "he") could be killed without there being a murder (Agamben 1998).

Although pieces of literature and thus imaginative reenactments of Icelandic events in general and juridical history in particular, the Sagas yield a significant analytic. Their characters serve as aesthetic subjects whose varying relationships to juridical space – being either inside or outside of it – reflect a relatively unfamiliar model of the administration of justice. Unlike the mechanism of confinement, which has characterized centuries of the European and American justice systems, medieval Iceland allocated justice by making the penalty a very precarious form of exclusion. For example, in *Njal's Saga*, both a well-intentioned character, the noble warrior Gunnar, who killed to protect himself, and an ill-intentioned character, the notorious Killer Hraap, who killed arbitrarily, end up outside the law and are killed by their enemies. At a minimum, the part-time administration of justice at the medieval Icelandic *Althing* (comprised as a yearly gathering of the clans) functioned to allocate bodies to a space "devoid of law" (to invoke another of Agamben's concepts) (*Njal's Saga* 2002).

By looking at the juridico–political system of medieval Iceland in the present, we are able to reflect on the historical trajectory of relationships between bodies and legal spaces and defamiliarize the current relationship. The outlawing practice in medieval Iceland was not predicated on the kind of security issues that are preoccupying the contemporary state. Outlawing was designed to disconnect wealth and violence and to regulate inter-clan violence. The almost certain consequence of being placed outside the law was death at the hands of one's enemies. Because there was no centralized system of revenge, retaliation for the alleged crime was strictly freelance; it was in the hands of the aggrieved parties and their allies. The result could be catastrophic because it was common for cycles of retaliation to develop and engulf the entire social order. Indeed, the justice system of the modern state was designed in part to avoid the escalating cycles of violence that have occurred in pre state political systems. By monopolizing retaliation, the state monopolizes and depersonalizes revenge.

However, as Fernand Braudel has pointed out, the history of forms is conjunctural rather than linear. As new forms develop, some of the older ones persist rather than being wholly surpassed (Braudel 1977). Thus, although the administration of confinement within a comprehensive array of "enclosure milieus" (Truby 2008: 43) for those citizen subjects "brought to justice" remains as the ultimate horizon of contemporary justice systems, the strategy of outlawing remains; it is invoked when a citizen (someone presumptively inside the law) is, by executive order, translated into an enemy status (for example the current U.S. practice of designating some Americans as "enemy combatants"). Such translations are increasingly the case. For example, once the "war on terror" reached its current level of expansion, it began functioning within the tripartite spatiality that Foucault ascribed to modern medicine; its locations included a nomenclature (a list of terrorist acts), interpreted bodies (e.g., those inscribed by psycho-biological discourses on the terrorist), and a proliferating set of surveilling and policing agencies. Some of those agencies lack killing power – for example the public health services that are now enjoined to heed the dangers of biological terrorism. However, after the September 11, 2001 attacks on The World Trade Center, President Bush, authorized the CIA, an agency *with* killing power, "to kill U.S. citizens abroad if strong evidence existed that an American was involved in organizing or carrying out terrorist actions against the United States or U.S. interests" (Harshaw 2010). But as one analyst points out, in some cases, "combat is not what we're talking about ..." Some people on the CIA's "'hit list' are likely to be killed while at home, sleeping in their bed, driving in a car with friends or family, or engaged in a whole array of other activities" (*ibid.*). In effect, the post-9/11 space–justice relationship has increasingly involved a mix of strategies, supplementing confinement with outlawing. But unlike the Icelandic practice of outlawing, it is the state's executive power that launches the killing. "Enemies" are enemies of the state rather than the unredeemed antagonists of individuals and groups with uncompensated grievances.

Nevertheless, the increasing use of such a supplement or "state of exception" has invited reactions in the form of counter discourses that contest the discursive practices that are complicit in outlawing citizens (for example the discourse on enemy combatants) which are used to warrant extra-judicial killing. As a result, the post-9/11 contentions over justice are expressed through what J-F. Lyotard calls a clash of "phrases regimes" (a conception to which I return below) (Lyotard 1988). However, in the case of the altered spatialization of justice after 9/11, a mere cataloguing of the different positions on the states of exception to juridical protections would not achieve a rendering of the micropolitical implications of clashes over juridical and/or extra-juridical deployments of punishment. Because, as Porumboiu's *Police, Adjective* shows, the tensions between senses of justice and the applications of official legal or extra legal authority are best appreciated when the subjects involved are mobilized into encounters that reveal the complexities of those tensions, it is aesthetic modes of apprehension, articulated in artistic texts – films and novels, for example – that often provide the most effective analytic. In what follows, I turn to the Italian writer Leonardo Sciascia's first crime novel, *The Day of the Owl* (Italian edition 1961), which contains aesthetic subjects whose encounters create the moments one needs to map the tensions as they unfold within a realistic scenario. The novel effectively articulates and contextualizes the conceptual basis of my analysis of the micropolitics of justice.

A policeman who needs no adjectives

> Political art ... means creating those forms of collision or dissensus that put together not only heterogeneous elements but also two politics of sensoryness. The heterogeneous elements are put together in order to provoke a clash.
>
> (Jacques Rancière)

Like all nation-states, Italy contains politically centrifugal regions, which embody diverse "structures of feeling," a concept invented and developed by Raymond Williams to refer to "affective elements of consciousness and relationships: not feeling against thought, but thought as felt and feeling as thoughts: practical consciousness of a present kind in a living and inter-relating continuity" (Williams 1977: 132). For purposes of understanding the epistemic implications of the encounters that Sciascia stages across two of Italy's diverse regions in his crime novel, Williams' observation that a structure of feeling is not universally shared and is often not "fully understood by living people in close contact with it" is especially *a propos* (Williams 1961: 49). The novel features an encounter between a investigator from Parma in the north of Italy, Police Captain Belodi, whose sense of justice in based on a commitment to the law as codified and applied to the country as a whole, and a Sicilian subculture whose sense of justice functions wholly outside of such a commitment. It is a regional sense of justice based on a historically deep structure of feeling rather than on an allegiance to Italy's centralized codifications of the law. As Captain Belodi ultimately recognizes as he struggles to consummate his case:

> The only institution in the Sicilian conscience that really counts, is the family; counts that is to say, more as a juridical contract or bond than as a natural association based on affection. The family is the Sicilian's State. The State, as it is for us, is extraneous to them, merely a de facto entity based on force; an entity imposing taxes, military service, war, police.
>
> (Sciascia 2003: 95)

Thus, as is the case with the justice systems in other nation-states, where centralized power has failed to impose completely a unitary legal culture, Italian justice deploys itself differently in incommensurate spaces of application. The differences in the law's reception, realized as a mosaic of justice subcultures across the regional spaces in Italy, is in evidence in other places that display complex cartographies of justice.

Although there are doubtless several examples, Thailand is exemplary among the places that have retained a markedly hybrid cartography of justice. There, the traditional justice system was based on "principles of control over people rather than the administration of geographically bounded units" (Engel 1990: 337). Because "space was defined in terms of hierarchical relationships between people and groups" that enjoined acts of ritual obligation (*ibid.*: 338) the system of justice functioned within a political culture that was based on "ceremonial acts of fealty." However, by the twentieth century the old royal legal structure in which juridical subjects were defined by their hierarchically structured, ritual obligations gave way to generalized legal obligations based on a centralized order administered from the capital (*ibid.*: 339). While the old decentralized system, in which there was a mosaic of localities, each with its own justice norms and enforcement procedures, was forced into a system of equivalence, the new system never completely displaced the traditional one. As a result, there remains an "interplay of multiple systems of dispute resolution," where one can observe competing normative systems based on heterogeneous (spiritually invested) social spaces (*ibid.*: 340).

Modern Italy manifests a similar heterogeneous legal cartography. The implications of the resulting centrifugal application of justice become evident once Sciascia's characters (his aesthetic subjects) encounter each other in dialogues. As in Porumboiu's film, contentious conversations are featured in the novel. And although the genre of the novel lacks cinema's image supplements, which (as I noted) are additional vehicles for representing corporeal and discursive dissensus with respect to justice, *The Day of the Owl*'s literary geography plays a role that is similar to *Police, Adjective*'s cinematic cartography. And what the novel lacks by way of visual images, it compensates for with characterizations of the passions and ideological commitments of its characters. The novel's grammatical style frequently turns psychological moments into abstractions by the use of nominalizations. For example a verb form that notes that Belodi thought X becomes something to the effect that Belodi's observed X. Whereas the cinematic grammar of Porumboiu's film operates with juxtapositions between the capitulating words elicited from Cristi, and shots of his body's resistance (based on part on the way his travel experience confirms his bodily sense of what is just), among the novel's primary vehicles are grammatical shifts that render psychic subject as aesthetic subjects whose remarks and actions articulate disjunctions between codified and cultural-spatial perspectives on justice. Ultimately both texts, using their respective genre forms, articulate the effects of culturally incommensurate legal spaces, senses of justice, and discursive styles.

Briefly, the novel, like most of those in the crime story genre, begins with a murder. But unlike many crime stories, the immediate post-murder scene is culturally elaborated. The victim, a building contractor named Salvatore Colasberna, is shot dead as he runs to catch a bus. Because it was known throughout the area that he had refused the mafia's demands for protection payments, the bus conductor's remark, "They've killed him" (Sciascia 2003: 9), represents the general consensus of everyone on the scene who witnessed the killing – the bus driver, the passengers, and nearby vendors. Yet once the *carabinieri* arrive and try to obtain the details of the killing from the witnesses, no one is willing to admit to having seen anything. George Scialabba effectively captures the cultural significance of the passivity of the local population in the face of such events. Referring to the witnesses who, as the novel describes them, "sat mute, their faces as if disinterested from the silence of centuries" (*ibid.*: 10), he suggests that it points to the "immemorial inertia of the local culture" (Scialabba 2003: ix). In short, as is the case of Thailand's cultural dispersion, some regions in Italy manifest a historically dense, cultural inertia that militates against being drawn into Italy's centralized system of justice.

Captain Belodi's arrival to the venue of the killing constitutes a disturbance to the region's "immemorial inertia" (*ibid.*). But a disturbance is also evinced for Belodi, who on the one hand has unalloyed respect for the centralized justice system and on the other has (like Sciascia himself) "affection for the region's landscape and literature" and thus its structure of feeling (*ibid.*: x). As a result, Belodi is a complex aesthetic subject, one with divided loyalties that generates ambivalence as he attempts to bring the perpetrators to "justice." A t the same time, however, his knowledge of the region allows him to recognize the spaces and genres of relevant evidence. While potential informants will not speak reliably about the events surrounding a crime, they often write (anonymously) about what they know or think: "'It's odd,' said the captain ... 'how people in this part of the world let themselves go in anonymous letters. No one talks, but luckily for us ... everyone writes'" (Sciascia 2003: 17). Nevertheless, once Belodi's investigation gets underway, he extracts oral reports (mostly unreliable) from a variety of local informants. And as the process unfolds, it becomes evident what the tension is between the codified system of justice that Belodi represents and the local senses of justice. At a minimum, there is no *sensus communis* in the sense that Immanuel Kant presents it – a shared "moral law within" (Kant 2002).

In order to provide a critical philosophical framing for what is involved in the novel's encounter between incommensurate modes of justice and the conversations that articulate the tensions in that encounter, we do well to heed Lyotard's neo-Kantian version of critical philosophy. In place of Kant's figuration of philosophy as a "tribunal," where "critical philosophy is in the position of a juridical authority," Lyotard substitutes the battlefield (Lyotard 1989: 93). Arguing that Kant's model cannot comprehend the negative events that engender "the exploding of language into families of heteronomous language games," Lyotard insists that "we need a philosophy of phrases rather than one of the faculties of the subject" (*ibid.*: 106). As he puts it in his extended treatment of a philosophy of language, *The Differend*:

> As distinguished from a litigation, a differend would be the case of conflict between (at least) two parties, that cannot be equitably resolved for lack of a rule of judgment applicable to both arguments. One side's legitimacy does not imply the other's lack of legitimacy.
>
> (Lyotard 1988: xi)

The "incommensurability" or "heterogeneity of phrase regimes" (*ibid.*: 128) that Lyotard posits as the fundamental basis of social encounter, is especially congenial with the novel form of Sciascia crime story, for as M.M. Bakhtin has famously put it, the novel is fundamentally "heteroglossic" in that it is constituted as many contending voices that pull against the verbal-ideological center of the nation (Bakhtin 1981).

142 Michael J. Shapiro

Among the most telling discursive encounters in the novel, which articulates the discursive contention it features, is between Captain Belodi and a mafia associate of the alleged mafia head, Don Mariano Arena, who is suspected of soliciting the murder. This local interlocutor challenges Belodi's model of the mafia's role in politics and crime by juxtaposing to the discourse of "justice," as it emerges from centralized state authority, "a sense of justice," as it operates within his Sicilian city:

> The Sicilian that I am and the reasonable man I claim to be rebel against this injustice ... D'you know him [the alleged mafia head]? I do. A good man, an exemplary father, an untiring worker ... Certain men inspire respect: for their qualities, their savoir-faire, their frankness, their flair for cordial relations, for friendship ... "These are heads of the mafia?" Now here's something you don't know: these men, the men whom public opinion calls the heads of the mafia, have one quality in common, a quality I would like to find in every man, one which is enough to redeem anyone in the eyes of God – a sense of justice ... naturally, instinctively ... And it's this sense of justice which makes them inspire respect ...
>
> (Sciascia 2003: 62–63)

When Belodi responds, "That's just the point. The administration of justice is the prerogative of the state; one cannot allow ..." his interlocutor interrupts, "I am speaking of the sense of justice, not the administration of justice ..." (*ibid.*: 63).

To appreciate the local understanding of the "administration of justice" (by Italy's central government-sanctioned crime enforcement agents), against which Belodi's interlocutor is juxtaposing "this sense of justice," we must heed another exemplary encounter, one between Belodi and a quasi professional "informant," Calogero Dibella, nicknamed *Parrinieddu* ("Little Priest ... due to the easy eloquence and hypocrisy he exuded") (*ibid.*: 29). Dibella, who like others in his city is forced to balance mafia demands with those of the crime-fighting establishment, has the typical local perspective on the law:

> To the informer the law was not a rational thing born of reason, but something depending on a man, on the thoughts and the mood of the man here [Belodi] ... To him the law was utterly irrational, created on the spot by those in command ... The informer had never, could never have, believed that the law was definitely codified and the same for all; for him between rich and poor, between wise and ignorant, stood the guardians of the law who only used the strong arm on the poor; the rich they protected and defended.
>
> (Ibid.).

Dibella's view of law enforcement expresses a politics of justice than transcends local structures of feeling. For example, Foucault's broadly applicable, critical perspective on the politics of juridical penalties is wholly in accord with Dibella's sentiments about the differential application of officially sanctioned justice:

Penalty would then appear to be a way of handling illegalities, of laying down the limits of tolerance, of giving free rein to some, of putting pressure on others, of excluding a particular section, of making another useful, or neutralizing certain individuals and of profiting from others, In short, penalty does not simply "check" illegalities; it "differentiates" them, it provides them with a general "economy." And, if one can speak of justice, it is not only because the law itself or the way of applying it serves the interests of a class, it is also because the differential administration of illegalities through the mediation of penalty forms part of the mechanisms of domination.

(Foucault, 1977: 272)

However, although Dibella's perspective represents a politics of justice that transcends the particular encounter, the clash of phrases involved in the conversation between him and Captain Belodi is also framed by the historical forces shaping the novel's aesthetic subjects. Captain Belodi "was by family tradition and personal conviction a republican, a soldier who followed what used to be called 'the career of arms' in a police force, with the dedication of a man who has played his part in a revolution and has seen law created by it" (Sciascia 2003: 30). Given his background and experiences, Belodi's affective connection with justice is one of righteousness; he sees himself as one with a sacred task of safeguarding liberty and justice. In contrast, Dibella's primary affective connection with the law is fear (figured as a "dog inside him" that "bit, growled, and bit again"). And Sciascia renders Dibella as an aesthetic subject with an aesthetic strategy (he is figured as a painter): As an informer by vocation, who must survive by balancing the mafia demand that he "inform" in a duplicitious way that keeps law enforcement from imperiling mafia's power structure and keeps him from being returned to prison (where he had already done time), Dibella is one who must "perform like a painter ... feverishly adding and retouching" creating a canvass that will satisfy the prosecutor, not betray the mafia, and ultimately and most importantly, not destroy its creator (*ibid.*: 28).

Sciascia's Dibella serves to gesture toward historical forces that have shaped the dilemmas of other types, informers among others. Indeed much of the novel's meditation on the problem of culturally and nationally divided senses of justice harks back to the fascist and immediately post-fascist periods. As Dibella, contemplates the problem of an informer, one whose vocation risks death daily, "he thought of other informers buried under a thin layer of soil and dried leaves high in the folds of the Apennines [nearby mountains]. Wretched dregs, soaked in fear and vice; yet they had gambled with death, staking their lives on the razor's edge of a lie between partisans and fascists" (*ibid.*). Here is the historical basis, not only of Sciascia's crime story but of other contemporary ones set in the fraught period of dramatic political change in post fascist Italy.

As the history of the period reveals, the frantic political positioning of informers during the events of political change is of a piece with that of law enforcement types. Carlo Lucarelli, who began as a scholar of the history of the police during the fascist period and ended up as a crime novelist, points to the perils of political choices at the point at which Italy is split in two ...

as the German army occupies that part of the country not yet liberated by the advance of the Anglo-American forces and puts Benito Mussolini in charge of a collaborationist government. This is one of the hardest and most ferocious moments in Italy's history. There is the war stalled on the North Italian front, where there is fierce fighting for a least a year. There is the dread of the Brigate Nere, the Black Brigades, and the formations of the new fascists political police who, together with the German SS, repress sabotage activities and resistance by partisan formations. There is, above all, enormous moral and political confusion that mixes together the desperation of those who know they are losing, the opportunism of those ready to change sides, the guilelessness of those who haven't understood anything, and even the desire for revenge in those who are about to arrive.

(Lucarelli 2006: 10–11)

Lucarelli ultimately found that the best way to capture that moral and political confusion was to focus on a man who had spent "forty years of his life in the Italian police force, during which with every change of government he found himself having to tail, to spy on, and to arrest those who had previously been his bosses." And in response to Lucarelli's query about his seemingly opportunistic political choices, responded, "What does that have to do with it? I'm a policeman." From this historical figure, Lucarelli invented "Comissario De Luca, the protagonist of a trilogy of crime novels; *Carte Blanche, The Damned Season* and *Via Delle Oche.* And as he puts it, "[I] lost myself in his adventures. And I never did write my thesis" (*ibid.*: 11).

The combination of political identity- and regional partitioning, to which Lucarelli's trilogy is addressed, surfaces in Sciascia's *Day of the Owl* as well. For example, it is revealed that the murder victim, Colasberna, had a "criminal record," but that fact is immediately dismissed in a discussion between Belodi and local police functionaries as an irrelevant aspect of his identity, because the "record" was acquired when he was reported for making a contemptuous remark about a patriotic statement during the war by a fascist Blackshirt, who had overheard him (Sciascia 2003: 15). Yet, as it becomes evident through the testimony of other characters in the novel, having a fascist past in Sicily does not attract the level of moral obloquy that it would in other parts of Italy because Sicily was less oppressed under Mussolini. It was "the only region given liberty during the fascist dictatorship, the liberty of safety of life and property" (Scialabba 2003: xi). Ultimately, as the novel shows, in addition to the diverse structures of feeling, it is political history that constitutes much of the basis for regional fault-lines.

It is a fraught history of political change that has yielded diverse political choices during the radical transitions in both centralized and local levels of control and has, as a result, witnessed the emergence of a historically invested identity matrix. Although Belodi's background is republican and partisan, he understands the special circumstances through which some of his interlocutors had embraced fascism. By the end of the novel, despite his disparate political background and the dissension between his legal vocation and the local sense of justice, Belodi finds a small window of consensus with his prime suspect, Don Mariano Arena, the alleged mafia head. As his interrogation of Arena proceeds, Belodi discovers, by dint of a corporeal moment of perception, that they share at least one dimension of a structural of feeling, a trans-regional sentiment about the importance of being a "man."

The novel's final interrogation pits Belodi's intellectual and experiential attachment to justice against a man who has lived a life of violence and has conducted it unapologetically:

> Beyond the pale of morality and law, incapable of pity, an unredeemed mass of human energy and of loneliness, of instinctive, tragic will. As a blind man pictures in his mind, dark and formless, the world outside, so Don Mariano pictured the world of sentiment, legality and normal human relations. What other notion could he have of the world, if around him, the word "right" had always been suffocated by violence and the wind of the world had merely changed the word into a stagnant, putrid reality?
>
> (Sciascia 2003: 102–103)

Although the Belodi–Arena encounter is primarily antagonistic, with accusations coming from the former and denials from then later, a degree of mutual respect arises when Arena, who feels that those who are less than men do not deserve justice, accords the quality of manhood to Belodi. Thus, although Arena's sense of justice is a deterritorializing one, accorded on the basis of character, while Belodi represents a territorialized version, based on the state's codification of justice, their encounter ends with a degree of harmony, for Belodi is pleased to be among those whom Arena calls men. When asked by a journalist to clarify what he, Arena, means when he refers to Belodi as a "man" – does he mean that like all men Belodi is fallible or "whether ... there was an adjective missing," Arena replies, "Adjective be damned! A man doesn't need adjectives ..." (*ibid.*: 115). Ultimately, as is the case with Porumboiu's *Police, Adjective*, Sciascia's *The Day of the Owl* raises onto-political questions about whose experiences, perspectives, and positions can entitle one to make claims about justice, while, at the same time, providing nuanced episodes of linguistic exchange.

Conclusion: "Italy is incredible" (and so is Romania): micropolitics and method

Jacques Rancière poses succinctly, the questions that the two texts I have explored raise about the politics of justice. After stating the obvious, "Politics is the public discussion on matters of justice among speaking people who are able to do it," he adds that there is a vexing "preliminary matter of justice: How do you recognize that the person who is mouthing a voice in front of you is discussing matters of justice rather than expressing his or her private pain?" In the case of *Police, Adjective*, what could have been recognized as a political event, an encounter between incommensurate senses of justice, became a matter of policing. Because he was unable to legitimate his sentiments about the injustice of arresting and prosecuting young hashish smokers within the narrow language of the policing vocation's obligations, Cristi's words were ascribed to the expression of "private pain." He was repositioned from one seeking to be able to speak about justice to one unwilling to carry out his policing obligations correctly.

If the clashes in both Porumboiu's film and Sciascia's novel are to be heeded as realistic encounters articulating the fault-lines in the structures of feeling within both Romania and Italy, a turn to Kantian shared moral sensibility has been impeached because it is evident that such sensibilities exist in a cultural dispersion. Rather than searching for a transcendent model of justice, I have turned to the post Kantian models offered by Lyotard and Rancière, which resonate well with encounters staged in both texts – where Lyotard displaces the Kantian tribunal and shared moral sense with a fight of phrases and Rancière displaces the Kantian aesthetic comprehension, predicated on a *sensus communis*, with a politics of aesthetics based on events of dissensus. Politics for both Lyotard and Rancière is not the exercise of power or authority within territorial assemblages. Rather for both, politics emerges in events of encounter – whenever a differend occurs for Lyotard or whenever an act of subjectification takes place (when those unheard demand that there words be regarded as political statements) for Rancière. However, instead of elaborating the frames that Lyotard and Rancière provide, I want to conclude by dwelling briefly on the problem of method by contrasting my turn to cinema and literature with the more familiar approaches in the social sciences, which turn to attitude surveys.

A remark by Sciascia's Captain Belodi near the end of *The Day of the Owl* inspires my reflections on method. After brooding because he sees his case dissolve when the confessions he extracted are withdrawn, new witnesses invent alibis for the accused, police operatives are reassigned, and the inquiry into the murder is reopened, Belodi remarks that "Sicily is incredible" and adds, "Italy is incredible, too" (Sciascia 2003: 117). Although given Belodi's understandable frustration, the ready-to-hand inference one might make about his remark is that Italy defies normal expectations about the administration of justice. However, I want to interpret the remark differently. I take it to mean that there is no such thing as "Italy," if it is meant to refer to a unitary national culture. What is credible on Sciascia's imaginative yet very realistic account is that there is no unitary ideational, justice-implemented Italy. To assay what Fredric Jameson refers to as "the existence of Italy" is to inquire into the extent to which it achieves a reality, which is necessarily always already mediated (as the complex and paradoxical phrase, "the representation of the real" implies) (Jameson 1992).

The methodological issue I want to pose involves a contrast among alternative methods: the social science attitude investigation, within which psychological subjects are constructed through interviews, with the aesthetic subjects invented and animated in film and literature. As an example of the former, I offer a brief gloss on Robert Putnam's investigation of "civic traditions in Italy, in which he is focused on what he calls "civic engagement." With elaborate interview protocols (applied to seven hundred interviewees – regional councilors," "community leaders," bankers and farm leaders, mayors and journalists, labor leaders and business representatives, as well as voters), Putnam investigates attitudes toward political institutions in a wide variety of Italian cities and regions and offers inferences about the attitudinal and participatory bases of regional democratic institutions (Putnam 1993).

In contrast with Sciascia's novel, the mafia plays no role in Putnam's survey; it is dismissed as an irrelevant criminal organization with no connection to civic life. However, the gaps in types of actors evident in Putnam's investigation are less significant than what his approach effaces more generally. Conceived within typical social science methodological conceits, Putnam refers to the importance of "careful counting," stating that "quantitative techniques" can correct misleading impressions derived from "a single striking case or two" (*ibid*.: 12). Putnam's statistical rendering of civic attitudes, which adds up his subjects to produce a view of the aggregate support for institutions, makes Italy incredible. It effectively negates the ideational fault-lines that become evident when subjects are located within the densities of their regional and city locales and are mobilized into encounters in which they have to defend their positions against alternative perspectives.

Putnam's investigation is thus insensitive to the politics of disparity that Sciascia's novelistic approach, with its mobilized aesthetic subjects reveals. Literature's (and film's) aesthetic subjects cannot be arithmetically assembled because their roles are aimed less at reflecting individual attitudes than at enacting the complex political and cultural cartography within which they strive to manage responsibilities and at manifesting the consequences of encounters with incommensurate perspectives as they strive to flourish, or to merely survive. While Putnam's Italy is incredible, Sciascia's (Belodi's remark to the contrary not withstanding) is credible. And ultimately, while Sciascia's crime story shows the multiplicity of structures of feeling that renders Italian justice as an encounter-ready dispersion by enacting a fight of phrases, Porumboiu's police procedural film achieves a similar account of such a dispersion in a Romanian city by rendering its aesthetic subjects with interrelated image frames, as an exemplary body resists the closural language of policing. As regards a unitary approach to justice, "Romania," like "Italy," is incredible.

References

Agamben, G. (1998) *Homo Sacer: sovereign power and bare life,* trans. D. Heller-Roazen, Palo Alto, CA: Stanford University Press.

Amiel, V. (1998) *Le Corps au Cinema: Keaton, Bresson, Cassavetes,* Paris: Presses Universitaires de France.

Bakhtin, M.M. (1981) 'Discourse and the novel', in *The Dialogic Imagination*, trans. C. Emerson and M. Holquist, Austin: University of Texas Press.

Braudel, F. (1977) *Afterthoughts on Material Civilization and Capitalism*, trans. P.M. Ranum, Baltimore, MD: Johns Hopkins University Press.

Corless, K. (2010) 'Lexicon of the Law: a conversation with Corneliu Porumboiu', *Sight & Sound* 20(10), pp. 40–42.

Deleuze, G. (1997) 'Bartleby; or the formula', in *Essays Critical and Clinical*, trans. D.W. Smith and M.S. Greco, Minneapolis, MN: University of Minnesota Press.

Eagleton, T. (1990) *The Ideology of the Aesthetic*, London: Basil Blackwell.

Engel, D.M. (1990) 'Litigation across space and time: courts, conflict, and social Change', *Law & Society Review* 24(2), pp. 333–344.

Foucault, M. (1973) *The Birth of the Clinic: an archaeology of medical perception*, trans. A. Sheridan Smith, New York: Pantheon.

Foucault, M. (1977) *Discipline and Punish: the birth of the prison*, trans. A. Sheridan Smith, New York: Pantheon.

Foucault, M. (1985) *The Use of Pleasure*, trans. R. Hurley, New York: Pantheon.

Fraser, N. (2010) 'Abnormal justice', on the web at: http://www.law.yale.edu/documents/pdf/Intellectual_Life/ltw_fraser.pdf.

Harshaw, T. (2010) 'Assassinating Americans, killing the constitution?' on the web at: http://opinionator.blogs.nytimes.com/2010/02/05/assassinating-americns-killing—the-constitution/?scp=1&sq=assassinating%20americans&st=cse.

Jameson, F. (1992) 'The existence of Italy', in *Signatures of the Visible*, New York: Routledge.

Kant, I. (2002) *Critique of Practical Reason*, trans. W.S. Pluhar, Indianapolis, IN: Hackett.

Lucarelli, C. (2006) 'Preface', in *Carte Blanche*, trans. M. Reynolds, New York: Europa Editions.

Lyotard, J-F. (1988) *The Differend: phrases in dispute*, trans. G. Van Den Abbeele, Minneapolis, MN: University of Minnesota Press.

Lyotard, J-F. (1989) 'The sign of history', in Benjamin, A. (ed.) *The Lyotard Reader*, New York: Basil Blackwell.

Melville, H. 'Bartleby, the scrivener: a story of wall street', online at: http://www.bartleby.com/129/.

Morrison, T. (1993) 'Nobel lecture', December 7, on the web at: http://nobelprize.org/nobel_prizes/literature/laureates/1993/morrison-lecture.html.

Njals Saga (1992) trans. R. Cook, New York: Penguin.

Panagia, D. (2000) 'Dissenting words: a conversation with Jacques Rancière', *Diacritics* 30, pp. 113–126.

Putnam, R.D. (1993) *Making Democracy Work: civic traditions in modern Italy*, Princeton, NJ: Princeton University Press.

Rancière, J. (2004a) 'Deleuze, Bartleby, and the literary formula', In *The Flesh of Words: The Politics of Writing*, trans. C. Mandell, Palo Alto, CA: Stanford University Press.

Rancière, J. (2005) 'The politics of aesthetics', on the web at: http://theater.kein.org/node/99 (accessed 5/18/2005).

Ruthrof, H. (1992) 'Differend and agonistics: a transcendental argument?' *Philosophy Today* 36(2), 324–335.

Sciascia, L. (2003) *The Day of the Owl*, trans. A. Colquhoun and A. Oliver, New York: New York Review of Books.

Truby, S. (2008) *Exit Architecture: between war and peace*, trans. R. Paynem, Vienna: Stringer-Verlag.

Veyne, P. (1982) 'The inventory of differences', trans. E. Kingdom, *Economy and Society* 11(2), pp. 173–198.

Virno. P. (2004) *A Grammar of the Multitude*, trans. I. Bertolleti, J. Cascaito and A. Casson, New York: Semiotext(e).

Williams, R. (1961) *The Long Revolution*, New York: Columbia University Press.

Williams, R. (1977) *Marxism and Literature*, Oxford, UK: Oxford University Press.

Žižek, S. (2006) 'Kate's choice, or, the materialism of Henry James', in Žižek, S. (ed.) *Lacan: the silent partners*, London: Verso.

9   The other is dead

Mourning, justice, and the politics of burial

Bonnie Honig

In political theory, the problem of the other is usually taken to be the problem of the foreigner, the immigrant, the refugee, perhaps the problem of sexual difference. In response to the problem so conceived, political theorists write books about the ethics and politics of multiculturalism, alien suffrage, the conflicting claims of cosmopolitanism and nationalism, internationalism and democracy, the politics of gender or sexuality in patriarchal societies. These are important, ongoing areas of inquiry.

But what if the other is dead?

That is, how should democratic societies relate to those others who are no longer around to make claims that need to be adjudicated, to those killed in the process of settlement or colonization, to the victims of civil wars, conflicts or genocide? In this essay, I look at two texts that deal with this question, a film and a play written over 2,000 years apart but which speak to each other across that temporal chasm. The film, *Sophie's Choice*, movingly explores the tragic outcome of the divergent pulls of mourning and justice in the aftermath of genocide. The play, *Antigone*, stages a reflection on the politics of mourning and justice, two conflicting political responses to the dead.

In "The Dead Body and Human Rights," historian Thomas Laqueur says there is "a tension" between mourning and justice, "between on the one hand truth for the purposes of remembering [or] communal therapy and medico-juridical truth, which grounds legal or political action." The bodies of the dead can serve either purpose but not both at the same time: "[I]t is not clear that the named bodies of the dead will serve us as both a corpus delecti [enabling justice] … and as the balm of closure" enabling mourning. Indeed, "the rhetoric of memory is manifestly different from the rhetoric of justice; the question is whether the one might serve as a substitute, an excuse, for not pursuing the other" (Laqueur 2002: 92).

Faced with this conflict between mourning and justice, Laqueur searches for a bridge between them: the "bridge between the two functions of the dead body" is "that these are not the bodies of beasts; they did not 'die like dogs' outside of law and culture." But, as Laqueur immediately realizes, this bridge will not support him, for the people in question here precisely did die like dogs. That is the very problem to which Laqueur's essay, which focuses on murders, massacres and genocides, is itself addressed. And so Laqueur corrects himself: "Or rather, they did 'die like dogs' despite the fact that they were human ..." This corrected claim is more accurate but it now fails to provide the sought after bridge. Instead it plunges us right back into the divide Laqueur sought to escape, as becomes clear when he adds: "which is why it is so important subsequently to determine their identities and their histories," so that "the named bodies of the dead" can serve as either "a *corpus delecti*" or "as the balm of closure." But not both. Justice and mourning are again at odds: "The will to prosecute may well be blunted by whatever peace remembering brings."[1] And the peace of remembering may well be disturbed by calls for justice. Neither justice nor mourning alone can offer the dead and those who survive them all they need and deserve. Laqueur does not offer a solution but he captures the problem that divides and unites the protagonists of *Sophie's Choice* and *Antigone*.

In *Sophie's Choice* and *Antigone*, the conflict between mourning and justice is explored by way of characters deprived of the opportunity to bury their dead. Might it be that the apparent incommensurability between mourning and justice explored in these texts is in some way connected to that deprivation? The question seems simple and yet it is also vexed. Recovering the dead enables those who survive them to believe they have passed on; death makes hyper-empiricists of us all. The recovered body enables the survivors to mourn those lost, sometimes to reconcile themselves with those who have done the harm or, other times, call for justice for those responsible.[2] At the same time, however, the focus on the dead named body, whether for purposes of justice or mourning, can be a distraction from, rather than a fulfillment of, ethical or political obligations. This last point is made forcefully by political scientist Thomas Hawley in a recent book about American POW/MIA recovery movements after the Vietnam War. Burial, dealing with the body of the dead, thus seems to trouble or unsettle the familiar opposition between mourning and justice. Before troubling that opposition, however, let us explore its workings in detail, as they are staged in *Sophie's Choice* and *Antigone*.

Sophie's Choice

In the film version of William Styron's *Sophie's Choice*, the fabulous Meryl Streep plays Sophie, a Polish Catholic woman who somehow ends up in Auschwitz and suffers unspeakable horrors. Before Auschwitz, Sophie was a secretary to her law professor father who demeaned and dominated her, a fate to which she re-consigns herself when she marries one of her father's disciples. That she married her father is further suggested in the film by her wedding photo, perched on a shelf behind her pre-war typewriter, in which Sophie stands in her wedding gown between two men and it is unclear which one is her father and which her husband. Both men are killed by the Nazis, but Sophie survives and after the war, in the U.S., Sophie tethers herself to the unpredictable rhythms of life with a schizophrenic, Nathan Landau (played by Kevin Kline), who by turns worships and torments her. In her hailstorm of a life, there is only one moment depicted in the film when Sophie seems to experience an autonomous pleasure. Soon after arriving in the United

States, seated in an English class for immigrants, Sophie is moved by a poem recited at the end of class. The instructor offers it as evidence that the English language is not just torturously difficult but also possessed of great beauty.

> Because I could not stop for Death,
> He kindly stopped for me;
> the carriage held just ourselves
> and Immortality.

Sophie asks a classmate for the name of the poet and jots it down. Then she takes herself to the New York public library and seeks out the book. "Excuse me, sir. Could you tell me what ... Where would be that listing in catalog file ... for ... nineteenth-century American poet ... Emile Dickens, please?" she asks the librarian in accented, broken English. "In the catalog room on the left," the librarian gestures roughly, exhibiting an unmistakable disdain for her, for her foreignness, for her ignorance. "... But you won't find any such listing," he adds, as she turns in the direction just indicated." "Oh, I won't find that listing? Why won't I ... find it?" she asks, her arched brow and her repetition registering an awareness of his disdain and the wherewithal to return his mockery, somehow. "Charles Dickens is an English writer," he sniffs. "There's no American poet by the name of Dickens." "I'm sorry. No," she insists, her eyes again on the scrap of paper where she has jotted down the name: "that is, I'm sure, American poet. Emile Dickens." The librarian explodes, fairly hissing at her, his bigotry or mere impatience palpable in the impropriety of his response (a librarian shouting in the library?): "Listen! I told you! There's no such person. Do you want me to draw you a picture?" And then, as she stutters to calm him and tries to leave his presence: "I'm telling you, you hear me?" Perhaps retraumatized by this reappearance of her father -a disdainful, demeaning, sarcastic, bullying, superior man-Sophie faints and then throws up as her head is cradled in the hands of a handsome stranger who comes to her rescue. It is Nathan, who takes her home, nurses her back to health and romances her with the poetry of Emily Dickinson, a volume of whose work he gives to Sophie as a gift on the night of their first meeting.

The mishap in the library is occasioned by the unimaginability to Sophie and to the librarian of a woman poet. It is not Dickens, after all, but rather-as Nathan rightly discerns-Dickinson that Sophie seeks; not Emile, but Emily. This scene of comic-gothic error in the library is filmed as Dickens would be or, indeed, has been filmed. Like the judge in the 1968 film version of Dickens' *Oliver Twist*, the librarian in *Sophie's Choice* is propped up on a large desk that communicates and enhances his (self-) importance. He is an impatient, pettily powerful male, less brutish than Mr. Bumble but echoing him nonetheless, and powerful only in relation to Sophie, an Oliver, that hapless, weak-bodied orphan, lost and running a fever in a cruel world, but soon to be saved by the kindness of a stranger. Sophie's kind stranger, Nathan, is no Mr. Brownlow; but then Sophie is no Oliver. Hers is a death-driven world, not merely an indifferent or cruel one. Her world is Dickinsonian, rather than Dickensian or, better, it is both. Perhaps that is the point of the film's staging of the confusion of the two names. Their merger unites the indifference and cruelty of Dickens' world with the thanato-eroticism of Dickinson's, and links Dickens's quest for a justice in which each gets his due with Dickinson's quest for proper mourning, in which death is not unwelcome.[3] In the merger as it is enacted here, the redemptions of Dickens and the light grace of Dickinson are lost. Moreover, both Nathan's and Sophie's quests, for Dickensian justice and Dickinsonian mourning, for a good life and a good death, will be for nought.

Whatever else it is, the story of Sophie and Nathan is also about literature and literariness. They meet in the library. On their first night together, Sophie reads to Nathan, at his request, from a Polish translation of Thomas Wolfe and he reads to her from a book of poems by Dickinson. The teller of their story, the film's narrator, Stingo, is an aspiring writer from the South who has moved to Brooklyn to write his first novel. Stingo enters into Nathan and Sophie's ill-fated relationship, and later records it for us. When Nathan welcomes Stingo to their rooming house, he does so by sending him Whitman's *Leaves of Grass*, with a card: "from one of Brooklyn's earliest bards to Brooklyn's newest one" (miming Emerson to Whitman, "I greet you at the beginning of a great career"). Stingo is moved into authorship by Nathan (who disparages and adores him by turns) and Sophie (who mothers and later sleeps with him before returning finally to Nathan). "I wanted to be and hoped or dreamed to be a writer," Stingo says in his narrator's voice at the film's beginning. "But my spirit had remained locked ... unacquainted with love and a stranger to death." These problems will be solved for Stingo by Sophie and Nathan.

The story Stingo had intended to write is about a twelve-year-old boy whose mother dies. (The story is his own, he admits at one point. His mother died "because I did not love her enough," he tells Sophie in a late night confidence. This confession gives the lie to his earlier claim in his narrator voice that he was "a stranger to death." Perhaps he was not acquainted with enough death to inspire writing. If so, Sophie will solve that problem for him, too.) Stingo's planned story of a motherless child (which the film audience never hears, although reams of paper are produced as Stingo types nightly), is replaced by "Sophie's Choice," the story of a childless mother, Sophie, whose two children died in Auschwitz. Subtly, the film suggests, the motherless child, Stingo, is America, willfully innocent, naive, and free of its past. The childless mother, Sophie, is Europe, a place with a past, but one that has no future.

The problem to which literature is here called to respond is that of stuckness in the face of horror or maybe merely of history. In post-World-War-II Brooklyn, Sophie, the European Catholic Holocaust survivor, and Nathan, the bipolar American Jew, cannot move past the war, Sophie because she suffered irreversible trauma in Auschwitz, and Nathan because he is, as Sophie says, "obsessed with the Nazis." The walls of Nathan's room are papered with pictures of Nazis not yet brought to justice. Nathan tortures Sophie with cruel interrogations about what she did to survive the war, when so many Jewish victims died. "Explain something to me," he says miming her Polish accent, "the reason maybe of why you are here

... walking the streets ... wearing this enticing perfumery ... while at Auschwitz, the ghosts of the millions of the dead ... still seek an answer." Sophie does not respond. She moans. The quest for justice in the face of the Holocaust cannot be satisfied. And Nathan is not wrong when he asks, did "the same anti-Semitism ... for which Poland has gained such a worldwide recognition ... did this similar anti-Semitism guide your own destiny, help you along ... protect you in a manner of speaking, so you became one of the miniscule ... handful of people who lived ... while the millions died?"

One might think that Nathan's personal quest to bring the Nazis to justice is a symptom of his madness. He is not in any position to really do this work; he is not a lawyer, not a politician, not a vigilante. But one could just as well infer that the film's point is that he who pursues justice for the Holocaust – or chooses to do so – must be mad or will surely be driven mad by the impossible quest.

Nathan cannot stop talking about the Nazis. But Sophie, like many survivors, cannot bring herself to speak of them at all. Bit by bit over the course of the film, her story comes out, in different iterations, half-truth by half-truth. The details do not matter here. What does matter is that both characters are haunted, one by her proximity to the violence, the other by the guilt (the guilt of American Jews) that comes from having been distant from it. Each suffers survivor guilt, expressed in him through madness, in her through melancholia.

And each loves Emily Dickinson, who provides the film with its leitmotif. The poem Nathan reads to Sophie on their first night together is a burial poem that might also have been (almost) a wedding song:

Ample make this bed
Make this bed with awe;
In it wait till judgment break
Excellent and fair.
Be its mattress straight
Be its pillow round;
Let no sunrise' yellow noise
Interrupt this ground

At the end of the film, when Sophie and Nathan have committed suicide together, Stingo will stand at their bedside, gazing at their bodies coupled in death, and his eyes will fall on the Dickinson volume on a nearby tabletop. He will open the book, and read the same poem, as their eulogy – "Ample make this bed ..." – re-performing the conjoining of marriage and death ritual that scholars have observed is a staple of Greek tragedy.[4]

Stingo then leaves the Brooklyn rooming house and as we watch him walk across the Brooklyn Bridge (referencing Whitman again: "Crossing Brooklyn Ferry") with the sun rising above him, his narrator's voice says:

And so ended my journey of discovery ... in a place as strange as Brooklyn. I let go the rage and sorrow for Sophie and Nathan and for the many others who were but a few … of the butchered and betrayed and martyred children of the Earth. When I could finally see again … I saw the first rays of daylight reflected in the murky river. This was not judgment day, only morning. Morning: excellent and fair.

This, the last line of the film, rewrites Dickinson: "Judgment … excellent and fair" becomes "morning, excellent and fair." Or perhaps, since it is a homonym, and the viewer cannot know, perhaps it becomes "mourning excellent and fair." Either way, or both, mo[u]rning replaces justice and Stingo walks toward a new day.

Taken as mourning, the line suggests Stingo is able to cross the bridge into a new future because he is now acquainted with but not broken by experiences of love and death. He is capable of the work of proper mourning. The eulogy of the poem and the telling of the story of Nathan and Sophie allow Stingo, an emerging writer, to work through the issues that trapped these bearers of justice and melancholy in their insane, impossible, death-driven romance. (Indeed, one critic refers to the novel as Stingo's *bildungsroman*.)[5]

Taken as morning, by contrast, the line suggests that Stingo represents a new world naivete, possibly willful. He lets go. He just moves on, leaving the past and its ruins behind. He has a future. This second reading is supported by the film's intimation, throughout, that Stingo is foreign to this place and its drama. He refers at the film's opening and close to these events as his "voyage of discovery in a place as strange as Brooklyn." To Stingo, Nathan and Sophie are exotics. He has never known people like this before. He is from the South. There is a bucolic home to which he can retreat (he is heir to a farm "south of Virginia" on which he might live), an option unavailable to Sophie and Nathan who are stuck in their historicity. That Stingo is not stuck in his, or does not see himself that way, is made clear when Nathan taunts Stingo, suggesting that because he is a child of the South, he knows something of racial violence or lynching. Stingo takes umbrage at the suggestion. He thinks himself entirely innocent of the charge. His is an American innocence, which is to say that by some force or chance he is positioned (or positions himself) as unimplicated in the racial history of his home, while Sophie is utterly implicated even in America in the European racist past that still destroys her. Indeed, a third reading of the film might play on the pun of mo[u]rning, and ask whether there isn't willful (i.e., American) naivete in the belief that it is possible to elide or overcome the difficulties surveyed here (the stuckness of justice and melancholy, of Dickens and Dickinson) by way of a healthy, proper work of mourning, in this instance, by way of storytelling or literature. As we shall see, Whitman himself gestures toward something beyond the stuckness of justice and mourning, by way of a difficult reconciliation not just with our enemies but also with our own shared condition of mortality. In *Sophie's Choice*, however, even Whitman is inadequate: if there is here a reference to a Whitmanesque openness to a new day, it is a repetition with a dismal difference: here the first rays of daylight are reflected not in the "gladness of the river and the bright flow" by which Whitman says he is "refreshed," but rather in a "murky river."[6]

Sophocles' Antigone

In Greek tragedy, all rivers are murky: no one is innocent, though many are blind to that fact. Everyone is known by the audience to be implicated in a history that precedes them and in a fate that is foretold yet is somehow not determinative. In Sophocles' great play, *Antigone*, Nathan's stuck, raging, impotent commitment to justice (or something like it) is represented by Creon.[7] Sophie's infinite, melancholic mourning (or something like it) is represented by Antigone – though the latter pair is importantly different: Antigone calls for her brother's death to be avenged and curses those responsible.[8] Sophie, perhaps because she feels responsible for her children's fate, does no such thing. (The call for justice or vengeance is made by Nathan and could in fact implicate Sophie.) Other readers of the play see Antigone as staging a struggle between conflicting principles yet to be worked out in the classical setting: between family and city, divine and human law, the bonds of kinship and citizenship, oral and written law, the city's gods and the gods of the underworld, or between authoritarian and democratic rule. But the text opens up to us in new ways when we approach it through the lens of a conflict between justice (Creon's principle of giving each his due as a matter of political and civic responsibility) and mourning (Antigone's principle of lamenting the loss of a life in order to usher the dead along to the next life, where the question of just desserts-a separate issue will be decided by gods, not men).

The play is set in Thebes, in the Bronze Age. With its spatial and temporal distance from fifth-century Athens, Bronze Age Thebes provided a way for Athenians to work through issues that might have been too close to home to be worked out safely in an Athenian setting.[9] The play's distant setting might have allowed Sophocles to broach for public consideration issues that would otherwise be dangerous to consider. It may be for this reason that, as Jean-Pierre Vernant points out, the hero of Greek tragedy is almost always alien and from a distant past.[10]

The play begins in the aftermath of near civil war. The conflict occurs in the wake of the rule of Oedipus who ruled Thebes wisely and well but who also, with his acts of patricide and incest (unintended, unknowing, but still his acts), polluted the polity and brought it to near ruin. As the Greek audience would have known, Oedipus's reign ends with his wife's/mother's suicide and his own exile. Left behind are the four children of his incestuous marriage to Jocasta: Eteocles, Polynices, Antigone, and Ismene. The sons, Eteocles and Polynices both claim the throne after their father leaves. Some versions of the story suggest they agree to rule by turns. Eteocles takes power first but refuses to hand the throne to Polynices when the time comes to do so. Polynices raises an army at Argos and besieges the city to claim what is his. The brothers do battle and each dies by the other's hand.

The play opens with Antigone telling her sister Ismene awful news; Ismene has not yet heard it: their brother Eteocles has been buried with full military honors by Thebes's new leader, their uncle Creon. But Polynices, their other brother, it has been decreed by Creon, is "to be left," as Antigone puts it "unwept, unburied, a lovely treasure for birds that scan the field and feast to their heart's content"

(Sophocles 1982: 35). Creon, Antigone rightly perceives, has "graced one with all the rites and disgraced the other."

In so doing, Creon means to do justice. Although the chorus welcomes Creon as "the new man for the new day" (Sophocles 1982: 174), Creon does not begin anew. He begins by orienting Thebes toward the past, to prepare it for a better future. The city must pass judgment over the events it has witnessed. It cannot turn a blind eye to the fact that one brother besieged the city ("he thirsted to drink his kinsmen's blood and sell the rest to slavery," says Creon of Polynices [Sophocles 1982: 225–226]), while the other sought to defend it. One brother is a friend of Thebes, a patriot, the other an enemy, a traitor (Sophocles 1982: 233; cf. 325). Creon means to stabilize Thebes in the aftermath of the brothers' conflict. To do justice, to give each brother his due, is also to broadcast the regime's determination to prevent the brothers' rift from permeating the regime and giving rise to ongoing sectarian conflicts between Eteocleans and Polyniceans. Thus, Creon promotes one as an honored son and denigrates the other as a traitor. In order to have the clarity that, in his view, a stable regime requires (this one more than most, perhaps, since it suffered from the lack of clarity that Oedipal incest introduced and symbolized), Creon does not inquire too deeply into the rights and wrongs of the situation. Had he done so, he might have found Eteocles in the wrong as well, for refusing to hand power to Polynices as promised. Even so, Creon might have said, we can acknowledge both wrongs while insisting that not all wrongs are equal. Eteocles may have been wrong to usurp power, but that does not rise to the same level of wrong as Polynices' action in attacking Thebes with a foreign army.

Most modern readers of the play consider Creon its villain and Antigone, who takes it upon herself to resist his edict and bury her brother, its heroine (Elshtain, Dietz, Butler, Irigaray, Euben). Most also see Creon as a representative of authoritarian power and Antigone as a democratic actor. But neither character lives up to these labels. Creon's authoritarianism is put in question from the beginning; he issues an important edict but he seems to lack the power to publicize or enforce it: news of it does not reach Ismene, until Antigone tells her about it, and the edict is violated, not once but twice.[11] For her part, Antigone may stand up to authority and so is in some way necessary to democracy, but she is not herself a democratic actor. Rather than mobilize a collectivity and inspire people to join together in common action, she alienates all potential supporters and allies in the course of the play.[12]

To pick either of the main characters as hero is to dilute the play's tragic quality. Tragedy, after all, is the form in which there is no right thing to do because whichever course is chosen, another, equally compelling, is left undone (Hegel 1979; Williams 1994). Besides, things are not so clear when it comes to heroes and villains in this play. Taking into account the brothers' destabilization of Thebes and the recent troubles under Oedipus, the reader may well begin the play with a certain appreciation for Creon's alertness to the politics of friendship and enmity. Rather than being blind to the importance of mourning and burial, Creon is highly aware of the implications of the practice. That is why he seeks to appropriate it for political purposes. He wants mourning to serve the cause of justice and justice to provide Thebes with stability. This is what leads him to prohibit the mourning and burial of Polynices, who after all went too far. Polynices pursued justice too far (*it was his turn*) and slipped into enmity.

In the end, Creon will pursue justice too far as well. He is not unlike Polynices. Creon too is immoderate. Dishonoring the dead is prohibited by conventional rules of warfare, themselves increasingly attenuated in this period and immediately after in the Peloponnesian Wars.[13] Creon seeks justice without measure (an irony, since justice for the Greeks is about measure: giving each his due). Creon slides therefore from being a potentially worthy captain of the "ship of state" into being an irresponsible navigator who will run it aground.[14] That Creon and Polynices share this same flaw is suggested by the fact that they suffer the same or similar fates. The play opens with Polynices who, deprived of burial rites, is unable to move from this world to the next, and it closes with Creon longing for death but stuck among the living, unable to move from this world to the next. The parallels continue. Just as Creon sought to prohibit anyone from clustering at Polynices' altar, so Creon finds at the play's end that no one is left to cluster at his, and it is this isolation that tortures him, though it is fit punishment: as Haemon earlier pointed out, Creon, who at that point would listen to no counsel, would be happiest ruling over a deserted island. Alone and bereft at the end of the play, Creon receives his just desserts. There is irony in this, too, since just desserts is what Creon and Polynices both told themselves they stood for.

Creon becomes, over the course of the play, a tyrant, but that need not be seen as his essence. In the end he learns his lesson, something that cannot be said of Antigone. Antigone mirrors Creon, but imperfectly. She represents the absolute imperative of mourning in opposition to Creon's principle of justice. In the absolutism of the imperative, we see her immoderation. She does not deliberate or equivocate any more than Creon does. Both are sure of themselves; too sure. She stands opposed to Creon's edict, but unlike Creon, she ends where she begins, staunchly supporting her cause. Her character does not change, though her cause does shift subtly. She begins speaking on behalf of the gods of the underworld. The dead must be buried regardless of their deeds in the human world. She ends claiming a particular devotion to her brother, Polynices, son of her mother. No child or husband, she says, could move her to the same self-sacrifice. Antigone's position shifts, perhaps as a result of her clash with Creon which may harden her, perhaps as a result of her disappointment with Ismene, who does not join her cause and offers only later to share her fate. While Antigone begins the play with the passionate declaration that the dead must be buried, and proclaims that all the dead are seen as equal by the gods of the underworld and must be so treated, she ends with a different claim, one that extols the singular importance to her of Polynices, to whom she refers as "son of my mother."[15]

These shifts and ambiguities notwithstanding, in her fundamental devotion to the cause of mourning, perhaps even stuck in melancholic yearning, Antigone does not waiver. Creon, by contrast, represents an absolute principle too, but his character changes: He begins in the voice of a measured lawgiver, then becomes a tyrant, and then learns to regret and tries to undo what he has done. There is no such curvature in Antigone, who dies unrepentant, albeit with some regret for her inability to claim entry into the kinship structure (which she, as a daughter of incest, surely troubles [Steiner, Butler]) by way of marriage and motherhood.

Most commentators comment upon the worth of Antigone's cause-the dead must be buried; the gods of the underworld must not be denied, the oral law must be respected; at the very least, she is said to help illustrate the idea that, as the blind seer Tiresias says later in the play, there must be a balance between human (Creon) and divine (Antigone) law (though Creon claims the gods too, for his side, and Antigone as the daughter and sister of previous kings is also identified to some extent with human law) (Gellrich 1988). That the play calls for balance is clearly right; but this message does not by itself argue only against Creon. Antigone herself seeks not balance but rather fulfillment of her duty to her brother, no matter the cost. The point of the play as a tragedy surely must be that disaster would have followed as well had Antigone had her way, had mourning triumphed over justice. Mourning Polynices would fulfill an obligation, but to grace him with such rites would have left justice (giving each his due) undone. And this is no small matter. Leaving justice undone was the omission of which Oedipus was accused, after all. It is only when Thebes is visited by a plague, after many years of Oedipus' rule, that Oedipus is finally led to open an inquiry into the death of Laius, the king whom Oedipus succeeded. Laius' murderer had never been found, had not even been actively sought, and had never been brought to justice. The plague is a sign: although the Thebans had mourned their king, they had not ever done him justice and, for this failure, Thebes is punished. It is as a result of the ensuing inquiry that Oedipus discovers a series of awful truths: the stranger he killed on the road to Thebes was in fact King Laius. Laius was Oedipus' true father. And Jocasta, the widowed queen whom Oedipus married upon his arrival in Thebes (the prize given to him for liberating Thebes from the terror of the Sphinx by solving her riddle), was none other than his own mother.

In sum, the play cannot be read as siding with either of its protagonists nor with either one's cause or principles. Instead, the play insists on the simultaneous necessity of justice and mourning. The play stages their conflict in a circumstance that renders the two incommensurable: In the context of treason, the two principles – the dead must be mourned; justice must be done – are incommensurable. The dead Polynices is left to die like an animal because he is a traitor. He is not left outside the city, like a true traitor, but rather inside its bounds. He is inside the city but not buried like a true member; rather he is left out to rot and to be fed upon by wildlife. Simon Goldhill points out: "[T]he tensions of the play are emphasized by having Polynices' body left on the land of the city."[16] Indeed. It is Polynices' liminality as both member of and traitor to Thebes that positions him in death as so deeply and troublingly productive of a non-negotiable incommensurability. Thus, the play calls the audience to interrogate the incommensurability that Laqueur reports on, to reflect on the circumstances in which incommensurability is produced, the circumstances in which people die like dogs, and their aftermath.

Burial rites

For some readers, Antigone's inflexible commitment to her cause is a shortcoming, but it is clearly also the source of her great power. Perhaps, however, we should read her inflexibility not as cause but rather as effect. What so many take to be a sign of backbone, or principle – Antigone's inflexibility – may be a sign of melancholic stuckness, an effect of her inability, given Creon's prohibition, to mourn Polynices properly, ritually. What Antigone may point us to, in other words, is not only the importance of mourning, and justice, but also their insufficiency. She may point us beyond that pairing to ritual burial. Burial is named as the second of the pair of acts forbidden by Creon: Recall Antigone says early in the play, that it has been decreed that Polynices must be left "unwept, unburied." Unwept, unburied is the condition as well of Sophie's children, whose mourning is not forbidden by a sovereign ruler but is rather disabled by the circumstances of genocide and by Sophie's own quest for some sort of life after the crime of infanticide in which she is horribly implicated. Both characters, deprived of the rituals of death, are stuck in melancholy and live out a death-identified existence. Neither really belongs among the living. Antigone's name, which means against generation, makes the point, as does her identification with the gods of the underworld. After Auschwitz, Sophie walks the line between life and death. Seduced into the English language by Dickenson's thanato-erotic poetry, Sophie does not care about living; she just does not want Nathan to die alone: "I don't care that I'll die. I'm afraid that he'll die without me" (as her children did).

Alongside the decree of justice and the edict against mourning, next to truth and reconciliation, rights and loss, lies-burial: those rites and rituals by way of which we inter the dead. Inter? The word comes from Middle English meaning, to put into the ground-in *terra*. For the nineteenth-century philosopher, G.W.F. Hegel, however, the function of burial, is not just to inter but also to inter-rupt the processes whereby the interred dead might become merely part of the mere organicism of nature. We, the living, put ourselves in the way, to interrupt the mere decomposition of death. With the word and deed of ritual, we insert ourselves into nature's processes and claim even the dead for the human community. In so doing, we humans take on the role of the gods in Homeric Greece, who were said to have warded off the decomposition and disfigurement of Greek heroes by way of active intervention. As Jean-Pierre Vernant explains, drawing on three episodes reported in the *Iliad* and elsewhere,

> In all three cases, the scenario is about the same. The gods miraculously save the hero from the shame of abuse that – by disfiguring, denaturing his body until it is no longer recognizable as his own, or even as a human body, or even as a body at all – would reduce him to a state of nonbeing. To preserve him as he was, the gods perform the human rituals of cleansing and beautification but use divine unguents: these elixirs of immortality preserve "intact," despite all the abuse, that youth and beauty which can only fade on the body of a living man [because, as this statement implies but does not aver, not only death but

also life itself involves decomposition]. [D]eath in battle fixes forever on the hero's form [his youth and beauty], just as a stele remains erect forever to mark a tomb.

(Vernant 1991: 74)[17]

What was then true for Greek heroes – that they would not be allowed to die like dogs – is true in Hegel's ideal state for all humans, and it generates an obligation to grant to all the right to have rites. We do not let humans die like dogs. (Of course, we ought not to let dogs do so, either.) We, the community, interrupt the decomposition of nature, (if not literally, with embalming, then figuratively with funerary practice), inserting the community into nature's process to mark the end of a life.[18]

The service we provide to the dead when we oblige their right to have rites is always also self-serving. Beth Knox, founder of a non-profit resource center for after-death care alternatives, says that, "During a time of mourning, especially after a sudden, unexpected death, people want to feel useful. But all too often, the expression of condolence – 'Is there anything I can do?' – has no response. In this country [the U.S.], where 99 percent of all deaths are handled by funeral directors, there's rarely anything of substance for friends and family to do. But ... giving people a task picking up the death certificate, buying more dry ice, building the coffin or digging the grave provides a physical way to work through grief" (Picard 2007).[19] Service to the dead provides survivors with the work needed to work through the death. This gives a literal and insightful cast to the current favored expression for grief: working through.

Burial, cremation, tending to the body, the rites of death are, as Antigone must have in some sense known, a way to work through, by working through (with physical labor), the loss of the other and the otherness of loss. If Antigone is stuck in melancholic mourning, that may be not because she is mourning a transgressive relation to her mother or the forbidden feminine (though these suppositions generate sharp readings of the text from Luce Irigaray and Judith Butler).[20] If Antigone is melancholic, stuck in her bereavement, that may be because the work that would allow her to work (physically) through grief is specifically denied to her.

The work of mourning and burial is increasingly the subject of various, sometimes conflicting political struggles in the U.S. and Europe. Some (consumer groups or advocates of green burial, for example) seek to resist the takeover of death rites by funeral homes and state institutions; others call on state institutions to enable death rituals to occur (as when family members demand that the government seek the return of lost soldiers' bodies from the battlefield). As the historian of Ancient Greece, Robert Garland, notes, dying practices have changed over the last one hundred years, from home deaths to hospitals, from death, in "the presence of one's closest kin [clustered] around a death-bed [which was] general in all ranks of society" to mid-twentieth century practices in which "the majority of people die alone in a hospital bed with only medical attendants for company" (Garland 1985: 16–17). Garland also notes that death rites are "the one ceremony in a person's passage through life invariably attended by a minister [and this] indicates that scruples and uncertainties continue to exist regarding death itself." It may. Or it may signal the existence of monopoly power in the death market.

When Garland concludes "I know of no popular reform movement to challenge the church's undisputed authority in this area," he unwittingly issues an invitation for further research. As it turns out, the politics of which he was unaware (in 1985, the year of the first edition of his book) has come into existence, albeit directed more toward the state than the church. Whether for reasons having to do with ignorance, indifference, or the power of the undertakers' lobby, misinformation about burial rites is rife, and some groups have arisen to address the problem. U.S. activists publicize the little known permissibility in most states of burying the dead on private property and keeping the body at home before burial. The Funeral Consumers Alliance warns that state officials routinely give out false information. In Vermont, for example, families are erroneously told that they may not transport their own dead for burial, that caskets are required for burial, (an "unsupported interpretation of Vermont statutes"), and that bodies crossing the Vermont border must be embalmed.[21] The errors regarding caskets and embalming are particularly egregious because they conflict with the religious tenets of Muslims and Jews who often bury their dead in direct contact with the earth and without embalming.[22] Proponents of green burial advocate similar practices for environmental rather than religious reasons.

Focusing on the body and burial can also be a way to avoid political engagement rather than stage it, however. This is the argument made by Thomas Hawley who analyzes the political consequences of demands of U.S. families that Vietnam war casualties, the bodies of their dead or missing family members, U.S soldiers and personnel, be accounted for and returned to the U.S. by the U.S. and Vietnamese governments after 1975. The focus on burial and the victorious retrieval of the body from (previously) enemy soil was, Hawley argues, a displaced way to experience victory in that already lost conflict. Moreover, it enabled the U.S. to avoid confrontation with the political aftermath of that war and its losses.[23] Hawley is right to ask after the effects of the national focus on repatriation, but that focus sometimes leads him to sound like he fails to appreciate the importance of the body to survivors. A political analysis of the nationalist and nationalizing effects of the POW/MIA movement can also at the same time affirm rather than undermine familial demands for the return of loved ones. Or better, such familial demands can be made otherwise.

In the realm of tragedy, Dickens and Dickinson meet in the aftermath of human cruelty, betrayal and genocide; it is the realm in which Sophie and Antigone dwell as living dead, in which Nathan and Creon cry out for justice but no one responds. At its best, mourning-work does not just retrench existing boundaries of self, community, and nation and condemn us to repeat our current traumas, as Hawley suggests is the case with the U.S. focus on repatriation after Vietnam. At its best, mourning-work also points us beyond ourselves. At its best, mourning-work asks us to extend ourselves in a kind of self-overcoming toward an other and toward a future, beyond the divide of nature and culture, the human and non-human, because in burial (as in life) all such distinctions slide and we are left not with the gladness of a new day but with a rather murky river. What lies beyond Stingo's mo[u]rning, beyond Antigone's revenge-seeking love for Polynices as philos, even though he is also an ekhthros to Thebes, beyond Laqueur's incommensurably coupled mourning and justice? Perhaps a different kind of mourning-work, not a working through but rather a loving letting go, such as that imagined by Whitman in "Reconciliation", where the sharedness of death itself, that ultimate other, and the power of the word, work some sort of a magic and draw the living to the dead in the moment of ritual burial. The encounter is intimate. The body here is neither a corpus delecti nor the basis of shared memory. Instead forgetting is invoked and the evanescence of time affirmed. There is here no Antigonean call for vengeance, no declaration of the satisfactions of justice, no triumphalism – just a sense of shared vulnerability and mortality, with a nod to literariness and its abundant powers:

Word over all, beautiful as the sky!
Beautiful that war, and all its deeds of carnage, must in time be utterly lost;
That the hands of the sisters Death and Night, incessantly softly wash again,
    and ever again, this soil'd world:
... For my enemy is dead-a man divine as myself is dead;
I look where he lies, white-faced and still, in the coffin-I draw near;
I bend down, and touch lightly with my lips the white face in the coffin.

Notes

1 The corpus delecti is a witness to the crime that "can be made to speak the truth by providing evidence about how it came to die," a status attributable to a corpse since 1941 and which originates, ironically, in the Nazis' exposure of Russian crimes at Katyn. Thomas Laqueur, 'The Dead Body and Human Rights,' in Scan Sweeney and Ian Hooder, (eds) *The Body* (2002), p. 92.
2 When there is no one left to testify, and even when there is, the speaking body is an important part of the apparatus of human rights protection, prosecution and public mourning. However, the public in question may be far from that to which the dead body might best have spoken, as is clear in the case of Gayatri Spivak's 'Can the Subaltern Speak?' (1988).
3 Upon hearing that Nathan has threatened to kill her and Stingo, Sophie says: "I don't care that I'll die. I'm afraid that he'll die without me" (as her children did). On thanato-eroticism and Greek tragedy, see Taxidou (2004).
4 On the conjoining of wedding and burial rites in Ancient Greece, see Taxidou (2004) and Rush Rehm (1994).
5 See Bertram Wyatt-Brown (2001).
6 In Crossing Brooklyn Ferry, Whitman says, "Just as you are refreshed by the gladness of the river and the bright flow, I was refreshed."
7 Is Creon not impotent? His first act of would-be power is to issue an edict which, though announced is at first not heard by everyone – Ismene is not aware of it until Antigone tells her – and is then grumbled about by the people and is finally disobeyed, not once but twice. Antigone, who melancholically mourns her irreplaceable brother, but calls children replaceable while knowing she will never have any of her own, mirrors Sophie, but also inverts her.

8 On the significance of Antigone's call for vengeance, see my 'Antigone's Laments,
   Creon's Grief: mourning, membership, and the politics of exception' (2009).
9 "Athens and Thebes in myth and tragedy have an interdependent relationship,
   Thebes usually standing in for the other of Athens, for all the things of which the
   democratic state wants to rid itself" (Taxidou 2004: 127). Louis Gernet suggests (in
   Michelle Gellrich's parsing) that tragedy's "orientation toward the social context is
   interrogative and even adversarial, for it holds us in the grip of conflicts that various
   mechanisms of the culture aim to neutralize and dissipate" (Gellrich 1988: 68).
10 I was reminded of this line of Vernant when I attended a talk by Viv Soni at Northwestern
   in January 2007. This paper owes a debt to our conversation after the talk, in which we
   argued for very different readings of the play. Much of my exposition of the play here
   is a continuation of that useful and enjoyable argument.
11 As Butler points out, the fact that Creon's edict is circulated orally (and imperfectly)
   makes it especially hard to sustain the notion that Creon stands for written law and
   Antigone for the unwritten (as Hegel claims).
12 Haemon does speak of the people's support for Antigone (690-700) but Antigone sees
   herself as friendless and alone (876–882, 916–920). Moreover, the death she gets,
   hidden, in a cave, is not the public glorious one she imagines for herself, when she
   says, "I will suffer nothing, So bad as to deny me a death with honor" [114–115].
13 Since violations of these rules were by this time not uncommon (and were soon to
   become even more common, during the Peloponnesian Wars), it may have been
   Sophocles' intent to call attention to this issue as well. On the increasing violation of
   rules of war after the Peloponnesian Wars and the ensuing controversies, see Jill Frank
   (2007).
14 Indeed, as Jill Frank points out in a comment on Nonet's Antigone, Tiresias will later
   say that Creon was a good ruler (Frank 2007: 994). Frank nicely observes that this
   suggests Ismene was not cowardly but astute when, early in the play, she chose to wait
   rather than to challenge Creon's edict. At the beginning of the play, it is not yet clear
   that Creon's edict is unjust, nor that he is a tyrant. He isn't, yet.
15 This phrasing leads some commentators (Irigaray, Butler) to suggest that the real
   object of Antigone's affection is not Polynices, but rather the forbidden feminine, or
   the mother, Jocasta, for whom Antigone yearns and with whom she could only have
   an attenuated relationship (mediated by a male figure, a brother) in this increasingly
   patriarchal society.
16 On this point, see Goldhill (1986: 89, n. 18).
17 Achilles' disfigurement of Hektor is discussed on p. 70, (citing *Iliad* 22, 401–403).
   The idea that decomposition begins in life (with aging) and is a source of anxiety
   (as it obviously is in our culture and as it surely was in Homeric Greece, a fact to
   which Priam, Hektor's father, is all too alert) suggests that in concerns about the
   decomposition of the dead, there may be a certain displacement (and vice versa).
18 Not all cultures seek to interrupt nature's processes in the same way. In Judaism and
   Islam, embalming is forbidden because it slows the processes of decomposition. For
   others, embalming is valued for that very reason, as in ancient Egypt and Homeric
   Greece. Notably, Thebes, the mythic Greek city, had been the capital of Egypt,
   thousands of years earlier, marking a point of contact in mythic and theatrical terms
   for a historical supposition (ventured by Vernant and noted above): that the Greeks
   may well have been familiar with Egyptian practices of embalming. The reference to
   oils and unguents as ingredients of physical restoration in Homer certainly suggests it.
19 Ken Picard's 'Dead Wrong: Are Vermonters getting stiffed on the facts about home
   funerals?' is available at: http://www.seven daysvt.com/features/2OO7/dead-wrong.
   html (accessed 03/18/07). Beth Knox says, "It's amazing the amnesia we have as a
   society. In every room I lecture in there's someone who says, 'We cared for my great
   aunt that way,' or whatever. In two generations, this information has been lost to us."
20 See Butler 2000, and Irigaray 1994.

21 Specifically, Slocum traces misinformation to Vital Statistics Director Richard McCoy and Chief Medical Examiner Stephen Shapiro. Slocum's documentations were in a seven-page letter to Vermont Attorney General William Sorrell and Vermont Commissioner of Health Sharon Moffatt. See Picard (2007).
22 In fact, Vermont law explicitly prohibits such conflicts between state and religious law in matters of burial. The statute reads: "A bylaw or regulation shall not be adopted to restrain a person in the free exercise of his religious sentiments as to the burial of the dead."
23 See Hawley (2005). I was first alerted to this book by an excellent review of it. See Joan Cocks (2007).

References

Butler, J. (2000*) Antigone's Claim: kinship between life & death*, New York: Columbia University Press.
Carlson, L. (1987) *Caring for the Dead: your find act of love*, Hinesburg, VT: Upper Access Books.
Cocks, J. (2007) 'Oh say can you see: looking for creepy-crawlies in American national identity', *Political Theory* 4(35), pp. 215–222.
Cox, R.S. (2005) 'A movement to bring grief back home: many bereaved opting to bypass funeral industry', *The Washington Post*, Sunday, 5 June, p. A01.
Darcangelo, V. (2007) 'Taking care of our own: Beth Knox educates the public on home death-care options', *Boulder Weekly*, available at http://www.boulderweekly.com/archive/110603/buzzlead.html (accessed 03/18/07).
Dickinson, E. (1960) *The Complete Poems of Emily Dickinson*, Johnson, T. (ed.) Boston, MA: Little Brown.
Dietz, M. (1985) 'Citizenship with a feminist face: the problem with maternal Thinking', *Political Theory* 13(1), pp. 19–37.
Elshtain, J.B. (1983) 'Antigone's daughters: reflections on female identity and the state', in Diamond, I. (ed.) *Families, Politics, and Public Policy: a feminist dialogue on women and the state*, New York: Longman.
Elshtain, J.B. (1989) 'Antigone's daughters reconsidered: continuing reflections of women, politics and power", in White, S. (ed.) *Life World and Politics*, South Bend, IN: University of Notre Dame Press.
Euben, P. (1997) *Corrupting Youth: political education, Democratic Culture and Political Theory*, Princeton, NJ: Princeton University Press.
Frank, J. (2007) 'Wages of war: on judgment in Plato's Republic', *Political Theory* 35(4), pp. 443–467.
Frank, J. (2006) '*The Antigone's* law', *Law, Culture, and the Humanities* 2, pp. 336–340.
Garland, R. (1985) *The Greek Way of Death*, London: Duckworth.
Gellrich, M. (1988) *Tragedy and Theory: the problem of conflict since Aristotle*, Princeton, NJ: Princeton University Press.
Gernet, L. (1955) *Droit et Société dans la Grèce Ancienne*, Paris: Recueil Sirey.
Goldhill, S. (1986) *Reading Greek Tragedy*, London–New York: Cambridge University Press.
Hawley, T.M. (2005) *The Remains of War: bodies, politics, and the search for American soldiers unaccounted for in southeast Asia*, Durham, NC: Duke University Press.
Hegel, G.W.F. (1979) *Phenomenology of Spirit*, A.V. Miller, trans. Oxford, UK: Clarendon Press.

Homer (2003) *The Iliad*, London: Penguin.

Honig, B. (2009) 'Antigone's laments, Creon's grief: mourning, membership, and the politics of exception', *Political Theory* 37(1), pp. 5–43.

Irigaray, L. (1985) 'The eternal irony of the community', in *Speculum of the Other Woman*, G.C. Gill, trans., Ithaca, NY: Cornell University Press.

Judith, C. and Morton, F.M.S. (2006) 'State casket sales and restrictions: a pointless undertaking?' NBER Working Paper No. W12012 Available at SSRN: http://ssrn.com/abstract=881246.

Laqueur, T. (2002) 'The dead body and human rights', in Sweeney, S. and Hooder, I. (eds), *The Body*, Cambridge, UK: Cambridge University Press.

Picard, K. (2007) 'Dead wrong: are Vermonters getting stiffed on the facts about home funerals?' in *Seven Days*, 01/31/07, available at: http://www.sevendaysvt.com/features/2007/dead-wrong.html (accessed 03/18/07).

Rehm, R. (1994) *Marriage to Death*, Princeton NJ: Princeton University Press.

Sophie's Choice DVD (1998), directed by Alan J. Pakula, North Vancouver, BC: Lion's Gate.

Sophie's Choice (script), available at: http://www.script-o-rama.com/movie_scripts/s/sophies-choice-script-transcript-streep.html (accessed 03/10/07).

Sophocles (1982) *The Three Theban Plays: Antigone, Oedipus the King and Oedipus at Colonus*, New York: The Viking Press.

Spivak, G. (1988) 'Can the subaltern speak?' in Nelson, C. and Grossberg, L. (eds) *Marxism and Interpretation of Culture*, Urbana, IL: University of Illinois Press.

Steiner, G. (1996) *Antigones: how the Antigone legend has endured in western literature, art, and thought*, New Haven, CT: Yale University Press.

Taxidou, O. (2004) *Tragedy, Modernity and Mourning*, New York: Columbia University Press.

Vernant, J.P. (1991) *Mortals and Immortals: collected essays*, Zeitlin, F.I. (ed.) Princeton NJ: Princeton University Press.

Vernant, J.P. and Vidal-Nacquet, P. (1990) *Myth and Tragedy in Ancient Greece,* New York: Zone Books.

Whitman, W. (1990) *Leaves of Grass*, Oxford, UK: Oxford University Press.

Williams, B. (1994) *Shame and Necessity*, Los Angeles, CA: University of California Press.

Wyatt-Brown, B. (2001) 'William Styron's Sophie's Choice: Poland, the south, and the tragedy of suicide', *The Southern Literary Journal* 34(1), pp. 56–67.

10 The elements of political reconciliation

Ernesto Verdeja

When the war in Bosnia and Herzegovina ended in 1995, the newborn country was in tatters. The conflict had killed tens of thousands of people, destroyed historical landmarks, ravaged cities like Sarajevo and Mostar, and resulted in the violent displacement of civilians through policies of terror and massacre. In the aftermath, the so-called international community, aware that it had failed in intervening to end the bloodshed or protect civilians, became heavily involved in the reconstruction of the country. The ensuing decade and a half has seen a remarkable and often strained attempt at creating a democracy through international fiat. However, the strategies of reconstruction and peacebuilding raise a host of challenging questions about what the future should look like in Bosnia.[1] Given the intensity of the fighting and the massive dislocations and bloodshed, what vision of reconciliation is morally appropriate?

This chapter attempts to sketch the elements of a viable normative theory of political reconciliation, with reference to Bosnia. It seeks to contribute to contemporary political theory debates about how best to conceptualize political reconciliation while taking seriously the obstacles these efforts face. I argue that *reconciliation is best understood as a condition of mutual respect among former enemies, which requires the reciprocal recognition of the moral worth and dignity of others. Political reconciliation is achieved when previous, conflict-era identities no longer operate as the primary cleavages in politics, and thus citizens acquire new identities that cut across those earlier fault lines.* This requires a number of corollary moral goods: an accurate understanding of the past, accountability, victim recognition and the rule of law. As a normative theory, it stipulates certain moral criteria while recognizing that the dynamics of reconciliation work in different ways depending on what levels, or dimensions, of society one is analysing. For instance, the dynamics of reconciliation among political elites are different than those among private individuals, and the political-institutional requirements of legal and juridical reform and economic development differ from the expectations and burdens of reconciliation in civil society. These different social levels draw our attention to the variety of ways in which reconciliatory efforts are manifested and develop.

The chapter proceeds in several steps. Part I briefly sketches events in Bosnia. Part II examines two general approaches to political reconciliation, minimalist and maximalist, and notes some problematic aspects of current formulations. Part III lays out and defends the normative elements of my account of reconciliation, based on moral respect, and Part IV adds further complexity to the theory by identifying various levels at which reconciliation may develop: among elites, institutionally, in civil society, and interpersonally. Part V concludes the chapter. The chapter draws on Bosnia to illustrate these various elements, though it is not meant to serve as a case study on Bosnia.

There are many types of transitions are sufficiently varied that that it is unlikely one can develop a nomothetic theory of reconciliation that would hold for every case. In some instances, such as Timor-Leste, partition may be appropriate where an oppressed group maintains a territorially distinct identity, seeks independence, and has little chance of securing political and economic protections under current conditions (Brilmayer 1991; Lehning 1998). But where political cleavages are not territorially demarcated, some form of acceptable coexistence is necessary. The Bosnian war achieved territorial separation only through massive bloodshed (Burg and Shoup 2000; Gagnon 2005), and even Bosnia today is not ethnically homogeneous. Thus, some form reconciliation is necessary.

Bosnia and Herzegovina

The Yugoslav wars of the early and mid nineties are the culmination of over a decade of economic stagnation, delegitimation of the centralized, Serb dominated central government, and the rise of extremist ethnicist forms of political discourse and identity. The wars of secession were particularly brutal in Bosnia, the most ethnically diverse of the former Yugoslav republics. The Bosnian war was fought between Bosnian Muslims (Bosniaks), Bosnian Croats – both of whom supported independence – and Bosnian Serbs, the latter enjoying support from the Yugoslav Army (dominated by Serbs). Bosniaks and Croats were occasional allies but also fought one another. All sides committed war crimes and crime against humanity, but the majority of violations were committed by Bosnian Serb paramilitary units, which employed 'ethnic cleansing' – mass murder and forcible deportation – to establish an ethnically pure Serb state. More than 100,000 people died, hundreds of thousands of persons were displaced from their homes and tens of thousands of women and girls were raped in the four-year war, which ended with the USA brokered Dayton Accords in 1995.

The Dayton Accords formalized the 1995 military boundaries between the major combatants. Under the Accords, the country became an international protectorate under UN and then EU control, though it maintained some internal autonomy. The country was divided into two entities: the Republika Srpska (RS), composed largely of Bosnian Serbs, and a federation of Bosnia and Herzegovina (FBH), which consists mostly of Bosnian Croats and Bosniaks. The internal boundaries between the entities reflect the military fronts at the end of the war and campaign of 'ethnic cleansing'. The country is still deeply divided and traumatized. In the fifteen years since the war, it has experienced significant periods of tension, and occasionally the danger of returning to war. RS leaders have continued to demand greater autonomy and even independence while protecting major war criminals and resisting federal integration. Secession is nevertheless unlikely and international actors continue to rule through the PIC (Peace Implementation Council), but some small yet important steps toward morally acceptable coexistence have been made. What kind of reconciliation, then, is both practical and morally acceptable?

Paradigms of reconciliation

There is significant disagreement over the definition and utility of the term reconciliation (Kymlicka and Bashir 2008). The numerous accounts include restorative (Philpott 2009; Llewellyn 2006; Kiss 2000; Graybill 2001); psychological (Bar-Tal 2000); religious (Torrance 2006; Burrell 2006; Tutu 1999); liberal and legalist (Osiel 1999; Hampshire 1989); and realist (Bhargava 2001; Dwyer 1999). Here I will focus on two important broad approaches, which I term minimalist and maximalist. These are not formal schools, but rather general understandings of the nature of social relations and solidarity. They have dominated much of the peace studies literature on reconciliation though received only scant attention in academic political theory. For this reason, I introduce them here.

The first identifies some basic, liminal conditions for coexistence rooted on the rule of law and the end of overt violence. The second, maximalist understanding emphasizes strong social solidarity and often mutual healing and forgiveness. While both approaches provide important insights, I believe that neither is satisfactory for deeply divided societies.

Reconciliation as minimalism

Minimalist approaches understand reconciliation as simple coexistence between former enemies, premised on a rejection of violence. Rajeev Bhargava discusses this shift toward 'minimal decency' as including 'negative injunctions against killing, or maiming or ill-treating others, and also a system of basic procedural due process' but no 'particular conception of the good life, including a substantive conception of justice' (2001: 45).

The central challenge is to establish basic norms for negotiation, contestation and decision-making, while suspending broader issues of social redistribution, punishment or explorations of historical memory. Anything more than basic procedural justice is likely to undermine a fragile state. Stuart Hampshire calls for a 'basic level of morality, a bare minimum, which is entirely negative' as the only realistic expectation. Indeed, procedural justice becomes the only means of achieving a tolerable coexistence between erstwhile enemies, 'without any substantive reconciliation between them, and without any common ground' (Hampshire 1989: 68, 72).

Minimalism is sensitive to post-conflict challenges, but leaves a number of issues undertheorized. By basing reconciliation on thin proceduralism, minimalists focus on the demands of the present to the near exclusion of the past.

In Bosnia, this has meant extensive focus on governance mechanisms and ensuring formal representation within the dual-entity federal structure, but also implicitly legitimizing the de facto borders at the end of the civil war (Hoogenboom and Vielle 2010). Given continued hostility and mistrust, the shortcomings of minimalist reconciliation are apparent: calls for thin proceduralism do not address continued impunity, triumphalist narratives, and the trauma of victims. Nor does this proceduralism say much about the substance of political discourse, or how it may contribute (or not) to reconciliation.

Maximalist reconciliation

Maximalist approaches to reconciliation stipulate more extensive requirements for morally acceptable coexistence. Maximalists call on perpetrators to acknowledge responsibility, repent, and ultimately be forgiven by their victims (Volf 2001; Schreiter 1997; Helmick 2008). Archbishop Desmond Tutu, former chairman of the South African Truth and Reconciliation Commission, is perhaps the strongest proponent of this position. Tutu argued that reconciliation required generating compassion and forgiveness among former enemies. 'In the act of forgiveness we are declaring our faith in the future of a relationship … we are saying here is chance to make a new beginning. It is an act of faith that the wrongdoer can change' (1999: 272). Similarly, Rodney Petersen argues that forgiveness establishes the grounds for a shared future among everyone affected by violence. Reconciliation thus becomes 'a restoration or even a transformation toward intended wholeness that comes with transcendent or human grace', 'grounded in a deep ontological understanding of life' (Petersen 2001: 13). This requires a great sacrifice on the part of the perpetrator and the victim: perpetrators must take responsibility for their crimes and repent, critically interrogating their identity and leaving themselves vulnerable to censure and reproach, while victims must move beyond 'insincere and grandiloquent language' of pity toward reimagining their violators 'in the present, not as encumbered in the past or prejudged in the future' (2001: 24; Cobban 2007).

The danger, however, is that the emphasis on transformation through forgiveness may be coercive, even if this is not the intention, a point eloquently made by Brudholm (2008). Certainly, the state cannot dictate forgiveness, and none of these thinkers argues this. But the de facto institutionalization of forgiveness in some truth commissions (such as in South Africa's [Wilson 2001]) or through official apologies provides victims with little opportunity to oppose it and instead demand some form of accountability.

Furthermore, and perhaps more problematically, these formulations of reconciliation risk defending a nominally apolitical understanding of coexistence. Claire Moon argues that maximalist theories, often heavily indebted to theological conceptions of moral renewal and community, rest on a narrative of return to a prelapsarian harmonious condition (Moon 2008: 118). The idea of a return to such condition (embedded in the term *re*-conciliation itself) is problematic not only for the way it understands the past, but also for the expectations it places on the present and future. It risks treating reconciliation as the substantive agreement on moral issues and perspectives, as well as a robust harmony between different groups that tends to smooth over real and legitimate differences – differences that are ineradicable elements of any political order. By underplaying dissension, these approaches face a difficulty in defining the difference between political conflict that may degenerate into violence and forceful political dissent, a basic element of democratic politics. This is partly because these theories fail to describe what post-atrocity politics should look like: they define permissible politics according to the likelihood of further violence, rather than the content of the claims being put forth by actors. But politics is more than the search for consensus or harmony; it also includes a distinctly agonistic element (Honig 1993a; Connolly 2002), and thus must allow for a distinction between legitimate political contestation and repression.

Elements of a theory of reconciliation

Deeply divided societies like Bosnia require a viable theory of reconciliation, one that take seriously the political, social and material challenges these societies face, but also one that is normatively defensible. Here, I argue for reconciliation as mutual respect, which entails reimagining the Other as a bearer of moral worth and dignity, but remaining sceptical of a deeply embracing conception of reconciliation through forgiveness or similarly ontologically transformative faculties. Bosnia, as well as other similar cases, raise the importance and urgency of establishing morally acceptable forms of coexistence which are more than merely the formal conception of proceduralism discussed earlier, which equates reconciliation with the presence of institutionalized rights and formal democratic praxis, but resistant to an apolitical idea of forgiveness. What, then, do we mean by respect?

Reconciliation as mutual respect

Reconciliation requires rejecting mutual estrangement and endorsing a condition of *respect* and tolerance of others, including, crucially, former enemies. *Reconciliation is the achievement of mutual respect across society*. The idea of respect pivots on a particular conception of moral personhood. A healthy identity develops from intersubjective recognition among equals, which includes reciprocal recognition of claims to moral worth and dignity. Dignity is a fundamental property of what it means to be a person, as it points to the value of autonomy that is at the core of a healthy sense of self, and its restoration is particularly important to victims and others who have suffered political abuse and stigmatization and remain mistreated and devalued. A society that seeks to be reconciled must create conditions for the recognition of all citizens as bearers of moral worth and dignity.

Respect is a reciprocal norm: it requires the mutual recognition of moral worth between subjects. Specifically, it assumes that in engaging with others, we have an obligation to give them reasons for our actions and values that could affect them.

We owe them, as moral beings whose dignity we recognize, an account of why we treat them the way we do. In this sense, reason (and justification) is not private, but intersubjective. It is not morally sufficient for me to be satisfied with my own reasons for values or actions that may affect others; it is not sufficient, in other words, to assume that the values we hold are agent-neutral. To respect another is to take seriously her ability to comprehend and judge my reasons and respond to them, but also to expect her to do the same for me. This does *not* mean – and I wish to emphasize this – that we should ultimately reach a consensus on ends or policies, nor does it point to deep solidarity or social harmony, since enacting these goals can be – and often are – deeply coercive. Nor does it assume that we are strictly rational creatures bereft of emotion. We are also emotional beings who experience pain and joy and develop meaningful commitments and relationships with others, and part of giving reasons is a recognition of the importance of these broader, complex relations for a healthy identity. Giving reasons to others, and expecting this from them, is an expression of this respect. One can show this respect while still remaining in agonistic relations with others.

How does mutual respect emerge? What is the primary mechanism for achieving and sustaining this form of political reconciliation? The deliberative democratic literature is useful here, though in a revised form that takes seriously the challenges posed by agonistic democrats. Mainstream deliberative democracy emphasizes the importance of reasoned argumentation and critical openness to persuasion among those actors who could be affected by the outcome of deliberation (Habermas 1996b). Through open-ended, public engagement with one another, myriad social groups form and reform public opinions, justify them in ways that appeal to common interests, subject them to public scrutiny and debate, reframe them, and raise counterarguments. The end result is the generation of so-called 'communicative power' that can influence political elites and the state. In this sense, deliberation is also transformative of participants, as it forces them to reform their positions and adjust their claims according to the criticisms raised by others. With these transformations, participants move toward achieving some degree of consensus on issues of public concern.

This understanding of deliberation is only partially suited to post-conflict societies, however, where deep distrust and antagonism are still evident. Bosnia is instructive here: the establishment of formal procedural democracy has failed to generate anything like rational deliberative discourse, much less a kind of 'constitutional patriotism'. Certainly, elite politics is still deeply sectarian and leaders consistently frame political demands in affective terms that privilege exclusivist ethnic membership. Simultaneously, however, some elites and civil society groups employ affective and emotionally evocative discourses to emphasize the suffering of all civilians during the war, recognizing that any meaningful reckoning with the past will require citizens to empathize with victims and acknowledge the scope of the violence.

We should accept, then, that the theoretical distinction between rational and emotional speech, central to much rationalist deliberative theory (Habermas 1996b) is empirically unsustainable and normatively problematic. The elevation of rationality and demotion of affect misrepresents the nature of deliberation, assumes that emotion contributes nothing of value to discourse, and delegitimizes interlocutors before they can even participate in politics. Following political violence, the demand for rationalist deliberation can serve to silence unpopular or critical claims and may be just as damaging to political life as calls for political forgiveness. In Bosnia this has taken the form of the EU Special Representative's and High Representative's frequent exercise of sovereign power to silence or overrule domestic leaders (Chandler 2000; Batt 2007). Furthermore, the assumption that rational deliberation can result in uncoerced consensus rests on a suspect teleology, particularly problematic where groups are deeply divided and disagree not only about specific interests but also moral orientations, ideologies and historical understandings. With so little in common, robust rational consensus is likely unattainable.

A more modest formulation of deliberation emphasizes the discussion and debate of politically relevant issues without turning to violence or threats of violence. Even securing this liminal state can be exceedingly difficult, as recent experiences of violence and terror may feed demands for vengeance and sow mistrust. In response, Dryzek (2005: 224) usefully identifies three tests that communication should satisfy: first, it should be capable of generating reflection among interlocutors; second, it should be non-coercive; and third, it should be capable of connecting particular experiences to more generalized principles (also see Verdeja 2009: 143–149). Crucially, this requires understanding political identities and claims as open to change through further deliberation and argument. A commitment to open participation and contestation is the scaffolding of this vigorous but peaceful conception of political life, but this conception remains wary of the integrative understanding of politics promoted by advocates of 'forgiveness in politics' or the consensus-seeking thrust of rationalist deliberative democracy.

Reconciliation as respect requires more than a commitment to open deliberation, however. A model of reconciliation that does not address fundamental moral demands and relies only on continued debate as an alternative to violence misses some of the pressing moral challenges transitional societies face. Here, I can only identify briefly the corollary moral norms: truth, accountability, victim recognition and the rule of law.

Societies need a basic understanding of past events to assign responsibility and resist continued impunity. Of course, *truth* alone will not reconcile former enemies. Bosnian survivors who publicly retell their experiences often desire more than merely being heard, though this is important to them; many seek reparations, justice for the guilty, and guarantees that their own rights will be protected in the future. And admittedly, new revelations may re-antagonize former enemies and threaten stability, at least in the short term. Certainly, how to frame the past has been one of the most contentious issues in post-war Bosnia. Most schools in the SR interpret the war as the outcome of Muslim and Croat aggression and separatism, and fail to address at all Serbian incitements to violence or the pervasive denigration of non-Serbs in the months leading up to the war. Bosnian and Croat schools are somewhat better, but even in 'integrated' schools student are divided into classes by ethnicity. Of course, in transitional settings, any historical inquiry is political charged. Making sense of what constitutes a 'fair' appraisal of the past is problematic because of the political and ethical stakes involved and the difficulty of combining a variety of truth claims and experiences claims in a coherent, convincing manner.

The expectation should not be to create a final 'truth', but instead work toward establishing factually informed historical narratives that are rooted in actual identifiable events, but acknowledge the contestability of their subject positions and remain open to change. We need a *critical* history that presents the past as accurately as possible, while also ensuring that the stories of victims are not erased, nor abuses minimized through ideological manipulation of the past to lessen responsibility. It interrogates given truths, and thus begin the admittedly difficult and politically delicate process of reconstructing a past that is not based on denials and self-serving justifications. This is a critical project, which remains sensitive to its own assumptions and justifications.

Accountability is also of particular importance to reconciliation. In its generic formulation, accountability requires publicly holding someone responsible and punishing him or her for an identifiable wrong. While accountability can take many forms, it has a constitutive element of sanction in it, and implies that victims are bearers of certain moral rights of dignity and worth (thus certain actions are seen as violations of these rights); and second, that perpetrators are also moral actors, to the extent that they are morally responsible for their actions and should thus be held accountable. For Bosnia, the International Criminal Tribunal for the Former Yugoslavia (ICTY) is the most explicit expression of this demand. It is also reflects many of the problems with formal accountability measures: it suffers from problems of selectivity, the creation of a rather rigid historical narrative that must satisfy the evidentiary requirements of a court of law, enormous expense, and the danger of being perceived as little more than victor's justice (Zolo 2009). Indeed, the ICTY as well as other justice mechanisms have in some cases contributed to further animosity between groups.

While all of these issues point to the limits of accountability, its importance should not be dismissed. Accountability is particularly important for ending culture of impunity, a particular problem in Bosnia where several high level perpetrators remain free. It may help promote the rule of law and provides at least some minimal recognition of victims, for it signals the importance of condemning violators while reinforcing values of human rights and dignity. Accountability is thus a crucial element in the larger project of reconciliation.

Survivors of political violence often continue to experience contempt and devaluation well after the conflict has ended. Continued devaluation makes it difficult for moral respect, and thus reconciliation, to develop, since these require that former enemies come to see one another as moral equals. In response, victim recognition efforts are important to recognize the moral status of victims as equals, restoring their sense of moral worth and establishing their legal rights as citizens.

Victim recognition rests on a broadly Hegelian understanding of identity formation based on a dialogical model of interaction. In this reading, recognition is a reciprocal relation whereby subjects see each other as equals entitled to respect. Beings become full individuals through mutual recognition, which emphasizes the essentially intersubjective (or social) nature of identity formation. Much of the recognition literature argues that recognition requires establishing the conditions for full ethical self-realization of the targeted community (Taylor 1994). Among the many criticisms of ethical recognition theories, we should note a tendency to assume that full recognition points to the creation of a harmonious, apolitical society (Schaap 2005: 47–55; also see Benhabib 2002; Fraser and Honneth 2003). Here, I use victim recognition more modestly to refer to establishing the conditions for mutual respect, which presumes continued political disagreement and contestation rather than the transformation of political identities into one common nation or claims of authenticity for subaltern groups. Thus, rather than resuscitating problematic reductive notions of ethnic political identities (Serb, Croat, etc.) as a way of recognizing victims, societies should engage in securing what Fraser and Honneth (2003: 29) calls 'reciprocal recognition and status equality', a goal that is unachievable if victims continue to find themselves excluded, marginalized, devalued and forgotten.

Victim recognition should include both material and symbolic components with the aim of securing status equality. In terms of symbolic recognition, it should emphasize the elimination of cultural views preventing individuals from recognizing each other as fellow citizens, to achieve what has termed the 'intersubjective condition' of parity of participation (Fraser and Honneth 2003: 36). This requires the positive revaluation of 'disrespected identities' and, more generally, cultural diversity, as well as the delegitimation of those social values which worked to justify violence and misrecognition (Fraser and Honneth 2003: 13, 47, 73). In terms of redistribution, it necessitates addressing economic marginalization that prevents individuals from participating as equal citizens, and securing the 'objective condition' of parity of participation. This may include a number of initiatives, such as monetary compensation and reparation for abuse, psychological and medical support, and increased development programs in places targeted by the violence (Verdeja 2008). The ultimate goal is to restore victims' dignity and self worth so that they may participate fully in social, economic and political life, and do so in a way that is morally sensitive to their experiences. Without both material and symbolic strategies to correct past injustices, such a goal will remain unrealized. Achieving this will require both symbolic and material (redistributive) claims of justice. I use the terms 'victim recognition' in this broader sense of status parity that includes both symbolic and material components.[2]

Victim recognition is a crucial element of reconciliation. Whereas a commitment to truth-seeking and accountability both have an impact on victims, a special focus needs to be given to individuals who suffered massive wrongs, not only as a way of reintegrating them into society as fellow citizens, but also as a means of recognizing their worth and dignity as fellow humans; that is, as a way of according them moral respect.

A final normative component of reconciliation as respect is the *rule of law*. The rule of law means more than the adoption of cogent general rules that constrain the actions of the state and establish minimum legal protections for the citizenry; it also means redrawing and reconstituting the boundaries of politics, which requires identifying some basic normative principles emphasizing that political differences will not be resolved violently. Rather, political contestation will remain bound within formal and informal spheres of deliberation, negotiation and contestation. To the extent that the rule of law is a normative concept, it also directly engages with the constitution of the political realm (Schaap 2005; Veitch 2007). How should we understand politics in a post-conflict scenario? What are the limits of political contestation, the normatively acceptable boundaries between non-violent politics and violent coercion? I have already discussed the importance of theorizing political reconciliation as open to contestation, argument and difference, rather than privileging notions based deep solidarity or 'apolitical' forgiveness. The rule of law is at least partly concerned with constituting and formalizing the boundaries of politics, though the boundaries are always contested, especially in transitional contexts (see Muldoon and Schaap, Chapter 11, this volume).

Disaggregating the model

Reconciliation as respect requires further disaggregation, however. While the concept of respect provides a normative point of evaluation for various processes and strategies of socio-ethical reconstruction, reconciliation does not develop uniformly across social space. Rather, it is more accurately understood as a multilevel process, characterized by specific logics and strategies operating at four (theoretically distinct) levels: political society, institutional, civil society and interpersonal. Curiously, much of the current reconciliation literature fails to ground actors, strategies and social processes in their relevant social and political contexts, thus providing a rather abstract and underspecified account of how reconciliation develops (Thomas 2009; Frayling 2009). A more viable approach distinguishes between these various levels to identify how different strategies and dynamics develop. *Political society* is the domain of political elites who control the state as well as major actors outside of government who represent defined social groups or sectors. It also includes formal politics, such as party politics, and serves as an important arena for presenting and shaping official accounts of the past. The transitional context, whether it was negotiated or imposed through military victory, is a constraint on how political elites pursue reconciliation.

The *institutional* level includes formal institutional mechanisms such as tribunals and truth commissions established to interrogate the past, address responsibility and formally recognize victims. State support separates these types of institutions from civil society efforts at investigating the past and examining responsibility, and also means that they are tied to the production of state legitimacy.

Civil society is a third important level of reconciliatory processes. Civil society actors can contribute to reconciliation by providing more complex and critical interpretations of the past and resisting statist accounts that distort or simplify responsibility. Non-governmental organizations (NGOs) and other groups may also help inform categories of bystanders, victims and perpetrators as well as redefine concepts such as justice, complicity and responsibility. Crucially, civil society is an important domain for deepening deliberative norms and promoting the principle of respect.

Finally, reconciliation occurs *interpersonally*. Individuals deal with the past by interpreting their own experiences as part of public narratives and discourses developed at other levels. Here, issues of accountability and recognition are transformed into concerns over personal responsibility, revenge, forgiveness and quotidian coexistence.

Granted, these various levels are only conceptually distinct: reconciliation across levels rarely develops uniformly, and the heuristic employment of a disaggregative approach is not meant to imply that all social processes can be neatly separated into their specific contexts. Reality is too complex, and actions and their consequences bleed across social space. But adopting a multi-level approach allows us to understand how varying strategies may work together across levels, or occasionally work at cross-purposes; more importantly, it permits us to think more systematically about the promise and limitations of reconciliation, about what we can and should expect from such complex undertakings.

The Bosnian case illustrates how reconciliatory efforts between certain actors, such as amnesties or official apologies among political leaders, may have only a mitigated and highly mediated effect on relations between individual citizens. Serbia recently apologized for the 1995 massacre of 8,000 Bosniak men and boys, but many Bosniaks saw the apology's timing as part of a strategy to facilitate Serbian entry into the EU, rather than expressing sincere remorse for the atrocity (*New York Times* 2010). A major source of popular frustration is Bosnia's dual entity federal structure, which many Bosniaks see as legitimizing the 'ethnic cleansing' campaign of Bosnian Serbs. While the country has become somewhat more institutionally integrated in recent years, the RS still retains significant autonomy. Many Bosnians feel that the political class has failed to promote justice or reconciliation.

Statist institutional responses, including reparations programs and employing official truth commissions to ascertain patterns of abuse and publicly promote reconciliation, may also have a complex and rather ambivalent reception among the population. This is evident in much of the qualitative and quantitative literature on truth commissions (Wilson 2001; Wiebelhaus-Brahm 2009), which finds that individuals only selectively adopt discourses of reconciliation and forgiveness. Trials, too, can be highly contentions and reinforce popular grievances and mistrust through selective prosecutions, evident in Bosnian Serbs' critical perceptions of the ICTY and partly domestic War Crimes Chamber. Both institutions have largely investigated Bosnian Serbs, with less attention paid to violations committed by Bosnian Croats and Bosniaks. Of course, this reflects the war's patterns of violence and responsibility, but dissatisfaction with both courts has meant that institutional efforts at promoting accountability have had only varied impact among individuals of different ethnicities, with few Bosnian Serbs considering them legitimate tools of justice. Although both courts may have had some positive impact on domestic human rights jurisprudence (Burke-White 2007), the upshot is general scepticism among Bosnian Serbs, as well as only tangential interest in the courts among Bosniaks and Bosnian Croats, many of whom see these institutions as removed from their everyday lives (especially the ICTY) (Drumbl 2007; Fletcher and Weinstein 2004).

Civil society also remains an important but contested site for reconciliation. In Bosnia, a number of educational organizations have worked to change school curriculum to be more inclusive (CEPOS 2010), and NGOs frequently provide basic services to civilians who were forcibly displaced during the violence and remain under or unemployed (Sejfija 2006; Vukosavljevic 2008). Other groups continue to press for accountability (Center for Policy Research and Development 2009). Nevertheless, civil society in Bosnia is hardly civil; numerous citizen organizations are essentially apologist groups for radically violent movements, and in many respects civil society remains deeply fragmented, no doubt a result of many regions remaining ethnically unintegrated (Civil Society Promotion Centre 2009).

The complexity of reconciliation is particularly evident, however, at the interpersonal level. Personal wartime experiences may dominate attitudes toward others, regardless of elite or institutional policies. Mahir P., a Bosniak I met in Sarajevo, spoke of how his Muslim family had been violently forced out of Mostar during the war by Croat militia. 'I am furious every day ... I simply hate these people who did this to us, and I doubt I'll ever change' (Verdeja 2009: 165). Others, of course, may be willing to forgive, motivated by personal convictions or a sense of needing to let go of the past. But forgiveness is rarely 'given' in one moment. It does not create a new relationship ex nihilo, but rather emerges partially over time, for new relationships take root through continued and sustained interactions between former enemies working together on common enterprises, slowly learning that they can trust one another. This process of rehumanization is often slow, tenuous and occasionally only partial. Jasmina I., a Bosnian Muslim whose brother and father were killed during the war, told me, 'We need to figure out how to move on. I don't forgive the people who killed my family, but I do understand that Bosnian Serbs are Bosnian, like me. We can't keep demonizing each other. We need to see each others as humans, as individuals' (Verdeja 2009: 175). Jasmina and Mahir's comments capture the ambiguity of interpersonal reconciliation, its tendency to shift between expectations of forgiveness, acceptance of morally acceptable coexistence, and resistance to renouncing a moral right to anger as a form of self-affirmation. In the end, we should remain wary of calls for transformative forgiveness as a matter of policy; while certainly some individuals will forgive, such calls can be read as demands on victims, and 'to coerce in any way a person already harmed or disrespected by a wrong into relinquishing her own need to grieve, reproach and make demands may itself be harmful or disrespectful' (Walker 2006: 179). The idea of respect at the interpersonal level is based on recognizing the moral worth of others, cultivated through practices that promote cooperation among former enemies.

These observations raise a deeper point: a normative theory of reconciliation requires sensitivity to the ways in which reconciliatory efforts develop and resonate at different social levels – political society, institutional, civil society and interpersonal.

Reconciliation develops through the contextually specific behaviour of actors, and thus any theory must retain sensitivity to the particular challenges, actors and logics operating at each level, and how events at one level interact with other levels. Furthermore, and perhaps more importantly, there is no guarantee that these different responses will work together smoothly. As Bosnia illustrates, they may work at cross-purposes with one another and thus undermine the broader aim of reconciliation. Trials may end in acquittals or focus only on certain groups and reactivate demands for private vengeance. Civil society actors may radicalize public opinions and make unachievable demands for justice, while interpersonal relations among former enemies may remain bitter and mistrustful, even as elites call for forgiveness and mutual understanding. Reconciliation, then, does not unfold smoothly across social space, but is instead best theorized as *disjunctured* and *uneven*, and its multivalent character means that formal and institutional responses are insufficient to guarantee its success. Reconciliation as respect also preserves the importance of the political domain by decoupling reconciliation from expectations of transformative forgiveness or non-contestation. This account of reconciliation recognizes the centrality of contestation in political life while providing grounds for normatively acceptable social solidarity.

Conclusion

Establishing whether reconciliation has occurred is, unsurprisingly, quite difficult. Sociological studies, anthropological ethnographies and surveys can offer much needed insights into overall patterns, but here I propose a basic way to assess progress: when conflict-era forms of political identification are no longer the primary ways of determining political loyalty, some success has been achieved. Political violence and the rhetoric surrounding it depend on a strongly binary logic of identity. In-groups use language that constructs a tightly knit community while simultaneously disparaging and dehumanizing out-groups, particularly evident in the case of the Bosnia. It is certainly impossible and undesirable to remove all distinctions and forms of differentiation from political life, since a constitutive element of politics is in fact differentiation. Thus, we can state that mutual respect has been achieved to the extent that previous loyalties (from the period of violence) are mitigated through the development of alternate, overlapping political identities. Thus, the prior in-group/out-group distinctions no longer obtain, or at least are no longer primary. This is not the same as requiring the end of political contestation, but it does mean that the most salient forms of political identity can no longer mobilize the passion and viciousness they once did. This is a sign that former enemies are working together, even if only for their new set of shared interests.

Reconciliation as respect is tied to the other normative concepts outlined in this chapter. A society that values tolerance and espouses peaceful forms of political contestation is unlikely to develop where the past is unexamined or where terrible crimes are justified. An honest and truthful understanding of the past is morally necessary, though this can be painful for victims and unsettling for those who supported the perpetrators. Accountability, too, is necessary, for a culture of impunity and language of superiority and contempt that often accompanies it signal a deep disdain for the rights of individuals. Related to this is the importance of recognizing victims as moral equals and fellow citizens. Without meaningful recognition efforts, they are likely to remain mistreated or ignored, receiving none of the respect and dignity they deserve. And the rule of law plays an important role in guaranteeing that personal rights will be respected, the state will remain bound by law, and that political differences should be resolved peacefully, if still contentiously. All of these normative concerns are important if reconciliation is to mean more than merely the temporary absence of violence where the powers of the past remain able to intimidate and coerce their opponents.

Notes

1   For the remainder of the chapter, I will refer to Bosnia and Herzegovina as Bosnia, the typical form of reference in scholarly, policy and journalistic accounts.
2   I use recognition in the sense of Fraser and Honneth's status parity, but restrict it to transitional societies. General social justice concerns in consolidated democracies require broader theorization, since they are not restricted to the period of conflict.

References

Amstutz, M. (2005) *The Healing of Nations: the promise and limits of political forgiveness*, Lanham, MD: Rowman and Littlefield Publishers.
Bar-Tal, D. (2000) 'From intractable conflict through conflict resolution to reconciliation: psychological analysis', *Political Psychology* 21(2).
Batt, J. (2007) 'Bosnia and Herzegovina: politics as war by other means: challenge to the EU's strategy for the Western Balkans', Institute Note, *Institute for Security Studies*, 19 November.
Benhabib, S. (2002) *The Claims of Culture: equality and diversity in the global era*, Princeton: Princeton University Press.
Bhargava, R. (2001) 'Restoring decency to barbaric societies', in Rotberg, R. and Thompson, D. (eds) *Truth v. Justice: the morality of truth commissions*, Princeton, NJ: Princeton University Press.
Brilmayer, L. (1991) 'Secession and self-determination: a territorial interpretation' Faculty Scholarship Series, paper 2434, online at http://digitalcommons.law.yale.edu/fss_papers/2434
Brudholm, T. (2008) *Resentment's Virtue: Jean Améry and the refusal to forgive*, Philadelphia, PA: Temple University Press.
Burg, S. and Shoup, P. (2000) *The War in Bosnia Herzegovina: ethnic conflict and international intervention*, Armonk, NY: M.E. Sharpe Press.
Burke-White, W. (2007) 'The domestic influence of international tribunals: the International Criminal Tribunal for the Former Yugoslavia and the creation of the state court of Bosnia and Herzegovina', *Columbia Journal of Transnational Law* 46, pp. 279–350.

Burrell, D. (2006) 'Interfaith perspectives on reconciliation', in Philpott, D. (ed.) *The Politics of Past Evil: religion, reconciliation and the dilemmas of transitional justice*, South Bend, IN: University of Notre Dame Press.

Center for Policy Research and Development (2009) 'The status of judicial efforts', available online at www.cpir.net, accessed 20 April 2010.

CEPOS: Center for Policy Studies (2010) 'Youth inclusion and empowerment: legal and institutional analysis', available at www.cepos.org.

Chandler, D. (2000) *Bosnia: faking democracy after Dayton*, London: Pluto Press.

Civil Society Promotion Centre (2009) 'Civil society today' available at www.cpcd.net.

Cobban, H. (2007) *Amnesty after Atrocity?: healing nations after genocide and war crimes*, Boulder, CO: Paradigm Publishers.

Connolly, W. (2002) *Identity/Difference: democratic negotiations of political paradox*, Minneapolis, MN: University of Minnesota.

Drumbl, M. (2007) *Atrocity, Punishment, and International Law*, Cambridge, UK: Cambridge University Press.

Dryzek, J. (2005) 'Deliberative democracy in divided societies', *Political Theory* 33(2), pp. 218–242.

Dwyer, S. (1999) 'Reconciliation for realists', *Ethics and International Affairs* 13, pp. 81–97.

Fletcher, L. and Weinstein, H. (2004) 'A world unto itself? the application of international justice in the Former Yugoslavia', in Stover, E. and Weinstein, H. (eds) *My Neighbor, My Enemy: justice and community in the aftermath of mass atrocity*, Cambridge, UK: Cambridge University Press.

Fraser, N. and Honneth, A.(2003) *Redistribution or Recognition?: a political-philosophical exchange*, London: Verso.

Frayling, N. (2009) 'Toward the healing of history: an exploration of the relationship between pardon and peace', in Quinn, J. (ed.) *Reconciliation(s): transitional justice in postconflict societies*, Montreal: McGill Queen's University Press.

Gagnon, V.P. (2005) *The Myth of Ethnic War: Serbia and Croatia in the 1990s*, Ithaca, NY: Cornell University Press.

Graybill, L. (2001) 'To punish or pardon: a comparison of the International Criminal Tribunal for Rwanda and the South African Truth and Reconciliation Commission', *Human Rights Review* 2(4), pp. 3–18.

Habermas, J. (1996b) *Between Facts and Norms: contributions to a discourse theory of law and democracy*, Cambridge, MA: MIT Press.

Hampshire, S. (1989) *Innocence and Experience*, Cambridge, MA: Harvard University Press.

Helmick, R.C. (2008) 'Seeing the image of God in others: key to the transformation of conflicts', *Human Development* 29(2), pp. 24–29.

Honig, B. (1993a) *Political Theory and the Displacement of Politics*, Ithaca, NY: Cornell University Press.

Hoogenboom, D. and Vielle, S. (2010) 'Rebuilding social fabric in failed states: examining transitional justice in Bosnia', *Human Rights Review* 11, pp. 183–198.

Kiss, E. (2000) 'Moral ambition within and beyond political constraints', in Rotberg, R. and Thompson, D. (eds) *Truth v. Justice: the morality of truth commissions*, Princeton, NJ: Princeton University Press.

Kymlicka, W. and Bashir, B. (eds) (2008) *The Politics of Reconciliation in Multicultural Societies*, Oxford, UK: Oxford University Press.

Lehning, P.B. (eds.) (1998) *Theories of Secession*, London: Routledge.

Llewellyn, J. (2006) 'Restorative justice in transitions and beyond', in Borer, T. (ed.) *Telling the Truths: truth telling and peace building in post-conflict societies*, South Bend, IN: University of Notre Dame.

Moon, C. (2008) *Narrating Political Reconciliation: South Africa's Truth and Reconciliation Commission*, Lanham, MD: Lexington Books.

New York Times (2010) 'Serbia apologizes for Srebrenica massacre', 30 March, p. A5.

Osiel, M. (1999) 'Making public memory, publicly', in Hesse, C. and Post, R. (eds) *Human Rights in Political Transitions*, New York: Zone Books.

Petersen, R. (2001) 'A theology of forgiveness: terminology, rhetoric, and the dialectic of interfaith relationships', in Helmick, R. and Petersen, R. (eds) *Forgiveness and Reconciliation: religion, public policy and conflict transformation*, Philadelphia, PA: Templeton Foundation Press.

Philpott, D. (2009) 'An ethic of political reconciliation', *Ethics and International Affairs* 23(4).

Schaap, A. (2005) *Political Reconciliation*, London: Routledge.

Schreiter, R. (1997) *Reconciliation*, Maryknoll, NY: Orbis Books.

Sejfija, I. (2006) 'From the "civil sector" to civil society?' In Fischer, M. (ed.) *Peacebuilding and Civil Society in Bosnia-Herzegovina*, Munster, Germany: Lit- Verlag.

Taylor, C. (1994) *Multiculturalism: examining the politics of recognition*, Princeton: Princeton University Press.

Thomas, L. (2009) 'Forgiveness as righteousness', in Quinn, J. (ed.) *Reconciliation(s): transitional justice in postconflict societies*, Montreal: McGill Queen's University Press.

Torrance, A. (2006) 'The theological grounds for advocating forgiveness and reconciliation in the sociopolitical realm', in Philpott, D. (ed.) *The Politics of Past Evil: religion, reconciliation and the dilemmas of transitional justice*, Notre Dame, IN: University of Notre Dame Press.

Tutu, D. (1999) *No Future Without Forgiveness*, New York: Doubleday.

Veitch, S. (ed.) (2007) *Law and the Politics of Reconciliation*, London: Ashgate Publishing.

Verdeja, E. (2008) 'A critical theory of reparative justice', *Constellations* 15(2), pp. 208–222.

Verdeja, E. (2009) *Unchopping a Tree: reconciliation in the aftermath of political violence*, Philadelphia, PA: Temple University Press.

Volf, M. (2001) 'Forgiveness, reconciliation, and justice: a Christian contribution to a more peaceful world', in Helmick, R. and Petersen, R. (eds) *Forgiveness and Reconciliation: religion, public policy and conflict transformation*, Philadelphia, PA: Templeton Foundation Press.

Vukosavljevic, N. (2008) 'Training for peacebuilding and conflict transformation: experiences of the Centre for Nonviolent Action in the western Balkans', Berghof Research Centre, available online at http://www.berghof-handbook.net.

Walker, M. (2006) *Moral Repair: reconstructing moral relations after wrongdoing*, Cambridge, UK: Cambridge University Press.

Wiebelhaus-Brahm, E. (2009) *Truth Commissions and Transitional Societies: the impact on human rights and democracy*, London: Routledge.

Wilson, R. (2001) *The Politics of Truth and Reconciliation in South Africa: legitimizing the post-apartheid state*, Cambridge, UK: Cambridge University Press.

Zolo, D. 2009. *Victor's Justice: from Nuremberg to Baghdad*, London: Verso Books.

11 Confounded by recognition

The apology, the High Court and the Aboriginal Embassy in Australia

Paul Muldoon and Andrew Schaap

In postcolonial states reconciliation processes can be understood as attempts to redress historical injustices arising from misrecognition. Reconciliation begins, or rather an appreciation of the need for it arises, with the acknowledgement of the denigration of the identity of Indigenous peoples. It is only when past practices are negatively re-evaluated in light of contemporary norms – norms based upon and a new appreciation of the value of Indigenous culture – that postcolonial states are drawn towards making symbolic and material reparations for historical mistreatment. In this context, reparations serve the dual function of making amends for the past and restoring trust in the institutions of the state. By initiating a process of reconciliation, the postcolonial state undertakes to do whatever can still reasonably be done to restore dignity to the victims of injustice. At the same time, it seeks to restore legitimacy to its own institutions by disavowing the racial or ethnocentric assumptions that led to discrimination in the past. To the extent that these belated acts of recognition help to heal the past away, reconciliation provides a new beginning for the postcolonial state, the true measure of which is the degree of unity evident in the population.

Generally speaking, however, none of this occurs without a bitter struggle. Attempts by identity groups to stake 'claims for recognition' – which, in this case, means recognition as 'victims' of certain hegemonic cultural practices – have tended to spark 'culture wars' in which the extent of the harm, the nature of the wrong and the appropriate mode of redress are all contested. Despite the fact that their telos lies in consensus, reconciliation processes tend to be of an agonistic nature precisely because they open up a space of contestation and disagreement in relation to the claims identity groups make as victims of injustice. Such disagreement is not, of course, inherently problematic. As Duncan Bell has noted, 'the struggle over interpretations of the past comprises a core dimension of agonistic politics' and provides a necessary corrective to unitary conceptions of collective memory (Bell 2008: 151). When questions of reparations are at stake, however, such contestation must eventually give way, even if it is not brought to a close, to a governmental decision (e.g. whether to apologise, pay compensation, recognize land rights). Public processes of reconciliation might thus reasonably be characterised as forms of civic contestation and adjudication in relation to the harms of the past. Positioning itself in the role of mediator, the postcolonial state enacts reconciliation as a way of establishing a consensus about the nature and meaning of Indigenous suffering.

Reconciliation processes can provide productive ways of responding to the ongoing legacy of colonial practices of dispossession and assimilation. Yet, in focusing upon the victim of injustice rather than the agent of injustice, such processes risk entrenching the view of the state as a neutral arbiter and diverting attention from the underlying source of identity-based harms. In line with Patchen Markell's more general critique of the politics of recognition, a potential problem with processes of reconciliation is that the meaning of misrecognition is only examined in relation to those who suffer it, not in relation to those who commit it. This leaves it open to treat misrecognition as an 'unfortunate fact', attributable to outdated belief systems, rather than interrogating its deeper sources in the desire for identity itself (Markell 2003: 21). Put differently, the transformative potential of the politics of reconciliation in postcolonial states might not lie in the recognition and reparation of indigenous suffering (though these are by no means insignificant). Rather it might lie in exposing the deeper sources of misrecognition in the identity-making practices of the colonial state itself. Viewed in a more antagonistic light, claims for the recognition of suffering present a challenge to existing social relations, not because their satisfaction requires the postcolonial state to engage in extraordinary acts of supplication, but because they draw attention to the deeper sources of misrecognition in the desire for sovereign unity.

In this chapter we seek to draw out some of the more agonistic (and antagonistic) dimensions of the demand for recognition by looking at the politics surrounding the two identity-based harms tangled up in the reconciliation debate in Australia: the removal of Aboriginal children from their families and the denial of Aboriginal sovereignty. As it unfolded in the 1990s, the reconciliation process gradually became identified with the tragedy of the 'Stolen Generations' and the poverty of the official response to the findings of *Bringing Them Home*, a report by the Human Rights and Equal Opportunity Commission into the removal of Aboriginal and Torres Strait Islander children from their families. By far the most publicly controversial aspect of the reconciliation process was the charge of genocide levelled in relation to such removals and the call for an official apology that would give due recognition to the suffering inflicted upon Aboriginal people through earlier policies of absorption and assimilation (Goot and Rowse 2007: 141). When the newly elected Rudd government finally delivered the apology in February 2008, therefore, it was officially hailed as the crowning achievement of the reconciliation process. What was largely obscured by the public celebration over this sovereign act of recognition, however, was the underlying cause of this terrible assault upon Aboriginal identity. While the apology provided a measure of recognition (both of the suffering endured by Indigenous people and of the value of their culture), it was marred by an ongoing failure on the part of the Australian state to properly acknowledge what the history of its relations with Indigenous people disclosed about *its* identity.

In principle revelations about the forced removal of Aboriginal children provided a perfect opportunity to focus critical attention upon the identity-making practices of the Australian state: the history of strategic attempts to incorporate the Indigenous peoples of the territory into the Australian nation as citizens. Ironically, however, the apology presumptively addressed Indigenous people as members of the nation, passing over the fact that it was precisely the attempt to turn them into 'fellow Australians' that was responsible for the tragedy of the 'Stolen Generations'. The ambiguity of this situation was heightened even further by Prime Minister Rudd's attempt to put the apology into the service of the very nation-building project to which it provided an implicit critique by declaring it the moment of arrival of a fully unified people. It is this ongoing inability on the part of the Australia state to properly acknowledge the underlying connection between its own pursuit of identity and the damage inflicted upon the identity of others that provides the critical impetus for our examination of the struggle for the recognition of Aboriginal sovereignty. Turning our attention to the High Court case of *Coe v Commonwealth* (1979) and the establishment of the Aboriginal Embassy in Canberra, we highlight the way claims for Aboriginal sovereignty press the Australian state to confront the deeper sources of misrecognition in its own desire for unity and sovereign control. We suggest that the Australian state must acknowledge the failure of identity making before it can do full justice to others.

The recognition of Aboriginal suffering

When newly elected Prime Minister, Kevin Rudd, delivered an apology to the Stolen Generations in 2008, it was widely viewed as an important act of recognition by Aboriginal and non-Aboriginal Australians. Rudd's apology was significant because it provided official acknowledgment of the injustice of child removal and its devastating impact on Aboriginal people. But the Prime Minister also attributed to his own apology a broader historic importance, claiming that it provided a rare moment in the nation's history, which had the potential to transform the identity of the Australian polity and the place of Aboriginal people within it (Rudd 2008: 172).

Rudd's claim about the power of the apology to reconstitute the identity of the polity is supported by recognition theory. Danielle Celermajer (2008: 31), for instance, observes that a political apology can function as an important 'mechanism of recognition'. An apology recognizes the hitherto denigrated identity of the group that has been wronged, reaffirming them as moral and civic equals while preserving the cultural difference that was previously devalued. But it also has the potential to transform the cultural identity of the nation that was complicit in the wrong due to its paradoxical structure. On the one hand, a political apology entails a shameful identification with the perpetrator of a wrong (Celermajer 2008: 26). Yet, on the other hand, in aligning oneself with 'concern for and recognition of the experience of the wronged other' an apology 'bespeaks in the present another identity' that transcends the identity of perpetrator (Celermajer 2008: 20). Indeed, following Levinas, Celermajer sees in political apologies the possibility of an 'ethical' or non-sovereign politics, predicated on the recognition of how our freedom is dependent on others. The 'constitutional shift in identity' that a political apology makes possible 'can only occur through [an identity] being called out of itself, towards the experience of the other, who has previously been excluded from our field of vision or definition of Australian identity' (Celermajer 2008: 26). Central to Celermajer's analysis is the insight elaborated by Charles Taylor (1995), among others, that our own self-understanding may be transformed through a struggle for recognition as we become of aware of the limits of our own cultural horizon by apprehending these from the perspective of the other (see Schaap 2004, 527f.).

While we agree that Rudd's apology provided an important official acknowledgement of the abuse of state power against Aboriginal people, we want to caution against too quickly endorsing Rudd's own rhetoric about its transformative power. As Noel Pearson (2008) observed in *The Australian* at the time of the apology: 'The imperative for the apology was a product of cultural war. If that was not its original intention, then it immediately became a weapon in this war.' Aboriginal people campaigned for over twenty years for an official apology to the Stolen Generations. However, the public debate that dominated the formal reconciliation process often seemed internal to the settler society. If the apology emerged from a struggle for recognition, this was often as not a struggle among non-Aboriginal people about how they should see *themselves* as it was a struggle between Aboriginal and non-Aboriginal Australians over how they see *each other*. The voices of many Aboriginal people, who sought recognition both of the *genocide* perpetrated by the settler society and of the *sovereignty* of Aboriginal and Torres Strait Islander peoples, were often marginalized within the mainstream debate about whether the Prime Minister ought to apologize or not (see Gunstone 2007; Short 2008).

In this context, Rudd's apology might be understood not only as an act *of recognition* of the suffering of Aboriginal people but a demand *for recognition* of the sovereignty of the Australian state and the unity of the people that it presupposes. As Patchen Markell (2003: 30) observes, a state's claim to sovereignty is less often perceived as a demand for recognition than are the claims of subaltern groups. More often, the sovereignty of a state is taken for granted, appearing as a pre-political or extra-political social fact. Indeed, this was evident in both PM Howard's refusal to say sorry and PM Rudd's apology in their invocation of national unity and shared citizenship between Aboriginal and non-Aboriginal people. The sovereignty of the Australian state over Aboriginal people was presupposed rather than acknowledged to be itself dependent on relations of recognition and therefore the potential object of politicization. As Markell also observes, despite the fact that the state can never fully realize the sovereignty it claims, the state commands substantial resources, which are partly due to the stabilized relations of recognition from which it derives its authority. Consequently, the political encounter between a subaltern group and the state is asymmetrical, often allowing the state to 'set the terms of exchanges of recognition, creating incentives for people to frame their claims about justice in ways that abet rather than undermine the project of state sovereignty' (Markell 2003: 30).

What terms of recognition, then, did Rudd's apology afford to Aboriginal people? To address this question we must situate the apology within the context of the reconciliation process that preceded it. The formal reconciliation process (1991–2001) was effectively inaugurated by Labor Prime Minister Keating in an extraordinary speech in 1992. Speaking in Redfern Park, the centre of Sydney's Aboriginal community, Keating (2000: 61) said that reconciliation 'begins with an act of recognition' that 'it was we [non-Aboriginal Australians] who did the dispossessing ... We brought the disasters ... We took the children from their mothers. We practised discrimination and exclusion.' An inquiry into the removal of Aboriginal children from their families was commissioned in 1994 as part of this reconciliation process. Relying extensively on the testimonies of people affected, the report produced by the inquiry described the devastating impact the practice had on Aboriginal individuals, families and communities and found that it amounted to genocide under the UN convention (HEROC 1997; see Orford 2006). Aboriginal people broadly embraced the term 'Stolen Generations' and endorsed the view that the removal of children from Aboriginal communities constituted an act of genocide against them (Behrendt 2001).

By the time the report was tabled in Parliament in 1997, however, there had been a change of government, with conservative John Howard elected as Prime Minister. The Howard government questioned the validity of the report's findings and dismissed most of its recommendations, including the call for an official apology. While governments, churches and police forces throughout Australia issued public apologies in response to the report, PM John Howard (2000: 90) insisted that 'Australians of this generation should not be required to accept guilt and blame for past actions and policies over which they had no control.' Howard objected to what he called a 'black arm band' view of history and a sentimental politics of shame embraced by the Left. Against what he derided as 'symbolic reconciliation' based on principles of reparative justice, Howard proposed 'practical reconciliation' based on principles of distributive justice. Rather than addressing particular historical wrongs, practical reconciliation would ensure that Aboriginal people have an equal opportunity to education, health, housing and employment, like other Australian citizens.

When Howard first articulated these views at a national Reconciliation Convention in 1997, a number of Aboriginal and non-Aboriginal people stood up and turned their backs on him. Incited by PM Howard's refusal to apologise, from 1998 there was a proliferation of unofficial apologies from ordinary Australians. Under pressure to respond to the report, Howard eventually tabled a 'Motion of Reconciliation' in Parliament in 1999. In contrast to Keating's act of recognition in Redfern Park 1992, Howard's Motion of Reconciliation appeared to most Aboriginal people and many non-Aboriginal Australians as a refusal to recognize the suffering of Aboriginal people. Rather than acknowledging the nature of the harm suffered by Aboriginal people through the practice of child removal, Howard offered only a 'generic' expression of regret for 'mistreatment of many indigenous Australians' in the past, during which 'mistakes had been made' (Howard 1999: 9205, 9207). His passing acknowledgment that 'injustices occurred' against

Aboriginal people was overshadowed by his concern about the injustice of judging *past* generations of non-Aboriginal Australians according to today's standards or of expecting *current* generations of non-Aboriginal Australians to be ashamed of events in which they did not participate (Howard 1999: 9207).

When the National Apology to the Stolen Generations was finally delivered by newly-elected Labor Prime Minister Rudd in 2008, it seemed a momentous occasion. Echoing Keating's Redfern Park address, it provided unequivocal acknowledgement of the injustice of child removal and the suffering it caused. Rather than a generic acknowledgment of mistakes made in the past, Rudd sought to recognize the specificity of the harms perpetrated by recounting the story of Nungala Fejo, a Waramungu woman who had been taken from her community in the 1930s. The apology clearly affirmed the moral equality of Aboriginal people in asking non-Aboriginal people to 'imagine for a moment that this happened to you' (Rudd 2008: 170). And the apology recognized the justified resentment of Aboriginal people for the harms perpetrated against them, asking non-Aboriginal people to 'Imagine how hard it would be to forgive' (Rudd 2008: 171). Rather than expecting that Aboriginal people accept the apology, Rudd asked only that 'this apology be received in the spirit in which it is offered as part of the healing of the nation' (Rudd 2008: 167). By recognizing the suffering of Aboriginal people, the apology both justified their feelings of anger and resentment and it provided grounds for relinquishing them (see Muldoon 2009).

What are we to make, then, of the transformative power of the apology as an act of re-cognition? In his analysis of the apology, Michael Fagenblat (2008: 16) concurs with Rudd's self-understanding that the apology entailed an extraordinary act of recognition in which the nation was imagined anew. Following Celermajer, he discusses how this involved a twofold process of identification. On the one hand, it was predicated on a shameful recognition (that transcended the juridical conception of responsibility) of how the identity of the Australian polity was constituted 'by denying and assimilating Aboriginal identity' (Fagenblat 2008: 20–21). This experience of shame arose through the reflexive self-understanding in which non-Aboriginal Australians retrospectively came to perceive their national identity from the moral perspective of Aboriginal people. 'By way of shame,' Fagenblat argues, 'a relationship of recognition, moral respect and the preservation of the otherness or particularity of Indigenous Australians was forged' (Fagenblat 2008: 22). On the other hand, it entailed an extraordinary assertion of sovereignty in the 'mode of contrition' (Fagenblat 2008: 16). The exceptional power of the sovereign was revealed in the act of re-imagining the identity of the people, by invoking a sense of community that transcended the constitutional order in order to reconfigure that order. Implicit in the apology was an enactment of sovereignty in terms of 'kenosis' – a 're-conception of the idea of sovereignty as a mode of radical humility' (Fagenblat 2008: 28). As such the '[a]pology attested to an abasement of the power of the sovereign to transcend the law by an extraordinary recognition of the violence of its own sovereignty' (Fagenblat 2008: 28).

But how deep did this recognition of sovereign violence go? Occluded in Fagenblat's analysis as, indeed, carefully omitted from the apology, is the naming of the wrong perpetrated against Aboriginal people as *genocide*. As Tony Barta (2008: 210) observes, the description of the practice of child removal as genocide provided Aboriginal people with a 'validating truth about their suffering in all the long years when their trauma had no public recognition' (see also Behrendt 2001: 146). The *Bringing Them Home* report supported this perspective, including a carefully researched section which argued that the removal policies amounted to genocide under the Genocide Convention ratified by Australia in 1949. This was the most controversial aspect of the report, which became the primary focus of the culture wars. Consequently, when Rudd came to power seeking to galvanize a consensus of the Australian people behind the apology he omitted any reference to genocide. It is, indeed, unlikely that Rudd's apology would have been 'felicitous' if it had recognized the wrong perpetrated against Aboriginal people as genocide. For its success depended perhaps more on eliciting public sympathy from the non-Aboriginal addressors on whose behalf it was offered than it did on being accepted by its Aboriginal addressees. Yet, in omitting any reference to genocide, Rudd's apology did not countenance the antagonism between the settler society and Aboriginal people on which the colonial state was predicated. In Jacques Rancière's (1999: 115–116) terms, we might say that, in this regard, the apology exemplified a mode of consensus politics that re-presents the political community as a classless society, denying the relations of non-community inherent to the particular form of community that it presupposes.[1] As such, it failed to properly recognize the injustice perpetrated against Aboriginal people as a *political* wrong – that is, how the suffering they experienced was part of a terrible historical event that was legitimized or, at least, excused, for the sake of the common good of the Australian people (Barta 2008: 210).

Rudd framed the apology as an extraordinary act of recognition by appealing to familiar tropes of reconciliation, resolving that: 'the injustice of the past must never, never happen again'; this 'be a new beginning for Australia'; and this should not be a moment of 'mere sentimental reflection' but 'one of those rare moments in which we might just be able to transform the way the nation thinks about itself' (Rudd 2008: 167–171). However, the potential of the apology to transform the terms of recognition between Aboriginal and non-Aboriginal people was diminished by the presupposition of a certain unity of the polity, the shared citizenship of Aboriginal people and of what they have in common (as Australians) with non-Aboriginal people. This is reflected in at least three further limitations of the apology. First, no tribunal was established to administer reparations to those affected. Instead Aboriginal people were left to seek compensation through the courts on a case-by-case basis, like any other citizens. This failure to provide material reparation reflects a failure to recognize that child removal was a general policy, enacted upon a specific minority group and legitimised in the name of the political community. Second, it sidelined the constitutional recognition of Aboriginal rights. If the government was serious about the promise 'never again' it should have made it a priority to enact constitutional amendments to ensure that such discriminatory laws cannot be made in the future rather than leaving this to be considered at an unspecified future time. Third, while important in itself, the policy announced of 'closing the gap' between Aboriginal and non-Aboriginal people (in relation to socio-economic indicators of well-being as health, housing, education, employment) addresses issues of distributive justice within an established body politic. In the absence of attention to how these distributive injustices are related to the historical legacy of colonization and ongoing colonial practices, the state risks reproducing those same practices through a form of rights paternalism (see Muldoon 2009).

In contrast to Celermajer and Fagenblat's account of the transformative power of political apologies, some critics argue that reconciliation in Australia and other settler societies is implicated in the further assimilation of Aboriginal people into the national community (e.g. Povinelli 2002; Motha 2007). As such, reconciliation is implicated in the same identity-making that underpinned the genocidal practice of child removal. Reconciliation is a new form of 'settler nationalism' (Moran 1998), the 'latest phase in the colonial project' (Short 2003), a 'more penetrating stage of occupation' (Gooder and Jacobs 2000: 245). By acknowledging their shame for the wrongs of the past, the settler society demands recognition from Aboriginal people of a newfound postcolonial identity, freed from the weight of the colonial past. In casting conflict between Aboriginal people and the settler society as already internal to the national community, reconciliation and the limited recognition it affords is implicated in the further colonization of Aboriginal people. Indeed, Alex Reilly (forthcoming) argues that while the apology *staged* a chastened, pluralistic sovereignty in its mode of supplication, it actually *perpetuated* the assumption of a monistic *sovereignty* that 'made possible the forced removal of Aboriginal children in the first place.' Reilly (forthcoming) agrees with Fagenblat that a genuine apology requires a certain loss of sovereignty. However, he suggests that Rudd's apology failed to reflect on the limits of the state's own sovereignty since it took for granted that it was within the (legitimate) power of the sovereign to pass those laws that made the practice of child removal lawful.

In failing to recognize the exceptional nature of the genocidal practices through which the state sought to ensure the unity of the Australian polity, Rudd's promise that such practices would 'never again' be perpetrated appeared hollow. Particularly troubling in this context, was the fact that Rudd came to power supporting the Howard government's controversial military and bureaucratic intervention in remote communities in the Northern Territory. The intervention (ongoing at the time of writing), was initiated in mid-2007, ostensibly to rescue Aboriginal children from sexual abuse and domestic violence (see Altman and Hinkson 2007). However, it appeared to be politically motivated as wedge issue prior to a national election and it has also been criticized by the affected communities and their supporters as a land grab (Behrendt 2009b). Among other special measures, it involved the extraordinary suspension of the Racial Discrimination Act, for which Australia has been criticized by the United Nations. The day prior to Rudd's apology saw a large protest at the Aboriginal Embassy in

Canberra against the intervention (Short forthcoming). And speaking against the intervention in Sydney in 2009, Larissa Behrendt (who had broadly welcomed Rudd's apology the previous year) asked: 'What are the words that he is going to use or a government is going to use in twenty years time when they have to apologize to this generation of Aboriginal people for these policies? How are they going to make up for the legacy of what they are doing today?' (Behrendt 2009b). Gary Foley (2008) argues that, in treating Aboriginal people as victims and ignoring their history of struggles for land rights and sovereignty, the apology helped to justify the intervention, which is 'a complete step backwards from Indigenous self-determination'.

Following this line of critique, the demand by Aboriginal people for recognition of the suffering inflicted on them through child removal served only (in Markell's terms) to 'abet rather than undermine' the sovereignty of the (post)colonial state. However, in a survey of public responses by Aboriginal people to the apology, Dirk Moses (2011: 146) finds these were 'overwhelmingly positive.' Overall, public comments by Aboriginal people indicated that they found the recognition of their suffering personally significant and welcomed being recognized as equal citizens of the Australian nation (e.g. Behrendt 2009a; cf. Behrendt 2009b). On this basis, Moses (2011, 146) takes issue with critics of the reconciliation process who presume 'the persistence of colonial domination, irrespective of legal and policy changes, by the tautological and essentialist reasoning that colonialism by definition cannot tolerate Indigenous alterity'. The problem with such radical critiques of reconciliation, he argues, is that they reduce the possibilities for Aboriginal agency to a choice between co-optation or resistance to the colonial state, which fails to account for the complexity of Aboriginal politics and the way in which Aboriginal people negotiate a 'sense of simultaneous national belonging and enduring difference' (Moses 2011, 155). Tim Rowse (2010) similarly takes issue with Damien Short's (2007) account of the reconciliation process in Australia, which he says fails to examine the variety of Aboriginal political actors' engagement with the formal reconciliation process – for instance, as part of the Council for Aboriginal Reconciliation or the Australian and Torres Strait Islander Commission throughout the 1990s. Consequently, Aboriginal political presence registers in Short's account of the politics of reconciliation only as 'thwarted sovereign', their political history reduced to a 'narrative of the settler colonial state's persistently limited concessions to the Indigenous grievance' (Rowse 2010: 72, 80). Moses and Rowse thus take issue with the tendency of critical approaches to reconciliation to reproduce and reinscribe the binary identities of colonizer-colonized even as they aim to overcome them.

Moses (2011: 155–156) suggests that agonistic pluralism provides a framework for conceptualizing the political agency of Aboriginal people outside the resistance/co-option binary, which he thinks prevails in much postcolonial theory. Indigenous agency, he writes, 'entails conflict in a space that constitutes a national political community while recognizing difference' (Moses 2011: 146). There is something in this. It is certainly important to avoid fetishizing either the alterity or the political agency of socially and politically marginalized people. The thematization of social struggle in terms of the ancient concept of the agon was recuperated by some political theorists who were concerned to find an adequate vocabulary in which to understand the praxis of new social movements, which neither emerged from nor could be reduced to the binary of class antagonism. And it has proved fruitful for understanding the ways in which plural identities are constituted through action, how freedom is always exercised within relations of power.

Yet neither should we too easily dismiss the antagonistic moment of struggles for recognition in the name of recognizing complexity or affirming plurality and contingency. Since antagonism is often a starting point for politicization, it is important politically and conceptually in order to understand the conditions of possibility for social transformation (Deranty and Renault 2009; Muldoon and Schaap forthcoming). Indeed, reconciliation often becomes ideological precisely to the extent that it domesticates or elides those antagonistic social relations that are constituted through material relations of power. Politicization depends on contesting the political unity in which the terms of recognition are inscribed, the possibility of making visible a rival image of the common. Rudd's apology may not have effaced Indigenous alterity by further assimilating Aboriginal people into the Australian nation, as a certain meta-political critique of reconciliation suggests. But neither could it redeem its own promise to fundamentally transform the Australian polity through the recognition of Aboriginal suffering as those committed to the ethical turn in political theory hoped. That possibility, we want to suggest, is better afforded by an ongoing and more antagonistic struggle for recognition of Aboriginal sovereignty waged by activists against the Australian state. For it shifts our attention to the identity-making practices of the state itself, its implication as a party to the struggle for recognition and its own history of thwarted sovereignty.

The recognition of Aboriginal sovereignty

It is indicative of the capacity of political initiatives to develop in unanticipated ways that the official reconciliation process should bring genocide forward as a question for the Australian state to address. No retrospective appreciation of the emergent radicalism of the reconciliation movement can, however, escape the fact that it was undertaken in the wake of (yet another) failed bid for Aboriginal sovereignty. When the Commonwealth Parliament voted unanimously to establish the Council of Aboriginal Reconciliation in 1991, it was responding in part to the collapse of a more ambitious proposal for a Treaty that had been a prominent feature of the national political landscape throughout the 1980s. The high point of the Treaty proposal came in June 1988 when Galarrwuy Yunupingu and Wenten Rubuntja presented then Prime Minister Bob Hawke with the Barunga Statement. Among other things, the Barunga Statement called on the Commonwealth Parliament to negotiate 'a Treaty or Compact' with Indigenous peoples recognising their 'prior ownership, continued occupation and sovereignty' (Attwood and Markus 1999: 317). The Prime Minister responded by declaring that '[t]here shall be a treaty negotiated between the Aboriginal people and the Government of Australia. We would expect and hope and work for the conclusion of such a treaty before the end of the life of this Parliament' (cited in Short 2003). In the face of hostile opposition, however, Hawke betrayed his earlier commitment, abandoning the Treaty proposal in favour of a ten-year process of reconciliation. If the creation of the Council for Aboriginal Reconciliation provided a new opening, therefore, it was also a moment of closure. In the face of a radical new possibility of shared sovereignty, reconciliation represented a return to the logic of nation building in which claims for recognition would be procedurally adjudicated in reference to the identity of the Australian state.

The way in which this forecloses on the possibilities of political transformation is perhaps best illustrated by returning to those instances where Aboriginal people have challenged the very terms of recognition by staking a claim to sovereignty. In the long and complex history of Aboriginal assertions of sovereignty, one of the primary sites for this claim-making has been the courts of the Crown. It is here that Indigenous people have challenged the presumption, legally known as the doctrine of *terra nullius*, that there was no *recognisable* legal or political organisation on the continent prior to the arrival of the British settlers and it is here that their aspirations for sovereignty have been repeatedly defeated. One of the most revealing of these challenges was the landmark case of *Coe v Commonwealth* (1979) in which the plaintiff, Paul Coe (a Wiradjuri man who played a central role in the Aboriginal Embassy and the Aboriginal Legal Service) disputed the accepted, legally entrenched, view that Australia was founded as a 'settlement.' In his wide ranging statement of claim Coe made three particularly controversial assertions: first, that '[f]rom time immemorial prior to 1770 the aboriginal nation had enjoyed exclusive sovereignty over the whole of the continent now known as Australia' (121); second, that the British Crown had accordingly acquired the territory by conquest rather than settlement (125); and third, that agents of the Crown had 'unlawfully dispossessed certain of the aboriginal people from their lands' (122). Taken together, these claims amounted to the suggestion that the Australian state was illegitimately founded and had unlawfully dispossessed the Indigenous people of their lands without fair compensation.

Given that the foundation of Australia as a 'settlement' was an established legal precedent dating back to the nineteenth century, it was not surprising that the majority judges took a dim view of Coe's line of reasoning. Though the court left open the possibility that Aboriginal people, *as citizens of the Commonwealth*, might be found to still enjoy certain rights and interests in the land arising from their original occupation, the assertion that Aboriginal people might once have exercised sovereignty was summarily dismissed. In his leading judgment, Gibbs suggested that the statement of claim contained allegations that were 'quite absurd' and had no hesitation in declaring that '[t]he contention that there is in Australia an aboriginal nation exercising sovereignty, even of a limited kind, is quite impossible in law to maintain' (129). Two separate rationales for this conclusion were offered based upon two different interpretations of the nature of the claim. If, suggested Gibbs, the plaintiff had intended to assert the existence of an Aboriginal nation with sovereignty *over the territory* of Australia (territorial sovereignty), the claim had to be denied on the basis that the acquisition of the Australian continent by the British Crown was an 'act of state' that could not be challenged in a municipal court. If, alternatively, the plaintiff had intended to assert the existence of an Aboriginal nation with sovereignty *over its own people* (domestic sovereignty), the claim had to be denied on the basis that Aboriginal people had 'no legislative, executive or judicial organs by which sovereignty might be exercised' (129).

Somewhat ironically, then, Gibbs invokes the very concept of domestic sovereignty used by Marshall CJ in *Cherokee Nation v State of Georgia* (1831) as a way of recognising that the Cherokee, while not sovereign in the territorial sense, still formed a 'distinct political society', only to refuse its application to the Aborigines. What first appears as an anomaly is, however, quickly accounted for by the pronouncement of the court on the matter of Coe's identity. As ultimately becomes evident, the distinction between the two forms of sovereignty – territorial and domestic – is in fact entirely superfluous in this case, because the Court rejects the idea that there is an 'aboriginal nation' in whom sovereignty *of any sort* could be vested. Towards the end of his judgment Gibbs finally raises the question 'whether the appellant has any standing to sue for the relief which he seeks.' 'That involves,' he goes on to add, 'whether there is a body of persons properly described as the aboriginal community and nation of Australia.' Gibbs, tellingly, refuses to endorse such a proposition. If, he suggests, acknowledging his reliance upon 'European standards', the term nation is taken to mean 'a people organised as a separate state or exercising any degree of sovereignty', its use in reference to the kinds of communal organisation evident among the Aborigines is a misnomer. From the perspective of the High Court, in short, the fundamental problem with Coe's claim for sovereignty, whether taken in its territorial or domestic form, is that it is not properly constituted 'as to parties'. Sovereignty, even of a limited kind, emerges as an 'impossible' legal proposition for the simple reason that 'there is no aboriginal nation' (131).

It is tempting, in light of this explicit refusal of recognition, to treat *Coe v Commonwealth* (1979) as a failure. Like other cases in which the question of Aboriginal sovereignty has been raised, however, Coe's case remains politically significant to the extent that it pressed the Australian state to acknowledge itself as a participant in, rather than simply an adjudicator of, the struggle for recognition. By re-asserting the prior claim of the Aboriginal nation to the territory *now known* as Australia, Coe drew attention to a forgotten antagonism, a struggle over the right to act as the sovereign power in which the Crown was not so much an agonist, as a combatant. Viewed as a strategic exercise in historical retrieval, in other words, Coe's case works to disinter the antagonism between the coloniser and the colonised buried under the legal fiction of *terra nullius* and, in that way, to make the political stakes of the colonial enterprise more visible. If nothing else, the act of challenging the established precedent of 'acquisition by settlement' brought to light the hidden dependence of the colonial sovereign upon the recognition of Indigenous people. Indeed Coe's action can be considered effective to the extent that it made visible the demand for recognition that the Australian state makes in all its dealings with Indigenous people – a demand that it (*and it alone*) be recognised as the legitimate sovereign.

Of course, part of what makes this case politically significant is the way in which the attempt to force to the state to acknowledge itself as a participant in the struggle for recognition – a struggle *between potential sovereigns* – is displaced in favour of its preferred image as an arbiter of struggles for recognition *among citizens*. Though Coe may have succeeded, albeit briefly, in making a displaced antagonism visible, his ambitious attempt to renew the struggle over the right to act as the sovereign power was quickly domesticated by the institutional setting in which he pursued his action. Coe's claim effectively fails before it begins since the identity he asserts for himself is incompatible with the terms of recognition available within the institutions of the Australian state. As the judgment of Gibbs makes clear, the only legal personality Coe is permitted to assert in the High Court is that of citizen of the Commonwealth of Australia. No other identity can be granted legal recognition without contradicting the foundations upon which the constitutional order (including its judicial arm) is built. Regardless of its historical merits, in other words, Coe's attempt to bring an action as a representative of a sovereign Aboriginal nation can be summarily dismissed on the grounds of procedural absurdity. His bid for recognition cannot be made intelligible to the court because it contradicts the judgments about identity that are built into the institutional setting – judgments that do not simply precede, but in fact ground, the legal judgment proper. Put simply, Coe's claim is confounded by the identity that the High Court pre-assigns to him as a claimant.

In its own way, then, *Coe v Commonwealth* (1979) illuminates Markell's point that it is not simply marginalised groups who practice the 'politics of recognition.' Though it has become customary to assume that such politics 'is a matter of how much or what kind of recognition *we* – speaking in the voice of universality, for the 'larger society' – ought to extend to *them*,' this characterisation conveniently forgets that 'it takes at least two to struggle' (Markell 2003: 6). As Markell highlights, those who speak in the name of the 'larger society' and its institutions are also practicing a politics of recognition. The only difference is that they are better placed to 'set the terms' under which any exchange of recognition takes place (Markell 2003: 6). Indeed, the mere fact that the state is not ordinarily understood to be engaged in the politics of recognition only serves to underline the institutional advantage it enjoys relative to the marginalised groups whose claims it is entrusted to adjudicate as an independent authority. The surest index of its superior position lies in its capacity to make its own demands for recognition disappear into the background as part of the already given nature of things. In the present context that capacity translates into a presumption on the part of the Australian state to exercise exclusive sovereignty over the territory and peoples of Australia. If there is a political lesson that must be drawn from Coe's case, therefore, it is that Indigenous people need to step outside the procedures of adjudication made available by the state in order to force it to acknowledge certain truths about itself.

Arguably, one of the most historically significant and symbolically evocative attempts to do precisely this took place on 26 January 1972 when four Aboriginal activists (Michael Anderson, Bertie Williams, Billie Cragie and Gary Williams) pitched a beach umbrella on the lawns of Parliament House in the national capital, Canberra, and named it the 'Aboriginal Embassy'. The initial impetus for the protest was a statement issued by Prime Minister McMahon on the previous day in which demands for Aboriginal land rights were rejected in favour of a much weaker (conditional and revocable) form of title called 'general purpose leases'. As Embassy activist Gary Foley (2001: 15) recalls, McMahon's rejection of land rights effectively relegated Aboriginal people to the status of 'aliens in our own land' and so 'as aliens we would have an embassy of our own'. From these humble beginnings the Aboriginal Embassy protest swelled into one of the largest and most significant demonstrations in Australia's history (see Peters-Little 1992; Robinson 1994; Foley 2001; Lothian 2007). As the movement gathered momentum, tents were erected in place of the original umbrella, the recently designed Aboriginal flag was flown, an office tent was established and a letterbox was installed which began receiving international mail. Although the Tent Ambassadors did not initially characterise the protest as a claim for sovereignty, the symbolism of the Embassy clearly implied a right of self-government and this gradually became the understanding of both the government and the protestors alike (Schaap 2009: 212).

If the act of taking political shelter under an umbrella revealed a refined comic sensibility, the naming of the protest as the Aboriginal Embassy also spoke to the tragic failure of the nation-building project in its existing form. Seen simply as the condition into which those best placed to call the country home had been delivered by colonisation (*Ab-origine* meaning literally, from the origin), the title 'alien' might have done little more than invite mournful reflection upon the themes of belonging and disinheritance. As the presentation of the Embassy as a political protest underscored, however, alien was also a symbolically enacted subject position, a conscious act of political self-identification, which served as a disavowal of the 'identity' of the Australian 'people'. When it is understood in this way, the Aboriginal Embassy becomes irreducible to a theatre of victimhood. By electing to describe themselves as aliens, the Ambassadors were not just lamenting their dispossession, but refusing to grant the state the recognition implicit in *its* characterisation of them as citizens. Making symbolic capital out of the oxymoron 'indigenous aliens', they conjoined a primordial right to belong with a political refusal to belong in order to rupture the assumed unity of the people and mark out a dissensus.

Officials at the time were inclined to interpret this refusal of identification as a demand for a separate state and this has been a consistent reflex of state authorities whenever the question of Aboriginal sovereignty is raised (see Schaap 2009: 212–213). The 'break-up' of Australia motif is, however, suspiciously ideological (itself one of the identity-making tools of the state) and frequently wholly insensitive to the actual demands being made by Indigenous people. No doubt the protest movement meant many different things to the Ambassadors and their supporters and it is not our intention (or place) to prescribe a single meaning. Yet, one can justifiably read the symbolism of the Tent Embassy, not as a refusal of inclusion *per se*, but as a refusal to be included in the kind of Australia that disavows its reliance upon the recognition of Indigenous people. For Aboriginal Ambassador Kevin Gilbert, this was one of the most important points to emerge from the struggle for Aboriginal rights. As he would later write, the Australian state 'cannot acquire a legal, valid title except by entering into a legal, binding TREATY of international status with Aboriginal People of this our country' (Gilbert 1995: 52). Understood in these terms, the Tent Embassy protest was not a secessionist movement, but an invitation to the Australian state to acknowledge the contingency of its own identity. By refusing their pre-assigned status as citizens, the Ambassadors were encouraging the Australian state to acknowledge the failure of its desire for sovereign unity and to begin from a different legal and political premise (see Muldoon and Schaap forthcoming).

Perhaps the most marked distinction between the Embassy and the various High Court challenges to the idea of 'acquisition by settlement' lies in its strategic relocation of the source of confusion over identity. As we have already seen, the difficulty faced by Coe in the High Court was that his identity as a claimant was pre-determined by the institutional setting. Put bluntly, the upshot of Gibbs's judgment in *Coe v Commonwealth* (1979) was that 'you' – meaning Paul Coe specifically and Indigenous Australians generally – do not understand who you are. You imagine yourself a member of an Aboriginal nation, but as a claimant in the High Court you are actually a citizen of the Commonwealth. In the case of the Tent Embassy, by contrast, the identity of the claimant does not prefigure the claim, but arises with it. By operating outside the procedural forms of adjudication available through the institutions of the Australian state, the Ambassadors were able to create their own terms of recognition. Theirs is not a plea *for* sovereignty, but a performative assumption *of* sovereignty. Viewed from the new perspective made available by the Tent Embassy, in other words, it is not Aboriginal people, but the colonists who do not understand who they are. The message of the Embassy is twofold: not only have you misnamed 'us' as citizens but that you have misnamed yourselves as sovereigns. Critically these two acts of misrecognition are intimately related: in effect, the Embassy says to the colonist, you do not recognise us *because* you do not recognise yourselves.

Conclusion

The point of this analysis is not to privilege the pursuit of sovereignty over the pursuit of reconciliation as a more 'real' or more 'authentic' expression of Aboriginal politics (as if the struggle against injustice could not be waged on different fronts and in different ways). It is rather to provide a clearer understanding of the possibilities and limits of each as a mode of political contestation. Contrary to those who are inclined to dismiss reconciliation as the latest phase in the colonial project, our analysis acknowledges it as an important mechanism of recognition. The apology to the Stolen Generations, justifiably regarded as the high point of the reconciliation process in Australia, simultaneously recognised Indigenous people as civic equals *in their difference* and undertook to build a new, more inclusive, political community. At no point, however, did the promise of a new beginning allow for critical questioning of the project of identity-making. Despite its self-presentation as an exceptional event, the assertion of sovereign power in the mode of contrition, the apology did not fulfil its ethical potential by identifying the desire for national unity as the source of misrecognition. By attributing the mistreatment of Indigenous people to outdated prejudices, the sovereign avoided implicating its own pursuit of sovereignty in the tragedy of the Stolen Generations and deflected critical scrutiny of the role of the apology in the continuation of that pursuit.

Our analysis follows Markell in assuming that the 'root of injustice is not identity, but the effort to make identity' (Markell 2003: 23). The value we ascribe to the struggle for Aboriginal sovereignty in this chapter derives from the fact that it allows the effort the colonial state makes in the name of identity – establishing it, preserving it, defending it – more clearly visible. Confronted by claims of Aboriginal sovereignty, the colonial state can no longer present its own identity as a given, as something which sits outside the contingency of intersubjective relations. On these occasions it discloses itself (albeit inadvertently and unwillingly) as an active participant in the struggle for recognition, at once dependent upon others for the security of its identity and deeply hostile to the admission of such dependence. The political implications of this are far from insignificant. To learn that the colonial state does not simply hear demands for recognition, but also makes them is to begin to appreciate that it has a strategic interest in misrecognition. Far from being simply the product of outdated belief systems, the misrecognition of others (and all the harms that result from them) is one of the forms taken by the identity-making practices of the state. That some Aboriginal activists chose to resurrect the Aboriginal Embassy in 1992 in protest against the substitution of the Treaty Proposal for Aboriginal Reconciliation speaks volumes about the limited forms of recognition such processes afford. By renewing the claim for sovereignty, these activists helped to expose the interests at stake in treating Indigenous people simply as mistreated citizens.

Notes

1 Rancière (1999: 115–116) writes, 'Consensus thinking conveniently represents what it calls 'exclusion' as the simple relationship between an inside and an outside. But what is at stake under the name of exclusion is not being-outside. It is the mode of division to which an inside and an outside can be joined. The 'exclusion' talked about today is a most determined form of such a partition. It is the very invisibility of the partition, the effacing of any marks that might allow the relationship between community and non-community to be argued about within some political mechanism of subjectification.'

References

Altman, J. and Hinkson, M. (eds) (2007) *Coercive Reconciliation: stabilise, normalise, exit aboriginal Australia*, Melbourne, Australia: Arena Publications.
Attwood B. and Markus A. (eds) (1999) *The Struggle for Aboriginal Rights: a documentary history*, Crows Nest, NSW: Allen & Unwin.

Barta, T. (2008) 'Sorry, and not sorry, in Australia: how the apology to the stolen generations buried a history of genocide', *Journal of Genocide Research* 10(2), pp. 201–214.

Behrendt, L. (2001) 'Genocide: the distance between law and life', *Aboriginal History* 25, pp. 132–147.

(2009a) 'Home: the importance of place to the dispossessed', *South Atlantic Quarterly* 108(1), pp. 71–85.

Behrendt, L. (2009b) 'Stop this intervention', public address in Sydney, 20 June, http://www.youtube.com/thejuicemedia#p/u/6/c1Vw4Qo47Oo.

Bell, D. (2008), 'Agonistic democracy and the politics of memory', *Constellations* 15(1), pp. 148–166.

Celermajer, D. (2008) 'Apology and the possibility of ethical politics', *Journal of Cultural and Religious Theory* 9(1), pp. 14–34.

Deranty, J-P. and Renault, D. (2009) 'Democratic agon: striving for distinction or struggle against domination and injustice', in Schaap, A. (ed.) *Law and Agonistic Politics*. Farnham, UK: Ashgate.

Fagenblat, M. (2008) 'The apology, the secular and the theologico-political', *Dialogue* 27(2), pp. 16–32.

Feltham, O. (2004) 'Singularity happening in politics: the aboriginal tent embassy, Canberra 1972', *Communication and Cognition* 37 (3/4), pp. 225–246.

Foley, G. (2008) 'Duplicity and deceit: Rudd's apology to the stolen generations', *Melbourne Historical Journal* 36, online at: http://www.kooriweb.org/foley/essays/essay_28.html

Foley, G. (2001) 'Black power in Redfern, 1968–1972', The Koori History Website, http://www.kooriweb.org/foley/essays/essay_1.html

Gooder, H. and Jacobs, J.M. (2000) '"On the border of the unsayable": the apology in postcolonizing Australia', *Interventions* 2(2), pp. 229–247.

Goot, M. and Rowse, T. (2007) *Divided Nation? indigenous affairs and the imagined public,* Carlton: Melbourne University Press.

Gunstone, A. (2007) *Unfinished Business: the Australian formal reconciliation process,* North Melbourne: Australian Scholarly Publishing.

Howard, J. (1999) Australian Commonwealth, *Parliamentary Debates*, House of Representatives.

Howard, J. (2000) 'Practical reconciliation' in Grattan, M. (ed.) *Reconciliation: essays in Australian reconciliation*, Melbourne: Bookman Press.

Human Rights and Equal Opportunity Commission (1997) *Bringing Them Home*, Report of the National Inquiry into the Separation of Aboriginal and Torres Strait Islander Children from Their Families, Canberra: Commonwealth of Australia, available at http://www.hreoc.gov.au/social_justice/bth_report/index.html

Keating, P. (2000) 'Redfern park speech', in Grattan, M. (ed.) *Reconciliation: essays in Australian reconciliation*, New York: Bookman Press.

Lothian, K. (2007) 'Moving blackwards: black power and the aboriginal tent embassy', in Macfarlane, I. and Hannah, M. (eds) *Transgressions: critical Australian indigenous histories*, Acton, ACT: ANU E-Press.

Markell, P. (2003) *Bound by Recognition*, Princeton, NJ: Princeton University Press.

Moran, A. (1998) 'Aboriginal reconciliation: transformations in settler nationalism', *Melbourne Journal of Politics* 25, pp. 101–132.

Motha, S. (2007) 'Reconciliation as domination' in Veitch, S. (ed.) *Law and the Politics of Reconciliation*, Farnham: Ashgate.

Moses, D. (2011) 'Official apologies, reconciliation, and settler colonialism: Australian indigenous alterity and political agency', *Citizenship Studies* 15(2), pp. 145–159.

Muldoon, P. (2009) 'Past injustices and future protections: on the politics of promising', *Australian Indigenous Law Review* 13(2), pp. 2–17.

Muldoon, P. and Schaap, A. (forthcoming) 'Aboriginal sovereignty and the politics of reconciliation: the constituent power of the aboriginal embassy in Australia', *Environment and Planning D: Society and Space*.

Orford, A. (2006) 'Commissioning the truth', *Columbia Journal of Gender and Law* 15(3), pp. 851–882.

Pearson, N. (2008) 'When words aren't enough', *The Australian*, 12 February.

Peters-Little, F. (1992) *Tent Embassy*, television documentary written and produced by F. Peters-Little, directed by D Sandy (ABC TV Factual Entertainment, Sydney).

Povinelli, E. (2002) *The Cunning of Recognition: indigenous alterities and the making of Australian multiculturalism* Durham, NC: Duke University Press.

Rancière, J. (1999) *Disagreement: politics and philosophy*, trans. J. Rose. Minneapolis, MN: University of Minnesota Press.

Reilly, A. (forthcoming) 'The sovereign's capacity to apologize' in Evans, J., Genovese, A., Reilly, A. and Wolfe P. (eds) *Sovereignty: frontiers of possibility*, Honolulu, HI: University of Hawai'i Press.

Robinson, S. (1994) 'The aboriginal embassy: an account of the protests of 1972', *Aboriginal History* 18(1), pp. 49–63.

Rudd, K. (2008) 'Apology to Australia's indigenous peoples', Parliament of Australia, House of Representatives, *Parliamentary Debates*, 13 February, pp. 167–177.

Schaap, A. (2004) 'Political reconciliation through a struggle for recognition?', *Social and Legal Studies* 13(4), pp. 523–540.

Schaap, A. (2009) 'The absurd proposition of aboriginal sovereignty' in Schaap, A. (ed.) *Law and Agonistic Politics*, Farnham: Ashgate.

Short, D. (2003) 'Australian "aboriginal" reconciliation: the latest phase in the colonial project', *Citizenship Studies* 7(3), pp. 291–312.

Short, D. (2008) *Reconciliation and Colonial Power: indigenous rights in Australia*, Farnham: Ashgate.

Short, D. (forthcoming) 'Australian reconciliation: when sorry isn't good enough', *Memory Studies*.

Taylor, C. (2005) 'The politics of recognition' in *Philosophical Arguments*, Cambridge, MA: Harvard University Press.

Verdeja, E. (2010) 'Official apologies in the aftermath of political violence', *Metaphilosophy* 41(4), pp. 563–581.

Court cases

Coe v Commonwealth (1979) 24 ALR 118

Cherokee Nation v State of Georgia (1831) 30 U.S 1

Select bibliography

Adorno, T. (1986) 'What does coming to terms with the past mean?', in Hartmann, G. ed. *Bitburg in Moral and Political Perspective*, Bloomington, IN: Indiana University Press.

Adorno, T. (2006) *Minima Moralia: reflections on damaged life,* London: Verso.

Agamben, G. (1999) *Remnants of Auschwitz: the witness and the archive.* New York: Zone Books.

Agamben, G. (2005) *The Time that Remains: a commentary on the letter to the Romans,* Palo Alto, CA: Stanford University Press.

Alexander, J. et al (eds) (2004) *Cultural Trauma and Collective Identity,* Berkeley, CA: University of California Press.

Alford, C.F. (2006) *Psychology and the Natural Law of Reparation,* Cambridge, UK: Cambridge University Press.

Althusser, L. (2001) *Machiavelli and Us,* London: Verso.

Altman, J. and Hinkson, M. (eds) (2007) *Coercive Reconciliation: stabilise, normalise, exit aboriginal Australia,* Melbourne, Australia: Arena Publications.

Améry, J. (1980) *At the Mind's Limits: contemplations by a survivor on Auschwitz and its realities,* Bloomington, IN: University of Indiana Press.

Amstutz, M. (2005) *The Healing of Nations: the promise and limits of political forgiveness,* Lanham, MD: Rowman and Littlefield Publishers.

Annan, K. (2004) 'The rule of law and transitional justice in conflict and post-conflict societies', Report of the Secretary General United Nations Security Council, 23 August.

Arditi, B. (2007) *Politics on the Edges of Liberalism: difference, populism, revolution, agitation,* Edinburgh: Edinburgh University Press.

Arditi, B. and Valentine, J. (1999) *Polemicization,* Edinburgh: Edinburgh University Press.

Arendt, H. (1948) *The Origins of Totalitarianism,* New York: Schocken Books.

Arendt, H. (1958) *The Human Condition,* Chicago, IL: University of Chicago Press.

Arendt, H. (1968a) 'On Humanity in Dark Times', in *Men in Dark Times,* New York: Harcourt Brace Jovanovich.

Arendt, H. (1968b) *Between Past and Future: eight exercises in political thought.* New York: Penguin Books.

Arendt, H. (1978) *Eichmann in Jerusalem: a report on the banality of evil,* New York: New Grove Press.

Arendt, H. (1982) *Lectures on Kant's Political Philosophy,* Chicago, IL: University of Chicago Press.

Arendt, H. (1987) *On Revolution,* New York: Penguin Books.

Aristotle (2000) *The Politics,* London: Dover Thrift.

Arnason, J and Murphy, P. (2001) *Agon, Logos, Polis,* Berlin: Franz Steiner Verlag.

Arthur, P. (2009) 'How transitions reshaped human rights: a conceptual history of transitional justice, *Human Rights Quarterly* 31, pp. 3221–3267.

Asmal, K.L. and Roberts, R. (1996) *Reconciliation Through Truth*, Cape Town, ZA: David Philip Publishing.

Assmann, J. (2006) 'Monotheism, memory, and trauma: reflections on Freud's book on Moses', in *Religion and Cultural Memory: ten studies*, Palo Alto, CA: Stanford University Press.

Attwood B. and Markus A. (eds.) (1999) *The Struggle for Aboriginal Rights: a documentary history*, Crows Nest, NSW: Allen & Unwin.

Badiou, A. (2007) *The Century*, Cambridge, UK: Polity Press.

Baer, U. (2000) *Remnants of Song: trauma and the experience of modernity in Charles Baudelaire and Paul Celan*, Palo Alto, CA: Stanford University Press.

Balfour, L. (2005) 'Reparations after identity politics', *Political Theory* 33.

Balfour, L. (2008) 'Act & Fact: slavery reparations as a democratic politics of reconciliation', in Bashir, B. and Kymlicka, W. *The Politics of Reconciliation in Multicultural Societies*, Oxford, UK: Oxford University Press.

Balibar, E. (1994) 'Rights of man and rights of the citizen: the modern dialectic of equality and freedom', in *Masses, Classes, Ideas: studies on politics and philosophy before and after Marx*, New York: Routledge.

Balibar, E. (2002) *Politics and the Other Scene,* London: Verso.

Barkan, E. (2001) *The Guilt of Nations: restitution and negotiating historical injustices*, Baltimore, MD: Johns Hopkins University Press.

Barker, D.W. (2009) *Tragedy and Citizenship: conflict, reconciliation, and democracy from Haemon to Hegel*, Albany, NY: SUNY Press.

Bar-Siman-Tov, Y. (2004) 'Introduction: Why reconciliation?', in *From Conflict Resolution to Reconciliation*, Oxford, UK: Oxford University Press.

Bar-Tal, D. (2000) 'From intractable conflict through conflict resolution to reconciliation: psychological analysis', *Political Psychology* 21(2).

Barta, T. (2008) 'Sorry, and not sorry, in Australia: how the apology to the stolen generations buried a history of genocide', *Journal of Genocide Research* 10(2), pp. 201–214.

Bartov, O. (2000) *Mirrors of Destruction: war, genocide, and modern identity*, Oxford, UK: Oxford University Press.

Bashir, B. and Kymlicka, W. (eds) (2008) *The Politics of Reconciliation in Multicultural Societies*, Oxford, UK: Oxford University Press.

Bass, G.J. (2000) *Stay the Hand of Vengeance: the politics of war crimes tribunals*, Princeton, NJ: Princeton University Press.

Batt, J. (2007) 'Bosnia and Herzegovina: politics as war by other means: challenges to the EU's strategy for the Western Balkans', Institute Note, *Institute for Security Studies*, 19 November.

Bauman, Z. (2000) *Modernity and the Holocaust*, Ithaca, NY: Cornell University Press.

Behrendt, L. (2009a) 'Home: the importance of place to the dispossessed', *South Atlantic Quarterly* 108(1), pp. 71–85.

Behrendt, L. (2009b) 'Stop this intervention', public address in Sydney, 20 June, http://www.youtube.com/thejuicemedia#p/u/6/c1Vw4Qo47Oo.

Behrendt, L. (2001) 'Genocide: the distance between law and life', *Aboriginal History* 25, pp. 132–147.

Bell, D. (2006) *Memory, Trauma, and World Politics: reflections on the relationship between past and present*, London: Palgrave Macmillan Press.

Bell, D. (2008) 'Agonistic democracy and the politics of memory', *Constellations* 15(1).

Benhabib, S. (ed.) (1996) *Democracy and Difference: contesting the boundaries of the political*, Princeton, NJ: Princeton University Press.

Benhabib, S. (2002) *The Claims of Culture: equality and diversity in the global era*, Princeton: Princeton University Press.

Benhabib, S. (ed.) (2010) *Politics in Dark Times: encounters with Hannah Arendt*, Cambridge, UK: Cambridge University Press.

Benjamin, W. (1996) 'The critique of violence', in Bullock, M. (ed.) *Walter Benjamin: selected writing, volume 1, 1913–1926*, Cambridge, MA: Harvard University Press.

Benjamin, W. (1998) *The Origin of German Tragic Drama*, New York: Verso.

Bennett, J. (2001) *The Enchantment of Modern Life: attachments, crossings, and ethics*, Princeton, NJ: Princeton University Press.

Berkowitz, R., Keenan, T. and Katz, J. (2010) *Thinking in Dark Times: Hannah Arendt on ethics and politics*, New York: Fordham University Press.

Berlant, L. (2002) 'The subject of true feeling: pain, privacy, and politics', in Brown W. and Halley, J. (eds) *Left Legalism/Left Critique*, Durham, NC: Duke University Press.

Bernard-Donals, M. and Glejzer, R. (eds) (2003) *Witnessing the Disaster: essays on representation and the Holocaust*, Madison, WI: University of Wisconsin Press.

Bernstein, R. (2002) *Radical Evil: a philosophical interrogation*, Oxford, UK: Blackwell Publishing.

Best, S. and Saidiya, H. (2005) 'Fugitive justice', *Representations* 9, 2005, pp. 1–15.

Bhargava, R. (2001) 'Restoring decency to barbaric societies', in Rotberg, R. and Thompson, D. (eds) *Truth v. Justice: the morality of truth commissions*, Princeton, NJ: Princeton University Press.

Blanchot, M. (1988) *The Unavowable Community*, New York: Station Hill Press, 1988.

Blanchot, M. (1995) *The Writing of the Disaster*, trans. A. Smock, Lincoln, NB: University of Nebraska Press.

Boraine, A. (2001) *A Country Unmasked: inside South Africa's Truth and Reconciliation Commission*, Oxford, UK: Oxford University Press.

Borer, T. (2006) *Telling the Truths: truth telling and peace building in post-conflict societies*, South Bend, IN: University of Notre Dame.

Botwinick, A. and Connolly, W. (eds) (2001) *Democracy and Vision: Sheldon Wolin and the vicissitudes of the political*, Princeton, NJ: Princeton University Press.

Breen, K. (2009) 'Agonsim, antagonism and the necessity of care', in Schaap, A. (ed.) *Law and Agonistic Politics,* Farnham, UK: Ashgate.

Brilmayer, L. (1991) 'Secession and self-determination: a territorial interpretation' Faculty Scholarship Series, paper 2434, online at http://digitalcommons.law.yale.edu/fss_papers/2434

Brooks, P. (2000) *Troubling Confessions: speaking guilt in law and literature*, Chicago, IL: University of Chicago Press.

Brown, N. (1992) *Apocalypse and/or Metamorphosis*, Berkeley, CA: University of California Press.

Brown, W. (1995) 'Wounded Attachments', in *States of Injury: power and freedom in late modernity*, Princeton, NJ: Princeton University Press.

Brown, W. (1999) 'Resisting left melancholia', *Boundary 2* 26(3), pp. 19–27.

Brudholm, T. (2008) *Resentment's Virtues: Jean Améry and the refusal to forgive*, Philadelphia, PA: Temple University Press.

Brudholm, T. (2009) *The Religious in Response to Mass Atrocity: interdisciplinary perspectives,* Cambridge, UK: Cambridge University Press.

Burg, S. and Shoup, P. (2000) *The War in Bosnia Herzegovina: ethnic conflict and international intervention*, Armonk, NY: M.E. Sharpe Press.

Burke-White, W. (2007) 'The domestic influence of international tribunals: the International Criminal Tribunal for the Former Yugoslavia and the creation of the state court of Bosnia and Herzegovina', *Columbia Journal of Transnational Law* 46, pp. 279–350.

Buruma, I. *Wages of Guilt: memories of war in Germany and Japan*, Los Angeles, CA: Phoenix Books.

Butler, J. (1998) 'Moral sadism and doubting one's own love: Klein's reflections on Melancholia', in Stonebridge, L. and Phillips, J. (eds) *Reading Melanie Klein*, London: Routledge.

Butler, J. (2000*) Antigone's Claim: kinship between life & death*, New York: Columbia University Press.

Butler, J. (2005) *Giving an Account of Oneself*, New York: Fordham University Press.

Butler, J. (2006) *Precarious Life: the power of mourning and violence*, London: Verso.

Card, C. (2002) *The Atrocity Paradigm: a theory of evil*, Oxford, UK: Oxford University Press.

Carlson, L. (1987) *Caring for the Dead: your find act of love*, Hinesburg, VT: Upper Access Books.

Caruth, C. (1996) *Unclaimed Experience: trauma, narrative and history*, Baltimore, MD: The Johns Hopkins University Press.

Castoriadis, C. (1997) *World in Fragments: writings on politics, society, psychoanalysis, and the imagination*, Palo Alto, CA: Stanford University Press.

Cavarero, A. 2005. *For More Than One Voice: towards a philosophy of vocal expression.* Palo Alto, CA: Stanford University Press.

Cavarero, A. (2008) *Horrorism: naming contemporary violence*, New York: Columbia University Press.

Celermajer, D. (2008) 'Apology and the possibility of ethical politics', *Journal of Cultural and Religious Theory* 9(1), pp. 14–34.

Center for Policy Research and Development (2009) 'The status of judicial efforts', available online at www.cpir.net, accessed 20 April 2010.

CEPOS: Center for Policy Studies (2010) 'Youth inclusion and empowerment: legal and institutional analysis', available at www.cepos.org.

Chakravarti, S. (2008) 'More than cheap sentimentality: victim testimony at Nuremberg, the Eichmann trial, and truth commissions', *Constellations* 15(2), pp. 223–235.

Chambers, S. (2003) *Untimely Politics*, New York: New York University Press.

Chandler, D. (2000) *Bosnia: faking democracy after Dayton*, London: Pluto Press.

Cheng, A. (2001) *The Melancholy of Race: psychoanalysis, assimilation, and hidden grief*, New York: Oxford University Press.

Christodoulidis, E. (1998) *Law and Reflexive Politics*, Norwell, MA: Kluwer Publishers.

Christodoulidis, E. (2000) 'Truth and reconciliation as risks', *Social and Legal Studies* 9(2), pp. 179–204.

Christodoulidis, E. (2001) 'The aporia of sovereignty: on the representation of the people in constitutional discourse', *King's College Law Journal* 12, pp. 111–133.

Christodoulidis, E. and Veitch, S. (eds) (2001) *Lethe's Law: justice, law, and ethics in reconciliation*, Portland, OR: Hart Publishing.

Clifford, J. (2007) 'Varieties of indigenous experience: diasporas, homelands, sovereignties', in Cadena, M. and Starn, O. (eds) *Indigenous Experience Today*, New York: Berg Publishing.

Cobban, H. (2007) *Amnesty after Atrocity? Healing nations after genocide and war crimes*, Boulder, CO: Paradigm Publishers.

Coetzee, J.M. (2000) *Disgrace*, New York: Penguin.

Cohen, S. (2001) *States of Denial: knowing about atrocities and suffering*, New York: Continuum.

Cole, C. (2010) *Performing South Africa's Truth Commission: stages of transition*, Bloomington, IN: Indiana University Press.

Coles, R. (2005) *Beyond Gated Politics: reflections for the possibility of democracy*, Minneapolis, MN: University of Minnesota Press.

Connolly, W. (1995) *The Ethos of Pluralization*, Minneapolis, MI: University of Minnesota Press.

Connolly, W. (2002) *Identity/Difference: democratic negotiations of political paradox*, Minneapolis, MN: University of Minnesota Press.

Connolly, W. (2005) *Pluralism*, Durham, NC: Duke University Press.

Copjec, J. (ed.) (1996) *Radical Evil*, London: Verso Books.

Corlett, W. (1989) *Community Without Unity: a politics of Derridian extravagance*, Durham, NC: Duke University Press.

Dallmayr, F. (1987) *Polis and Praxis: exercises in contemporary political theory*, Cambridge, MA: MIT Press.

De Greiff, P. (2010) *Transitional Justice and Development: making connections*, New York: Social Science Research Council.

Deleuze, G. (1990) *The Logic of Sense*, New York: Columbia University Press.

Deranty, J-P. and Renault, R. (2009) 'Democratic agon: striving for distinction or struggle against domination and injustice', in Schaap, A. (ed.) *Law and Agonistic Politics*, Farnham, UK: Ashgate.

Derrida, J. (1989) 'Force of law: The Mystical Foundation of Authority', *Cardozo Law Review* 11.

Derrida, J.(1994) *Spectres of Marx: the state of the debt, the work of mourning, and the new international*, New York: Routledge.

Derrida, J. (2001) *On Cosmopolitanism and Forgiveness*, New York: Routledge.

Derrida, J. (2004) *Rogues: two essays on reason*, Palo Alto, CA: Stanford University Press.

Derrida, J. (2005) 'On Absolute hospitality: the cause of philosophy and the spectre of the political', in *The Politics of Friendship*, London: Verso.

Des Forges, A. (1999) *Leave None to Tell the Story: genocide in Rwanda*, Washington, DC: Human Rights Watch.

Deveaux, M. (2000) *Cultural Pluralism and Dilemmas of Justice*. Ithaca, NY: Cornell University Press.

Digeser, P. (2001) *Political Forgiveness*, Ithaca, NY: Cornell University Press.

Doxtader, E. (2003) 'Reconciliation: a rhetorical concept/ion', *Quarterly Journal of Speech* 89, pp. 267–292.

Doxtader, E. (2009) *With Faith in the Works of Words: the beginnings of reconciliation in South Africa, 1985–1995*, Cape Town, ZA: David Philip/Michigan State University Press.

Doxtader, E. and Villa-Vicencio, C. (eds) (2003) *The Provocations of Amnesty: memory, justice and impunity*, Cape Town, ZA: David Philip Publishers.

Drumbl, M. (2007) *Atrocity, Punishment, and International Law*, Cambridge, UK: Cambridge University Press.

Dryzek, J. (2005) 'Deliberative democracy in divided societies', *Political Theory* 33(2), pp. 218–242.

Dryzek, J. (2006) *Deliberative Global Politics: discourse and democracy in a divided world*, New York: Polity.

Du Bois F. and du Bois-Pedain, A. (ed.) (2009) *Justice and Reconciliation in Post-Apartheid South Africa*, Cambridge, UK: Cambridge University Press.

Durrant, S. (2004) *Postcolonial Narrative and the Work of Mourning: J.M. Coetzee, Wilson Harris, and Toni Morrison*, Albany, NY: SUNY Press.

Düttmann, A. (2000) *Between Cultures: tensions in the struggle for recognition*, London: Verso.

Dwyer, S. (1999) 'Reconciliation for realists', *Ethics and International Affairs* 13, pp. 81–97.

Edkins, J. (2003) *Trauma and the Memory of Politics*, Cambridge, UK: Cambridge University Press.

Elshtain, J.B. (2003) 'Politics and forgiveness', in Biggar, N. (ed.) *Burying the Past: making peace and doing justice after civil conflict*, Washington, DC: Georgetown University Press.

Elster, J. (2004) *Closing the Books: transitional justice in historical perspective*, Cambridge, UK: University of Cambridge Press.

Eng, D. and Kazanjian, D. (eds) (2003) *Loss,* Berkeley, CA: University of California Press.

Engel, D.M. (1990) 'Litigation across space and time: courts, conflict, and social change', *Law & Society Review* 24(2), pp. 333–344.

Enright, R. and North, J. (1998) *Exploring Forgiveness*, Madison, WI: University of Wisconsin Press.

Euben, P. (1990) *The Tragedy of Political Theory: the road not taken*, Princeton, NJ: Princeton University Press.

Euben, P. (1997) *Corrupting Youth: political education, democratic culture and political theory*, Princeton, NJ: Princeton University Press.

Fagenblat, M. (2008) 'The apology, the secular and the theologico-political', *Dialogue* 27(2), pp. 16–32.

Felman, S. (2002) *The Juridical Unconscious: trials and traumas in the twentieth century*, Cambridge, MA: Harvard University Press.

Ferguson, M. (2008) 'Aporetic Democracy', unpublished essay, presented at the Western Political Science Association, San Diego, cited with author's permission.

Fish, S. (1999) 'Mutual respect as a device of exclusion', in Macedo, S. (ed.) *Deliberative Politics: essays on democracy and disagreement,* Oxford, UK: University Press.

Floyd, J. and Stears, M. (eds) (2011) *Political Philosophy versus History? contextualism and real politics in contemporary political thought*, Cambridge, UK: Cambridge University Press.

Foley, G. (2008) 'Duplicity and deceit: Rudd's apology to the stolen generations', *Melbourne Historical Journal* 36, online at: http://www.kooriweb.org/foley/essays/essay_28.html

Foley, G. (2001) 'Black power in Redfern, 1968–1972', The Koori History Website, http://www.kooriweb.org/foley/essays/essay_1.html

Forst, R. (2002) *Contexts of Justice: political philosophy beyond liberalism and communitarianism*, Berkeley, CA: University of California Press.

Foucault, M. (1970) *The Order of Things*, London: Tavistock Press.

Frank, J. (2009) 'Staging dissensus: Frederick Douglas and we, the people', in Schaap, A. (ed.) *Law and agonistic politics*, Burlington, VT: Ashgate.

Fraser, N. and Honneth, A.(2003) *Redistribution or Recognition?: a political-philosophical exchange*, London: Verso.

206   *Select bibliography*

Fraser, N. (2009) *Scales of Justice: reimagining political space in a globalizing world*, New York: Columbia University Press.

Frayling, N. (2009) 'Toward the healing of history: an exploration of the relationship between pardon and peace', in Quinn, J. (ed.) *Reconciliation(s): transitional justice in postconflict societies*, Montreal: McGill Queen's University Press.

Gagnon, V.P. (2005) *The Myth of Ethnic War: Serbia and Croatia in the 1990s*, Ithaca, NY: Cornell University Press.

Gellrich, Michelle (1988) *Tragedy and Theory: the problem of conflict since Aristotle*, Princeton, NJ: Princeton University Press.

Geuss, R. (2008) *Philosophy and Real Politics*, Princeton, NJ: Princeton University Press.

Girard, R (1996) 'Mimesis and violence', in Williams, J. (ed.) *The Girard Reader*, New York: Crossroad.

Glover, J. (2001) *Humanity: a moral history of the twentieth century*, New Haven, CT: Yale University Press.

Goot, M. and Rowse, T. (2007) *Divided Nation? Indigenous affairs and the imagined public,* Carlton: Melbourne University Press.

Gorringe, T. (1996) *God's Just Vengeance: crime, violence, and the rhetoric of salvation*, Cambridge, MA: Cambridge University Press.

Govier, T. (2002) *Forgiveness and Revenge*, London: Routledge.

Graybill, L. (2001) 'To punish or pardon: a comparison of the International Criminal Tribunal for Rwanda and the South African Truth and Reconciliation Commission', *Human Rights Review* 2(4), pp. 3–18.

Griswold, C. (2008) *Forgiveness: a philosophical exploration*, Cambridge, UK: Cambridge University Press.

Gutmann, A. and Thompson, D. (1990) 'Moral Conflict and Political Consensus', *Ethics* 101(1), pp. 64–88.

Gutmann, A. and Thompson, D. (1998) *Democracy and Disagreement*, Cambridge, MA: Harvard University Press.

Gutmann, A and Thompson, D. (2000) 'The moral foundations of truth commissions', in Rotberg, R. and Thompson, D. (eds.) *Truth v. Justice: the morality of truth commissions*, Princeton, NJ: Princeton University Press.

Habermas, J. (1990) *Moral Consciousness and Communicative Action*, Cambridge, MA: MIT Press.

Habermas, J. (1996a) 'Three normative models of democracy', in Benhabib, S. (ed.) *Democracy and Difference: contesting the boundaries of the political*, Princeton, NJ: Princeton University Press.

Habermas, J. (1996b) *Between Facts and Norms: contributions to a discourse theory of law and democracy*, Cambridge, MA: MIT Press.

Hall, S., Morley, D. and Chen, K-H (eds) (1996) *Stuart Hall: critical dialogues*, London: Routledge.

Hamber, B. and van der Merwe, H. (1998) 'What is this thing called reconciliation?', *Reconciliation in Review* 1(1).

Hampshire, S. (1989) *Innocence and Experience*, Cambridge, MA: Harvard University Press.

Hampshire, S. (1999) *Justice is Conflict*, Princeton, NJ: Princeton University Press.

Hatzfeld J. (2004) *Machete Season: the killers in Rwanda speak*, New York: Picador.

Hawley, T.M. (2005) *The Remains of War: bodies, politics, and the search for American soldiers unaccounted for in Southeast Asia*, Durham, NC: Duke University Press.

Hayner, P. (2002) *Unspeakable Truths: facing the challenge of truth commissions*, New York, NY: Routledge.

Hegel, G.W.F. (1979) *Phenomenology of Spirit*, trans. A.V. Miller, Oxford, UK: Clarendon Press.

Heidegger, M. (1992) *Parmenides*, Bloomington, IN: Indiana State University Press.

Heidegger, M. (2000) *Introduction to Metaphysics*, New Haven, CT: Yale University Press.

Hess, C. and Post, R. (eds) (1999) *Human Rights in Political Transitions: Gettysburg to Bosnia*, New York: Zone Books.

Hirsch, A.K. (2009) 'Ruling the agon', *Law, Culture and the Humanities* 5(3), pp. 456–460.

Hirsch, A.K. (2011) 'Fugitive reconciliation: the agonistics of respect, resentment and responsibility in post-conflict society', *Contemporary Political Theory* (10)2, pp. 166–189.

Hobsbawm, E. (1996) *The Age of Extremes: a history of the world, 1914–1994*, New York: Vintage.

Homer (2003) *The Iliad*, London: Penguin.

Honig, B. (1993a) *Political Theory and the Displacement of Politics*, Ithaca, NY: Cornell University Press.

Honig, B. (1993b) 'The politics of agonism: a critical response to "beyond good and evil: Arendt, Nietzsche, and the aestheticization of political action", by Dana R. Villa', *Political Theory* 21.

Honig, B. (1995) 'Toward an agonistic feminism: Hannah Arendt and the politics of identity', and 'Afterword: agonism versus associationism?', in Honig, B. (ed.) *Feminist Interpretations of Hannah Arendt*, Philadelphia, PA: Pennsylvania State University Press.

Honig, B. (2003) *Democracy and the Foreigner*, Princeton, NJ: Princeton University Press.

Honig, B. (2009) 'Antigone's laments, Creon's grief: mourning, membership, and the institution of exception', *Political Theory* 37(1), pp. 5–43.

Honig, B. (2011) 'Undazzled by the ideal? Tully's politics and humanism in tragic perspective', *Political Theory* 39, 138–144.

Honneth, A. (1995) *The Struggle for Recognition: the moral grammar of social conflicts*, Cambridge, UK: Polity Press.

Ignatieff, M. (1998) *The Warrior's Honor: ethnic war and the modern conscience*, New York: Owl Books.

Ingelaere, B. (2008) 'The Gacaca Courts in Rwanda', in Huyse, L. and Salter, M. (eds) *Traditional Justice and Reconciliation after Violent Conflict: learning from African experiences*, Washington, D.C.: IDEA Books.

Institute for Justice and Reconciliation (2003) *The Provocations of Amnesty: Memory, justice, and impunity*, David Philip.

Irigaray, L. (1985) 'The Eternal Irony of the Community', in *Speculum of the Other Woman*, Ithaca, NY: Cornell University Press.

Jankélévitch, V. (2005) *Forgiveness*. Chicago, IL: University of Chicago Press.

Kalyvas, A. (2009) *Democracy and the Politics of the Extraordinary: Max Weber, Carl Schmitt, and Hannah Arendt*, Cambridge, UK: Cambridge University Press.

Kant, I. (2002) *Critique of Practical Reason*, trans. W.S. Pluhar, Indianapolis, IN: Hackett.

Karagiannis, N. and Wagner, P. (2005) 'Towards a theory of synagonsim' *Journal of Political Philosophy* 13(3), pp. 235–262.

Keane, J. (2004) *Violence and Democracy*, Cambridge, UK: Cambridge University Press.

Keenan, A. (2003) *Democracy in Question: democratic openness in a time of political closure*, Palo Alto, CA: Stanford University Press.

Kirkpatrick, J. (2008) *Uncivil Disobedience: studies in violence and democratic politics*, Princeton, NJ: Princeton University Press.

Klein, M. (1975) 'Love, guilt, and reparation', in *Love, Guilt, and Reparations and Other Works 1921–1945*, New York: Delacorte.

Kristeva, J. (2011) *Hatred and Forgiveness*, New York: Columbia University Press.

Krog, A. (1998) *Country of My Skull: guilt, sorrow, and the limits of forgiveness in the new South Africa*, New York: Random House.

Kurasawa, F. (2007) *The Work of Global Justice: human rights as practices*, Cambridge, UK: Cambridge University Press.

Kymlicka, W. and Bashir, B. (eds) (2008) *The Politics of Reconciliation in Multicultural Societies*, Oxford, UK: Oxford University Press.

LaCapra, D. (2000) 'Reflections on trauma, absence, and loss', in Brooks, P. and Woloch, A. (eds) *Whose Freud? The place of psychoanalysis in contemporary culture*, New Haven, CT: Yale University Press.

Laclau, E. (2007) *Emancipation(s)*, London: Verso.

Laclau, E. and C. Mouffe (1985) *Hegemony and Socialist Strategy: towards a radical democratic politics*, London: Verso.

Laqueur, T. (2002) 'The Dead Body and Human Rights', in Sweeney, S. and Hooder, I. (eds) *The Body*, Cambridge, UK: Cambridge University Press.

Lara, M. (ed.) (2001) *Rethinking Evil: contemporary perspectives*. Berkeley, CA: University of California.

Latour, B. (2007) *Reassembling the Social: an introduction to actor-network theory* Oxford, UK: Oxford University Press.

Lederach, J-P. (1997) *Building Peace: sustainable reconciliation in divided societies*, Washington, DC: United States Institute of Peace Press.

Leebaw, B. (2011) *Judging State-Sponsored Violence, Imagining Political Change*, Cambridge, UK: Cambridge University Press.

Lefort, C. (1988) *Democracy and Political Theory*, Minneapolis, MI: University of Minnesota Press.

Lehning, P.B. (eds.) (1998) *Theories of Secession*, London: Routledge.

Levi, P. (1989) *The Drowned and the Saved*, New York: Vintage.

Levinas, E. (1994) 'Politics after', in *Beyond the Verse: talmudic readings and lectures*, Bloomington, IN: University of Indiana Press.

Lindahl, H. (2008) 'Democracy, political reflexivity, and bounded dialogies: revisiting the monism-pluralism debate', in Christodoulidis, E. and Tierney, S. (eds) *Public Law and Politics: the scope and limits of constitutionalism*, Aldershot, UK: Ashgate.

Lingis, A. (2011) *Violence and Splendor*, Chicago, IL: Northwestern University Press.

Little, A. (2004) *Democracy and Northern Ireland: beyond the liberal paradigm?*, London: Palgrave.

Little, A. (2007) 'Between disagreement and consent: unravelling the democratic paradox', *Australian Journal of Political Science* 42(1), pp. 143–159.

Little, A. (2008) *Democratic Piety: complexity, conflict and violence*, Edinburgh, UK: Edinburgh University Press.

Llewellyn, J. (2006) 'Restorative justice in transitions and beyond', in Borer, T. (ed.) *Telling the Truths: truth telling and peace building in post-conflict societies*, South Bend, IN: University of Notre Dame.

Loraux, N. (1998) 'Of amnesty and its opposite', in *Mothers in Mourning*, Ithaca, NY: Cornell University Press.

Loughlin, M. and Walker, N. (eds) (2007) *The Paradox of Constitutionalism: constituent power and constitutional form*, Oxford, UK: Oxford University Press.

Lyotard, J-F. (1988) *The Differend: phrases in dispute*, Minneapolis, MN: University of Minnesota Press.

Lyotard, J-F. (1989) 'The sign of history', in Benjamin, A. (ed.) *The Lyotard Reader*, New York: Basil Blackwell.

MacKay, D. (2003) 4,835th Meeting of the UN Security Council, 30 Sept, 2003, available online at https://www.civcap.info/fileadmin/user_upload/UN/S_PV_4835.pdf.

Mamdani, M. (1996) 'Reconciliation without justice', *Southern Review* 10(6), pp. 22–25.

Mamdani, M. (1996) *Citizen and Subject: contemporary Africa and the legacy of late colonialism*, Princeton: Princeton University Press.

Mamdani, M. (2002) *When Victims Become Killers: colonialism, nativism, and the genocide in Rwanda*, Princeton, NJ: Princeton University Press.

Mani, R. (2002) *Beyond Retribution: seeking justice in the shadows of war*, Cambridge, UK: Polity Press.

Mann, M. (2004) *The Dark Side of Democracy: explaining ethnic cleansing*, Cambridge, UK: Cambridge University Press.

Markell, P. (2003) *Bound by Recognition*, Princeton, NJ: Princeton University Press.

Marion-Young, I. (1990) *Justice and the Politics of Difference,* Princeton, NJ: Princeton University Press, 1990.

Marion-Young, I. (2006) *Global Challenges: war, self-determination and responsibility for justice*, London: Polity Press.

Marion-Young, I. (2011) *Responsibility for Justice* Oxford, UK: Oxford University Press.

Martel, J. (2007) *Subverting the Leviathan: reading Thomas Hobbes as a radical democrat*, New York: Columbia University Press.

Martel, J. (2008) '*Amo Volo Ut Sis*: love, Williand and Arendt's reluctant embrace of sovereignty' *Philosophy and Social Criticism* 34(3).

McAdams, J. (ed.) (1997) *Transitional Justice and the Rule of Law in New Democracies*, South Bend, IN: University of Notre Dame Press.

Meister, R. (2010) *After Evil: a politics of human rights*, New York: Columbia University Press.

Milbank, J. (2003) *Being Reconciled: ontology and pardon*, London: Routledge.

Minow, M. (1999) *Between Vengeance and Forgiveness: facing history after genocide and mass violence*, Boston, MA: Beacon Press.

Minow, M. (ed.) (2003) *Breaking the Cycles of Hatred: memory, law, and repair*, Princeton, NJ: Princeton University Press.

Moon, C. (2008) *Narrating Political Reconciliation: South Africa's Truth and Reconciliation Commission*, Lanham, MD: Lexington Books.

Moses, D. (2011) 'Official apologies, reconciliation, and settler colonialism: Australian indigenous alterity and political agency', *Citizenship Studies* 15(2), pp. 145–159.

Motha, S. (2007a) 'Reconciliation as Domination' in Veitch, S. (ed.) *Law and the Politics of Reconciliation*, Farnham: Ashgate.

Motha, S. (2007b) *Democracy's Empire: sovereignty, law, and violence*, London: Blackwell.

Mouffe, C. (ed.) (1996a) *Dimensions of Radical Democracy: pluralism, citizenship, community*, London: Verso.

Mouffe, C.(1996b) 'Democracy, power, and the political', in Benhabib, S. (ed.) *Democracy and Difference: contesting the boundaries of the political*, Princeton, NJ: Princeton University Press.

Mouffe, C. (2000a) 'For an agonistic model of democracy', in *The Democratic Paradox*, London: Verso.

Mouffe, C. (2000b) *The Democratic Paradox*, London: Verso Books.

Mouffe, C. (2006) *The Return of the Political*, London: Verso Books.

Mujawayo, E. and Belhaddad, S. (2004) *Survivantes: Rwanda, historie d'un* genocide, Paris: Editions de l'Aube.

Mukayiranga, S. (2004) 'Sentimens de rescapés', in Coquio, C. (ed.) *L'histoire trouée: négation et témoignage*, Paris: L'Atlante.

Muldoon, P. (2003) 'Reconciliation and political legitimacy: the old Australia and the new South Africa', *Australian Journal of Politics and History*, vol. 49(2), pp. 182–196.

Muldoon, P. (2009) 'Past injustices and future protections: on the politics of promising', *Australian Indigenous Law Review* 13(2), pp. 2–17.

Muldoon, P. (2010) 'The very basis of civility: on agonism, conquest and reconciliation', in Bashir, B. and Kymlicka, W. (eds) *The Politics of Reconciliation in Multicultural Societies*, Oxford, UK: Oxford University Press.

Murphy, J. (2004) *Getting Even: forgiveness and its limits*, Oxford, UK: Oxford University Press.

Nancy, J-L. (2000) *Being Singular Plural*, Palo Alto, CA: Stanford University Press.

Nancy, J-L. (2002) *Hegel: the restlessness of the negative*, Minneapolis, MN: University of Minnesota Press, 2002.

Nancy, J-L. (2010) *The Truth of Democracy*, New York: Fordham University Press.

Neiman, S. (2004) *Evil in Modern Thought: an alternative history of philosophy*, Princeton, NJ: Princeton University Press.

Ngai, S. (2005) 'Irritation', in *Ugly Feelings*, Cambridge, MA: Harvard University Press.

Nietzsche, F. (1989) *On the Genealogy of Morals and Ecce Homo*, New York: Vintage Press.

Nino, C. (1998) *Radical Evil on Trial*, New Haven: Yale University Press.

Norton, A. (2001) 'Evening Land', in Botwinick, A. and Connolly, W. (eds) *Democracy and Vision: Sheldon Wolin and the Vicissitudes of the Political*, Princeton, NJ: Princeton University Press.

Norval, A. (2002) 'Memory, identity, and the (im)possibility of reconciliation: the work of the South African Truth and Reconciliation Commission', *Constellations* 5(2), pp. 250–265.

Osiel, M. (1999) 'Making public memory, publicly', in Hesse, C. and Post, R. (eds) *Human Rights in Political Transitions*, New York: Zone Books.

Owen, D. (2009) 'The expressive agon: on political agency in a constitutional democratic polity', in Schaap, A. (ed.) *Law and Agonistic Politics*, Farnham, UK: Ashgate.

Panagia, D. (2004) 'The force of political argument', *Political Theory* 32(6), pp. 825–848.

Petersen, R. (2001) 'A theology of forgiveness: terminology, rhetoric, and the dialectic of interfaith relationships', in Helmick, R. and Petersen, R. (eds) *Forgiveness and Reconciliation: religion, public policy and conflict transformation*, Philadelphia, PA: Templeton Foundation Press.

Pettit, P. (1999) 'Contestatory Democracy', in Shapiro, I. and Hacker-Cordon, C. (eds) *Democracy's Value*, Cambridge, UK: Cambridge University Press.

Phillips, A. (1989) *The Politics of Presence*, Oxford, UK: Oxford University.

Philpott, D. (2006) *The Politics of Past Evil: religion, reconciliation and the dilemmas of transitional justice*, South Bend, IN: University of Notre Dame Press.

Philpott, D. (2009) 'An ethic of political reconciliation', *Ethics and International Affairs* 23(4).

Pitkin, H. (1991) 'Justice: on relating public and private', *Political Theory* 9(3), pp. 327–352.

Posner, E. and Vermeule, A. (2003) 'Transitional justice as ordinary justice', *Harvard Law Review* 117.

Postone, M. and Santner, E. (eds) (2003) *Catastrophe and Meaning: the Holocaust and the twentieth century*, Chicago, IL: University of Chicago Press.

Povinelli, E. (2002) *The Cunning of Recognition: indigenous alterities and the making of Australian multiculturalism*, Durham, NC: Duke University Press.

Ramsbotham, O. (2010) *Transforming Violent Conflict: radical disagreement, dialogue and survival*, New York: Routledge.

Rancière, J. (1995) *On the Shores of Politics*, London: Verso.

Rancière, J. (1999) *Disagreement: politics and philosophy*, Minneapolis, MN: University of Minnesota Press.

Rancière, J. (2001) 'Ten these on politics', *Theory and Event* 5(3).

Rancière, J. (2004a) 'Deleuze, Bartleby, and the literary formula', in *The Flesh of Words: The Politics of Writing*, trans. C. Mandell, Palo Alto, CA: Stanford University Press.

Rancière, J. (2004b) 'Who is the subject of the rights of man?' *The South Atlantic Quarterly* 103(2/3), pp. 297–310.

Rancière, J. (2005) *The Politics of Aesthetics: the distribution of the sensible*, London: Continuum.

Rancière, J. (2009) *Hatred of Democracy*, London: Verso.

Rawls, J. (1971) *A Theory of Justice*, Cambridge, MA: Harvard University Press.

Rawls, J. (1993) *Political Liberalism*, New York: Columbia University Press.

Rawls, J. (2001) *Justice as Fairness: a restatement*, Boston, MA: Harvard University Press.

Ricoeur, P. (1967) *The Symbolism of Evil*, New York: Harper and Row.

Ricoeur, P (2004) *Memory, History, Forgetting*, Chicago, IL: University of Chicago Press.

Roht-Arriaza, N. and J. Mariecruzana (eds) (2006) *Transitional Justice in the Twenty-First Century: beyond truth versus justice*, Cambridge, UK: Cambridge University Press.

Rorty, R. (1993) 'Justice as a Larger Loyalty', in Cheah, P. and Robbins, B. (eds) *Cosmopolitics: thinking and feeling beyond the nation*, Minneapolis, MI: University of Minnesota Press.

Rose, J. (2003) 'Apathy and accountability: the challenge of South Africa's Truth and Reconciliation Commission to the intellectual in the modern world', in *On Not Being Able to Sleep: psychoanalysis and the modern world*, Princeton, NJ: Princeton University Press.

Rosoux, V. (2009) 'Réconcilier: ambitions et pièges de la justice transitionnelle. Le cas du Rwanda', *Droit et sociétés* 73, pp. 613–633.

Rotberg, R. and Thompson, D. (eds) (2000) *Truth v. Justice: the morality of truth commissions*, Princeton, NJ: Princeton University Press.

Rousseau, J-J. (1997) 'The Social Contract', in *Discourses and Other Early Political Writings*, Cambridge, UK: Cambridge University Press.

Sanders, M. (2007) *Ambiguities of Witnessing: law and literature in the time of a truth commission*, Palo Alto, CA: Stanford University Press.

Santner, E. (1990) *Stranded Objects: mourning, memory, and film in postwar Germany*, Chicago, IL: University of Chicago Press.

Sarat, A. and Kearns, T. (1986) 'A journey toward forgetting: toward a jurisprudence of violence', in A. Sarat and T. Kearns (eds) *The Fate of Law*, Ann Arbor, MI: University of Michigan Press.

Scarry, E. (1987) *The Body in Pain: the making and unmaking of the world*, Oxford, UK: Oxford University Press.

Schaap, A. (2004) 'Political reconciliation through a struggle for recognition?' *Social and Legal Studies* 13(4), pp. 523–540.

Schaap, A. (2005) *Political Reconciliation*, London: Routledge.

Schaap, A. (2006) 'Agonism in divided societies', *Philosophy and Social Criticism*, 32(2), pp. 255–277.

Schaap, A. (2007) 'Political theory and the agony of politics', *Political Studies Review* 5(1), pp. 56–74.

Schaap, A. (ed.) (2009) *Law and Agonistic Politics*, London: Ashgate Press.

Schaar, J. (1981) *Legitimacy in the Modern State*, New York: Transaction Publishers.

Schmitt, C. (1985) *The Crisis of Parliamentary Democracy*, Cambridge, MA: MIT University Press.

Schmitt, C. (1996) *The Concept of the Political*, Chicago, IL: University of Chicago Press.

Schmitt, C. (2003) *The Nomos of the Earth in the International Law of the Jus Publicium Europaeum*, New York: Telos.

Schift, A. (ed.) (2005) *Modernity and the Problem of Evil*, Bloomington, IN: Indiana University Press.

Schoolman, M. (2001) *Reason and Horror: critical theory, democracy, and aesthetic individuality*, New York: Routledge.

Schreiter, R. (1997) *Reconciliation*, Maryknoll, NY: Orbis Books.

Sebald, W.G. (2003) 'Against the irreversible: on Jean Amery', in *On the Natural History of Destruction*, New York: Random House.

Sejfija, I. (2006) 'From the "civil sector" to civil society?', in Fischer, M. (ed.) *Peacebuilding and Civil Society in Bosnia-Herzegovina*, Munster, Germany: Lit- Verlag.

Shapiro, I. (2010) *The Real World of Democratic Theory*, Princeton, NJ: Princeton University Press.

Shapiro, M. (1997) *Violent Cartographies: mapping cultures of war*, Minneapolis, MI: University of Minnesota Press.

Shapiro, M. (2009) *Cinematic Geopolitics*, London: Routledge.

Shklar, J. (1964) *Legalism: law, morals, and political trials*, Cambridge, MA: Harvard University Press.

Simmel, G. (1964) *Conflict and the Web of Group Affiliations,* New York: Free Press.

Sontag, S. (2003) *Regarding the Pain of Others*, New York: Farrar, Straus and Giroux.

Sophocles (1982) *The Three Theban Plays: Antigone, Oedipus the king and Oedipus at Colonus*, New York: The Viking Press.

Soyinka, W. (1999) *The Burden of Memory, the Muse of Forgiveness*, Oxford: Oxford University Press.

Stow, S. (2010) 'Agonistic homecoming: Frederick Douglas, Joseph Lower, and the democratic value of African American public mourning', *American Political Science Review* 104(4), pp. 681–697.

Taxidou, O. (2004) *Tragedy, Modernity and Mourning*, New York: Columbia University Press.

Taylor, C. (1994) *Multiculturalism: examining the politics of recognition*, Princeton: Princeton University Press.

Taylor, C. (2005) 'The politics of recognition', in *Philosophical Arguments*, Cambridge, MA: Harvard University Press.

Teitel, R. (2000) *Transitional Justice*, Oxford, UK: Oxford University Press.

Teitel, R. (2003) 'Transitional justice genealogy', *Harvard Human Rights Journal* 16.

Ternon, Y. (2001) *L'Innocence des victims: au siècle des genocides*, Paris: Desclee de Brouwer.

Thomas, L. (2009) 'Forgiveness as righteousness', in Quinn, J. (ed.) *Reconciliation(s): transitional justice in postconflict societies*, Montreal: McGill Queen's University Press.

Thomson, A. (2005) *Deconstruction and Democracy*, London: Continuum Publishers.

Thomson, A. (2009) 'Polemos and agon', in Schaap, A. (ed.) *Law and Agonistic Politics*, Burlington, VT: Ashgate.

Thompson, J. (2003) *Taking Responsibility for the Past: reparation and historical injustice*, New York: Polity Press.

Tilly, C. (2003) *The Politics of Collective Violence*, Cambridge, UK: Cambridge University Press.

Tønder, L. and Thomassen, L. (eds) (2005) *Radical Democracy: politics between abundance and lack*, Manchester, UK: Manchester University Press.

Torpey, J. (ed.) (2003) *Politics and the Past: on repairing historical injustices*, Lanham, MD: Rowman and Littlefield.

Torrance, A. (2006) 'The theological grounds for advocating forgiveness and reconciliation in the sociopolitical realm', in Philpott, D. (ed.) *The Politics of Past Evil: religion, reconciliation and the dilemmas of transitional justice*, Notre Dame, IN: University of Notre Dame Press.

Tully, J. (1995) *Strange Multiplicity: constitutionalism in an age of diversity*, Cambridge, UK: Cambridge University Press.

Tully, J. (1999) 'The agonic freedom of citizens, *Economy and Society* 28(2), pp. 166–182.

Tully, J. (2009) *Public Philosophy in a New Key*, Cambridge, UK: Cambridge University Press.

Tutu, D. (1999) *No Future without Forgiveness*, New York: Doubleday.

Unger, R. (2004) *False Necessity: anti-necessitarian social theory in the service of radical democracy*, London: Verso.

Vazquez-Arroyo, A. (2008) 'Responsibility, violence, and catastrophe', *Constellations* 15(1), pp. 98–125.

Veitch, S. (2007) *Law and the Politics of Reconciliation*, London: Ashgate Publishing.

Veltesen, A.J. (2006) 'A case for resentment: Jean Améry versus Primo Levi', *Human Rights* 44(5).

Verdeja, E. (2008) 'A critical theory of reparative justice', *Constellations* 15(2), pp. 208–222.

Verdeja, E. (2009) *Unchopping a Tree: reconciliation in the aftermath of political violence*, Philadelphia, PA: Temple University Press.

Verdeja, E. (2010) 'Official apologies in the aftermath of political violence', *Metaphilosophy* 41(4), pp. 563–581.

Villa, D. (1992) 'Beyond good and evil: Arendt, Nietzsche and the aestheticization of political action', *Political Theory* 20.

Villa, D. (1999) *Politics, Philosophy, Terror: essays on the thought of Hannah Arendt*, Princeton, NJ: Princeton University Press.

Villa, D. (2008) *Public Freedom*, Princeton, NJ: Princeton University Press.

Villa-Vicencio, C. (2009) *Walk with us and Listen: reconciliation in Africa*, Washington, DC: Georgetown University Press.

Vogler, C. and P. Markell (eds) (2003) 'Violence and redemption,' special edition, *Public Culture* 15(1).

Volf, M. (2001) 'Forgiveness, reconciliation, and justice: a Christian contribution to a more peaceful world', in Helmick, R. and Petersen, R. (eds) *Forgiveness and Reconciliation: religion, public policy and conflict transformation*, Philadelphia, PA: Templeton Foundation Press.

214   *Select bibliography*

Waldron, J. (2002) 'Redressing Historic Injustice,' *University of Toronto Law Journal* 52(1), pp. 135–160.

Walker, M. (2006) *Moral Repair: reconstructing moral relations after wrongdoing*, Cambridge, UK: Cambridge University Press.

Wallace, R. (1994) *Responsibility and the Moral Sentiments*, Cambridge, MA: Harvard University Press.

Walzer, M. (1983) *Spheres of Justice*, Oxford, UK: Robertson.

Weber, M. (1948) 'Politics as a vocation' in Gerth, H. and Mills, C.W. (eds) *From Max Weber: essays in sociology*, London: Routledge.

Wenman, M. (2003) 'Agonistic pluralism and three archetypal forms of politics', *Contemporary Political Theory* 2, pp. 165–186.

Warner, M. (2005) *Publics and Counterpublics*, New York: Zone Books.

White, S. (2008) 'Uncertain constellations: dignity, equality, respect and …?', in Campbell, D. and Schoolman, M. (eds) *The New Pluralism: William Connolly and the contemporary global condition*, Durham, NC: Duke University Press.

Wiebelhaus-Brahm, E. (2009) *Truth Commissions and Transitional Societies: the impact on human rights and democracy*, London: Routledge.

Williams, Bernard (1994) *Shame and Necessity*, Berkeley, CA: University of California Press.

Wilson, R. (2001) *The Politics of Truth and Reconciliation in South Africa: legitimizing the post-apartheid state*, Cambridge, UK: Cambridge University Press.

Wood, N. (1999) *Vectors of Memory: legacies of trauma in postwar Europe*, New York: Berg Books.

Wolin, S. (1989) *The Presence of the Past: essays on the state and the constitution*, Baltimore, MD: Johns Hopkins University Press.

Wolin, S.1996. 'Fugitive Democracy', in S. Benhabib (ed.) *Democracy and Difference: contesting the boundaries of the political*, Princeton, NJ: Princeton University Press.

Wolin, S.(2008) *Democracy Incorporated: managed democracy and the specter of totalitarianism*, Princeton, NJ: Princeton University Press.

Wyschogrod, E. (1990) *Spirit in Ashes: Hegel, Heidegger, and man-made mass death*, New Haven, CT: Yale University Press.

Wyschogrod, E. (1998) *An Ethics of Remembering: history, heterology and the nameless others*, Chicago, IL: University of Chicago Press.

Zerilli, L. (1998) 'This universalism which is not one', *Diacritics* 28(2), pp. 3–20.

Ziarek, E. (2003) 'Evil and testimony: ethics "after" postmodernism', *Hypatia* 18(2), pp.197–204.

Zizek, S. *Tarrying with the Negative: Kant, Hegel, and the critique of ideology*, Durham, NC: Duke University Press.

Zizek, S. (2008) *Violence: six sideways reflections*, London: Picador.

Zolo, D. (2009) *Victor's Justice: from Nuremberg to Baghdad*, London: Verso Books.

Index

Taylor & Francis

eBooks

FOR LIBRARIES

ORDER YOUR FREE 30 DAY INSTITUTIONAL TRIAL TODAY!

Over 23,000 eBook titles in the Humanities, Social Sciences, STM and Law from some of the world's leading imprints.

Choose from a range of subject packages or create your own!

Benefits for **you**

▶ Free MARC records
▶ COUNTER-compliant usage statistics
▶ Flexible purchase and pricing options

Benefits for your **user**

▶ Off-site, anytime access via Athens or referring URL
▶ Print or copy pages or chapters
▶ Full content search
▶ Bookmark, highlight and annotate text
▶ Access to thousands of pages of quality research at the click of a button

For more information, pricing enquiries or to order a free trial, contact your local online sales team.

UK and Rest of World: **online.sales@tandf.co.uk**

US, Canada and Latin America:
e-reference@taylorandfrancis.com

www.ebooksubscriptions.com

ALPSP Award for BEST eBOOK PUBLISHER 2009 Finalist sponsored by

Taylor & Francis eBooks
Taylor & Francis Group

A flexible and dynamic resource for teaching, learning and research.

10409773R00134

Printed in Great Britain
by Amazon.co.uk, Ltd.,
Marston Gate.